THE STATESMAN
AND THE FANATIC

JASPER RIDLEY

THE STATESMAN
AND
THE FANATIC

THOMAS WOLSEY
AND
THOMAS MORE

CONSTABLE
LONDON

First published in Great Britain 1982
by Constable and Company Ltd
10 Orange Street London WC2H 7EG
Copyright © 1982 by Jasper Ridley
All rights reserved
ISBN 0 09 463470 X
Set in Monophoto Baskerville 11pt by
Servis Filmsetting Ltd, Manchester
Printed in Great Britain by
St Edmundsbury Press Ltd
Bury St Edmunds

To CHRISTOPHER SMALL

CONTENTS

ILLUSTRATIONS

PREFACE

CARDINAL WOLSEY and Sir Thomas More represent two opposite extremes, the two conflicting types of political leaders who throughout history have influenced the lives of their fellow-men. Today, Wolsey is usually regarded as an unscrupulous politician, and More as a saint. A hundred years ago, Protestant England, at the height of its imperial power, acclaimed Wolsey as one of the founders of national greatness, and was less than enthusiastic about More; but on 7 February 1978, the five-hundredth anniversary of More's birth, the *Times* leader-writer wrote: 'If the English people were to be set a test to justify their history and civilization by the example of one man, then it is Sir Thomas More whom they would perhaps choose'. After considering the rival claims of Churchill, Gladstone, Dr Johnson, Shakespeare, Elizabeth I and King Alfred to be the greatest figure in English history, the leader-writer expressed the opinion that none of them was as great as More. If, in the twentieth century, even Churchill cannot compete with More, what chance has Wolsey?

But it is surely time to make a different assessment. Wolsey, for all his faults – and he had many – was a great statesman, a man of natural dignity with a generous temperament, who preserved a relatively tolerant régime until he fell from power and was succeeded by More. A careful examination of More reveals that the accusations of Foxe and his successors have not been disproved as effectively as is generally believed; that More's love for his family is largely a myth; and that the saint was the worst kind of intolerant fanatic, an idealist gone astray, who began as a brilliant intellectual but developed first into a sycophantic courtier and then into a persecuting bigot, before he redeemed himself, at the eleventh hour, by a brave if muted stand for his principles which cost him his life.

Like all students of More's works, I am profoundly in the debt of the founders of the St Thomas More Project of Yale University and to the learned editors of the Yale University Press edition of More's Collected Works. Although they will profoundly disagree with my view of More, I hope that this will not make them regret the fact that their researches and achievement were of so much help to me. I must also thank the Yale University Press for allowing me to cite certain passages from their edition of More's Works. Where I have quoted from one of More's Latin works, I have used the Yale translation, and I make no apology if this has occasionally meant translating More's medieval Latin with a word which was in use in America in the 1970s but not in England in the 1930s.

I wish to thank Miss Ann Hoffmann of Authors' Research Services, Mrs Jeanne Stoddard, Miss Brigid Allen, and Mr Stephen Parker, for their help with research; Dr Michael Smith, for his information on sixteenth-century medicine; Mrs Winifred Champion, Mrs Kay Coutin, Mr Vincent Cronin, Mrs Moyra Heffer, Mr Ernst Lowe, Mr Marcel Pressburg and Mr Tim Tatton-Brown for their information and advice, though none of them, of course, has any responsibility for the opinions expressed in this book; the staffs of the London Library, the British Library, the Public Record Office, the Northamptonshire Record Office and the Suffolk Record Office; my wife Vera for her advice on my typescript; and my son John for his help with the proofs.

Grateful acknowledgment is made to the following for permission to reprint copyrighted material: Princeton University Press: Selections from *The Correspondence of Sir Thomas More*, edited by Elizabeth Frances Rogers. Copyright 1947 by Princeton University Press, Copyright © renewed 1974 by Elizabeth Rogers; Yale University Press: Selections from *The Complete Works of St. Thomas More*, from *St. Thomas More: Utopia*, edited by Edward Surtz, and from *St. Thomas More: Selected Letters*, edited by E.F. Rogers. Used by permission of Yale University Press.

Jasper Ridley
Tunbridge Wells,
18 July 1982

CHAPTER 1

THOMAS WOLSEY OF IPSWICH

In the 1470s, in the reign of Edward IV, two very intelligent children were born, Thomas Wolsey and Thomas More. Both of them grew up to be men of outstanding ability. Both became Lord Chancellor of England; both were close personal friends of Henry VIII; and both were ultimately arrested at his orders and charged with high treason, though Wolsey, unlike More, escaped execution by dying a natural death before he could be tried and convicted.

In other respects they differed. Wolsey became a priest, but More remained a layman. The layman, More, was a learned theologian and a deeply religious man; the priest, Wolsey, was no theologian, and became religious only on his deathbed. More was an intellectual, a philosopher; Wolsey was an administrator and diplomat. More wrote books; Wolsey wrote state papers. Wolsey's character was straightforward, More's was complex and bewildering. Wolsey was unashamedly ambitious; in More, ambition and principle were in conflict. Until the last few months, Wolsey led a happy life; More was always tortured by doubts, frustrations and guilt.

They had another thing in common: both were very skilful liars. Wolsey lied without compunction in the interests of his king's diplomacy; More lied quite as unscrupulously in the interests of the Catholic Church.

Wolsey was the son of a butcher of Ipswich, More of a London barrister. Wolsey was probably about five years older than More. As in the case of most of his contemporaries, we do not know the date of Wolsey's birth, and have to deduce it from a number of conflicting statements by people who knew him; but the weight of evidence suggests that he was born during the winter of 1472–3.[1] In More's case, we know much more exactly when he was born, for by a lucky chance a document has been preserved in which his father noted that his son Thomas was born between two and three o'clock in the morning on the Friday after the feast of the Purification of the Blessed Virgin Mary in the seventeenth year of the reign of King Edward IV. This was Friday 6 February 1478. More's father afterwards added an insertion in the document stating that the day of his birth was 7 February, which introduces a contradiction, for 7 February was a Saturday in 1478. The reference to 7 February may well have been added in later years, when the father's memory was fading. In the fifteenth and early sixteenth centuries men usually dated their letters and events by the day of the week, the nearest saint's day, and the year of the king's reign, rather than by the day of the month and the *Annus Domini*; so the original date is probably correct, and 7 February an error. On the other hand, a man who sits up on a Friday night while his wife is in labour might well overlook the fact that when his son was born at 2.30 a.m. it was no longer Friday but already Saturday. The evidence for the year 1478, not 1477, is overwhelming, and we can say with virtual certainty that we know within twenty-four hours the date of the birth of Thomas More, between 2 and 3 a.m. on either 6 or 7 February 1478.[2]

Like all their contemporaries, Wolsey and More were given only one Christian name, and both were baptised 'Thomas'. So were hundreds of other boys in their generation, including Thomas Cromwell, Thomas Cranmer, Thomas Howard, Duke of Norfolk, Thomas Boleyn, Thomas Wyatt, Thomas Audley and Thomas Wriothesley. It had become as common as the traditional English 'John', because of the veneration felt by the people for Thomas Becket, St Thomas of Canterbury, murdered in his cathedral by four knights at the command of Henry II in 1170 because of his resistance to the king's attack on the privileges of the Church. The indignation of England and Europe had forced the king, four years later, to do public penance and submit to a flogging from the monks of Canterbury; and in 1220 another Archbishop of Canterbury, Stephen Langton, had officiated at a great ceremony when Becket's body was placed in a magnificent tomb in the cathedral, which for the next three hundred years was a shrine to which pilgrims came from all over England and Europe. St Thomas of Canterbury was the only saint, apart from the Virgin Mary, who was commemorated in England by more than one holy day in the year – the major feast day on 7 July, the anniversary of Henry II's penance in 1174 and the translation of the relics in 1220, and the lesser feast in the middle of the Twelve Days of Christmas on 29 December, the anniversary of the martyrdom in 1170.

Wolsey's enemies during his lifetime attacked him as an upstart son of a butcher, and after his death the chroniclers were fascinated by the story of his rise from the lowest to the highest rung of the social ladder, which was all the more dramatic and poignant because of his eventual fall. No such stories were told about the low birth of Thomas More. After he was executed, a government propagandist made a hostile reference to his humble origin; but as More never achieved the power, pomp or unpopularity of Wolsey, the allegation was forgotten.

The son of a barrister who later became a High Court Judge has been regarded as coming from a higher social background than a butcher's son; but one generation further back there was little to choose between the families in social status; for Wolsey's grandfather was a farmer and More's was a butler.

Thomas Wolsey's father, Robert Wolsey – who, like his son, always spelt his name 'Wulcy' – was a yeoman farmer in the Suffolk village of Sternfield, near Farnham. He was a pushing, forceful man who was determined to get on in life. He was brought up in the lawless age which preceded and followed the outbreak of the Wars of the Roses. The wars were fought by the royal and noble families with their bands of armed retainers, and were confined to a few counties; there was no fighting or marching of armies in East Anglia. But though Sternfield was eighty miles from the nearest battlefield, it suffered from the widespread breakdown in law and order during the wars. When noblemen and members of the royal family were fighting each other and murdering their captured cousins, yeomen farmers of Robert Wolsey's temperament saw no reason why they should obey the local by-laws.

Robert Wolsey married Joan Daundy, a member of the wealthy and influential Daundy family. The Daundys were not gentlemen, but they were the dominant family in several Suffolk villages which, like many other villages in England, had no local squire in residence. Robert Wolsey saw a chance of making money, and rising in the world, by opening a butcher's shop in Ipswich, and by 1466 he had moved with his family to the St Nicholas ward of the busy county town.[3] Ipswich had about five thousand inhabitants. Its access to the sea down the River Gipping and the Orwell made it a centre of the wool trade with the great duchy of Burgundy, which stretched from the Lake of Geneva to the Zuyder Zee and included modern Belgium and the southern part of modern Holland. When Wolsey and More were children, Burgundy was acquired by the house of Habsburg, and became part of the territories of the Holy Roman Emperors Maximilian I and Charles V. The trade with the Netherlands was one of the most important factors influencing the foreign, and even the domestic, policies of the emperors and the kings of England. It brought prosperity to Suffolk and its port of Ipswich.

Like most other butchers of the time, Robert Wolsey had his own livestock, which he probably brought to Ipswich from his farm at Sternfield. He kept his pigs and cattle before slaughter at his house and shop in Ipswich. The urban population in the fifteenth century were used to seeing animals in the streets of the towns being driven on their way to market or straying from their owners' premises; but the Ipswich borough council tried valiantly to restrict the filth in the streets, and the epidemics which resulted, by ordering butchers and other householders

3

to fence and keep their animals in. Robert Wolsey was one of a number of Ipswich tradesmen who was fined in the Mayor's Court for allowing his pigs to roam in the streets. He was fined more than once for allowing his house to be used for illegal purposes. It is not clear what had been going on at the house, but it was probably gaming; if it had been a brothel, he would have been brought before the ecclesiastical court and more severely punished.

He was also fined on several occasions for selling bad meat and for selling meat and skins above the prices fixed by law. Butchers were usually tanners as well, for animal skins could be sold for leather at a higher price than the meat would fetch for food. The high prices put butchers under a temptation to receive stolen cattle from the cattle-thieves. Robert Wolsey's son Thomas knew enough about this for him to present a bill to Parliament when he was Lord Chancellor which forbade butchers to carry on the trade of a tanner because of the number of butchers who dealt in stolen cattle.

Robert Wolsey's offences were dealt with lightly by the Mayor's Court in Ipswich. Even after he had been convicted several times he was still fined only twopence, though on one occasion he was fined tenpence and on another twelve pence. As unskilled labourers were paid threepence or fourpence a day, and meat was sold at $1\frac{1}{2}d.$ a pound, this amounts to fines of only about £5, £25 and £30 in terms of the value of money in 1982. Despite his repeated flouting of the law, Robert Wolsey was willing to resort to the courts to enforce his own rights, and on one occasion brought an action in the courts against a fuller who he claimed had broken his contract to dye some cloth for him.

Robert Wolsey never became a freeman of the borough of Ipswich, perhaps because of his criminal record; but he was considered to be sufficiently respectable to be chosen as one of the two churchwardens of his parish church of St Nicholas. In this capacity, too, he became involved in litigation, when he and his fellow-churchwarden brought an action against one of the parishioners who had not paid his tithe to the church.[4]

By the time his son Thomas was born, the Wars of the Roses were over, and the country was settling down under Edward IV to a new era of economic prosperity and the restoration of internal peace amid a general spirit of optimism. The new wealth and confidence showed itself in the houses that were built. Not only gentlemen but prosperous yeomen and merchants like Robert Wolsey were building stone houses, which were much more durable than the earlier wooden houses; a few of them are still standing today after five hundred years. Their chief novelty was a 'solar', a separate private bedroom for the master of the house, standing by itself on the first floor apart from the common room where the rest of the household ate and slept. Robert Wolsey's house in Ipswich is said to have been in St Nicholas Street, at the corner of the little alley leading to the church. As it was pulled down in the eighteenth century, we know nothing about it; but his son Thomas acted in the spirit of the age when he engaged in building projects as a means of showing his opulence and gaining prestige.

Robert and Joan Wolsey had at least three more children after the birth of their eldest son Thomas, who we know had two brothers and a sister; but Robert's hopes centred on his eldest son, who from his childhood showed exceptional precocity. He presumably received his first education at the Ipswich Grammar School, after which it was decided to send him to Oxford University, not at the usual age of fourteen, but when he was only eleven. We do not know who was responsible for this step, the first and most decisive in Thomas Wolsey's career, which alone made it possible for the Ipswich butcher's son to become, forty years later, the most powerful man in Western Europe. Robert Wolsey may have been in touch with some well-wisher who had connections with Oxford, for Cambridge would have been a more obvious choice for a Suffolk man; but there can be very little doubt that the ambitious father, who had pushed his own way to success in trade, had visions of much greater prospects for his very intelligent son. The university fees came to about four pounds a year, about £2,500 in terms of today's prices. From his will, it appears that Robert Wolsey could have found this money, but only at the cost of a considerable sacrifice. In about 1484 the eleven-year-old Thomas Wolsey went as an undergraduate to Magdalen College, which had been founded twenty-six years before, though the building of the college had still not been completed when he first went there.[5]

Admission to the university and entry into the Church would open up unlimited possibilities for Thomas Wolsey. Men from humbler homes than the house of a prosperous Ipswich butcher-grazier had risen through the Church to the highest positions in the land. The Church offered a career, not only to parsons and curates in every parish in England, but to canons in the cathedrals, to the chantry-priests singing private masses several times a day for the souls of the founders, and to the chaplains of the nobility. The scholars who spent their lives in study at the universities had usually been ordained as priests. The ecclesiastical courts, which dealt with all matrimonial causes, with probate of wills, and with offences against morality, as well as with those matters concerning church administration which are tried in the ecclesiastical courts today, employed a large staff of canon lawyers, who were mostly priests. A bishop's diocese was administered by a number of clerics, from his ordinary (his deputy) downwards. Noblemen employed priests as their secretaries and as their land agents and officials.

Most important of all, the king's government was very largely carried on by priests. His chief minister, the Lord Chancellor, was nearly always a priest; there had only been two cases in history of a layman holding the office.* About half the members of the Privy Council – the equivalent of the modern Cabinet – were bishops. Ambassadors were usually bishops or deans. The lower ranks of the government administration were manned partly by priests and partly by laymen.

This link between the Church and what we today would call the civil service was one of the reasons why the Church, by the end of the fifteenth century, had become completely corrupt. It was not merely that there were isolated cases of corruption; the corruption had become endemic, as it is in the civil service in some countries today. With a few exceptions, nearly every priest was corrupt; people expected a priest to be corrupt, and thought him a fool if he was not corrupt. When nearly everyone is corrupt, it becomes almost misleading to speak of corruption, for no one thinks that it is wrong to act in the usual way in which everyone else is acting.

Corruption is especially likely to take hold in a society where people's lives are beset by regulations, and when licences are needed before anything can be done. Englishmen in the days of Wolsey and More were subject to a large number of regulations and could not engage in many activities without licences granted by priests in the civil and ecclesiastical administration. It was the bishops and nobles in the Privy Council who fixed the maximum price which Robert Wolsey and the other butchers could charge for their mutton, beef, pork and poultry between Easter and Michaelmas and between Michaelmas and the Feast of St John the Baptist next coming (24 June). It was priests who granted the passports permitting the holders to leave the realm, and the licences to export wool, to export and import gold, silver, and English and foreign coin, and to marry a foreigner. It was also priests who granted dispensations from the fasting laws. These laws forbade the eating of meat or cheese on Wednesdays, Fridays and Saturdays, on all days in Lent and Advent, on a number of Ember Days scattered throughout the year, and on the eve of every holy day – those national holidays, about forty in the year, when the people stayed away from work, went to mass, and then spent the rest of the day eating and drinking. It was not difficult to get dispensations to eat meat on the fast days, and these were much sought after, for gluttony was said to be the national vice of the English, as drunkenness was the national vice of the Germans and lechery of the French. The dispensations were needed, as the sheriff's

---

* Sir Thomas Beaufort in 1409, and Richard Neville, Earl of Salisbury, in 1454.

men and the mayor's officers were always liable to enter the people's houses at dinner time to see what they were eating. The ecclesiastical officials who granted the dispensations expected to be given a little gift in return.

The priests in the civil service needed the gifts, as they did not receive any salary, though when they travelled on diplomatic missions and government business they were paid a generous expense allowance; at the highest level, when a bishop was sent abroad as an ambassador, this might be as high as twenty shillings a day. The gifts from grateful members of the public were one of their main methods of remuneration. The other was a grant to them of an ecclesiastical benefice. This was only feasible if they obtained a dispensation for pluralities which allowed them to hold more than the maximum number of benefices permitted by law, and another dispensation for non-residence. A parish priest was not permitted to be the parson of more than two benefices at the same time, and was expected to reside in his parish. Both requirements could be waived by a dispensation which would allow a priest to be the parson of several parishes in the north or the west, a week's ride from the place where he performed his duties as the king's secretary or as a bishop's chancellor. He could then live on the tithes paid by the parishioners, out of which he provided a small salary for a less eminent priest who acted as his curate and carried out his priestly duties in the parish.

The priesthood was a career which appealed more to practical men, especially those with an eye to feathering their own nests, than to spiritual individuals with a religious temperament, who usually preferred to retire to one of the many monasteries which were to be found in both town and country all over England. Indeed, the word 'religion' was used exclusively to refer to monks and nuns. When a man in the fifteenth century spoke about 'the religious', he meant monks and nuns; and when the authorities called a meeting to discuss 'matters appertaining to religion', they talked only about the state of the monasteries and nunneries. The priests, by contrast with the monks, were very appropriately called the 'secular clergy'. But it was these priests of the secular clergy who alone held the power, not only to grant licences and dispensations, but to save souls by granting absolution after confession and penance, and to perform the miracle of transforming bread and wine at mass into the Body and Blood of Christ, which no monk could do, unless he had also been ordained as a priest. The Catholic theologians, distinguishing between the 'reality' of the substance of the bread and wine and the 'accidents' of their taste, smell and texture, taught that they had been transubstantiated by the words of the priest during mass, and that Christ's Body and Blood were 'really' present in them. Wycliffe and his Lollards had denied this at the end of the

7

fourteenth century; but anyone who believed their doctrine was a 'sacramentary', the worst kind of heretic. If a sacramentary refused to recant, he was condemned as a heretic by his bishop or the bishop's ordinary, and was delivered to the secular arm – the local sheriff and justices of the peace – to be burned alive at the stake under the provisions of the Act for the Burning of Heretics of 1401.

Within the priesthood, there was fierce competition for the higher prizes which were there to be won by priests with the necessary qualities – ability, energy, ruthlessness, and the knack of making useful friends. But there was a complication. Men who are attracted by the competitiveness and the rewards of a public career, which the priesthood offered at the end of the fifteenth century, often enjoy the pursuit and conquest of women; and priests had been required to be celibate ever since Pope Gregory VII, the great Hildebrand, introduced the rule in the far more zealous and rigid eleventh century. At one time, priests had taken a vow of celibacy at their ordination, but by the fifteenth century they no longer did so, though novices had to take the oath before becoming monks or nuns. The distinction was significant; while monks and nuns were required to be celibate because of their vows, priests were forced to observe the rule only because it was a regulation imposed by the popes and the Church. This had the effect, on the one hand, of underlining the authority of the Church, which could compel a priest to remain celibate although he had never taken any vow to do so; on the other, it emphasized the different way in which the Church and the people regarded 'the religious' and the secular clergy. A monk who broke his vow of celibacy was considered to be guilty of a far more heinous offence than a priest who committed fornication.

The offence was so common among the secular clergy that the Church tacitly accepted it, and even decided unofficially to try to restrict it by winking at the practice of concubinage. By the time of More and Wolsey, many priests lived more or less openly with a woman who kept house for the priest and whom everybody knew was his 'concubine', just as they knew that the children in his home were the illegitimate sons and daughters of the priest and the concubine. It was not at all unusual for these children to follow their father's example by becoming priests, after the necessary dispensations for illegitimacy had been obtained; and if their father had by this time become an influential bishop, they could expect to be given a lucrative ecclesiastical benefice. From time to time some reforming zealots would denounce concubinage and succeed in getting a synod to pass a regulation against it; but the decree was ignored or evaded, and concubinage continued unchecked.

Even in the monasteries and nunneries life was not as devout as it should have been. There were 513 monasteries in England. The largest,

Christchurch in Canterbury, had seventy monks, but most were much smaller, only thirty-seven of them having more than twenty monks, and only 115 more than ten.[6] In the monasteries with only two or three inmates, discipline tended to be laxer than in the larger houses. It is difficult to discover the truth about the morals of the monks and nuns from the reports of the commissioners whom Henry VIII and Thomas Cromwell sent to visit the houses in 1535, because they were certainly biased, and wanted to present the houses in the worst possible light in order to justify their dissolution and the confiscation of their property by the king; but there can be no doubt that in many houses homosexuality between monks was practised, and in some cases winked at. In others, some of the monks, or more often the abbot, kept a mistress hidden on the premises; and in several nunneries the nuns and the abbess were regularly visited by their lovers. In many more, religious discipline was lax. Dispensations were granted to ignore or relax the fasting laws; and wine, which Christ had clearly sanctioned by the miracle at the feast in Cana, was often consumed in very large quantities.

But despite the jokes about drunken and lecherous monks and friars which were told and sung in the taverns and at the dinner tables of the aristocracy and the merchants, there were still religious houses where the discipline of earlier times was applied in all its rigour. The strictest fasting laws were enforced; the brothers rose repeatedly during the night to pray in the cold chapel; and, with the permission of the superior, a monk could indulge in special acts of mortification of the flesh.

Life in a devout, well-disciplined religious house had a great attraction for Thomas More. The priesthood offered great possibilities to Thomas Wolsey.

CHAPTER 2

THOMAS MORE OF LONDON

IN the fifteenth century, as in more recent times, good food and wine were appreciated in the Bar mess; and the barristers of Lincoln's Inn had a high regard for their butler, John More, who supervised the arrangements at their dinners. In 1470 they rewarded him for his many years of service by making him an honorary member of the Inn. He lived till about the end of the century, but not long enough to see his son John become a High Court judge and his grandson, Thomas, Lord Chancellor of England.

Soon after the butler was made a member of the Inn, he was promoted to be chief steward, and his son John succeeded him as butler. But young John was ambitious, and persuaded the benchers of the Inn to admit him as an ordinary member of the Inn with a view to his being called to the Bar. We have no record of when this took place, and whether he was a butler or a barrister when his son Thomas was born. Before he was twenty-four, John had married Agnes Granger, the daughter of a prosperous London merchant who afterwards became one of the sheriffs. John More and Agnes lived in a house in Cripplegate, either within, or just outside, the City walls. Here their first child, a daughter, Joan, was born in March 1475. John More was aged twenty-seven when Thomas, his second child and eldest son, was born in February 1478. Then came Agatha in January 1479, John in June 1480, Edward in September 1481, and Elizabeth in September 1482. Two of the six children, Agatha and John, probably died in infancy.

John More did well at the Bar, and by 1503 had joined Serjeants' Inn as a serjeant-at-law, which was the highest class of barrister until the title became extinct in the twentieth century. About fifteen years later, when he was well over sixty, he was appointed a High Court judge in the court of Common Pleas, and was later promoted to the court of King's Bench. As the butler of Lincoln's Inn he was no higher in rank than Robert Wolsey the butcher; but when he became a barrister he automatically became an esquire and a gentleman. At some date – perhaps when he was first appointed a judge – he was knighted.[1]

Even if he had not married Thomas Granger's daughter, John More would have been closely connected, as a London barrister, with the commerce of the City. The growth of trade and the removal of the restrictions on the conveyance of land which followed the end of feudalism, increased the demand for barristers, particularly in London, and made it possible for some of them to acquire a lucrative practice at the Bar. Barristers played an important part in business life and in local government in the City, but not yet in national politics or in government administration, which was in the hands of the priests. There was a good deal of antagonism between the priests in the civil service and the barristers, for these priests were usually canon lawyers, who had studied not only the canon law but also the Roman civil law which had developed in ancient Rome and had been codified by the Emperor Justinian in Constantinople in the sixth century. It had survived in some form or other in Europe for nine hundred years, and was the basis of the legal system of most of Western Europe, including Scotland.

The English common law had developed on different lines, and there was no love lost between the common lawyers, on the one side, and the canonists and 'civilians' on the other. The common law relied on the evidence of witnesses called by the parties to a dispute – in criminal cases, by the crown and the defendant. The civil law was inquisitorial, and compelled the defendant to submit to interrogation. The emperor Constantine, with the best intentions, had issued a decree which provided that no one could be convicted unless he admitted his offence; but the result was to introduce the practice of interrogating the defendant under torture. By the fifteenth century, torture was freely used in political cases brought before the Privy Council, where the civilians – most of them priests – conducted the proceedings. The common lawyers did not approve of this procedure, though it was not until a hundred years after Wolsey's and More's time that they ventured to say so. They disapproved even more of the arbitrary intervention by the Lord Chancellor – nearly always a priest and a canonist – who in his High Court of Chancery applied his principles of equity to modify the rigid rules of the common law when he thought that they caused injustice. The court of Chancery, though hated by the common lawyers, was very popular with litigants.

Thomas More was sent to St Anthony's School in the City of London, where he learned Latin. It was the language of the priests and intellectuals of Western Europe, the language in which the mass and church services were held, in which international treaties were drafted, in which learned books were written, in which intellectuals of different nations wrote and spoke to each other. It removed all language barriers between educated men, and separated them from the uneducated masses and from the women of their own families, for not many women could understand Latin. Like all his friends, More learned to speak it fluently. In later life, he wrote books sometimes in Latin and sometimes in English; but, according to the learned editors of the Yale edition of his collected works, his literary style and his handwriting indicate that he found it easier to write in Latin, at least when dealing with scholarly subjects.[2]

By 1490, if not earlier, John More was a rising barrister, and sufficiently influential to give his son an advantage which was not available to the son of an Ipswich butcher. When Thomas was twelve, he became a page in the household of John Morton, Archbishop of Canterbury and Lord Chancellor of England. The practice of placing young boys as pages in great households had survived from the age of feudal chivalry; and to be a page in Morton's household was a splendid opportunity which Thomas More did not waste. He waited on Morton at the dinner table, and acted in plays in the household during the Twelve Days of Christmas.[3] The Archbishop supervised his education, and introduced him to a circle of acquaintances whose level of culture was very different from that of John More's legal and commercial friends in the City of London. Thomas More acquired the greatest admiration for Morton, and when, twenty-five years later, he wrote his *History of King Richard III*, he praised Morton with an enthusiasm which went far beyond the formal respect which he was expected to show when writing about his old master.

This great ecclesiastical statesman, who became the prototype and ideal of Thomas More, had been far more concerned with politics than with religion during his chequered career. Morton was born into a humble family at Bere Regis in Dorset in about 1420. He was educated at a local monastery and went to Oxford University. He became a priest, and a very able and successful lawyer, practising as a canonist and civilian in the ecclesiastical courts in London. He became a high government official under Henry VI, and was appointed a canon of Lincoln and of Salisbury cathedrals with a dispensation to hold both positions at the same time. He was with Henry VI and his queen, Margaret of Anjou, when they were defeated by Edward IV at Towton and were forced to escape into Scotland. Most of the Lancastrian officials made their peace with the victorious Yorkists; but Morton remained loyal to the Lancastrian cause, and went into exile with his king and queen. He stayed with them through thick and thin, remaining at their side during their exile in Scotland, returning with them when they invaded Northumberland, and escaping with the queen to France while Henry VI was captured and held as a prisoner in the Tower of London. In 1470 he returned with her and her army to England, when the Lancastrian cause triumphed for six months; but in the spring of

1471 Edward IV was again victorious, and this time made sure of things by murdering Henry VI and his son, the Prince of Wales.

It was at this point that the loyal John Morton decided that enough was enough. He had remained faithful to Henry VI as long as Henry had any chance of success; but when he was sure that his King's cause was hopeless, he made peace with his murderer. His old friend, Archbishop Bourchier, had long since joined the Yorkists, and it was probably thanks to the archbishop that Edward IV took Morton into his service. Morton's combination of loyalty and expediency had proved very successful; by holding out longer, he had obtained better terms than many who had gone over to Edward ten years earlier. Next year he was appointed Master of the Rolls, and, beginning a new life at fifty-one, he prospered. He was duly appointed Bishop of Ely, and a member of Edward IV's Privy Council, and as an Executor of the King's Will he became a member of the Council of Regency of the boy king, Edward V.

Edward IV's brother, Richard, Duke of Gloucester, immediately took steps to get rid of the boy and make himself king. After cutting off the heads of the queen mother's brothers, he decided to strike down the powerful Yorkist nobleman, Lord Hastings. Shakespeare's version of this incident in his play *Richard III* is historically accurate. A meeting of the Council was held in the Tower at which Hastings was present along with Morton and the other Privy councillors. Richard, knowing that Morton was the only one of them who would dare to stand up to him, asked him to go to his house in Holborn, in the suburbs of London, and tell his servants to bring some strawberries for the councillors. While Morton was absent on this errand, Richard denounced Hastings as a traitor and had him taken out from the Council chamber to the Tower green and immediately beheaded before Morton returned from Holborn. It was a strange suggestion that a member of the Council should withdraw from its deliberations in order to make arrangements for strawberries to be brought, but it was very advantageous for Morton to have been away while Hastings was arrested and executed. In fact, the incident was so strange and so convenient for both Richard and Morton that it may have been the result of a secret agreement between them; but if so, this was never discovered, and a few weeks later, Richard arrested Morton and placed him in the custody of Richard's powerful ally, the Duke of Buckingham.

Morton afterwards told More how he had handled the situation. By very skilful conversation, which More describes in detail in his book *Richard III*, he made Buckingham believe that Richard was planning to double-cross him and destroy him.[4] Buckingham became so alarmed that he rose in revolt against Richard and sent Morton on a mission to the Lancastrian pretender, Henry, Earl of Richmond, in France.

Buckingham's revolt failed, and he was captured and executed; but two years later, Richmond landed with a force of Bretons at Milford Haven, defeated and killed Richard III at Bosworth, and became King Henry VII. Morton was appointed Archbishop of Canterbury and soon afterwards Lord Chancellor. In 1493, just after More had left his household, he was created a cardinal.

As Henry VII's chief minister, he was traditionally thought to be the originator of the device which became known as 'Morton's Fork', by which the king's subjects were asked to pay a 'voluntary contribution' to the royal Exchequer. If a man lived ostentatiously, the commissioners told him that as he was obviously very rich, he could afford to contribute a large sum; if he lived simply and frugally, they argued that as he evidently did not spend much money, he would not miss it if he gave it to the king, so that either way the taxpayer was caught on one or other of the two prongs of the fork. But after Morton's death, More himself told this same story to Erasmus about Morton's successor as chief minister, Richard Foxe, Bishop of Winchester. In More's version Foxe, not Morton, was the author of this trickery, and historians have therefore believed that Morton had nothing to do with it. But the fact that More told the story about Foxe does not mean that Morton did not also do it; and there is no doubt that Morton was ruthlessly efficient in enforcing Henry VII's authority, and resorted to arbitrary methods of government. He reached what was, in the fifteenth century, the great age of eighty, and died in 1500.

Morton was a very cultured man and a patron of the new studies in Greek which had become fashionable in intellectual circles in Italy and spread to England in Henry VII's reign. Until the middle of the fifteenth century the literature of ancient Greece had been almost ignored in Western Europe, for the New Testament and the works of Aristotle were the only Greek books that had been translated into Latin. Then the influx of Greek scholars into Italy, which had increased as Turkish armies overran the Eastern Roman Empire; the development of printing in the Netherlands and in Germany in the 1450s, and its introduction into England by Caxton in the year of More's birth; and the efforts of the influential Italian scholar, Lorenzo Valla, caused the works of Euripides, Sophocles, Plato, and the writers of the Silver Age to become available in the West. Many churchmen did not approve, for the writers of these books had been pagans, and the study of their work distracted scholars from pursuing the studies in divinity which, apart from medicine, had hitherto been almost the only subjects taught at the universities. Valla and his supporters argued that it was justifiable to study humanistic writings as long as divinity was not neglected, and they became known as 'humanists'. In the fifteenth century the word did not mean, as it does today, a freethinker who does not believe in any established religion, but a Catholic who thought that it was permissible to study other subjects as well as divinity, and to read the writings of authors who had lived before the birth of Christ.

The opponents of the humanists who disapproved of the study of Greek – the humanists nicknamed them the 'Trojans' – might have crushed the humanists if it had not been for the sympathy felt for the new culture by the highest authorities in Church and State. The bishops' ordinaries and the teachers in the universities might disapprove of reading the old pagan authors, but popes, cardinals and kings were interested in them. The humanists were encouraged and protected by the princes of the Church, and were welcomed at the courts of the temporal princes, and as a result became strong supporters of the spiritual and temporal authority. Intelligent and cultured humanists like Erasmus and More might be well aware of the abuses in the Church and the vices of kings and emperors, and sometimes denounced or satirised them; but they did not wish to weaken the authority of popes and kings who protected them from their persecutors, gave them financial help, and made it possible for them to proceed with their studies and creative work.

More first discovered the attraction of Renaissance culture in Morton's household, and this was doubtless one of the reasons for his admiration of Morton. But it is clear from his *Richard III* that he was also fascinated by Morton's political ingenuity and diplomatic finesse. It was probably during his residence in Lambeth Palace that More first felt the attraction of political life, with its excitement, its unscrupulousness, and its capacity for doing good, that afterwards drew him, with such unfortunate results, into the service of Henry VIII.

In 1492 Morton arranged for More, who was then fourteen, to go to the university at Oxford, probably to Canterbury College, of which Morton, as Archbishop of Canterbury, was patron, and which occupied the site of the modern college of Christ Church. Not far away, at the other end of the High Street, Wolsey was in residence at Magdalen College. More stayed only two years at Oxford, which was not long enough for him to take a degree. It is not quite clear what he did there. Canterbury College, which was under the control of Benedictine monks, provided facilities for the study of Greek, which Morton encouraged; but More did not learn Greek until about seven or eight years after he left Oxford. His life at Oxford was very hard. The undergraduates were brought up in very Spartan conditions; and his father, who thought that this was good for Thomas, did not provide him with any money with which he could have alleviated his situation. He did not have enough money to have his shoes repaired.[5]

In 1494 More returned to London to study at the New Inn of the Court of Chancery before following his father and grandfather and becoming a member of Lincoln's Inn.[6] John More was very eager that Thomas should practise as a barrister at the common law Bar, and it shows his breadth of view that he was prepared to keep him for two years in Morton's household and for two more years at Oxford, while he absorbed the culture of the Renaissance, which was of no practical use to him as a barrister, and then to send him to the New Inn to study the rival system of equity. But Thomas, as a result, felt the pull of the two conflicting interests: on the one side, the world of which he had caught a glimpse at Lambeth Palace – politics, Greek, the priesthood as a road to office in the king's government, the stimulus of intellectual cynicism and the friendship of the leading thinkers of the age; on the other, the world in which his father moved, the common law, the Bar, Lincoln's Inn, the City of London, and good opportunities for making money.

It was probably through his contacts in Morton's household that he met the young Lord Mountjoy, who was the same age as Thomas More. Mountjoy was a courtier, soldier and intellectual who, by the age of nineteen, had served with distinction in the suppression of Perkin Warbeck's rebellion, and had learned Greek in Paris as a pupil of Erasmus of Rotterdam. It was Mountjoy who introduced More to two men who in their very different ways were to have a great influence on his life – Henry VIII and Erasmus. More had already been presented to the little Henry, Duke of York, who later became Henry VIII, before the late summer of 1499 when he met Erasmus for the first time. He and his friend, the young barrister Edward Arnold, called at Lord Mountjoy's country house near Greenwich, where Erasmus was staying during a visit to England. More, Arnold and Erasmus walked over to the king's palace in the nearby village of Eltham, where all the royal children – except the eldest, Arthur, Prince of Wales – were being educated by their tutor, John Skelton. More presented Erasmus to Henry, Duke of York, aged eight; to Princess Margaret, who was nearly ten, and afterwards married James IV of Scotland; to Princess Mary, aged three, who married Louis XII of France and later the Duke of Suffolk; and to the baby Prince Edmund, who was a few months old and died next year.

More and Arnold delivered some written work to the Duke of York; but More had forgotten to warn Erasmus that he would be expected to do the same. After More and his friends had been entertained to dinner in the palace, the eight-year-old prince sent a note to Erasmus asking him to present him with something in writing; and three days later Erasmus duly sent him a flattering ode in praise of Henry VII and his children.[7]

In January 1500 Erasmus returned to Paris in a vile temper and thoroughly incensed against the English, for he had forgotten to obtain a licence to export English coin, and all his money was confiscated by the authorities at Dover.[8] But he retained at least one happy recollection of England – his meeting with Thomas More.[9]

CHAPTER 3

THE AMBITIOUS PRIEST

ACCORDING to George Cavendish, who was a gentleman usher in Wolsey's household during the last eight or nine years of his master's life, Wolsey told him that he took his degree as a Bachelor of Arts at the very early age of fifteen, which so impressed the scholars at Oxford that he was called the 'boy-bachelor'.[1] As the degree could only be taken after a four-year course, this means that he must have gone to Oxford when he was only eleven; and if, as seems likely, he was born in 1473, that he was in residence at Magdalen for sixteen years. But we have no record of what he was doing between the ages of fifteen and twenty-five. At some date during this period he took his degree as Master of Arts, which was usually taken three years after the B.A. degree. He probably studied divinity, but he did not take his degree as a Doctor or even as a Bachelor of Divinity. By 1497 he had become a Fellow of Magdalen, and had been appointed headmaster of Magdalen school, which adjoined the College premises. He also acted as tutor to a number of boys.[2]

After his remarkable achievement in becoming a B.A. at fifteen, his progress was not especially rapid. He was not an academic by nature, and almost certainly regarded his university studies and qualifications as a stepping-stone to a career in the Church and in government as a priest and civil servant. But to a butcher's son from Ipswich, without many useful contacts or influence, success came slowly.

At the beginning of October 1496 his father died. Robert Wolsey made his will on 30 September, a few days before the end. He appointed his son Thomas and a man named Thomas Cady to be his executors. He made a number of bequests to church charities. He directed that if his son Thomas became a priest within a year of his death, he was to receive ten marks (£6.13s.4d.) for singing masses for his soul for a year. If Thomas had not become a priest within the year, some other priest was to be asked to sing the masses for the ten marks fee. Robert Wolsey then bequeathed all his property to his wife, who remarried soon after his death; but by the law then in force, his freehold land must have passed to Thomas as his eldest son.[3]

Thomas was almost certainly aged twenty-three when his father died.

18

By the canon law, no one could be ordained a priest before his twenty-fourth birthday, though it was not very difficult to obtain a dispensation to be ordained during the previous year at any time after the twenty-third birthday. If Thomas Wolsey was born during the winter of 1472–3, his dying father in October 1496 could be sure that he would be ordained within a year, even if he could not obtain a dispensation to be ordained under the canonical age. Yet for some reason, this did not happen, and Thomas, despite his incentive to keep the ten marks in the family, did not take orders until five months after the expiry of the time limit fixed in his father's will. On 10 March 1498 he was ordained at Marlborough by the Bishop of Salisbury's suffragan, who bore the title of Bishop of Lydda,[4] one of the sees 'in infidel parts' which were awarded for titular purposes to suffragan bishops.

Was Wolsey, for some reason, reluctant to become a priest? And did his father insert the provision about the ten marks in his will in order to overcome this reluctance? If Wolsey hesitated to take orders, the most likely explanation would be that he had fallen in love and wished to marry; and this is quite possible, for we know that he was attracted to women, and some years later had a mistress who bore him at least two children. Or was the delay in his ordination due not to him but to some unusually rigid official in the diocese of Salisbury who made difficulties about the women?

For a year after he was ordained he could not obtain any benefice, and then was appointed only to the very subordinate position of rural dean in the diocese of Norwich, in which Ipswich was situated. At Oxford he did not attain any of the university offices, but in 1498 he was appointed Junior Bursar of his college, and next year became Senior Bursar. As Bursar of Magdalen, he was concerned with the financial arrangements for the building of the great college tower which was being erected in the last years of the fifteenth century. According to a tradition at Magdalen, he was dismissed from his office of bursar because he broke some regulation while collecting funds for the building of the tower.[5] This would be quite in keeping with the tendency which he showed in later years to cut through red tape and take irregular shortcuts in order to get things done.

His lucky break came at last when he was nearly twenty-seven. Among his pupils at the college school at Magdalen were the three youngest sons of the Marquess of Dorset, and in December 1499 he was invited to spend the Christmas vacation with Dorset and the boys at Dorset's mansion at Bradgate in Leicestershire. Dorset was not only the second nobleman in England after the Duke of Buckingham, but as Elizabeth Woodville's son by her first marriage he was the half-brother of Henry VII's queen, Elizabeth of York. Wolsey made a favourable impression on Dorset, who soon afterwards appointed him as Rector of Limington near Ilchester in Somerset, of which Dorset was patron. Wolsey was inducted as rector on 10 October 1500.[6]

He took up residence in his parish, and came into conflict with Sir Amyas Paulet, a knight who lived ten miles from Limington at Hinton St George and after a distinguished military career had been appointed Sheriff of Somerset. According to Cavendish, Paulet put Wolsey in the stocks. Cavendish did not know what offence Wolsey had committed, but eighty years later Sir Roger Wilbraham, Elizabeth I's Master of Requests, stated that it was for fornication. Sir John Harington, who, as Sheriff of Somerset, held the office which Paulet had occupied a hundred years earlier, wrote that it was because Wolsey had got drunk at a fair. Cavendish adds that many years later, when Wolsey was Lord Chancellor, he revenged himself on Paulet by ordering him to remain within the confines of the Middle Temple, of which Paulet was Treasurer, and forbidding him to leave the Inn for five or six years, or even longer. Paulet spent these years supervising the building of a splendid gatehouse to the Inn, and adorning it with Wolsey's arms and badge, in the hope of appeasing Wolsey's anger. The gatehouse was burned down in the Great Fire of London in 1666.

'Now may this be a good example and precedent', wrote Cavendish:

to men in authority, who will sometimes work their will without wit, to remember in their authority how authority may decay. And whom they punish of will more than of justice may after be advanced in the public weal to high dignities and governance – and they based as low – who will then seek the means to be revenged of old wrongs sustained wrongfully before. Who would have thought then that when Sir Amyas Paulet punished this poor scholar, that ever he should have attained to be Chancellor of England, considering his baseness in every condition? These be wonderful works of God and fortune.[7]

It is a surprising story, and it is unlikely to be true in every detail. Cavendish states on several occasions in his book that an incident which he relates was told to him by Wolsey himself; but, not surprisingly, he does not claim that he heard about this scandalous episode from the cardinal. On the contrary, he says that he does not know for what reason Paulet put Wolsey in the stocks, which suggests that the story was current gossip in Wolsey's household which no one ventured to discuss with their master. The stocks were regularly used as a punishment for members of the lower classes who had committed some comparatively minor misdemeanour which was not sufficiently serious to deserve a prison sentence; but it would be most unusual and irregular to set the

Richard Foxe, Bishop of Winchester, after the portrait by Hans Corvus

Catherine of Aragon, by an unknown artist

parish rector in the stocks. In 1501 Wolsey was no longer a 'poor scholar' with 'his baseness in every condition', but one of the most important people in Limington who enjoyed the patronage of the queen's half-brother. Paulet held an important position in the king's service, but he knew that Dorset was much more influential than he was.

If Wolsey had committed fornication, as Wilbraham thought, Paulet's proper course would have been to report him to his bishop, not to set him in the stocks. The stocks were the proper punishment for being drunk and disorderly at a fair, which was probably why the tradition arose that this was Wolsey's offence; but though it is easy to believe, from what we know of Wolsey, that he may have discreetly committed fornication in Limington, it seems very unlikely that he would have been drunk and disorderly within a few months of having at last obtained a benefice and the favour of a very powerful patron whom it would have been folly to antagonise by a scandal of this kind.

Dorset could hardly have overlooked the matter if Paulet had put his rector in the stocks. He would have heard about it either from Paulet or from Wolsey, and would either have supported Paulet and disgraced Wolsey, or the incident would have led to one of those clashes between Dorset and Paulet which from time to time occurred among powerful personages and had repercussions at the highest level, but of which there is no record whatever in connection with Wolsey in 1501.

From our very scanty knowledge of the episode, we can only deduce that Wolsey, with his proud, independent and arrogant self-assertiveness, annoyed the local magnate, Sir Amyas Paulet; that there was an unpleasant incident of some kind, perhaps a threat from Sir Amyas, in a moment of anger, to put Wolsey in the stocks; that Dorset accepted Wolsey's side of the story and continued to favour him; that Wolsey resented Sir Amyas's conduct, and did him an ill turn when he was Lord Chancellor; and that the members of Wolsey's household, knowing about this resentment and about Wolsey's mistress and bastards and his low social origin, embroidered the story about youthful peccadilloes and his punishment as a low-born fellow for his misconduct.

In September 1501 Wolsey suffered what might have been a blow to his hopes when Dorset died; but he had already made useful contacts through Dorset, and very soon after Dorset's death was appointed chaplain to Henry Deane, the Archbishop of Canterbury. Deane had succeeded Morton both as Archbishop and in performing the office of Lord Chancellor, though he had been given only the more modest title of Keeper of the Great Seal. Just about the time that Wolsey became his chaplain, he married Arthur, Prince of Wales, to Catherine of Aragon, the daughter of the king and queen of Spain; but Arthur died within five months of the wedding. Next summer Deane resigned his office as

Keeper of the Great Seal on account of his age, for he was over seventy.

As soon as Wolsey was appointed to be the Archbishop's chaplain, he obtained a dispensation from the Pope allowing him to hold three benefices simultaneously and not to reside in any of his parishes.[8] He lived with Deane in Lambeth Palace, an impressive building which had recently been enlarged and made more splendid by Morton, and continued as Rector of Limington, which he probably never visited again.

He held his position as Deane's chaplain for less than eighteen months. In February 1503 Deane died, having appointed Wolsey and one of his other chaplains as his executors. They carried out the archbishop's elaborate instructions about his funeral, for which Deane had allocated £500. They arranged for the body to be carried by water from Lambeth to Faversham by thirty-three sailors, and then taken on a hearse to Canterbury to be buried with great pomp in the cathedral.[9] Wolsey had again lost a patron, but again he turned ill luck to his own advantage. He was appointed chaplain to Sir Richard Nanfan, the Governor of Calais.[10] This was a less impressive position than being chaplain to the Archbishop of Canterbury, but it gave Wolsey a wide experience of many sides of government, especially of relations with foreign countries, and a foothold in the government service.

The Marches of Calais had been English territory ever since they had been conquered by Edward III a hundred and fifty years before. Since 1453 they were the only territory in France which was still in English hands, and were a useful military and commercial strongpoint, as well as justifying the continued use of the title 'King of France' by the English kings. The territory stretched along the coast for about twenty-five miles, and inland for some six miles; it contained the town and harbour of Calais, the fortress of Guisnes on the French border, and a number of villages. It was surrounded to the south and west by France, and on the east by the Holy Roman Emperor Maximilian's territories in the Netherlands, which extended as far as the emperor's border towns of Gravelines and St Omer. At the time of the conquest of 1347, the French population had been expelled and replaced by Englishmen, and in 1503 many of the inhabitants were descended from these English settlers; but there were also many foreigners in Calais, chiefly Flemings who had come to trade. There was a permanent military garrison both in the town of Calais and in Guisnes, and in the government of the territory the mayor and corporation and the local government bodies were subordinated to the King's Deputy. The territory was in the diocese of Canterbury, and ecclesiastical affairs, including the investigation into cases of heresy, were conducted by the Archbishop of Canterbury's commissary in Calais.

There was often friction with the French garrison in the fortress of

Ardres, just across the French border not far from Guisnes, and at times there were more serious clashes with French troops sent out to reconnoitre from Boulogne. As relations with the emperor were usually better than those with France, there was a much more relaxed atmosphere along the border with the Netherlands. Calais was the staple for wool, tin and other commodities through which all exports from England had to pass on their way to the Netherlands and to other foreign countries. Most of the English overseas trade passed through Calais, though Venetian and other foreign merchants had licences to bring their wares in their own ships to London, Southampton and other English ports. English and foreign travellers between England and the Continent usually crossed by the Dover-Calais route. In good weather with a favourable wind the crossing took only three hours, but it could take more than twenty-four hours in bad conditions, and travellers were sometimes delayed for three days or longer in Dover or Calais before the wind and weather made it possible for their ship to sail.

The four years that Wolsey spent in Calais between 1503 and 1507 gave him the opportunity to learn about the problems of many aspects of government administration and to show his efficiency in dealing with them. The king's government in London had constantly to be reminded of the need to make money available in Calais to pay the soldiers' wages; and when the harvests in England were bad, it was not always easy to ensure that food supplies were sufficient for the garrison and the civil population in Calais. The merchants who operated the staple had to be pressed to pay their customs dues to the king; seditious utterances among the soldiers were viewed with particular suspicion in view of the importance of Calais as a defensive stronghold; there was the need to watch the movements of the French garrison at Ardres and to report any border incidents to the government in London. A vigilant eye was kept on any French spy who was thought to have come to Calais, and reports were often received from English spies who had discovered important intelligence in France, Flanders or further afield about hostile military preparations or the actions of 'White Rose' – the Yorkist pretender to the crown of England, Edmund de la Pole – who was living as a refugee in Germany. Twice a year, in May and November, the Deputy of Calais received the king's pensions from France. These were the payments of the half-yearly instalments of 25,000 francs of the total of 745,000 francs which the kings of France had agreed to pay, under their peace treaties with Edward IV and Henry VII, on condition that the king of England did not enforce his claim to the throne of France.

The ability with which Wolsey discharged his duties at Calais led to him being taken directly into the king's service. In January 1507 Nanfan died, having appointed Wolsey as his executor;[11] and at about this time

Wolsey was appointed a royal chaplain, and took up residence at Henry VII's court. It was intended from the first that he should play his part in the king's government as well as in the Chapel Royal, and he became one of the assistant secretaries to Richard Foxe, Bishop of Winchester, the Lord Privy Seal, who was in charge of Henry VII's foreign policy. Foxe, who was fifty-nine in 1507, had been a close friend of Henry VII for nearly thirty years, having been with him in France in the days of Richard III. Wolsey also became friendly with another veteran in the royal service, Sir Thomas Lovell, who had been appointed Chancellor of the Exchequer for life as a reward for his valour at Bosworth Field.[12] William Warham, who had succeeded Deane as Archbishop of Canterbury, was Lord Chancellor; and Thomas Ruthall, the Dean of Lincoln, was the King's Secretary.

But a more powerful and sinister role was played by two men of lower status, Sir Richard Empson, the Chancellor of the Duchy of Lancaster, and Sir Edmund Dudley, who had been Speaker of the House of Commons, but in 1507 held no official position except some minor sinecures. Dudley, who was a Sussex gentleman by birth, and Empson, a Northamptonshire man of lower rank, had both been called to the Bar and after a successful career as common lawyers had entered Henry VII's service, and were employed by him, with Lovell, in the tax-raising activities of the Court of Exchequer. They became the most hated men in England because of their ruthlessness in extracting money from the taxpayers, their offensive manners, and their personal corruption.

Wolsey, with his experience of financial administration and of foreign relations at Calais, and his friendship with both Foxe and Lovell, could have been equally suitably employed in handling either the financial or the diplomatic side of the king's government; but he was appointed to deal with foreign policy. Whether this was pure chance, or through skilful manipulation on his part, it turned out in a few years' time to be lucky for him, for he thus avoided being too closely associated with the hated activities of Dudley and Empson.

In the spring of 1508 he was sent on a difficult diplomatic mission to Scotland. The king of Scots, James IV, had raised the prestige of his remote kingdom to a height which it had never reached before in its history, and would never attain again while it remained an independent country. Having for long been regarded in England and Europe as a backward, poor and lawless land almost beyond the frontiers of Christendom, it had emerged under James IV with a powerful navy, the largest and most modern cannon in its land armies, and with a king who was a cultured Renaissance prince and a force to be reckoned with in international diplomacy.

Henry VII and James IV had put an end to the years of warfare between England and Scotland by making peace and cementing it with the marriage of Henry's daughter Margaret to James; but James wished to keep his options open, and did not, as Henry had hoped, repudiate the 'old alliance' between France and Scotland which had lasted for more than three hundred years. He sent his cousin, the Earl of Arran, and Arran's brother Patrick Hamilton to France to negotiate a renewal of the alliance. The Scots always faced the problem of how to maintain contact with their French ally, for their envoys had either to obtain permission to go by land through England, or, if they went by sea, they might be forced to put in to an English port in bad weather. Arran and Hamilton took the risk of travelling through England without a safe-conduct from Henry VII. They reached France safely, but on the way home were arrested when they landed in Kent, and were taken to Henry's court, where there were treated as honoured guests but were not allowed to return to Scotland. As James IV strongly complained about the detention of his envoys, apart from objecting to the failure of the English authorities in Northumberland to surrender Scottish fugitives from justice, Henry sent Wolsey to Edinburgh to smooth things over.

The journey from London to Edinburgh took at least a fortnight in ordinary circumstances, and sometimes longer.

> . . . Haste away,
> For we must measure twenty miles today,

cries Portia in Shakespeare's *Merchant of Venice*. On the rough and muddy roads, forty miles a day was the furthest that a traveller would normally go. Government officials who went to Scotland usually took their time, and carried out other duties on the way. After travelling up the Great North Road by Ware, Huntingdon and Grantham, they made arrangements at York with the Abbot of St Mary's, who acted as the government's banker, for the payment of the wages and for the supply of provisions to the Border garrisons; in Newcastle and Alnwick they discussed with the Earl of Northumberland his rather ineffectual attempts to suppress the lawlessness in the Border country; and they inspected the fortresses at Berwick and Norham. It was probably on this journey to Scotland that Wolsey became friendly with Lord Darcy, the Warden of the Eastern Marches, for some years later Darcy wrote to Wolsey, calling him his 'bedfellow', and reminding him of how they had discussed their private and personal problems.[13] From Berwick it was a two-day journey by Dunbar and Haddington to Edinburgh along a road which was more often travelled by invading English armies than by English diplomatic envoys.

After waiting five days in Berwick for his safe-conduct, Wolsey reached Edinburgh on 28 March 1508; but the king was inspecting a gunpowder factory, and kept him waiting for another five days before granting him an audience on 2 April. This was undoubtedly a calculated gesture of coolness on James's part. Wolsey saw James every day during the next eight days, and reported to Henry VII that he found him very moody and changeable; but though James was sometimes pleasant and sometimes stiff, he made it clear to Wolsey that he would not negotiate any treaty of friendship until Arran and Hamilton were released, and Wolsey returned home, having accomplished nothing. On leaving Edinburgh he was given the usual 'reward' paid to envoys, receiving £54 Scots from the king for his trouble, and £41.14s.7d. Scots for his lodging and other expenses in Edinburgh.*[14] Arran and Hamilton were not set free until after Henry VII's death a year later.

It was probably a few months later, in July 1508, that Wolsey was sent on another diplomatic mission by Henry VII which he accomplished with a speed of which he was very proud and about which he told Cavendish more than twenty years later. Henry was negotiating with the Emperor Maximilian about the possibility of marrying as his second wife Maximilian's daughter Margaret of Austria, the widowed Duchess of Savoy, who was Maximilian's Regent in the Netherlands, though Henry was simultaneously discussing with King Ferdinand of Spain the possibility of his marrying Ferdinand's daughter, the mad Queen Juana. Maximilian was sympathetic to the idea of a marriage between Henry and Margaret, but Margaret herself was reluctant.

One morning, when the court was at Richmond, Henry instructed Wolsey to go on a mission to the Netherlands; but if it was in the summer of 1508, it could not have been to Maximilian himself, as Cavendish says, for the emperor was not in the Netherlands at this time. Henry told Wolsey that the mission was urgent, and ordered him to leave as soon as possible. Wolsey left Richmond the same day about noon, and, riding to London, took a barge to Gravesend, which he reached three hours later. He rode through the night from Gravesend to Dover, a distance of fifty miles; it was one of the few good roads in England, and a supply of post-horses was always available at Rochester, Sittingbourne, Faversham and Canterbury for travellers on the king's business. He reached Dover early in the morning, and as wind and weather were favourable, crossed to Calais in three hours, presumably getting some rest and sleep on the ship. He left Calais at once, and with post-horses reached the emperor's court that same evening. This would hardly have been possible if the court was at Bruges or Courtrai, which are sixty miles from Calais; but

---

* The English £1 sterling usually exchanged in Scotland for £5.14s.0d. Scots pounds.

perhaps it was at Gravelines, or some other place not far from the frontier.

Next morning Wolsey had audience with the emperor, and, impressing on him the urgency with which King Henry wanted the business to be concluded, received the emperor's reply by noon, and, leaving at once, reached Calais that night. He sailed early next morning, again made the crossing in three hours, was in Dover by 10 a.m., and with relays of horses reached Richmond late that night. On the road between Dover and Richmond he met a messenger whom the king had sent after him with further instructions, and Wolsey sent the messenger on to the emperor's court. Next morning Wolsey went to court, four days after he had received his orders from Henry. When the king saw him, he reprimanded him for having not yet set out on his journey, but was most favourably impressed when Wolsey gave him the emperor's letters and explained that he had already been and returned.[15]

The truth of the story has been doubted by many historians. Certainly Cavendish must have got some of the details wrong, for his information dates the journey at a time when Maximilian was not in the Low Countries. It is also quite possible that Wolsey may have exaggerated the speed at which he travelled, like the modern motorist who assures his friends that he has motored down from London in a time which would be possible only if he had averaged sixty m.p.h. through the West End in the rush hour. Perhaps the two journeys took one more day than Wolsey said or Cavendish wrote. But it is not impossible that with favourable weather conditions Wolsey might have travelled from Richmond to some place in Flanders not far from Calais, and back again to Richmond, in three and a half days; and there is no reason to doubt that with his strong physical stamina, his drive, and his determination to impress and succeed, he accomplished the remarkable achievement.

Wolsey was again in the Netherlands in October 1508, when he spent a month at the Emperor's court at Malines; but he was unable to arrange a marriage between Henry VII and Margaret of Austria.[16]

Meanwhile the ecclesiastical benefices were accumulating, and with them the income from the tithes. While Wolsey was in Calais with Nanfan in June 1506, the Abbot of Bury St Edmunds, no doubt after the usual requests from Nanfan, appointed him Vicar of Redgrave in Suffolk. In July 1508 he received a dispensation from the Pope to hold a maximum of four benefices simultaneously with leave of absence from all of them, and was appointed Vicar of Lydd on Romney Marsh near Dungeness by the Abbot of Tintern, who held the presentation. There is a local tradition at Lydd that he enlarged the church tower; but this is unlikely, as the local records show that the work was carried out in 1445.[17]

On 2 February 1509 he was appointed Dean of Lincoln in succession to the king's secretary Ruthall, who was promoted to be Bishop of Durham.[18] This was the last preferment which Wolsey received from Henry VII. The king died on 21 April, and Henry VIII became king two months before his eighteenth birthday. The accession of a handsome and dashing young king in place of his cautious and money-grasping father was welcomed by the people, but boded ill for Henry VII's unpopular ministers. The popular clamour was directed against Empson and Dudley. They were arrested in July and charged with high treason, being accused of having plotted to place the new king under restraint in order to prevent their removal from power. In January they were attainted in Parliament and sentenced to death. Henry VIII was reluctant to sign the warrant for their execution, but did so at last, and to the joy of the people they were both beheaded on Tower Hill in August 1510.

The death of the two scapegoats saved the others. Wolsey's patron Foxe survived and continued as Bishop of Winchester and Lord Privy Seal on Henry VIII's Privy Council. His other friend, Lovell, who had been close to Dudley and Empson at the Exchequer, also managed to emerge unscathed after some anxious weeks, and was reappointed Chancellor of the Exchequer by Henry VIII. Wolsey was equally lucky. A butcher's son who had become a royal chaplain, Dean of Lincoln, and a second-rank official in the king's government, was much less resented by the nobles and the people than knights of the shire like Dudley and Empson, who, instead of performing their proper functions in local government administration, had been so ambitious as to set themselves up in the national government in a more powerful position than the nobles and bishops of the king's Council.

In December 1509 Wolsey was appointed to be the king's Almoner. He even managed to pick up some of the plums which had become available through the fall of Dudley and Empson, for in October 1509 he was granted the long lease of the vicarage of St Bride's church in Fleet Street which had been held by Empson and which he had resigned to the Abbot of Westminster in an attempt to curry favour with the king a few months before it would in any case have been forfeited by his attainder. Before the execution of Empson and Dudley, Wolsey had also been appointed a canon of Hereford cathedral, holding this prebend along with his position as king's Almoner, Dean of Lincoln and Vicar of Lydd, though he resigned the rectory of Limington.[19] He had weathered the storm, and at the age of thirty-six his prospects under Henry VIII seemed to be even better than his achievements under Henry VII.

CHAPTER 4

LAWYER, HUMANIST OR MONK?

WHILE Thomas Wolsey, overcoming all handicaps and setbacks, was single-mindedly devoting his energies and abilities in advancing his career, Thomas More, with advantages which Wolsey would have envied, could not make up his mind what career he wished to choose – still less could he decide what career God wished him to choose. Should it be the priesthood, the government service, life at the king's court, the friendship of Lord Mountjoy and Erasmus, and the study of Greek; or his father's profession, Lincoln's Inn, the common law, and municipal politics in the City of London? More's solution of the problem was to leave his father's house and take up residence in the Carthusian monastery not five minutes' walk away, just outside the City walls in Cripplegate. He did not take his vows, and become a monk, but lived in the monastery as a guest for four years while on the one hand he lectured on the common law at Furnival Inn, a centre for legal education, and on the other learned Greek from Grocyn and Linacre, two of the leading Greek scholars in Europe, and lectured on St Augustine's *City of God* in the church of St Lawrence in Old Jewry.[1]

But his stay in the Charterhouse created further complications. He loved the spiritual peace of the Carthusian monastery, and thought of taking his vow of chastity and spending the whole of his life as a Carthusian monk. The London Charterhouse was one of the most strictly disciplined religious houses in England; even Henry VIII's commissioners in 1535 could find no trace of moral delinquency in it. The monks not only observed the fasting laws in all their strictness, but ate no meat at all even on other days, and to a large extent observed a rule of silence in the monastery.

More was greatly attracted by monastic life, for there was a deep spirituality in his nature which filled him with a strong desire to withdraw from the competitiveness of the rat-race which took place both in the world of priests, court and scholarship, and in the law and commerce of London. Instead of merely having to choose between the priesthood and the law, there was now a third choice – the spiritual contentment of life in a monastery.

For four years he managed to have all three at the same time, living in the Charterhouse, lecturing on both the common law and St Augustine, and learning Greek from Grocyn; but the choice could not be indefinitely postponed. In the end, at the age of twenty-six, he chose the law, leaving the Charterhouse, beginning a practice at the Bar, and contributing in his spare time to humanistic studies. He also got married. There were two reasons why he chose law – the influence of his father, and his decision, as Erasmus put it, 'to be a chaste husband rather than a licentious priest'.[2]

More's attitude to sex, as to other matters, was contradictory, revealing the two sides of the complex character of this Catholic fanatic and cultured humanist. One thing is clear: he had a very different attitude towards sex and family life than that held by anyone brought up in a society which has been influenced by nineteenth-century ideas of romantic love and by twentieth-century views of equality between the sexes. More believed, with his contemporaries, that woman, ever since the time of Eve, had been Satan's instrument in tempting man to sin, at worst to commit fornication and adultery, and at best to fill his heart with lustful thoughts which distracted him from his prayers and studies. Sex was sinful, but because of man's wickedness God had decreed that it was to be his only method of reproduction. The best form of life was to renounce sex completely by taking, and observing, a vow of chastity; but as the capacity to observe the vow was granted only to some, the rest of mankind had better marry and contain themselves within the bounds of matrimony rather than indulge in fornication and adultery. All this was accepted Catholic doctrine. Most Catholics in Western Europe in 1500 did not take it very seriously in practice. More did, just as he took seriously all aspects of his Catholic faith – or rather, one side of him took it seriously, for the other More could take it, or appear to take it, as lightly as did his worldly humanist friends.

It was a young woman who finally caused More to take the decision about his career. He knew the family of Mr John Colt, a gentleman in the village of Netherhall near Harlow in Essex. Colt, who had married three times, had eighteen children, including two daughters who in 1504 were aged seventeen and sixteen and were both unmarried. More fell in love with the younger sister. He thereupon proposed to the elder sister, Jane; he was accepted, and married her. Roper writes that he married Jane because he thought that it would be a disgrace for her if her younger sister married before she did.[3]

It was not a solution which would have appealed to every man, but it was a satisfactory compromise for More. The charms of the younger sister were distracting him from the law, from Greek, and from monastic life, and were causing him to have grave doubts as to whether he would always be able to resist the temptations of the flesh. He felt unable to make the sacrifice which a vow of chastity would have entailed; but he could at least make a lesser sacrifice by marrying a girl whom he did not love and not the sister for whom he lusted. The unselfishness of his decision must surely be admired even by twentieth-century readers who may think that it was mistaken. Young men of More's generation had not been brought up in the ethical code of nineteenth and twentieth-century novelists, of Verdi's librettists and Hollywood script-writers. In 1504 romantic love was glorified only when, like Tristan and Isolde, it involved sacrifice and unfulfilled desires.

Colt, like other English gentlemen, had not given his daughters any education; unlike their brothers, gentlemen's daughters were usually not taught to read and write. More tried to educate Jane in letters and music, but she was unresponsive. When he tried to make her learn by heart and recite long sermons which he had read to her, she burst into tears and bewailed her lot in leaving her Essex country home and living with More in his learned establishment in London. So he took her on a visit to her father at Netherhall. In Jane's presence, More told Colt about her reluctance to learn. Colt advised him to give her a good beating. More replied that he would prefer it if Colt, her father, administered the beating himself, whereupon Jane ran to More for protection, and promised him that she would never again complain about his treatment of her. More was very pleased with himself for the way he had handled the situation, and told Erasmus, who wrote about it in one of his books.[4]

Jane was in the same position as other sixteenth-century wives: she knew that in the last resort her husband would use a cudgel to compel her to obey him. But not many women of her generation had married a man who despised worldly vanities as much as More did. According to Erasmus, he played a trick on Jane; for More's friends and contemporaries believed that he was the unidentified husband in Erasmus's story in the *Praise of Folly*. He

made his new bride a present of some jewels which were copies, and as he had a ready tongue for a joke, persuaded her that they were not only real and genuine but also of unique and incalculable value. Now, if the young woman was just as happy feasting her eyes and thoughts on coloured glass, what did it matter to her that she was keeping such trinkets hidden carefully away in her room as if they were some rare treasure? Meanwhile her husband saved expense, enjoyed his wife's illusion, and kept her as closely bound in gratitude to him as if he'd given her something which had cost him a fortune.[5]

Jane gave birth to three daughters and a son. Margaret, Elizabeth and Cecily were probably born in 1505, 1506 and 1507, and the fourth surviving child, John, in 1509. In 1511, Jane died at the age of twenty-four.[6] More's biographers have consoled themselves with the thought that, despite all her initial tears at being forced to learn sermons by heart, she had several very happy years with him. One must hope so, but the evidence for it is slight. It rests only on the testimony of Erasmus about More's happy home life when he was staying with More shortly before Jane's death, and the statement in the epitaph which More composed for his own tomb more than twenty years later in 1532.[7] As Erasmus spent all his time in the More household talking Latin to More, a language which Jane did not understand, it is difficult to see how he could have known whether she was happy or not; he probably deduced it from her submissive attitude and from what More told him about how he and her father had tamed her after she had shown resentment at his treatment of her. As for More's statement in his epitaph, this was a document which was designed, as he himself wrote to Erasmus, to 'show off' his achievements to posterity, and he could hardly have said anything else about Jane. He also stated in this same epitaph that he had always lived happily with his second wife, which is contradicted by many other statements. But as it is almost impossible for anyone else to know whether or not a married couple are living happily together, it would be unwise for a biographer nearly five hundred years later to try to answer the question.

Within a month of Jane's death More approached his parish priest in Bucklersbury and asked him to obtain a dispensation which would allow him immediately to marry Alice Middleton, the widow of a London merchant who had died two years before. Erasmus says that More married her because he needed a woman to look after his children.[8] She had the additional advantage for More of being utterly devoid of any sexual attractions, so that no one could think that he had married her in order to indulge in the lusts of the flesh. Erasmus says that she was a good housekeeper, but More himself never had a good word to say for her, except, of course, in his epitaph. He used often to say, jokingly, that she was 'in no way beautiful, or a girl',*[9] for she was no longer young when she married him, and bore him no children.

More was a great success at the Bar. With his logical mind, his profound knowledge of law, his capacity for clear exposition, and his pleasant personality, he had all the necessary qualities for a barrister, and his father's reputation and contacts gave him a useful start. Within a

---

* Chambers retained the rhyme in Erasmus's Latin, 'nec bellam admodum nec puellam', by translating it as 'neither a pearl nor a girl'.

few years he was earning about £400 a year at the Bar, though this is hardly possible if, as Harpsfield says, he never broke the regulation which forbade a barrister to take a fee or more than three groats (one shilling) from a client for each case. He always tried to persuade litigants to settle their actions out of court.[10]

In view of his contacts in the City, and his success as an advocate, it is not surprising that at the age of twenty-six he was elected to the House of Commons at the general election of 1504. As the election returns have been lost, there is no record of which constituency he represented; but there is some evidence that it was the City of London, and this is overwhelmingly probable, for it was not until the end of the sixteenth century that the practice arose of MPs sitting for constituencies where they did not live or own property, and More had no connections in any part of England outside London.

The only matters which really interested MPs and their constituents in 1504 were questions of taxation, and the chief duty which the voters expected their MP to perform was to oppose and restrict, within the bounds of possibility and prudence, the financial demands of the king and his government. Henry VII asked Parliament for a subsidy of three-fifteenths – that is to say, a capital levy of twenty per cent of the taxpayer's property – to meet the expenses of the marriage of his daughter Margaret to James IV. The king's demand was vigorously pressed in the House of Commons by Dudley, who had been chosen by the MPs as their Speaker in accordance with the usual practice of electing the king's nominee to this office.

More played a leading part in opposing the grant, and as a result of his efforts and the general feeling among MPs, the demand for the three-fifteenths, which would have brought in £115,000, was rejected. Instead, the House voted Henry a subsidy of £40,000, but continued to complain to such effect that the king eventually agreed to waive £10,000 and be content with £30,000. We may well believe the story told by Roper and Nicholas Harpsfield that Henry was very annoyed with More, and complained to his ministers that a 'beardless boy' had frustrated his plans, even if the expression 'a beardless boy' seems inappropriate in the case of a man of twenty-six in an age when all men were cleanshaven; but other parts of the story told by Roper and other biographers are less convincing. They state that Dudley told More that if they could have interpreted his speech in such a way as to prove that he had directly criticised the king, he would have been beheaded for high treason, but that as More had not much property – he was only just beginning his successful career at the Bar – Henry and his advisers decided to strike not at him but at his father. John More was therefore imprisoned in the Tower of London and not released until he had agreed to pay a fine of £100 for some imaginary offence. Some years later, Foxe told More that if he expressed his regret for the incident the king would forgive him and show him favour; but on leaving Foxe, More was warned by Foxe's chaplain, Richard Whitford, not to trust anything that Foxe said, for Foxe would agree to his own father's death if this would be useful to the king.[11]

Certainly More did not like Foxe, for he told Erasmus of the tricks to which Foxe would resort to extract money for the king from both wealthy and poor men, which has led historians to think that this is the origin of the legend of 'Morton's fork' which has been wrongly attributed to Morton. More was on much better terms with Foxe's colleague Ruthall, the King's Secretary.[12]

Alongside his legal practice and his activities as an MP, More found time for his studies in Greek, and for writing. He wrote a book of Latin epigrams, and a number of poems on suitable subjects – on Childhood, Manhood, Venus and Cupid, and on Death; a respectful and sympathetic ode on the death of the queen, Henry VII's wife, Elizabeth of York; a love poem to 'Eliza', who cannot be identified and may never have existed;[13] and an amusing venture in comic verse, 'A merry jest how a Serjeant would learn to play the Friar'. It tells a story, in a cantering verse, of how a serjeant-at-law, hearing that a debtor has taken refuge in a friary where his creditor cannot pursue him, offers to catch the debtor, and in order to do so disguises himself as a friar.

> So was he dight
> That no man might
> Him for a friar deny;
> He dopped and dooked,
> He spake and looked,
> So religiously.

But there is a glorious misunderstanding, and the serjeant is eventually knocked down by a maidservant and a housewife. They pull his friar's hood over his face, and

> While he was blind
> The wench behind
> Lent him laid on the floor.
> Many a jowl
> About the mowle
> With a great battledore.

The wife came yet
And with her feet
She help to keep him down,
And with her rock [distaff]
Many a knock
She gave him on the crown.[14]

It was just the kind of joke, at a friar's expense, that appealed to the English people and to the humanist intellectuals in 1505; but More, who at the time that he wrote the verse was half-longing to retire to a monastery, did not make a friar the butt of his humour, but a serjeant disguised as a friar.

About this time, he translated into Latin three stories by the Greek writer Lucian, who had written in the second century after Christ. No one thought that Lucian was a writer in the class of Euripides or Sophocles, but his amusing anecdotes appealed to the Renaissance scholars, who thought that his works were well worthy of being translated into Latin. The first story, *The Cynic*, is a justification by a cynic of his going around with long hair and beard and wearing no shirt; why wear a shirt when it is possible to eat, walk and live without a shirt, which is therefore a superfluous luxury? The second story, *Menippus*, is a journey to Hades, where the visitors find that the Senate and people of Hades have made a law that all rich men who oppressed the poor during their lives should be punished by becoming donkeys for 250,000 years, bearing burdens and being driven around by the poor. The third story, *The Lover of Lies*, is a frivolous discussion on the advantages of telling lies, and the motives which induce men to lie; it draws the conclusion, among others, that it is pointless to tell lies and resort to stratagems in order to seduce another man's wife when it is possible quite honestly to buy a whore in the market for twenty drachmas.[15] The translator of these amusing witticisms, who shocked the straitlaced traditionalists by making the immoral writings of the pagan author available to readers of Latin, was the same man who had yearned for the discipline of one of the strictest monasteries in the country, and who had married a woman whom he did not love for fear of yielding to the temptation of sexual lust.

The fourth story is the most interesting intellectually. *Tyrannicide* tells the story of an imaginary state where anyone who kills a tyrant is paid a large monetary reward by the Senate. As a tyrant has seized power in the state, a man decides to kill him and claim the reward. He climbs up into the Acropolis, the tyrant's fortress, intending to assassinate him, but at the last moment his nerve fails him, and he turns and flees. In his flight he meets the tyrant's son, and kills him, leaving his sword in the body. Soon afterwards the tyrant passes by, and, seeing the corpse of his son with the assassin's sword in it, is so overcome with grief that he commits suicide by stabbing himself with the sword. Is the killer of the son entitled to the reward offered for killing the tyrant? Lucian argues that he is, as the tyrant's death is the direct consequence of his act in killing the son. He left the sword in the dead son's body in the hopes that the tyrant would find it and commit suicide with it in his grief; and if, instead of killing the tyrant himself, he subjected him to the agony of seeing his beloved son killed, this is a fitting punishment for his tyranny for which the son's assassin should be all the more rewarded.[16]

It was a nice exercise in logic and in the principles of causation, and Erasmus was delighted with More's translation when he read it while he was in England during the winter of 1505–6. More was a very exact and literal translator, and did not fall into the temptation of embellishing or adapting the text.

More suggested to Erasmus that they should both compose a reply in Latin to Lucian's *Tyrannicide*, putting the contrary case with arguments as to why the son's assassin was not entitled to the reward for killing the tyrant. Erasmus accepted the challenge, and asked their mutual friend Whitford to judge which of them had written the best reply. Erasmus translated into Latin a fifth story by Lucian, and his translation, and More's translations of the other four stories, and the replies by More and Erasmus to *Tyrannicide*, were published in one volume in Paris in November 1506. If Whitford expressed an opinion in favour of either More or Erasmus, it was not published in the book and we do not know which he thought was the best. The book was acclaimed by scholars all over Western Europe, and was reprinted eight times, in Paris, Venice, Basle, Florence and Lyons, during More's lifetime.[17]

More argued, simply and forcefully, that the assassin did not kill the tyrant; he killed the tyrant's son, and could not reasonably have expected that the consequence of killing the son would be the suicide of the father. It was the gods, not the man, who caused the tyrant to commit suicide. The state should save money by not paying the reward, and thank the gods for the liberation of the city.[18]

This was, of course, just an ingenious intellectual exercise. Some of the learned doctors of the Church, like John of Salisbury and Thomas Aquinas in the twelfth and thirteenth centuries, had discussed whether tyrannicide was justifiable, at a time when emperors and kings were in bitter conflict with the Church and the Papacy. John of Salisbury, who was Becket's friend and had been with him in Canterbury cathedral when he was murdered, had argued that a Christian was entitled to kill a tyrant; Aquinas had been much more cautious, but had conceded that it was justified in exceptional circumstances. But no question of morality came into More's counter-arguments to Lucian's about cause and effect.

Within fifty years of More's death, tyrannicide had again become a controversial issue, with John Knox arguing that it was justifiable to kill a Catholic sovereign, and the Jesuit theologians praising Catholics who had assassinated William the Silent and Henry III of France. But in 1506 More could as safely justify tyrannicide, placing his arguments in the setting of ancient Greece, as he could thank 'the gods' – that is to say, the Greek pagan gods – for the overthrow of tyranny.

He returned to the realities of the contemporary world in his dedicatory preface to Ruthall. He took the opportunity to condemn those who mislead 'the common herd' by inventing stories about a saint 'or a horrendous tale of Hell to drive some old woman to tears', or who 'with pious intent, to be sure', think that Truth cannot stand by itself without being bolstered up by lies. This was only one of many of his early doctrines which More rejected in later years. He then proceeded to praise Ruthall for his learning and skill in government and in diplomacy. 'Unless he had regarded this as tried and tested, a sagacious prince would never have appointed you to be Secretary.'[19]

Apart from his poems and his humanist flippancies, More also translated a serious book containing some of the writings of Giovanni Pico, Count of Mirandola, near Ferrara, which had been published in Latin, with a short biography of Pico, by Pico's nephew. Pico della Mirandola, after a dissolute youth, had written a book on theology and philosophy which had been condemned as heretical in certain points by the ecclesiastical authorities in Rome, chiefly because he denied that Christ had descended into Hell in bodily form between His crucifixion and resurrection, and because he claimed that the truth of Christian doctrines could be proved by passages from the Jewish *Kabbala*. In due course, Pico was pronounced not guilty of heresy by Pope Alexander VI (Rodrigo Borgia). The shock of finding himself accused of heresy transformed Pico from a lecherous young gallant into a virtuous ascetic. He gave away to the poor nearly all the property that he had inherited, and henceforth his love poems were written, not to a mistress, but as the expression of his love for Christ and His Church. The book published by Pico's nephew contained a number of these poems, three of Pico's letters, his *Exposition of the Fifth Psalm*, and the biography by the nephew. More translated them all into English, rendering the poems into English rhyming verse.[20]

In Florence, Pico came under the influence of Savonarola, who was then in control of the city; but he died of fever at the age of thirty-one before Savonarola's fall. In the biography, Pico's nephew quoted from a sermon by Savonarola, in which Savonarola revealed that he had told Pico that God intended him to enter the Church, but that Pico, for all his piety, had not obeyed the divine command. Savonarola said that for this

37

he would be punished by being burned with fire for a long time in Purgatory, but would in the end enter the kingdom of Heaven.

When the nephew published the Latin edition of his book in Bologna in 1496, two years after Pico's death, Savonarola was still in power in Florence; but in 1498 he was overthrown at the instigation of the same Pope, Alexander VI, who had exonerated Pico from the charge of heresy, and was condemned by the Pope's commissioners as a heretic, and executed. It is interesting that More, twelve years after Savonarola's execution, should have published a translation of a biography of Pico in which Savonarola is described as 'a man as well in cunning [subtlety] as holiness of living most famous', and as 'this holy man Jerome, this servant of God',[21] especially as More made a number of cuts in the original Latin, as well as adding a few passages of his own. The remarks about Savonarola in this translation are the nearest which More ever came to supporting heresy.

More dedicated his translation to a nun, Joyeuse Lee, a Poor Clare of the Minorites of Aldgate. She was the sister of Edward Lee, who afterwards became Archbishop of York. More sent her the manuscript as a New Year's gift, probably in 1505, for he had completed the translation several years before it was published in 1510.[22] His great-grandson, Cresacre More, who write a biography of him in 1631, states that when More decided to marry and not to become a priest or a monk, he decided to base his own life on the example of Pico della Mirandola, who had combined Christian asceticism with humanist scholarship.[23] Obviously the words of Savonarola about Pico's refusal to obey God's will and enter the Church had a personal significance for More after he chose marriage instead of the cloister.

We can understand why he added a paragraph of his own, at the end of the biography by Pico's nephew, which was not in the original Latin. In this he stated that Pico had been sentenced to burn in Purgatory before entering Heaven, and no one knows how long he shall burn there, but that it may be a shorter time if Christians pray for him; so he calls on all Christians, doubtless with his own case in mind:

> to help to speed him thither where, after the long habitation with the inhabitants of this dark world (to whom his goodly conversation gave great light) and after the dark fire of Purgatory (in which venial offences be cleansed) he may shortly (if he be not already) enter the inaccessible and infinite light of Heaven, where he may in the presence of the sovereign Godhead so pray for us that we may the rather by his intercession be partners of that unspeakable joy which we have prayed to bring him speedily to. Amen.[24]

CHAPTER 5

THE CARDINAL OF YORK

THANKS to the taxation imposed by Henry VII with the help of Dudley and Empson, Henry VIII was one of the richest kings in Europe. He began at once to spend the money on banquets, tournaments, masques, and extravagant dress and jewels. These activities took up a considerable amount of his time. He also went hunting nearly every day, and resented having to attend meetings of his council and writing letters. The government was dominated by Foxe and Ruthall; in May 1510, the Spanish ambassador reported that the Bishop of Winchester and the Bishop of Durham managed all business. He also complained that they were very slow in dealing with it.[1]

The king's Almoner, Thomas Wolsey, continued to attach himself to Foxe, and carried out his duties with great efficiency. As Almoner he came into personal contact with the king, and was soon exerting his influence over Henry, who preferred him to Foxe. Whereas Foxe and the other Privy Councillors urged Henry to preside at Council meetings, as his father had done, and to devote his time to affairs of state, Wolsey offered to carry out all the work of government while Henry hunted and amused himself. While Foxe and Ruthall were very slow, Wolsey was very quick.[2]

All the facts fit the story which Cavendish tells, and which so exactly complies with the traditional sixteenth-century picture of the good counsellors who make themselves unpopular with their prince by urging him to do his duty, and the evil counsellor who wins his favour by encouraging him to indulge in his vices. According to Cavendish, the other councillors urged the king to heed their advice as to what policy he should pursue, but the Almoner found out what the king wanted, and did it.

So fast as the other Councillors advised the King to leave his pleasure and to attend to the affairs of his realm, so busily did the Almoner persuade him to the contrary. Which delighted him much, and caused him to have the greater affection and love to the Almoner. Thus the Almoner ruled all them that before ruled him: such did his policy and wit bring to pass. Who was now in high favour but Mr Almoner? Who had all the suit but Mr Almoner? And who ruled all under the King but Mr Almoner?[3]

Wealth and promotion now came quickly for the Almoner. He lived in Bridewell, the house in Fleet Street which had belonged to Empson, with a considerable number of servants. In April 1510 he asked Oxford University to grant him degrees as Bachelor of Divinity and Doctor of Divinity by virtue of his position without the need for any further study or examinations. In July he was appointed a canon of Hereford; in November, Vicar of Torrington in Devon; in February 1511, a canon of Windsor; and, a few months later, the Registrar of the Order of the Garter. Next year he was made Dean of Hereford, but resigned this office when he was appointed a canon of York in January 1513 and Dean of York in February. He held all these offices simultaneously as well as being Dean of Lincoln and the king's Almoner, with dispensations for pluralities and non-residence.[4]

In the autumn of 1511 he was appointed a member of the Privy Council. He immediately obtained an ascendancy in the council by volunteering to carry out work and by doing it very ably. He was the clearest thinker and the most lucid and eloquent speaker among the councillors, and so was usually chosen to draft and deliver speeches on the council's behalf. He was always ready to ignore formalities, and, as later generations of civil servants would have put it, to cut through the red tape.

Soon after he became a member of the council, he caused some resentment by by-passing the proper channels for the issue of letters patent. The recognised procedure was for the king to sign an authorisation to his secretary; the secretary sent a warrant to the Lord Privy Seal; the Lord Privy Seal sent another warrant under the privy seal to the Lord Chancellor; and the Lord Chancellor sent an order under the Great Seal to the Master of the Rolls, who issued the letters patent. Wolsey, knowing that the king wished the letters patent to be issued, wrote directly to Warham and told him that it was the king's wish that he should give the orders under the Great Seal to the Master of the Rolls. Warham complied with some reluctance, noting that 'Dominus Wulcy' had assured him that this was the king's pleasure.[5] Such methods annoyed the other councillors, but pleased the king.

Tournaments were not enough for Henry VIII. He wanted a war with France in which he could win glory on the battlefield and regain the crown of France. Less than eighty years before, Henry VI had been crowned king of France in Paris, and the gallant young King Henry VIII should surely be able to reconquer his French kingdom when confronted with the old invalid French king, Louis XII. Henry was encouraged in his warlike ambitions by his father-in-law, King Ferdinand of Spain, who through Henry's queen, Catherine of Aragon, exercised a strong influence over him. England's natural ally, Burgundy, now the territory of the Emperor Maximilian, was also ready for war with France; and so, most of all, was the Pope, Julius II, who feared the French designs in Italy, where French armies and puppets had been in control of Milan for nearly twenty years. By 1511 England, the Empire, the Netherlands, Spain, the Pope, and the states of Italy had lined up against France; only Scotland sided with her French ally.

Henry VII had succeeded in keeping England out of war in Europe for the last seventeen years of his reign, and Foxe and Ruthall urged Henry VIII to pursue the same peaceful and cautious policy. They were supported by the Lord Chancellor, Archbishop Warham, who publicly spoke in favour of peace in the House of Lords, and by the other bishops on the council. But the nobles on the council were for war; they wished to distinguish themselves in battles in France, as their ancestors had done. The leaders of the war party were George Talbot, Earl of Shrewsbury, and the sixty-eight-year-old veteran, Thomas Howard, Earl of Surrey, the Lord Treasurer. Surrey, after fighting in the Wars of the Roses, had followed his father in supporting Richard III and had been on the losing side at Bosworth; but after spending some years in the Tower, he had been restored to his earldom of Surrey, though he was not permitted to inherit his father's title of Duke of Norfolk.

Wolsey played a double role in the divisions in the council. He continued to support his ecclesiastical colleagues against the noblemen, and to help Foxe's attempts to weaken Surrey's influence; but alone among the churchmen on the council, he encouraged Henry to go to war. Here again, his action in supporting the war party can be interpreted as the action of the evil counsellor who pandered to the king's bad inclinations. It has also been cited as proof of his subordination to the Papal See, of his desire to gain popularity among the cardinals in Rome, of his sacrificing English interests to further Julius II's war plans. These factors were doubtless present in his mind; but he also realised that the grand alliance against France which the Pope was forging provided England with the best opportunity she had had for many years, and was likely to have in the future, for reconquering France.

Foxe and the bishops could not hold out against the Papal pressure. Julius II proclaimed a holy war for the liberation of the Pope and the Church, and excommunicated all who fought for the king of France, who had summoned a schismatic General Council of the Church at Pisa without the Pope's authority, and had sent his troops to besiege the Pope in Bologna. Henry VIII's Council and Parliament unanimously endorsed the military alliance between England, Spain, the Pope and Venice which was signed at Windsor on 13 November 1511.

It took a long time in the sixteenth century to make the necessary preparations for a large-scale invasion by an 'army royal' commanded by the king himself and supported by a large force of his subjects and of foreign mercenaries; for men, equipment, naval transport, and above all money had to be obtained well in advance. But King Ferdinand persuaded Henry to send a smaller force in the meantime to help the Spaniards drive the French from Navarre and conquer Guienne. Seven thousand men sailed from the port of London and from Southampton to San Sebastian in April 1512, under the command of the Marquess of Dorset, the son of Wolsey's former patron.

The expedition was a disaster. Though Henry had given Dorset instructions to place himself and his men wholly at Ferdinand's disposal and to obey him as if he were the king of Spain's subject, the English refused to follow the plan of campaign devised by the Spanish generals; they were only prepared to besiege Bayonne, and refused to invade Navarre and march on Pamplona. In the hot summer the English soldiers at the camp at Fuentarrabia, unable to get beer in Spain, drank Spanish wine and cider, to which they were not accustomed, in large quantities, with disastrous results to their health. They refused to serve unless they were paid wages of eightpence a day, and when the money was not forthcoming, they mutinied, and threatened to sail home. Dorset then decided to bring them back to England. Henry was very indignant at the disgrace which Dorset and the troops had brought upon him and his kingdom. His first impulse was to hang the mutineers; but he contented himself with forcing their commanders to beg forgiveness on their knees from the Spanish ambassador.[6]

Wolsey was in close touch with the events at Fuentarrabia. He carried on the government's correspondence with the commanders in Spain, and their reports were addressed to him. The soldiers considered him to be responsible for their plight, and for the war, though we have no idea as to how, in the days before the appearance of the first newspapers, the men in Spain became aware of the influence which he was exercising at court. On 5 August the English ambassador in Madrid, Dr Knight, who was visiting the army at Fuentarrabia, wrote to Wolsey and informed him that many of the soldiers had spoken against him.[7] This was potentially a dangerous situation for Wolsey: if public opinion held him responsible for an unsuccessful war, he might be sacrificed to appease the discontent.

He tried to strengthen his links with Foxe and the peace party. On 30 September he wrote to Foxe from Windsor mentioning that Surrey had

withdrawn from court after some contention with Henry, and expressing the hope that the withdrawal would be permanent. He complained
of the attempts by the war party to waste the king's money on military
expeditions, and of Surrey's son, Sir Edward Howard, the Lord
Admiral, who was inciting the king to go to war with the Scots. He urged
Foxe to return to court as soon as possible. By Howard's 'wanton means
His Grace spendeth much money and is more disposed to war than
peace. Your presence shall be very necessary to repress this appetite.'[8]

But the plan for the great invasion went on, with the greatest
publicity, which was designed to arouse the martial enthusiasm of the
English people and to impress foreigners with Henry's power. Rumours
of an army of 60,000 men which would cross to Calais by Easter 1513
were circulating all over Europe. The Emperor Maximilian would
simultaneously invade from the Netherlands and link up with Henry's
army near Calais, while Ferdinand and the Spaniards invaded Navarre
and Guienne from Spain, and the Pope and his Italian allies and the
Spanish armies in Naples attacked the French in Italy. The project cost
a great deal of money, for in the sixteenth century, as at other periods of
history, war was the most expensive form of activity in which a
government could engage. In the first two years of Henry VIII's reign,
his total government expenditure was £3,640 and £5,706, most of it
spent on tournaments and court festivities; in the third year, the war
preparations brought the expenditure up to £111,455.[9] The money was
raised by taxes and subsidies from the loyal laity and clergy, and by
loans from German and Flemish bankers. The whole supervision of the
financial arrangements, as well as of the military and naval preparations, was conducted with the greatest efficiency by the king's Almoner,
the Dean of Lincoln, Thomas Wolsey.

The humanists, from their studies of ancient history and philosophy,
and their cosmopolitan intellectual milieu, were opposed to war. Colet,
the Dean of St Paul's, who was a leading scholar of Greek and a friend of
More's, openly preached pacifism at Paul's Cross, the open-air pulpit in
the churchyard in front of the cathedral which was the chief place from
which government propaganda was disseminated to the people. He
declared that a Christian prince should never bring the miseries of war
to his subjects except in those few cases which could be justified by
Christian theology as a just war. Colet's sermon angered many patriotic
Englishmen and government officials; but the king, after a long talk with
Colet, expressed his high regard for him, and asked him only to refrain
from preaching pacifism too loudly while preparations for the invasion
of France were going ahead.[10]

Erasmus, who was living partly at Cambridge and partly in More's
house in London, was also opposed to war, having become particularly

conscious in the Netherlands of the damage that mercenaries could do in wartime to peaceful citizens. More reacted differently. He wrote a patriotic tract attacking the French humanist, Germain de Brie (Brixius), who had written a treatise showing the superiority of the French over the English in war. More claimed, on the contrary, that the English would always thrash the French in a fair fight.[11] Unlike Colet, he was not the man to advocate an unpopular policy in the face of public opinion. He was in every way a conservative by temperament, what we today would call a man of the Right, and never a man of the Left. He was a traditionalist, an authoritarian, a nationalist, a supporter of the established Church and of the royal authority, an enemy of revolution, sedition, and of any major innovation. If he had not written *Utopia*, this could hardly be doubted, for all his other books, and all the actions in his life, show this very clearly; but *Utopia* does not really conflict with his profound conservatism.

The invasion had not taken place by Easter, nor by the end of May, which was the new date substituted by the rumour-mongers after Easter had passed; but on 30 June Henry crossed to Calais in perfect weather in three hours. The fine weather in Northern France did not last into August, when heavy rain hampered troop movements and military operations. It was three weeks after Henry's arrival before he and his army marched out of Calais and invaded French territory, and he then settled down in the rain to besiege Therouanne.

Henry had left behind in England his queen, Catherine of Aragon, as Regent with a Regency Council consisting of Warham, Foxe and Ruthall and most of the Privy Councillors, including Surrey, who at the age of seventy had been left to guard the kingdom against the Scots; but Wolsey went to Calais with the king. The Earl of Shrewsbury and most of the other nobles were with Henry. So was Charles Brandon, a gentleman of the court who was one of Henry's closest friends, and who had been created Viscount Lisle a few weeks before the army sailed for France, and put in charge of operations under Henry with the office of Marshal of the Camp. The financial arrangements for the army, and the organisation of supplies, were controlled by Wolsey. Philippe de Bregilles, who was the emperor's liaison officer with the English army, had the usual disagreements with his allies on various minor matters, and on 2 August wrote complainingly from the camp at Therouanne to Margaret of Austria that everything there was controlled by 'two obstinate men', Lisle and Wolsey.[12] It was Wolsey who carried on the correspondence with the queen and the Regency Council in England. Catherine of Aragon, not wishing to distract Henry by writing to him when he was facing the enemy, addressed her letters to Wolsey, asking him for news of Henry and beseeching him to prevent her lord from risking his life too recklessly.[13]

After Therouanne had been besieged for a fortnight, a relieving French army appeared and fought a battle against the English on 16 August. A few salvoes of artillery and one cavalry charge were sufficient to scatter the French, who fled, leaving several high-ranking prisoners in English hands, including the famous Bayard. Meanwhile James IV invaded England. He captured the Border castles of Norham and Ford, but dallied for three weeks at Ford – according to the chroniclers, making love to the 'lady of Ford', who used her woman's wiles to keep him there and prevent him from driving home his advantage against the English. The queen and the Regency Council in London sent Surrey at the head of an army to fight the Scots. On 9 September they met the enemy near Ford and fought a battle which the English named Branxton and the Scots Flodden. In two hours the prestige which James IV had acquired for Scotland was shattered, never to be revived. The English infantry outmatched the Scottish pikemen, and the English archers, as in so many earlier battles, slaughtered and scattered their enemies. The king of Scots and nearly all his nobles were killed, and the remnants of his army fled in disorder into Scotland. Surrey was rewarded for his victory by being granted the title of Duke of Norfolk which his father had forfeited.

After taking Therouanne, Henry visited Margaret of Austria at Lille and then besieged the flourishing French city of Tournai on the border with the Netherlands. One of the chief difficulties with sixteenth-century sieges was the inefficiency of the supply services and the shortage of provisions; but this did not apply at Tournai with Wolsey in charge of the arrangements. Brian Tuke, the Clerk of the Signet, wrote from Tournai that 20,000 men were living in the camp more cheaply in wartime than they lived at home in peacetime because of the abundance of supplies.[14]

In the camp before Tournai, Henry heard of the victory at Flodden, and the city surrendered on the same day. When Henry sailed for England on 21 October, he was acclaimed in his own realm and in Europe as the conqueror of the French and the Scots. Tournai was annexed by Henry as part of his kingdom; he appointed More's friend, Lord Mountjoy, to be Governor there. The Bishop of Tournai, like all the supporters of the King of France, had been excommunicated by the Pope, and was now deprived of his see, and Wolsey was appointed Bishop of Tournai. A few months later he was also created Bishop of Lincoln.[15]

The position looked very dangerous for France, but she was saved by the divisions among her enemies. No one had been more responsible than Ferdinand of Spain for inciting Henry to war with France; but

Ferdinand had been infuriated by the English fiasco at Fuentarrabia. It so happened that the weather in September and October 1512 turned out to be exceptionally favourable for campaigning, and Ferdinand was sure that only the English mutiny and desertion had prevented him from conquering all Navarre and Guienne. This gave him the excuse to double-cross his son-in-law. In April 1513, just as the plan for the great invasion of France from Calais, Flanders, Italy and Spain was about to be put into operation, Ferdinand signed a truce for six months with Louis XII, leaving Henry and Maximilian to fight without his help.

There was more enthusiasm for the war in England, both among the nobility and the people, than in any of the other allied countries. Of all the allies, Henry had most to gain from the war. The Pope and the Italians wished to deprive the French of Milan. Ferdinand wished to seize Navarre and Guienne from them. Maximilian hoped to recover the provinces of Burgundy which France had taken in 1482. But Henry intended to obtain the crown of France and conquer the whole kingdom. There could be no possible compromise between him and Louis on this issue. Ferdinand therefore believed that he could rely on England to go on fighting France, if necessary alone, and he decided to let the English beat the French for him, giving them ardent support in words, but contributing at most a token force to help Henry, and then pick up Navarre and Guienne from the wreckage after England had annexed the rest of France.

After the English victories at Therouanne, Flodden and Tournai, Ferdinand assured Henry that he had made his truce with France, not because he had cooled in his enthusiasm for the holy war in defence of the Church but only to gain a breathing space because, having fallen ill, he did not wish his successor to succeed to the throne, in the event of his death, at a time when Spain was involved in the hazards of war. His envoy signed the treaty between Henry and Maximilian which was made at Lille in October 1513, renewing the military alliance between England, the Empire and Spain, and providing for a joint invasion of France in the early summer of 1514; but at the same time he carried on secret peace negotiations with Louis XII, hoping that Louis would cede him Navarre, and perhaps Brittany after Louis's death, if Ferdinand could persuade Henry to forgo his claim to the French throne and join in a general peace. In April 1514, immediately before the new invasion of France was to begin, Ferdinand again made a six-months' truce with France as he had done the year before.

From Henry's point of view, Maximilian's conduct was only marginally better than Ferdinand's. The emperor had met Henry in the camp at Therouanne, but he and his daughter Margaret had contributed nothing to Henry's victories in Northern France. He was really more interested in settling his scores with the Venetians than in defeating France, and because of this the Venetians were receptive to the friendly overtures from Louis XII, who was urging them to abandon the anti-French alliance.

Wolsey now advised Henry to out-do Ferdinand and Maximilian, and leave them in the lurch by making a separate peace with France. If Henry was France's most uncompromising and dangerous enemy, this gave Louis XII an incentive to make concessions to Henry and to snap his fingers at Ferdinand and Maximilian. While Henry and Wolsey ostensibly adopted a very intransigent stand against France, refusing Ferdinand's suggestions that they should agree to a general peace, they were themselves secretly negotiating with the French. Instead of invading France in the summer of 1514, they signed a peace treaty at St Germain-en-Laye on 9 July. Louis agreed to cede Tournai to Henry and to pay him a million francs for his forbearance in not enforcing his claim to the crown of France; the money was to be paid over ten years in half-yearly instalments of 50,000 francs payable at Calais in May and November. Louis, who was a widower of over fifty, and ill and decrepit, was to marry Henry's beautiful young sister Mary, who was aged eighteen. This caused much ribald laughter at every court in Europe; people said that if Louis tried to consummate the marriage the effort would kill him.[16] It was agreed, in the peace treaty, that the French Bishop-elect of Tournai would withdraw his claim to the see, and that France would recognise Wolsey as Bishop of Tournai; and Louis also agreed to pay pensions of 1,000 écus d'or per annum to Wolsey and other English courtiers as a reward for their part in negotiating peace.[17]

The separate peace with France annoyed the emperor, King Ferdinand, and Pope Leo X, who had succeeded Julius II. As the French Bishop of Tournai had been excommunicated, Leo could hardly refuse to issue the bulls for Wolsey's consecration as bishop; but he would not waive the annates payable on his consecration as Bishop of Lincoln. By the canon law, the Pope was entitled to the first year's revenue of the see whenever a new bishop was installed; but this was sometimes waived as a favour to the king and the new bishop, especially if suitable gifts were given to the cardinals in Rome who influenced the Pope's decision. When Henry asked Leo to waive the annates for Lincoln, he refused, and to Henry's arguments about Wolsey's great services to the allies during the war, he stubbornly insisted that the see of Lincoln was very rich and could afford to pay.

For the last five years, Cardinal Bainbridge, the Archbishop of York, had been residing in Rome as Henry's agent at the Papal court. He was assisted by Cardinal Gigli and Cardinal Hadrian, who had been appointed bishops of Worcester and of Bath and Wells in return for

47

advancing English interests in Rome, though they had never set foot in England. Bainbridge died suddenly in July 1514. His secretary Richard Pace – a humanist and Greek scholar, who was a friend of More – suspected that he had been poisoned by one of his chaplains. The chaplain was arrested, and after being savagely tortured, confessed that he had been paid by the Bishop of Worcester to poison Bainbridge. The chaplain then committed suicide to save himself from further torture. Gigli denied the accusation, and said that it had been wrung from the priest by torture; he also said that the chaplain was mad. After an investigation, the Pope and the Consistory accepted his denial, and he was exonerated.

When Henry heard of Bainbridge's death, he immediately asked the Pope to create Wolsey a cardinal in his place and to issue the bulls for his consecration as Archbishop of York, with the usual dispensation for non-residence. Leo issued the bull for York in September 1514 after there had been some haggling about the annates: he eventually agreed to remit 2,000 ducats of the annates due on the bulls for Lincoln if the annates were paid in full for York.[18] He made more difficulties about making Wolsey a cardinal. It was usual to create a batch of cardinals at the same time, after thorough consultations with the emperor and the King of France and other rulers with a view to preserving the balance of power between them in the College of Cardinals. Henry asked Leo to take the unusual, but not unprecedented, step of creating Wolsey a 'cardinal sole', by himself. The demand was not unreasonable, as he would be replacing Bainbridge, who was likewise Henry's nominee. Writing to Leo on 12 August 1514, Henry stated that he esteemed Wolsey above his dearest friends and could do nothing of importance without him. But Leo replied that there were great difficulties about complying with his request, and that Wolsey would have to wait for his cardinal's hat until the next creation of cardinals.[19]

In October Princess Mary sailed for France and married Louis XII at Abbeville. In November she entered Paris and was crowned queen of France in Notre Dame. Within two months she was a widow. Louis XII died on New Year's Day 1515 and was succeeded as king by his cousin and son-in-law, François, Count of Angoulême, who became King François I after Mary had declared on oath that she was not pregnant by Louis XII. Henry had sent his great friend Charles Brandon as ambassador to France after creating him Duke of Suffolk, and he fell in love with Mary. Wolsey, like many other people, had been expecting Louis to die, and as soon as he heard the news he wrote to Mary urging her to take care not to take any step which could commit her in any way to a second marriage; but when Suffolk confided in him that he wished to marry Mary, he promised to use all his influence with Henry to further the match. Then, on 5 March, Suffolk wrote and told Wolsey that he had already secretly married her, that she was pregnant by him, and that he dreaded that Henry should hear of it.[20]

To marry a princess without the king's consent was a very serious offence. It was made worse in Henry's eyes because he had suspected that Suffolk was falling in love with Mary before they left England, and he had made Suffolk promise, in Wolsey's presence at Eltham, that he would not attempt to woo her. But though Henry's first reaction was an outburst of anger, he quickly forgave his friend and his sister. Wolsey used his influence in Suffolk's favour. His self-indulgent nature made him tolerant towards the lovers, and he undoubtedly realised that he would be complying with Henry's wishes by doing so. The new king of France also intervened on Suffolk's behalf although he himself had fallen in love with Mary. The Duke of Suffolk and the 'French queen', as Mary was called for the rest of her life, returned to England and lived happily ever after as husband and wife at court and at their country house at Westhorpe in Suffolk, though there were arguments about who should have the jewels which Mary had taken to France when she married Louis XII. It was the money aspect which interested Henry most. Suffolk had taken the precaution of enclosing a pearl with the letter in which he first informed Wolsey that he had married Mary; and he agreed to repay the value of the jewels to Henry by instalments over the years.[21] It was one of the very few stories in the reign of Henry VIII which had a happy ending.

The good relations between England and France did not long survive the death of Louis XII. Instead of the doddering old king, there was François I, a dashing young man not yet quite twenty-one, who was as eager as Henry to win glory in war. Within eight months of becoming king he had invaded Italy and, encountering an army of seasoned Swiss mercenaries in the Pope's pay at Marignano near Milan, he won a great victory in which he showed himself to be as gallant in war as in love.

Henry and Wolsey immediately reacted adversely to this renewed threat from France; but it was not so easy to revive the anti-French alliance of 1511. King Ferdinand again joined the alliance and did nothing; and after his death in February 1516 his sixteen-year-old grandson Charles, who succeeded him as King of Spain and was soon to become the Emperor Charles V, was for the first few years of his reign under the influence of his pro-French Council in the Netherlands, where he lived. Charles's other grandfather, the Emperor Maximilian, was more ready to oppose France; but Venice, still at loggerheads with Maximilian, hastened to support François's armies as they advanced into Italy. Leo X lacked the energy and pugnacity of Julius II, though he and the other Italian states, except Venice, were anti-French. Best of all from the French point of view, the mistrust and resentment between England, Spain and the Empire, following on their mutual double-crossing activities during the previous war, made it difficult for them to unite now.

In these circumstances, England did not declare war on France, but resorted to a policy which would today be called 'cold war'. In the last war, the English alone had done the fighting; this time they would leave the fighting to others. Henry and Wolsey used all diplomatic means to thwart French policy, and, making use of the fact that Henry was the richest prince in Christendom after the king of Portugal, offered financial aid to any power which opposed France by military or political action.

The Pope's first reaction to the French invasion of Italy was to draw closer to Henry. In September 1515, after more urging from Henry and from Wolsey himself, he created Wolsey a cardinal sole. Wolsey sent Gigli a 'reward' of 1,000 ducats for his services in the matter, and assured him that nothing could have given greater pleasure to his king, who had been much more eager for it than he himself, and had asked every day for news of the Pope's decision.[22] The Pope sent Wolsey not only the red hat but also a valuable ring, though a ring was not usually sent with the hat. They were brought to England in great state by the Pope's Protonotary, Cardinal Gambara. On his journey from Dover, Gambara was received at Blackheath by the Bishop of Lincoln, the Earl of Essex, and other dignitaries, and rode through the streets of London escorted by Essex and the bishop and the lord mayor to Westminster Abbey, where the hat was received by the Abbot of Westminster and eight other abbots.

The delivery of the hat to Wolsey took place in the abbey on Sunday 18 November. The three archbishops of Canterbury, Armagh and Dublin sang mass, assisted by eight bishops and eight abbots. Colet, as Dean of St Paul's, preached the sermon. He said nothing about peace and war, but urged the new cardinal to put his trust in the Holy Trinity and not in worldly powers, and to do equal justice to rich and poor. Wolsey prostrated himself while the Papal bull was read, and Warham then placed the red hat on his head. After the ceremony the cardinal was escorted by the Dukes of Norfolk and Suffolk and by a large number of officers and gentlemen to his house at York Place near Charing Cross, where he entertained the king and queen and all the nobles and prelates who had officiated in the abbey, and the judges and the barons of the Exchequer, to a magnificent banquet.[23]

Wolsey was now supreme in the Privy Council, and personally directed all aspects of both home and foreign affairs. His old protector, Foxe, was reduced to being his subordinate, but seems not to have resented it; he spent more time in his diocese at Winchester, congratulated Wolsey on his abilities, and urged him not to work after 6 p.m.[24] Ruthall was still the king's secretary, but in effect was Wolsey's secretary, drafting the diplomatic despatches for Wolsey to correct and approve. Wolsey still encouraged Henry to hunt and pursue his other pleasures while he himself worked twelve hours a day; but he consulted Henry on all important decisions. The king and the cardinal were nearly always in agreement on what to do, and worked excellently as a team. On the rare occasions when they disagreed, Henry sometimes forced Wolsey to give way, and sometimes gave way to him.

Wolsey was not content with the realities of power; he wanted all the honours of his position, the grandeur and the ostentation as well. It was not only his vanity, but the proprieties and efficiency of government administration that made it necessary to regularise his relationship with Warham. As Archbishop of Canterbury and Lord Chancellor, Warham had precedence over Wolsey in both Church and State. A month after Wolsey received the red hat, Warham resigned the Great Seal, and on Christmas Eve Wolsey replaced him as Lord Chancellor. On 2 January the Venetian ambassador in London, Giustiniani, wrote to his government that Wolsey was 'ipse rex' – the king himself.[25]

It was not so easy to get rid of Warham's ecclesiastical pre-eminence, for this needed the assistance of the Pope. Both the Archbishop of Canterbury and the Archbishop of York, by virtue of their offices, held the rank of legatus natus, along with a number of other archbishops in Europe. But on exceptional occasions the Pope would send a legate a latere* to visit a country on his behalf, and during the visitation the legate had supreme ecclesiastical authority, as the Pope's representative, over all the archbishops, bishops and abbots in the realm. In 1515 Henry and Wolsey began pestering the Pope to appoint Wolsey as his legate a latere in England, not merely during a short visitation, but permanently. Leo X's desire to please Henry had been countered, after Marignano, by his fear of François I, which caused Wolsey to complain to the Venetian ambassador that as long as the French armies dominated Italy, the Pope would be nothing but the French king's chaplain. He raised objections to making Wolsey legate a latere for fear of offending the French; but in 1518 he agreed to appoint him legate for a year, with a half-promise to extend the term.[26] It was regularly extended until 1524, when Wolsey was appointed legate a latere for life. As legate he could, and did, overrule the decisions of the ecclesiastical officers and courts in the province of Canterbury, just as he interfered, as

---

* For the respective powers of a legatus natus, a legatus delegatus, a legatus nuncius apostolicus, and the highest rank of a legatus a latere, and the origin of the terms, see Hinschius, Kirchenrecht, I.498, ff.; and see Pollard, pp.165–70.

Lord Chancellor, with the decisions of the common law courts in his Court of Chancery.

During the years of the cold war after 1515, he was in sole charge of foreign policy, subject only to Henry's intervention. He directed every move of the struggle against France from the Po to the Tay. The Emperor Maximilian raised an army of Swiss mercenaries and fought the French in Lombardy with some success in 1516. Wolsey sent Pace to make arrangements for paying him the money which he needed for his soldiers' wages; but while Henry and Wolsey hinted that England would soon enter the war, they instructed Pace to keep a tight hold on the money and only to pay it over to Maximilian by degrees and in so far as it was being used efficiently. Apart from paying the emperor's Swiss mercenaries, Wolsey tried to persuade the governments of the Swiss cantons to join the war against France. His chief ally here was the Cardinal of Sion, whose predecessors for five hundred years had been the secular as well as the ecclesiastical rulers of the canton of Valais, with the rank of princes of the Holy Roman Empire. Since the fourteenth century the bishopric had become hereditary in the Duke of Savoy's family. The Cardinal of Sion travelled through Italy, Switzerland, Germany, the Netherlands and England, instigating princes and republics to resist the French and offering them the king of England's money if they did.

'The King and the Cardinal' – the phrase was coming into general use in the language of European diplomacy – exerted their influence to detach Venice from her alliance with France. England and Venice had close commercial ties. The Venetian merchants brought spices and other commodities from the East to England, being granted special licences to bring them in their own ships through the Mediterranean and by the ports of Spain and Portugal to Southampton and London. They sailed home with English wool without passing through the staple at Calais. A number of Venetian merchants and bankers lived in London, often for years at a time before being moved to Smyrna or to some other overseas trading centre. The trade with England was beneficial to both nations, but especially to Venice.

In many interviews, which were often stormy, Henry and Wolsey put the strongest pressure on the Venetian ambassadors to break their alliance with France, to settle their differences with the emperor, and to line up with the other Italian states in the anti-French alliance. They were unsuccessful. The Venetians tried to appease their anger, made excuses, and assured Wolsey that they were even more friendly to England than they were to France, but explained that they could not defy a king whose armies were on their borders, and pleaded the emperor's enmity as their excuse for supporting the French. Wolsey at times did

Thomas Wolsey, by an unknown artist

Erasmus, by Holbein

not hesitate to hint at economic sanctions against Venice; but though this alarmed the Venetians, it was bluff, for it would have hurt England to lose the Venetian trade.

In Scotland geographical proximity gave England an advantage over France which Henry and Wolsey exploited to the full. After the death of James IV at Flodden, he was succeeded by his son, James V, who was seventeen months old. During his minority, the realm fell into a state of complete lawlessness. Henry's sister Margaret, the queen mother, wished to pursue a policy of friendship towards England; but loyalty to the old alliance with France induced the Scottish lords and Parliament to appoint John Stewart, Duke of Albany, as Regent instead of Queen Margaret. Albany's name and title were the only Scottish things about him. He had lived in France since he was a boy of four; he spoke French much better than Scots or English; and only his duty to the king of France persuaded him to leave the pleasures of the French court to undertake the dangerous service to which he was assigned in cold, far-off Scotland among a people whom Pope Leo described as 'savages'.*[27]

Henry and Wolsey sent money to Queen Margaret's partisans in Scotland. They encouraged her to marry Archibald Douglas, Earl of Angus, whose family had always been enemies of the Stewarts, and gave the Douglases all the financial and diplomatic support that they needed, including the very useful promise of asylum in England if they were ever in danger of being punished for an unsuccessful rebellion. The petty feuds on the lawless Borders gave Henry and Wolsey many opportunities to protest and threaten the Scots; and when the Scots made proposals to improve relations and establish friendship with England, they were told that King Henry would not negotiate as long as Albany remained in Scotland. François I encouraged the Scots to resist England, but gave them no military, financial or other assistance.

To the great annoyance of Henry and Wolsey, Maximilian made peace with France at Christmas 1516, leaving Milan in François's hands and selling Verona to Venice for 60,000 ducats. Henry and Wolsey felt that the money they had given Maximilian had been wasted. They tried to persuade the emperor that he had gravely weakened his position in Italy by selling Verona to the ally of France, and at the same time told the Venetians that François was plotting to double-cross them and to join with Maximilian to recapture Verona and destroy Venice. Meanwhile King Charles of Spain signed the Treaty of Noyon with France, and under the influence of his ministers in the Netherlands established friendly relations with François. Henry and Wolsey failed to persuade Maximilian to remove Charles's pro-French ministers.

* 'Gentibus horridiusculis.'

There was not much that Henry and Wolsey could do against France as long as neither Maximilian nor Charles, nor Henry and Wolsey themselves, were prepared to go to war. François I, on his side, knew that if he aimed at any further aggrandisement, he would revive the great alliance against him. There was therefore a good basis for peace negotiations. An additional spur to peace was the threat from the East. A new young Sultan of Turkey, who in due course became known to history as Soleiman the Magnificent, came to the throne in 1516, and immediately made military preparations for the invasion of Hungary and the Christian strongholds in the islands of the Eastern Mediterranean. Leo X, instead of calling for war against France like his predecessor, summoned all the princes of Christendom to make a universal peace amongst themselves and to unite in a new crusade to save Europe from the Turk.

There were prolonged diplomatic negotiations and journeyings. In July 1517 the emperor's ambassador came to London for talks about peace with the king and the cardinal. In the ceremonies and festivities, unprecedented honours were granted to Wolsey. At a banquet for the ambassador he dined at the king's table with the king, the queen, Henry's sister the French queen, and the emperor's ambassador, with the dukes and other nobles in their usual places at a lower table.[28]

The universal peace was at last established in the summer of 1518. France retained Milan, but agreed that Spain should retain Navarre. Henry surrendered Tournai to France, in return for a further 600,000 *écus d'or* to be added to the pensions already due to him from France under earlier treaties. Wolsey resigned as Bishop of Tournai, in favour of the French nominee, and received a pension payable annually out of the income of the see. François's son, the Dauphin, who was four months old, was to marry Henry's two-year-old daughter Mary, when they reached marriageable age. Albany remained in France, and François agreed that he should not return to Scotland.[29]

Wolsey acquired a new bishopric in place of his see of Tournai. Cardinal Hadrian, the Bishop of Bath and Wells, was suspected of being involved in a plot to poison the Pope. As the evidence against Hadrian was unsatisfactory, Leo agreed to take no action against him, and to hush up the scandal if Hadrian paid him 25,000 ducats. Henry and Wolsey insisted that Hadrian should be prosecuted in the courts in Rome and deprived of his see, claiming that the king's honour was involved when his representative at the Papal court was suspected of having tried to poison the Pope. At this point, Hadrian fled from Rome to Venice. The Pope thereupon excommunicated him, and deprived him of his see. The Pope and the cardinals were discussing whom to choose as his successor when a demand arrived from Henry and Wolsey that Wolsey should be appointed Bishop of Bath and Wells with a dispensation to hold the see together with the archbishopric of York. After the usual bribes and a compromise over the annates, Wolsey's bulls for Bath and Wells were issued in July 1518.[30]

England had lost, rather than gained, by the cold war of 1515–18, but thanks to the skill with which Wolsey handled the diplomatic negotiations, she had enhanced her prestige. The peace treaties culminated in a treaty signed in London on 2 October 1518, in which all the powers of Christendom agreed to unite, at the Pope's request, to make a universal peace amongst themselves and to launch a crusade against the Turk. If any of the parties to the treaty committed an act of aggression against another party, all the other parties would go to the help of the victim of aggression. Wolsey, as Papal legate and Henry's minister, was universally considered to be the chief architect of the peace; and he played a leading part in the ceremonies with which the peace was proclaimed in London with unprecedented pomp and extravagance, officiating at mass at the Te Deum in St Paul's.[31] It was one of the very rare occasions on which he celebrated mass.

English foreign policy had changed for the third time in four years. Once again, as in 1514, France was no longer an enemy but a friend linked to England by a royal marriage engagement. But there was no change in the fortunes, and no check to the advancement in power, honours, wealth and international fame, of the Lord Legate, the Cardinal of York.

CHAPTER 6

UTOPIA AND RICHARD III

THOMAS MORE, like nearly all his fellow-countrymen, enthusiastically welcomed the accession of Henry VIII. He wrote a poem in which he applauded the overthrow of the 'tyranny' of Henry VII's ministers, bestowed a few grudging praises on the dead king, and lauded the qualities of the new king to the skies. In an accompanying letter to Henry VIII, he praised his virtues, and ended the letter: 'Farewell, Prince, the greatest, the best, and (to use a new and very honourable title for a king), the most loved.'[1] The poem shows how greatly he disliked Henry VII's government, but his biographers are almost certainly wrong in stating that at the time of the old king's death he was planning to escape abroad to avoid the king's fury. More did in fact go abroad in 1508, and spent a short time studying at Paris and Louvain Universities; but he had returned to England before Henry VII died.[2]

Henry VIII was determined to add to the lustre of his throne by making England the greatest artistic and literary centre in Europe. In 1490 Renaissance culture was almost unknown in England; but within a few years of the young king's accession no country could boast of having more eminent intellectuals than Colet, Linacre, Grocyn, William Latimer and More. These famous humanists could ignore the carping criticism of the obscurantists of the Church, safe under the protection of the most brilliant prince in Christendom. Apart from the king, Archbishop Warham was a great patron of the arts, as was John Fisher, the Bishop of Rochester, a member of Henry VIII's Privy Council, who found time, amid all his duties to the State and the Church, to learn Greek when he was over fifty years of age. The king's Almoner, Thomas Wolsey, now rapidly rising to the highest power in the government, soon established his reputation as another leading patron of culture. Here again he knew what the king wanted, and outdid his rivals in achieving it; but apart from this, he was by nature a man of sensibility and good taste.

Erasmus, who had spent a few months in England in 1499 and in 1505–6, came again in 1509 at the king's invitation and stayed for five years.[3] He needed the protection of powerful patrons more than any other humanist, for he had the misfortune to be that despised creature of sin, the illegitimate son of a monk, conceived through the violation of a vow of chastity. The special circumstances which made his case almost excusable were well known throughout Europe in his lifetime, and were often retold during the next five centuries, most notably by Charles Reade in the novel *The Cloister and the Hearth* in 1861. Erasmus's father was originally not a monk but a young artisan of the Dutch town of Gouda in the Duchy of Burgundy. He fell in love with the daughter of a wealthy physician of Gouda. She reciprocated his love, but her father despised him for his low birth, and refused his consent to their marriage. They therefore fell into temptation and committed the sin of fornication. Repenting of their sin, the young man went on a pilgrimage to Rome to expiate it. While he was away, the girl realised that she was pregnant, and wrote and told him; but her father intercepted the letter, and destroyed it, and wrote himself to the young man telling him that she was dead. In his grief and remorse, the broken-hearted lover became a monk. When he discovered the truth, and realised that he had taken his vow of chastity in ignorance of the true facts, he nevertheless felt bound to observe the vow. He never saw the girl again, but made provision for the maintenance of their child, who was baptised Erasmus, the consequence of a tragic love which could move the hearts of the men of the fifteenth and sixteenth centuries.

Some people did not believe this story. They said that Erasmus had invented it to cover up a common and sordid case of a lecherous monk who violated his oath and seduced a respectable young girl. There was, in fact, one unfortunate detail which Erasmus never mentioned and was not generally known: Erasmus had an elder brother named Peter. If there was any truth at all in the moving story, it applied to the birth of Peter; and after his birth the erring couple did meet again, and again committed fornication, although the male partner was now a monk who had taken his vows. It was after this second and far more heinous sin that the physician's daughter gave birth to Erasmus.

Erasmus was almost certainly born in Rotterdam, for he was known throughout his life as 'Erasmus of Rotterdam', although he spent his childhood in his mother's house at Gouda. He always celebrated his birthday on 28 October, the Feast of St Simon and St Jude; but the year of his birth is something of a mystery. In one of his earlier works he wrote that he was aged fourteen when he left school at Deventer in 1484, and that he was just thirty when he first met Colet on his visit to England in the autumn of 1499. This means that he was born on 28 October 1469; but afterwards, on thirteen occasions, he wrote that he was born in 1466. Once he said that he was born in 1467. During the last decade of his life, he stated eight times that he was born in 1464. The most likely explanation is that he was born in 1469, but falsely gave the earlier dates to make it appear that he was conceived before his father became a monk.

In 1486 both Erasmus and his brother Peter entered monasteries. It was a fitting atonement for their father's sin. They both became Augustinian canons, Erasmus entering the monastery at Steyn, one mile from Gouda, and Peter a monastery near Delft. Peter remained in his monastery for forty-two years until his death in 1528; according to Erasmus, he was nearly always drunk, and broke his vow of chastity even more often than his father had done. Erasmus did not like monastic life and made up his mind to find a way of escaping from it if he could do so without incurring punishment.

After five years in the monastery, he was appointed secretary to the Bishop of Cambrai, a leading member of the Privy Council of Philip of Habsburg, the ruler of the Netherlands. Erasmus was granted a dispensation to leave his monastery and live in the bishop's palace in Brussels. He also became a priest, being granted a dispensation to take holy orders despite his illegitimate birth. The bishop himself held his bishopric by dispensation, for he was the bastard son of the Count of Bergen-op-Zoom, who had had ten legitimate and thirty-six illegitimate children. After four years in the bishop's service, Erasmus received a further dispensation to absent himself from his monastery while he studied at the Sorbonne, the divinity school of Paris University. He never again returned to the monastery, his leave of absence being regularly renewed for the rest of his life.

Many monks with similar dispensations were to be seen in the streets of Paris and the corridors of the Sorbonne, as well as in university towns all over Europe, wearing their monks' robes and cowls. But Erasmus did not like the idea of wearing monkish garments, and obtained a dispensation which allowed him to wear layman's clothes. He also disliked eating fish, which he claimed was bad for his ailment of the stone from which he suffered in later years. At the beginning of the sixteenth century it was not very difficult to obtain dispensations from the fasting laws; but after Luther and the Protestants attacked the doctrine of fasting and flagrantly broke the law by eating meat on fast days, the Church became more reluctant to grant these dispensations from fasting. Erasmus succeeded in obtaining the dispensations to the end of his life, after he had amused the Pope by explaining that although his doctrine was Catholic, his stomach was Lutheran.

Erasmus had of course to pay for all these dispensations, but he could afford to do so out of the money which was paid to him by his various patrons – Henry VIII, the king of France, a number of Italian dukes, a larger number of cardinals and bishops, and by the most generous of them all, Anne de Veere, the widow of the bastard son of the Duke of

Burgundy, to whom he wrote the most adulatory dedications of his books. But the obvious source of income was the tithes of some ecclesiastical benefices. He was appointed as the parish priest of a number of places in several countries of Western Europe, including Aldington in Kent, a benefice in Archbishop Warham's gift. He was given dispensations for pluralities and non-residence in every case.

He published his first book, *Adages*, in 1500; it was a collection of proverbs and sayings, many of which are still in common use today. He then studied and taught at the University of Louvain, and afterwards resided in the universities and cities of Northern Italy, writing and publishing other books. He was in Rome in 1509 when he heard from his former pupil, Lord Mountjoy, that Henry VIII had come to the throne and had invited him to come and live in England. Erasmus accepted the invitation with some reluctance, for he preferred Italy to England. He thought that the English, because of their cold climate and the abundance and cheapness of timber, tended to overheat their houses; and he hated the sea voyage across the Channel. As he rode through Italy and France to Calais, he was composing in his mind a new book, the *Praise of Folly*. When he reached London he visited his friend Thomas More, and stayed in More's house in Bucklersbury where he wrote the *Praise of Folly*, in Latin. It was published in Paris in 1511.

It was the most daring book that Erasmus or anyone else had written against the Church within living memory. The theme was that nothing can be achieved without fools, and it was an excuse for Erasmus to ridicule groups and institutions that he did not like. No sensible man would ever fall in love with a girl and marry a wife, with all the suffering and worry that love and marriage entails; but unless fools did so, mankind would not continue. No sensible man would spend his life studying lawsuits that took place hundreds of years ago; yet unless foolish lawyers did this, we would have no law. No sensible man would spend many hours writing books when he could be enjoying himself; yet unless foolish authors did so, there would be no literature. Continuing in the same light-hearted vein, and cleverly interweaving it with other passages, he asks what sensible man would spend his life arguing about the precise nature of the bread and wine in the eucharist, and how far it has changed after consecration by the priest; but unless foolish priests did so, our holy religion would not continue. This was sailing near the wind, and some people objected, and criticised him for writing it; but princes and cardinals laughed, and enjoyed the book, and it was not until after the advent of Luther that it was condemned by the Catholic Church.

The *Praise of Folly* was the most successful book that Erasmus had so far written, and a second edition, which was published in 1515 with comic illustrations drawn by his friend Hans Holbein the younger, was even more successful. It was dedicated to More, and its Latin title, *Encomium Moriae* – from the Greek word for 'folly' – was a pun on More's name. Some years later, Erasmus wrote that it was More who suggested that he should write the book, by which he doubtless meant that it was More who urged him to write down the ideas that had been simmering in his mind during the journey from Rome.[4] More enjoyed and admired the *Praise of Folly*. In 1515 he wrote a very long letter to a Flemish theologian, Martin van Dorp, who had criticised it, in which he vigorously defended Erasmus and the book.[5]

Erasmus stayed in London for two years. For much of the time he lived in More's house, though he also stayed with the king's Latin secretary, the Italian Ammonio. In 1511 Fisher, who was Chancellor of Cambridge University, appointed him to the chair of Greek at the university, and he moved to Cambridge; but he usually stayed with More on his visits to London. The acquaintanceship and intellectual collaboration of More and Erasmus developed into a deeper friendship during these years. It was a strange friendship, for the two men were very different in character.

The relationship was perhaps a little one-sided. On several occasions Erasmus praised More's virtues in his usual enthusiastic style; but More, who had a deeper insight and a much colder personality than Erasmus, never eulogised Erasmus as Erasmus eulogised him. More strongly defended Erasmus against the criticisms of his enemies; but though he emphasized Erasmus's intellectual achievements and integrity, he did not praise him as a person. He was probably conscious of the lack of moral fibre in Erasmus's character.

Erasmus's attitude to More was influenced by his obsession with Greek. The Greek language and culture meant everything to Erasmus. He was not interested in the geographical discoveries in the New World which fascinated his contemporaries, or in the work of Copernicus in astronomy. Although he was a personal friend of Holbein, Dürer and Matsys, he seems to have had very little appreciation of their art. Like other sixteenth-century travellers, he did not notice the landscapes through which he passed on his journeys. He tried to learn Hebrew, but gave it up because it distracted him from his studies of Greek. He left the study of Hebrew to the German scholar, Reuchlin. When the former Jewish rabbi, Pfefferkorn, who had converted to Christianity, demanded that all Hebrew books should be seized and burned except for the Old Testament, Erasmus supported Reuchlin's opposition to the anti-Hebrew campaign; but he said in private that he personally would prefer every Hebrew book to be destroyed rather than one Greek manuscript.

If a man was a Greek scholar, he could do no wrong in Erasmus's eyes. In his letters he often praises the character of unscrupulous politicians like Pace, Campeggio and Wolsey, mentioning only that they were scholars or patrons of Greek.

In July 1519 Erasmus wrote to the German poet Ulrich von Hutten, who was soon to become a leading Lutheran, and described More and his way of life in his home in London. He was a little below middle height. His hair was black or dark brown, but his complexion was pale. By 1519, when beards were just coming into fashion, he had a very thin beard. His eyes were grey and covered with specks, which, Erasmus wrote, was much admired in England as a sign of genius. His right shoulder was slightly higher than his left when he walked, not from any natural defect, but from a habit which he had acquired of walking in this way. His hands were a little clumsy. He was always careless in his dress. Although he was not robust, his health was good, and as his father was still active at the age of sixty-eight, and had just married his third wife, Erasmus believed that Thomas More was likely to live to a good old age. He was not fussy about food. He usually drank water, but when toasts were drunk, as they often were in England, he would add a little weak beer to the water. His favourite dishes were beef, salted meat, eggs, milk and vegetable foods, and coarse brown bread well fermented. His voice was penetrating and clear, and his speech distinct, but not musical, although he was fond of music.

He particularly liked watching animals and noting their habits, and had a monkey, a fox, and a ferret in his house. He disliked tennis, dice and other games. He enjoyed leisure and relaxation, but no one was more hardworking and painstaking when this was necessary. He was very fond of jokes, including those at his own expense. He was friendly and enjoyed conversation. He was equally at home with both the wise and the foolish, and was especially liable to make jokes when in female company. He was more inclined to joking than to gravity, but was quite free from buffoonery.[6]

Erasmus's account of More is very different from the picture of him presented a generation later by his biographers Roper, Harpsfield and Stapleton. Erasmus was writing about a humanist friend during his lifetime; the others were making Catholic propaganda about a martyr who had given his life for their cause. But we know that already in 1509–11, when Erasmus stayed in Bucklersbury, there were other sides to More than the Greek scholar whom Erasmus admired. One wonders whether Erasmus was really aware of this. He was not a good judge of character, and he probably never understood that he and More were utterly different people.

Erasmus was sceptical, tolerant, easy-going. Although in no way sensuous or addicted to gluttony, he valued his own quiet comforts, disliked over-exerting himself, and always sought to avoid risks and physical danger. More was profoundly religious, intolerant, abstemious, deliberately undergoing the discomfort of a hairshirt and the pain of the flagellant's whip, and always ready to torture himself and others for the Faith. Erasmus seems to have been almost entirely devoid of sexual desires; More's sexual desires were probably strong, and his knowledge of the fact disturbed and frightened him. Erasmus, as he himself often said, was not the stuff of which martyrs are made; More was, and despite all his hesitations and reluctance, he ultimately proved it at the cost of his life. Perhaps Erasmus saw only one side of More, and wrongly thought that his friend was very like himself; but Holbein, who knew them both and painted their portraits, reproduced two very different types of men. His Erasmus is a patient, sad cynic; his More is a tight-lipped fanatic. Holbein the artist saw further than Erasmus the scholar.

In 1513 More was appointed Under-Sheriff of London. It was a judicial appointment which involved sitting as a judge to deal with minor criminal and civil cases in the City. As the court sat only on Thursdays, More was free to carry on his legal practice and literary activities on other days in the week.[7]

Two years later, he was entrusted by the City of London with a more unusual duty. He was attached, on the recommendation of the City authorities, to a diplomatic mission that was sent to the Netherlands to negotiate about political and commercial matters with the representatives of the Council who governed the country for the fifteen-year-old Prince Charles of Castile – soon to be king of Castile and the Emperor Charles V – to whom the Emperor Maximilian had recently given the Netherlands. The English delegation was headed by the Archbishop of Canterbury's Chancellor, Cuthbert Tunstal, and included several canon lawyers who were regularly employed as diplomats and who, like Tunstal, afterwards became bishops. More, the most junior member of the delegation, was the only one of them who was not a priest.[8]

Tunstal and his colleagues had important and tricky matters to negotiate. To the great annoyance of Henry and Wolsey, Charles's Council in the Netherlands insisted on pursuing a pro-French policy, despite the fact that Maximilian and King Ferdinand of Spain were encouraging Henry to go to war with France; and Maximilian was evading the English requests to him to remove the pro-French ministers on Charles's Council, who Henry and Wolsey believed were in the pay of François I. Maximilian was playing a double game. He was hiring mercenaries to fight the French in Italy, but he could not afford to raise another army to fight them in Flanders at the same time, and he was particularly eager to prevent a French invasion of the defenceless

Netherlands, especially as he knew that he could not rely on Henry and Wolsey to send an army to Calais if the French marched on Bruges or Cambrai. It suited him very well if people believed that the leading members of Charles's Council in Brussels had been suborned by French money, and he encouraged them to be, or to appear to be, pro-French.

The Council of the Netherlands supported the French nominee in his dispute with Wolsey over the bishopric of Tournai. Maximilian and the government of the Netherlands were not too pleased that Henry, after capturing Tournai, had kept it for himself, though they had officially acquiesced in this term of the peace treaty. They permitted the ecclesiastical authorities in the Netherlands to recognise the French Bishop of Tournai; and while Wolsey's rights as bishop were enforced in the city of Tournai by Lord Mountjoy and the English authorities there, he was unable to collect his rents in the other parts of the diocese which were in the territory of the Netherlands, although his position as Bishop of Tournai was recognised by the Pope. When Sampson, as Wolsey's representative, tried to act on his behalf in the diocese, he was excommunicated and threatened with arrest by the ecclesiastical and temporal authorities in the Netherlands.[9]

Compared with these disputes, the commercial disagreements between the London merchants and the government of the Netherlands were of comparatively minor importance; but More was sent to the Netherlands with Tunstal, Knight and Sampson to try to smooth them out. There were allegations on both sides of breaches of the commercial treaty of 1506; the London merchants objected to being forced to send all their exports to the Netherlands through Bruges; and an English ship had been detained at Antwerp on the grounds of non-payment of customs duties.

More and his colleagues left England in May 1515 and met the Netherlands representatives at Bruges. After some weeks' negotiations, the Netherlands representatives returned to Brussels to receive further instructions from their government. While they were away, More went off to Antwerp to deal with some business for the London merchants there.[10] He stayed in the house of Peter Gilles, the town clerk of Antwerp, with whom he became friendly. The English envoys did not return to England until November 1515, and during the long intervals between the negotiating sessions More spent the time writing. It was at Antwerp that he began his book *The Best State of a Commonwealth and the New Island of Utopia*, writing the second part of the book during his stay in the Netherlands, and afterwards writing the first part in London at the beginning of 1516.[11]

Nothing that More did in his lifetime – not his actions as Lord Chancellor, his religious writings, or his martyrdom for the Catholic

Church – has done as much to ensure his immortal fame as writing this book, which he himself undoubtedly considered to be far less important than his service to God and his king. His *Utopia* added a new and important word to every language in the world. For twentieth-century readers, it has placed him in a different category from all the other statesmen and martyrs of the Tudor era. It has made him appear, quite incorrectly, to have been a man with the outlook of a twentieth-century socialist.

To us today, the adjectives 'Spartan' and 'Utopian' have nothing in common; but the system of government which was established in Sparta – according to a doubtful tradition, by Lycurgus in the ninth century B.C. – was not only the origin of the word 'Spartan' as we use it, but also the inspiration, through Plato's *Republic*, of More's *Utopia*. In ancient Greece, the two strongest states, Athens and Sparta, had presented the contrast between a tolerant, oligarchic, cultured society, and a harsh, egalitarian, military one in which the guiding principle was the complete subordination of the individual to the state. The society portrayed in *Utopia*, though it differed in many respects from ancient Sparta, was based on the Spartan view of the relationship of the state and the individual. There was nothing in this view which conflicted with the outlook of More and the thinkers of his generation. The modern idea that the state should exist to serve man, not man to serve the state, which did not develop until the Enlightenment of the eighteenth century, would have seemed strange to More, who believed that the individual must serve first God and then his prince, and not seek his own prosperity or happiness. It is an irony that modern socialists and communists, whose theoretical doctrines developed out of the libertarian and hedonistic thought of the eighteenth century, should have created a society which in many respects resembles, not the future envisaged by Marx in the nineteenth century, but the Utopian tyranny described by More in the age of Tudor despotism.

When More considered the political doctrines of Lycurgus and Plato, he knew that they had been rendered obsolete by Christianity. Since the days of ancient Greece, God had revealed the truths of Christianity to the peoples of Europe; and the Christian Church, after surviving for its first three hundred years under persecution and with a form of organisation necessitated by its illegal underground existence, had been granted the most perfect form of government which God had devised for mankind – the rule of an autocratic Christian prince who was led by his conscience and the behests of the Church and the Pope to rule for the glory of God and the welfare of his subjects. Speculation about forms of government and ideal societies were limited by the fact that nothing could be better than the rule of a Christian prince, and such speculation could only be justified in a world in which government by a Christian prince was excluded from consideration. This had applied in Plato's time, before the advent of Christ; but in 1515 it was possible only in a world which did not know about Christianity, in which the inhabitants could not be damned as infidels or heretics if they preferred some alternative form of government to the rule of a Christian prince.

The recent voyages of discovery, which had disclosed the existence of unknown territories in Southern Africa and a whole new world in America, made it possible for More to invent an imaginary country which he named Utopia, from the Greek word for 'nowhere', though he pretended that the name was derived from King Utopus, the founder of the state. After describing, in the opening pages of the book, his diplomatic mission to Bruges and his visit to Antwerp, and taking the opportunity to insert a flattering eulogy of both Henry VIII and Tunstal,[12] he pretended that while he was staying with Peter Gilles in Antwerp, and attending mass in the cathedral, he met a man whom he called Raphael Hythlodeus, from the Greek word meaning 'learned in nonsense'. Hythlodeus had travelled to the New World on one of Amerigo Vespucci's voyages, but had become separated from the main body of the expedition, and, straying off course, discovered the island of Utopia.

As the inhabitants of Utopia had never heard of Christianity, no sixteenth-century writer could blame them for choosing their own form of government rather than submitting to the autocracy of a Christian prince. They were in the position of the men and women who had lived before the Christian era and who, in the opinion of More and the Christian theologians of his time, could not go either to Heaven, Hell or Purgatory. Their souls would rest in Limbo, along with those of infants who had died in Christendom before they could be baptised. They could not go to Heaven, not having been baptised into the Christian Church; but though eternal joy would be denied to them, they would sleep for ever in Limbo, and would not suffer what More called 'any sensible pain in the fire of Hell' at the hands of those 'grisly fiends' who 'daily look and long for us in Hell for ever to torment us' with 'pain a thousand times more horrible' than any known pain on earth, 'of which terrible torment they be sure they shall never have end'.[13] Like all his contemporaries, he believed that this was a literal description of what occurred in Hell.

The book is in the form of a dialogue between More and the fictitious traveller Hythlodeus, who tells More about the laws and society in Utopia, with More expressing the surprise which would be felt by any sixteenth-century Englishman and pointing out the obvious objections to such laws, and Hythlodeus in reply explaining why they work satisfactorily in Utopia. At one point the account of Utopia is interrupted by a lengthy digression in which Hythlodeus tells More of a journey which he once made to England and an argument which he had with an English lawyer in the presence of Cardinal Morton about the laws of the Polylerites – 'the People of Much Nonsense' – who are said to inhabit an autonomous part of Persia but are as imaginary as the Utopians.

Erasmus, who read the manuscript before publication and was delighted with it, wrote to Ulrich von Hutten that More had written the book to expose the evils of contemporary governments, and that he had the government of England particularly in mind.[14] Erasmus was referring to the criticisms in *Utopia* of certain aspects of English life. More attacked the enclosures of agricultural land for the rearing of sheep; the maintenance by the nobility of large numbers of superfluous servants, retainers and hangers-on who, if they were disbanded for any reason, were liable to become vagrants or criminals; the idleness of the nobility and wealthy classes; and the death penalty for all forms of stealing. This was the first thing about *Utopia* to strike Erasmus and other contemporary readers; but these passages form only a small part of the book, most of which is devoted to a description of a perfect society – or rather, what would be a perfect society if pure reason was the only factor to be taken into consideration.

The case against capital punishment for theft is put forward by Hythlodeus in his debate with the lawyer in Morton's household. He uses exactly the same arguments, in reverse, as do the supporters of capital punishment today when they call for the restoration of the death penalty in cases of murder committed in the course of robbery. Hythlodeus argues that if thieves are going to be put to death for stealing, they have every incentive to kill anyone who can bring about their arrest and conviction, as they have nothing to lose by committing murder in addition to the theft.

When the lawyer in Morton's household objects that, if capital punishment is abolished, there would be no effective deterrent to prevent stealing, Hythlodeus refers to the laws in force in the land of the Polylerites. Instead of hanging thieves, the Polylerites employ them as slaves working in forced labour camps, or as slaves hired out to private individuals. These slaves are forced to do a hard day's work by the threat and use of the whip. They cannot escape, because they are forced to wear special clothes and a badge which it is a capital offence to remove; their hair is cropped short above their ears, and a piece of one ear is cut off in order to identify them. As an additional precaution to prevent escape, no one is allowed to give them money on pain of death both for the man who gives it and for the slave who accepts it. They cannot plot a slave insurrection with the slaves in other parts of the territory because they are put to death if they are seen speaking to a slave from another district.[15] In reading about these horrific measures suggested by More as a means of enforcing discipline and preventing revolts among criminals sentenced to forced labour, we must remember that he was putting forward arguments to show that there were other deterrents than death as a punishment for stealing, and that cutting off all or part of a criminal's ear was an accepted method of punishment in sixteenth-century England.

In *Utopia*, More does not only criticise isolated aspects of sixteenth-century society, but the very basis of the established social order. In Utopia, everyone works six hours a day. This is enough, because there are no idle classes of noblemen and their servants, of priests and monks, and of women, who do no work at all and live on the labour of others. It is not a country like those in Europe where working men labour for long hours like beasts of burden and receive almost nothing for their work, while the idle classes live in luxury. In Utopia every man and every woman is compelled to work. Goods are owned in common. Gold is so despised that only the slaves wear it. The sick are carefully looked after, but if they become incurably ill they are encouraged by the authorities to starve themselves to death. There are no lawyers, as they have all been expelled from the country. No idle games such as dice are played. The Utopians do not hunt, as they consider it degrading to derive pleasure from the sufferings of hunted animals whose plight ought to arouse compassion; so the necessary work of hunting animals for food is carried out by slaves.

Utopia is a planner's dream. It is divided into fifty-four city-states, almost equidistant from one another. The Utopians live in families of approximately equal size, each family having between ten and sixteen adults. If families rise above, or fall below, this size, members are moved from one family to another to make up the correct numbers. The Utopians live in houses with flat roofs, as these are the most healthy. All the houses are exactly alike, and exactly the same distance from the next house. From time to time the inmates are moved to other houses, presumably so that no trace of individuality can develop in any dwelling. All the towns are exactly alike, and are divided into districts of equal size. Everywhere there is perfect symmetry.

The Utopians eat sparingly and sensibly, for the good of their health, not for pleasure. They take great care to remain physically healthy. At meals they sit together at two or three long tables. The men sit on the inside with their backs to the wall, and the women on the outside, so that any woman who feels sick, as women sometimes do during pregnancy, can retire from the table without disturbing the other diners. The seating arrangement, like everything else, is planned for everyone's

67

benefit, and nothing is left to individual choice.

The men and women marry one wife or husband only, choosing their spouse after viewing them naked to make sure that they have no physical blemish. Fornication before marriage is severely punished, and the guilty parties are forbidden to marry. Divorce is authorised by the state, either for adultery or for psychological incompatibility, or by mutual consent; in cases of adultery, the guilty parties are sentenced to slavery in a labour camp, and for a second offence suffer death. If a married man and a married woman commit adultery together, their innocent wife and husband are paired off and married to each other, unless they prefer to marry someone else, for they are, surprisingly, allowed this degree of choice. If the innocent spouse does not wish to divorce the guilty partner, this is permitted on condition that the innocent spouse accompanies the guilty one to the forced labour camp and works there as a slave.

The country is governed democratically, each thirty families electing a representative to a body which elects its own representatives, and these elect a governor who rules the country for life with the advice of an elected Senate. Rules are laid down about the hours of debate and procedure in the Senate to ensure that decisions are reached in the most rational way. No one may discuss politics outside the Senate on pain of death.[16]

There are normally no fixed punishments for crimes, as the sentence is left to the discretion of the judges in every case. Ordinarily husbands punish their wives and parents punish their children, unless 'it is to the advantage of public morality'[17] to have the offence punished publicly. For serious crimes slavery, rather than death, is the punishment, because the treatment of the slaves is so severe that slavery is as great a deterrent as capital punishment, and enables the criminal to be of service to the community. The death penalty is apparently inflicted only for rebellion by slaves, for the second offence of adultery, and for discussing politics outside the Senate.

The Utopians are reluctant to go to war, but do so to revenge injuries to their merchants. Their chief reason for going to war is to colonise foreign territory, for they consider it their duty to do this if the inhabitants of the territory are not making the best economic use of their land. When they do go to war, the Utopians wage it in a most logical and ungentlemanly way. They hire mercenaries from a neighbouring mountainous state where the inhabitants are ferocious savages – the description of them convinced More's sixteenth-century readers that he had the Swiss in mind – and only volunteers from the native Utopians join the army. They offer bribes to anyone who will assassinate the enemy king and leading generals, and publicise their offer in order to spread alarm and suspicion in the enemy camp. When they capture a city, they kill the bravest of the enemy soldiers and employ the others as slaves. They make their defeated enemies pay an indemnity to cover the cost of the war.[18]

The Utopians place travelling restrictions on their people, as in sixteenth-century England and in the most totalitarian twentieth-century states. If anyone wishes to go to another part of Utopia, either to visit a friend or to see the country there, he may do so with a licence from the authorities. On his arrival there, he must report to the local authorities, who will ensure that he does a day's work in the district before he is allowed to pursue his pleasures or his own business. If he travels without a licence, he is 'severely punished', and is sent as a slave to a forced labour camp for the second offence.

> Now you can see how nowhere is there any licence to waste time, nowhere any pretext to evade work – no wine shop, no alehouse, no brothel anywhere, no opportunity for corruption, no lurking hole, no secret meeting-place. On the contrary, being under the eye of all, people are bound either to be performing the usual labour or to be enjoying their leisure in a fashion not without decency.[19]

Hythlodeus describes the religion of Utopia. There are a number of different religions; some Utopians worship the sun, some the moon, and other gods; but most of them worship the god Mithras. They all believe in one Supreme Being who created the world and governs all events that occur in it. Religious toleration is granted to all these religious sects, but they are not allowed to proselytise and attack the beliefs of the other sects. When Hythlodeus and his companions told the Utopians about Christianity, they were very attracted to it, especially because of the practice of Jesus and His apostles in owning their few goods in common and rejecting private property. Several Utopians became Christians and were baptised by Hythlodeus and his party. But when one of them began to proselytise, and preached sermons attacking the native religions, he was eventually arrested and sentenced to banishment, not for expressing his religious opinions but for inciting a riot. Although all religions are tolerated, no one is allowed to hold any public office in the state unless he believes in a life after death, for otherwise he has no incentive to do good and to avoid doing evil in this world.[20] Not even in Utopia will More forgo that most basic of all his beliefs – the 'grisly fiends' who 'daily look and long for us in Hell for ever to torment us'.[21] Those who deny a life after death are forbidden by the Utopians to express their opinions in the presence of the common people, but they are permitted to do so before the priests and 'important personages'.[22]

Utopia vividly exposes the strange contrasts in More's character and opinions. The lawyer who in 1515 and 1516 was at the height of his successful career states that lawyers are banned in Utopia. The man who wore a particularly uncomfortable hairshirt and flogged himself tells us that the sensible Utopians consider such activities to be ridiculous and to serve no true religious purpose.[23] The man who had yearned for monastic life states that it is possible for men to work only six hours a day in Utopia because they have no idle priests and monks. The king's minister and Lord Chancellor who in a few years' time will be persecuting heretics more savagely than any of his colleagues praises the Utopians' policy of religious toleration.

There are even some contradictions, or apparent contradictions, in the book itself. Despite the strictures on the uselessness of idle priests and monks, the Utopians have priests. Women as well as men may be priests; and the male priests are given 'the very finest women'[24] as their wives. Like the members of the government of Utopia, they alone are exempted from the duty of daily labour; and the priests have the additional privilege of being immune from all punishments, whatever crime they may commit, because the Utopians' respect for anyone who has held the office of priest is too great for them to punish him even if he commits the most serious offence. The Utopians are sure that in nearly every case the virtue and conscience of a priest will prevent him from misbehaving; and as there are only thirteen priests, and thirteen churches, in every one of the fifty-four cities of Utopia, the number of priests is sufficiently small that it does not greatly matter if they do misbehave. There is also a class of persons who voluntarily undertake to do the most laborious and degrading work out of devotion to the community. Some of these choose to practise chastity, but others prefer to marry. The Utopians believe that the latter group are more sensible, but that the celibates are holier.[25]

More ends *Utopia* with a strong attack on sixteenth-century class society.

What brand of justice is it that any nobleman whatsoever or goldsmith-banker or moneylender or, in fact, anyone else from among those who either do no work at all or whose work is of a kind not very essential to the commonwealth, should attain a life of luxury and grandeur on the basis of his idleness or his non-essential work? In the meantime, the common labourer, the carter, the carpenter, and the farmer perform work so hard and continuous that beasts of burden could scarcely endure it and work so essential that no commonwealth could last even one year without it. Yet they earn such scanty fare and lead such a miserable life that the condition of beasts of burden might seem far preferable. . . . Now is not this an unjust and ungrateful commonwealth? It lavishes great rewards on so-called gentlefolk and banking goldsmiths and the rest of that kind, who are either idle or mere parasites and purveyors of empty pleasures. On the contrary, it makes no benevolent provision for farmers, colliers, common labourers, carters and carpenters without whom there would be no commonwealth at all.[26]

Moreover, the rich use their power to enact laws which oppress the poor and benefit the rich.

What did More really believe about Utopia? The contrast between his own practice in England and the régime that he describes in *Utopia*, along with the form in which the book is written, with Hythlodeus arguing against More in favour of the Utopians' system, has led many to believe that More did not favour the system in Utopia but put it forward merely as an intellectual exercise. On the other hand, More's biographer, Chambers, in 1935 pointed out the irony of the fact that the word 'Utopia' has come to mean an ideal society which is incapable of realisation, whereas More's Utopia is 'a sternly righteous and puritanical State where few of us would feel quite happy' but has many features which have been applied in practice in the twentieth century.[27] But for More, his Utopia was exactly what the word has come to mean today. He knew that it was not practicable to introduce such a system into the Europe of 1516, but he believed that it was the perfect society – or rather, that it was the kind of society which pure reason would lead him to believe was the perfect society if pure reason was the only factor involved, which he knew was not the case. The title of More's book was *The Best State of a Commonwealth and the New Island of Utopia*; but it was the best state of a commonwealth, not of a Christian kingdom.

At the end of *Utopia*, More makes two statements which surely indicate quite clearly what he felt about the society which he described. One of these statements, significantly, is made by Hythlodeus, and the other, equally significantly, by More himself. 'Nor does it occur to me to doubt', says Hythlodeus:

that a man's regard for his own interests or the authority of Christ our Saviour – who in His wisdom could not fail to know what was best and who in His goodness would not fail to counsel what He knew to be best – would long ago have brought the whole world to adopt the laws of the Utopian commonwealth, had not one single monster, the chief and progenitor of all plagues, striven against it: I mean Pride. Pride measures prosperity not by her own advantages but by others' disadvantages. Pride would not consent to be made even a goddess if no poor wretches were left for her to domineer over and scoff at, if her good fortune might not dazzle by comparison with their miseries, if

71

the display of her riches did not torment and intensify their poverty. . . . Pride is too deeply fixed in men to be easily plucked out. For this reason, the fact that this form of a commonwealth, which I should gladly desire for all, has been the good fortune of the Utopians at least, fills me with joy.[28]

To which More adds his own comment, speaking himself:

When Raphael [Hythlodeus] had finished his story, many things came to my mind which seemed very absurdly established in the customs and laws of the people described – not only in their method of waging war, their ceremonies and religion, as well as their other institutions, but most of all in that feature which is the principal foundation of their whole structure. I mean their common life and subsidence, without any exchange of money. This latter alone utterly overthrows all the nobility, magnificence, splendour and majesty which are, in the estimation of the common people, the true glories and ornaments of the commonwealth.

He finally closes the book by stating that Hythlodeus

though in other respects he is a man of the most undoubted learning as well as of the greatest knowledge of human affairs, I cannot agree with all that he said. But I readily admit that there are very many features in the Utopian commonwealth which it is easier for me to wish for in our countries than to have any hope of seeing realised.[29]

More wrote *Utopia* in Latin, as he intended it to be read by the intellectuals of Europe, not by the common people. It was published in Louvain in December 1516, and was acclaimed by scholars throughout Christendom. According to More, some readers took it so seriously that they believed that the island of Utopia really existed, and one of them suggested to More that missionaries should be sent to convert the Utopians to Christianity.[30] Five more editions were published in Paris, Basle and Vienna during the next three years. It was not translated into English until 1551, sixteen years after More's death.

It was almost certainly just after More had finished writing *Utopia*, and probably before it was published, that he wrote another and very different book, his *History of King Richard III*. There has been considerable doubt about the date of the book, and whether More was indeed the author, for it was not published until after his death. It first appeared in English, when it was printed by Richard Grafton in London in 1544 as part of Harding's *Chronicle* without mentioning More's name, at a time when More's family were in no position to prevent this pirating of a book written by an author who had been executed as a traitor. It was reprinted in English as More's book in London during Queen Mary's reign in 1557, and published in Latin in Louvain in 1565. Various Latin manuscripts of the book are in existence. All the evidence shows that it was certainly written by More, probably in English and at some date between 1515 and 1518. As More was busy writing *Utopia* until the middle of 1516, he probably wrote *Richard III* at the end of 1516 or the beginning of 1517.[31]

It is the earliest book written about the king who had died just over thirty years before, and it has been regarded as the source of the story which was later passed down by Holinshed and other writers to Shakespeare, and which has represented Richard to history as the monstrous crookback murderer and usurper. Richard III's admirers have denounced it as Lancastrian and Tudor propaganda, which is at best a gross over-simplification. It has also been seen, by Chambers and other admirers of More, as a tract against Machiavellian doctrines of statecraft,[32] though in many ways it is a handbook of Machiavellianism. It is a denunciation of Richard III, a justification of Edward IV, and a glorification of Cardinal Morton, while it tactfully avoids expressing any opinion about More's old enemy, Henry VII. For the biographer of More, its interest is not what it tells us about Richard but what it reveals about More.

There is no doubt that More must have obtained a great deal of his information from Morton; but Morton's influence has probably been exaggerated. More was a page in Morton's household for two years when he was between the ages of twelve and fourteen, and no doubt remembered many things that he had heard Morton say at the time; but it is very unlikely that more than a small proportion of the facts related in the book had been told to More when he was a child and remembered by him for the twenty-five years that elapsed before he wrote the book. We know that he made inquiries from other sources, for with the scrupulousness of the serious historian he distinguishes between facts which he was told by eye-witnesses and those which he heard only at second hand.[33]

It is almost as surprising that the author of *Richard III* should have written *Utopia* as it is that he should have composed the religious books and epistles which More wrote during his last days in prison in the Tower. If it was More the witty humanist who wrote the reply to Lucian's *Tyrannicide* and the early poems; More the socialist planner who wrote *Utopia*; and More the Catholic saint and martyr who wrote the Tower tracts, it was More the worldy-wise politician, soon to enter the king's service, who wrote *Richard III*.

73

The book begins with a tribute to Edward IV, who, though a Yorkist enemy of the house of Lancaster, was Henry VIII's grandfather and the father of the queen who by her marriage to Henry VII united the red and white roses of Lancaster and York. More acknowledges that Edward IV won the throne by a rebellion, committing high treason against his lawful sovereign Henry VI, but lightly brushes this aside, saying that Edward afterwards showed himself to be a good king who restored law and order in the realm and was loved even by Henry VI's supporters. More is equally tolerant towards Edward's notorious lechery. Adultery might be severely punished in Utopia and in More's household, but it was a forgivable peccadillo in Henry VIII's grandfather. In his youth, writes More, he was 'greatly given to fleshly wantonness'; but healthy, rich and successful men hardly ever refrain from this vice, unless they are exceptionally virtuous. The people did not mind very much, because it was impossible for one man to seduce many men's wives, because he never raped a woman by force, and because he became less lascivious in later years.[34]

After giving due praise to Richard's courage in battle and his military ability, More describes his murder of Henry VI in the Tower and his usurpation of power after Edward IV's death, including the incident of Morton and the strawberries and Lord Hastings's summary execution, and the assassination of the princes in the Tower. As part of Richard's campaign to discredit the children of Edward IV and to persuade the people to accept his story that they were illegitimate, he compelled Edward's mistress, Jane Shore, who was also Hastings's mistress, to do public penance for her adultery at Paul's Cross. More's account of this incident is difficult to reconcile with the hero of Roper, Harpsfield and Stapleton.

He begins by commenting sarcastically on Richard's motive in forcing her to do penance 'as a goodly continent prince, dear and faultless of himself, sent out of Heaven into this vicious world for the amendment of men's manners'. When she walked, slowly and 'demure so womanly', dressed only in her petticoat, she blushed to see the people gazing at her, for she looked 'so fair and lovely'. What was intended to put her to shame won her great praise, both among those who were 'more amorous of her body than curious of her soul', and among other good folk who were glad to see sin corrected, yet pitied her because of her penance and of Richard's motives in ordering her to perform it. More then proceeds to tell his readers that Jane Shore, after being properly brought up, was married when very young to a wealthy young citizen of London whom she never loved, 'which was haply the thing that the more easily made her incline unto the king's appetite when he required her. Howbeit the respect of his royalty, the hope of gay apparel, ease, pleasure, and other wanton wealth was able soon to pierce a soft tender heart.'

After she had become the king's mistress, her husband, being an honest man who knew what was good for him, 'not presuming to touch a king's concubine, led her up to him altogether'. When the king died, she became the mistress of Lord Hastings, the Lord Chamberlain, who 'in the King's days, albeit he was sore enamoured upon her, yet he forbore her, either for reverence or for a certain friendly faithfulness. Proper she was and fair'; according to those who knew her in her youth, there was 'nothing in her body that you would have changed', except that she might have been a little taller. More writes that some people who see her now (for she is still alive) say that she is not beautiful, but as she is aged about seventy this is hardly surprising, and he does not think that her past beauty should be judged on her present appearance. In any case, men loved her not only for her beauty, but for her

> pleasant behaviour. For a proper wit she had, and could both read well and write, merry in company, ready and quick of answer; neither mute nor full of babble, sometime taunting without displeasure, and not without disport. The king would say that he had three concubines, which in three divers properties diversely excelled. One the merriest, another the wiliest, the third the holiest harlot in his realm, as one whom no man could get out of the church lightly to any place but it were to his bed.

More does not identify the other two harlots, whom he says were of higher rank than Jane Shore, but he says that it was she who was the merriest.

He then praises her for the good that she did in Edward IV's reign by interceding with him to remit forfeitures of the property of his political opponents, which she did without expecting to be paid bribes, either out of a wish to do good or because 'she delighted to be sued unto, or to show what she was able to do with the king, or for that wanton women and wealthy be not always covetous'. More ends by lamenting the present poverty of Jane Shore, who, after her past grandeur, is reduced to begging for financial help.[35]

More's account of Jane Shore has been described by several of his biographers and other writers as a moving example of the saint's tolerance and forgiveness for the sinner; but it reads much more like the sympathy and admiration which a worldly and at least mildly sensuous courtier or author feels for a pretty and charming woman. Still more revealing is the admiration which More expresses in the book for Morton, whom he had already praised at some length in *Utopia*. More undoubtedly admired Morton as a kind master who had befriended him when he was a page in his household and had persuaded his father to allow him to go to Oxford, and he also respected him as a patron of Greek and humanist studies; but it is quite clear from his *Richard III* that there was another aspect of his admiration for Morton. He was fascinated by Morton's political cunning. 'This man', he wrote, 'had gotten by great experience, the very mother and mistress of wisdom, a deep insight in politic worldly drifts.'[36]

He quoted at length from Morton's conversation with Buckingham when Morton was the duke's prisoner at Brecon, by which he persuaded his jailor to revolt against King Richard. More wrote *Richard III* more than fifteen years after Morton's death and probably twenty-five years after Morton told him about the incident; so it is unlikely that More quoted the exact words which Morton used to Buckingham in 1483. If, as is quite possible, the wording is more More's than Morton's, this only emphasizes the extent to which More identified himself with Morton's subtle intrigue.

Morton told Buckingham about his change of allegiance from the Lancastrians to the Yorkists.

If the world would have gone as I would have wished, King Henry's son had had the crown and not King Edward. But after that God had ordered him to lose it, and King Edward to reign, I was never so mad that I would with a dead man strive against the quick. So was I to King Edward faithful chaplain, and glad would have been that his child had succeeded him. Howbeit if the secret judgment of God have otherwise provided, I purpose not to spurn against a prick, nor labour to set up that God pulleth down. And as for the late Protector and now king –

and here Morton paused, as if unwilling to make any comment about King Richard, and only continued when urged by Buckingham.

He then told Buckingham a story which More, in his book, says is one of Æsop's fables, but which in fact does not appear in Æsop and was probably invented either by Morton or More, though it faintly resembles a story which had been sung in a ballad in 1308 and was published in yet another variation in 1604. It was probably a popular fable in More's time. The lion ordered that no animal with a horn in his head should remain in the wood on pain of death, whereupon an animal who had no horn, but had a lump of flesh on his forehead, fled from the wood in great haste. The fox stopped him and asked him why he fled, for he had no horn, and the lion's proclamation did not apply to him. 'No, marry,' replied the fleeing animal, 'that wit I well enough. But what and he call it a horn, where am I then?' Buckingham 'laughed merrily at the tale', but began to draw the conclusions that Morton intended he should.

Then Morton said to Buckingham that he would not dispute King Richard's title:

> but for the weal of this realm, whereof His Grace hath now the governance, and whereof I am myself one poor member, I was about to wish that to those good abilities whereof he hath already right many, little needing my praise, it might have pleased God, for the better store, to have given him some of such other excellent virtues, mete for the ruler of a realm, as our Lord hath planted in the person of Your Grace.[37]

The result of this talk was that Buckingham set Morton free and revolted against Richard III, with disastrous results for Buckingham, but with excellent long-term benefits for Morton.

At the time when More was writing *Richard III*, he had just completed his first diplomatic mission abroad, and was undoubtedly considering the possibility of entering the king's service. He discussed the principles which this involved in *Utopia*, in a conversation that he pretended Peter Gilles and he had had with Hythlodeus. Gilles urges Hythlodeus to put his experience and abilities to good use by entering the service of some prince. But Hythlodeus replies that this would be servitude; and when Gilles explains that he is speaking of service, not servitude, Hythlodeus replies that 'servitude' is only one syllable more than 'service'.* Finding Hythlodeus unmoved by Gilles's argument that if he enters a king's service he will be in a position to obtain favours for his relatives and friends, More tells him that it is his duty to enter his prince's Council, and to use his abilities to persuade the prince and the government to do good, or, if this is impossible, at least to persuade them not to do too much harm. Hythlodeus replies that kings always wish to be advised to go to war, not to make peace.[38]

The arguments in *Utopia* between Hythlodeus and More on this point are the familiar ones in every century on whether or not to enter politics. It will involve compromises of principle and the use of questionable moral tactics. Should a conscientious citizen opt out of politics in order to preserve his moral purity, thus relinquishing any opportunity to influence the government to do good; or should he take part in the game and do the best he can for his country and the people, at the risk of contaminating himself and sinking by degrees into moral corruption and iniquity?

* In More's original Latin, *'inservias'* has one more syllable than *'servias'*.

In the summer of 1517 More had occasion to render a service to the king and the government in his capacity as Under-Sheriff of London in a way which brought him prominently into the public eye. There was a widespread resentment against foreigners in London which throughout the sixteenth century made England, and especially its capital city, notorious in Europe for nationalist intolerance. At the end of April 1517 a speaker harangued an open-air meeting in the fields just outside London, and denounced the foreign merchants and their servants who, he alleged, robbed, cheated and exploited the native inhabitants of London and seduced their wives and daughters. The foreigners and the government became alarmed, especially as 1 May was approaching, and the May Day festivities were always an occasion for Morris dances, Robin Hood games, and other noisy disorders.

On 30 April a band of about two thousand Londoners attacked the houses of the Venetian, Flemish and German merchants in London, and a number of City officials, including the Under-Sheriff Thomas More, hurried off to see Wolsey at Hampton Court and urged him to take action. Wolsey told them to ban the usual all-night festivities on the eve of May Day and to enforce a curfew that night; but the order merely enraged the apprentices, who defied the curfew.

More, with his officers and men, patrolled the streets during the night. He encountered a group of rioters, and was apparently on the point of persuading them to disband and go home when one of them threw a stone at More and his party. More's serjeant and his men charged the rioters with their staves, and More could do nothing further to prevent a full-scale riot from developing. The streets were eventually cleared next day by the Duke of Norfolk and his soldiers.

The king and the cardinal took a very serious view of the riot on 'Evil May Day'. They thought that it was necessary to make an example of the rioters, in order both to enforce respect for the royal authority and to show foreign merchants that they would be protected if they came to London to trade. Fifteen of the rioters were hanged on gibbets which were erected in various parts of the city. Another batch of rioters were sentenced to death, but were pardoned in a ceremony which was often performed after riots and rebellions in the sixteenth century. The condemned men were brought before the king in Westminster Hall with halters around their necks. More was present, with other representatives of the city, and they pleaded with Wolsey to intercede with Henry to show mercy to the men. Wolsey knelt to Henry and begged for mercy, and was followed by Queen Catherine, who likewise pleaded with Henry on her knees. The king then agreed to pardon them.[39]

More's courage in trying to appease the riot, and his plea for the lives of the rioters, were remembered to his credit in London for many years, even after the Londoners had become staunchly Protestant and supporters of the party which More had persecuted and which had applauded his execution. The incident was commemorated more than eighty years later in a play, *Sir Thomas More*, which may have been written by Shakespeare.[40]

More's role in 'Evil May Day', his success as a diplomat in Flanders, and his international reputation after the publication of *Utopia*, made it certain that he would be invited to join the king's government. According to Roper, the immediate cause of the invitation was a legal dispute which arose when Henry and his council detained at Southampton a ship belonging to the Papal States, which they claimed was forfeit as prize for some offence under maritime law. The Papal Nuncio in England briefed More to appear on his behalf before the Prize Court, and More argued the case so ably that the court gave judgment in the shipowner's favour. Henry and Wolsey then decided that they must ensure that More's legal talents would in future be employed for them, not against them.[41] So More, after being employed on a second diplomatic mission on behalf of the City of London when he was sent to Calais to argue with the envoys of the Netherlands over wine duties,[42] was appointed Master of Requests in the summer of 1518, when he was aged forty. The duty of the Master of Requests was to receive petitions presented to the king, and involved living at court and travelling with the king on his progresses through the country. A few months later, More was appointed a member of the Privy Council. He resigned his office as Under-Sheriff of London.[43]

Harpsfield tells a story, which came to him from Roper and More's family, of how More's wife, Dame Alice, urged More to take office in the king's government and go to court, despite his reluctance to do so. She told More that she could not believe that he would be so foolish as to refuse to join the government, because if she were in his place she would prefer to rule than be ruled. More replied that he could well believe it, as he had never yet seen her consent to be ruled about anything.[44] We can be sure that he was chiefly influenced, not by Dame Alice, but by the arguments that he had put forward in his own name against Hythlodeus in *Utopia*, just as he was very conscious of the force of Hythlodeus's arguments on the other side.

He must also have been influenced by the attitude of his fellow-humanists, especially Erasmus. Although Erasmus, who moved from one country to another throughout his life, never took an active part in politics, he strongly believed that the evils which were threatening Christendom, especially wars and intolerance, could be abolished if humanists and Greek scholars became the secretaries of state and the ambassadors of the most powerful European princes. But there was an even stronger influence affecting More's decision. If one Thomas More wished to practise at the Bar and play his part in the City of London; if a second Thomas More wished to write books about perfect rational societies in imaginary countries; and if a third Thomas More wished to withdraw into the contemplative life of a strictly regulated monastery; a fourth Thomas More, the Thomas More who wrote *Richard III*, was fascinated by the skill, the finesse and the excitement of the political chess-game. He longed to try his hand at playing it, despite all the hazards that it entailed both for the necks and for the immortal souls of those who became involved in it.

CHAPTER 7

THE FIELD OF CLOTH-OF-GOLD

IN 1516, the year in which More published his *Utopia*, with its picture of an utterly new society in complete contradiction to the accepted ideas of his time, Erasmus published a new edition of the most orthodox and accepted book in Christendom. More's *Utopia* aroused no adverse criticism; Erasmus's Greek New Testament was violently denounced, and caused turmoil in Church and State.

The New Testament had been translated from Greek into Latin by St Jerome in the fourth century, and for over a thousand years the Church in Western Europe had read it in his translation, which was known as the Vulgate. When the humanists learned Greek at the end of the fifteenth century, they were able to use their knowledge of the language not only for their studies of the pagan writers of ancient Greece, but also to read the New Testament in the original Greek and to contemplate making a new Latin translation of it. This idea disturbed the conservative churchmen even more than the study of Euripides and Lucian. It was a little disconcerting to be reminded that the Vulgate, which had for so long been accepted as the Word of God, was in fact a Latin translation, and possibly an inaccurate translation, of the Word of God.

Erasmus had begun work on a new translation of the Greek New Testament as early as 1506, working from a fifteenth-century Greek manuscript containing the text used in the Christian Churches of Eastern Europe until the Turkish conquest. He realised that his translation might be controversial, for he translated several words in a different way from the Vulgate, including the Greek word ἐκκλησία, which Jerome had retained in its Greek form as *ecclesia* in his translation. Erasmus usually translated it as *congregatio*, and sometimes as *concio*. *Ecclesia* had become the accepted Latin word for 'the Church', and to replace it by 'the congregation' was likely to cause trouble. When Erasmus came to England in 1509, he showed his work to several scholars and leading churchmen. Colet was enthusiastic, but others were more doubtful, and Richard Bere, the Abbot of Glastonbury, warned him so strongly about the dangers which would follow from the publication of his translation, that he decided to abandon the project.

In Spain, Cardinal Ximenes embarked on a plan to publish the text of the Old and New Testaments in the original Hebrew and Greek. As the idea of publishing the Greek text of the New Testament had thus obtained official approval, Erasmus decided to produce his own version based not on the fifteenth-century Greek text of the Eastern Church but on earlier Greek manuscripts, written between the twelfth and the fifteenth centuries, which he found in libraries in Basle and in England. After he had studied nine of these manuscripts, Reuchlin showed him a tenth, and much older, manuscript, which Erasmus believed was the original first-century text, though later scholarship suggests that it dates from the tenth century.

Erasmus was able to steal a march on Cardinal Ximenes's scholars. Their Greek New Testament was printed at Alcalá in January 1514, but its publication was held up until they had prepared a Greek vocabulary which was to accompany it, and until the new Pope, Leo X, found time to compose an official bull approving the publication, which was to be printed as a foreword to the book. Erasmus, who was a friend of Leo's, obtained his informal consent to his own project, and decided to publish it without waiting for an official bull. His Greek New Testament, with his accompanying notes and a Latin translation, was published by the printer Froben in Basle in February 1516. In the hope of appeasing the controversies which were likely to arise, the Latin translation was almost identical with the Vulgate, and did not contain the changes which Erasmus had made in his unpublished translation of 1506.

The book aroused a storm of criticism. Erasmus, relying on what he believed was the first-century Greek manuscript, claimed that several passages in the accepted text of the New Testament were later additions, and therefore, by implication, not the Word of God. The most important was the passage in 1 John 5:7: 'For these are three that bear record in Heaven, the Father, the Word and the Holy Ghost; and these three are one.' Erasmus said he had not found this passage in any Greek manuscript, and believed that it was inserted in the Latin text by Priscillian in 380. He included in his text the last twelve verses of the last chapter of Mark's Gospel, which describe Christ's actions between the Resurrection and the Ascension, and the famous passage in John 8: 1–11 concerning Christ's forgiveness of the woman taken in adultery; but he stated in the notes that he believed that these passages, too, were later insertions.

Erasmus made matters worse by publishing three years later a new edition of the Greek New Testament, after he had consulted new manuscripts found in the Netherlands and Hungary. He made four hundred alterations to his text of 1516. He added a Latin translation, which was not, this time, almost identical with the Vulgate, but was his own translation of 1506 which he had not ventured to publish before. Where the Vulgate had 'the Church', he had 'the congregation'; where the Vulgate, in John 1:1, had 'In the beginning was the Word' (*verbum*), he had 'In the beginning was the sermon' (*sermo*), meaning, in medieval Latin, the spoken word as used in sermons, which seemed to imply divine approval for the preaching of the sermons which were so popular with heretical sects. In Matthew 3:2, the Vulgate had: 'Do penance (*poenitentiam agite*), for the kingdom of Heaven is at hand'; he had: 'Come to your senses (*ad mentem medite*), for the kingdom of Heaven is at hand.'[1]

Leo X wrote a letter to Erasmus approving of the first edition of his Greek New Testament, but this did not save him from widespread condemnation. Fisher liked it very much, and wrote to Erasmus that his only criticism was that it did not differ more widely from the Vulgate; but Cambridge University, of which Fisher was Chancellor, banned the book. Edward Lee, a canon of Lincoln and a future Archbishop of York, who was a childhood friend of More's, published a book attacking Erasmus, and starting a violent personal controversy between the two which More and other mutual friends were unable to heal. Foxe, the old Bishop of Winchester, supported Erasmus; Standish, the Bishop of St Asaph, denounced him. More liked the Greek text and Erasmus's translation, and enthusiastically defended his friend. He wrote letters to several critics of Erasmus, taking them to task for attacking him, and urged Wolsey to use his influence on Erasmus's side.[2]

Apart from the New Testament, Erasmus was in some other trouble with the authorities in 1516. The matter was hushed up so effectively that we do not really know what it was; but it seems likely that the authorities had discovered that he had lied on many occasions when he had stated that he had been born in 1466 and had been conceived before his father became a monk. He had therefore obtained all his dispensations by false pretences. He was very worried for some time before he extricated himself from his difficulties with the help of his friend Ammonio, who as Henry VIII's Latin secretary was very influential at the court of Rome. Erasmus was granted absolution and pardoned after he had repented of his sin, and all his dispensations were renewed and extended; but this cost him a great deal of money.[3]

Erasmus had strongly objected to Pope Julius II's war policy; he deplored the fact that, when peace had been established in Europe in 1511, the 'trumpet of Julius' had summoned the nations of Christendom to war. When Julius died in 1513, and Erasmus's friend Cardinal de Medici succeeded him as Pope Leo X, Erasmus wrote a funny tract, *Julius at the Gates of Heaven*, which he took care not to publish. It described how, when Julius reaches the heavenly gates, he finds there the souls of all the men slain in the wars which he had instigated, and these souls persuade St Peter not to admit him. Julius thereupon becomes very angry at the impudence of a mere fisherman like St Peter who presumes to refuse admission to a Pope, and he threatens to summon his soldiers and order them to capture the gates of Heaven by storm. In 1517 the young humanist and Greek scholar, Thomas Lupset, who was a friend of Erasmus and More, rashly published *Julius at the Gates of Heaven* in Paris, as the work of an anonymous author. Though Lupset took care not to give any hint that Erasmus had written it, his style was recognised, and he was widely accused of being the author, which he denied.[4]

After Erasmus came Luther. Martin Luther, nearly six years younger than More, eleven years younger than Wolsey, fourteen years younger than Erasmus, was born at Eisleben in Saxony in 1483, the son of a peasant who, soon after his birth, moved to the growing industrial town of Mansfeld to work as a miner in the tin mines. Martin became a monk and a priest, went on a pilgrimage to Rome – the only time in his life that he left Germany – and in his Augustinian monastery at Erfurt learned Greek and Hebrew as well as Latin, read the leading humanist authors, and became more and more indignant at the corruption of the Church. He read Erasmus's books, and admired them, but was suspicious of his lack of religious and reforming zeal. He said that *Julius at the Gates of Heaven* was 'so amusing, so learned, and so ingenious, in other words, so entirely Erasmian, that it makes the reader laugh at the vices of the Church, whereas every true Christian ought to feel angry about them'.[5]

Albert of Brandenburg, the brother of the Margrave of Brandenburg who ruled the extensive territories between the Netherlands and Poland, was in 1515, at the age of twenty-five, Archbishop of Magdeburg and Bishop of Halberstadt. He was eager also to become Archbishop of Mainz, an archbishopric which would bring him not only the revenues of the see but would also make him, like his brother the Margrave, one of the seven Electors of the Holy Roman Empire. As the Emperor Maximilian was old and ill, his death and the election of a new emperor could not be long delayed. When the election took place, all the candidates for the imperial crown would pay very large sums in bribes to the Electors; and Maximilian was already promising an enormous amount of money to those of them who undertook to vote, after his death, for his grandson Charles, the prince of Castile.

To obtain the vacant archbishopric of Mainz, Albert of Brandenburg needed two dispensations – one to hold three bishoprics simultaneously, and another to be consecrated as a bishop before he reached the canonical age of thirty, though he had already been granted dispensations for age for the two bishoprics which he already held. In view of

Thomas More, by Holbein

The Field of Cloth-of-gold, by an unknown artist

Albert's financial prospects if he obtained Mainz, the Pope demanded an unusually high price for the dispensations, and insisted on 10,000 ducats. Albert approached the Fuggers of Augsburg, the biggest bankers in Europe; but they would not lend him the money without good security.

The Pope thought of a way of helping Albert. He would issue an indulgence to anyone who contributed money to the building of a new cathedral of St Peter's in Rome, and would widely publicise the fact in Germany. The effect of the indulgence would be to shorten the stay in Purgatory of the souls of those who contributed and of all their relations, and to enable them to pass forthwith from the pains of Purgatory to the joys of Heaven. By an agreement with the Fuggers which was to be kept secret, half the proceeds from the sales of the indulgences in Germany were to be handed over to the Pope for the building of St Peter's, while the other half was to be paid to the Fuggers, ostensibly as their bankers' commission for transferring the money from Germany to Italy, but also as repayment of their loan to Albert of Brandenburg.

The duty of raising the money in Germany was entrusted to Johann Tetzel, the prior of the Dominican monastery in Leipzig, who had considerable learning and a great sense of humour. He was a splendid mob orator. At great meetings all over Germany he painted a vivid description of the appalling tortures which were inflicted on souls in Purgatory, and told his audience that by putting their money into his collecting boxes they could immediately relieve their loved ones from these tortures and enable them to enter Heaven at once. Luther first heard about Tetzel's activities when local residents came to him in his monastery to confess their sins to him as their priest. When he told them, as usual, that they must repent before he could give them absolution, they replied that they had bought indulgences from Tetzel, who had told them that this would entitle them to absolution whether they repented or not.

On the evening of 31 October 1517, All-Hallows Eve, Luther nailed his Ninety-five Theses to the door of the church at Wittenberg. The theses put forward the doctrine that absolution granted by a priest, and even by the Pope himself, could only remit the necessity of penance by the sinner, and could not absolve him from the sin itself; nor could such absolution have any influence on the fate of souls in Purgatory. When the theses were read by the scholars of the university and the people of Wittenberg next morning, they aroused great enthusiasm, and soon they were being discussed all over Germany. During the next year Luther wrote a number of tracts criticising the Papal indulgences, the doctrine of Purgatory, and the corruptions of the Church. He had launched a national movement in Germany, supported by princes and peasants alike, against the Pope, the Church of Rome, and its economic exploitation of the German people.[6]

Erasmus sympathised with Luther. When he read his Ninety-five Theses, he wrote to More and to Fisher and told them that he agreed with all of them except a few about Purgatory. He very much hoped that the Church would not condemn Luther, for he was sure that this would not only drive a virtuous and learned man from the Christian fold, but ran the risk of losing all Germany for the Church. But he himself was in a difficult position, in view of the criticism which his Greek New Testament had caused. Already the saying was heard throughout Europe which was to be repeated again and again during the next thirty years – that Erasmus laid the eggs which Luther hatched. While Erasmus was eager to prevent the condemnation of Luther, he was also anxious about his own safety. He wrote to his Basle publisher, Froben, who had published some of Luther's tracts, and asked him not to publish any more of Luther's works, as this would compromise Erasmus. He wrote to his Lutheran friends urging them to be careful not to antagonise the Pope and the princes of Christendom, and not to encourage the people to take the reformation of the Church into their own hands; if necessary, they should submit to the authority of the Pope and recant their doctrines. He wrote to Wolsey, assuring him that he had nothing in common with Luther.[7]

But Wolsey had other matters to deal with. The Emperor Maximilian died in January 1519, and the election campaign began at once. Two candidates offered themselves for the imperial crown – Charles of Castile and François I. Of the seven Electors, the twelve-year-old King Ladislaus II of Bohemia was engaged to marry Charles's sister Mary and was inseparably linked to the House of Habsburg. Maximilian had bought the votes of the Margrave of Brandenburg, of his brother Albert, Archbishop of Mainz, and of the Archbishop of Cologne, by promises of very large cash payments, annual pensions, and a marriage into the royal family for the Margrave. The Count Palatine of the Rhine, the Duke of Saxony and the Archbishop of Trier were uncommitted, and François I made large offers to them. Hearing this, Albert of Brandenburg went back on his promise to Maximilian and told Charles that he had raised his price. Charles offered him and the other Electors enormous sums which far exceeded the highest bid that François I could make, for, unlike François, Charles had secured the backing of the Fuggers. He also had the support of public opinion in Germany, which made it difficult and risky for any Elector to support the French; and as the time for the election in Frankfurt-am-Main approached, Charles's supporters assembled a force of German mercenaries nearby to prevent François's election, if necessary by force. The only serious obstacle to Charles's success was the Pope, who let it be known that he favoured François's candidature, because Charles was King of Naples, and it was a maxim of Papal policy that the king of Naples should not become Holy Roman Emperor.

In the new era of universal peace in Christendom, Henry and Wolsey were equally friendly to both Charles and François, and ready to play them off against each other; but commercial ties with the Netherlands and the traditional anti-French feeling in England drew them to Charles's side. Wolsey told both Charles and François that Henry supported them in the election, and sent Richard Pace, a friend of More and Erasmus, to Frankfurt in May 1519, a month before the voting was due to begin, with orders to do nothing to help either candidate, but to tell the supporters of both that he was working on their behalf. Henry thought of the possibility of standing as a candidate himself. His counsellors were conscious that the Empire, with its troublesome princes and free cities, would be a burden and an expense, not an asset, to him and to England; but Wolsey instructed Pace to try to borrow money from the German bankers so that he would be able to bribe the Electors to vote for Henry.

Pace persuaded the Cologne banker, Hermann Rinck, to give him credit, but found that the Electors would not accept any bribes which were not paid in hard cash or were formally guaranteed by Henry under his seal; and Pace had not brought any such formal guarantees with him. In any case, Charles was offering sums that far exceeded anything that Henry would have been willing to pay. Pace therefore contented himself with offering smaller bribes to the Electors if they promised to say that Henry had urged them to vote for Charles, and not to reveal that he had hoped to bribe them to vote for him. Pace wrote to Wolsey that he could have done a great deal for Henry's candidature if arrangements had been made with the bankers at an earlier date.

The Electors spent only one day in conclave, partly because plague had broken out in Frankfurt and they wished to leave the town as soon as possible. Their last hesitations were removed when news came that the Pope had reached an agreement with Charles and had withdrawn his opposition to his candidature. On 28 June they unanimously elected Charles as king of the Romans, which would be his official title until he was crowned emperor by the Pope in the traditional manner. Henry and Wolsey hastened to congratulate Charles on his success and to commiserate with François on his failure. They told neither of them that Henry had himself been a candidate.[8]

François put a brave face on his defeat, and set about trying to form an alliance with Henry against Charles. He proposed to Henry that they should meet at some place near Calais to demonstrate their friendship to the world. Charles got to hear of this, and tried to dissuade Henry from agreeing to the meeting. Wolsey adopted a neutral attitude between Charles and François to make them both bid for Henry's support. He agreed in principle to the meeting between Henry and François, but raised all sorts of difficulties. The French had suggested that the meeting should take place in August or September 1519; but Wolsey said that a longer time would be needed to make the arrangements, and that it could not be held before the summer of 1520.

The intervening winter was spent discussing the arrangements for the meeting, for both the English and the French were determined to ensure that their king's prestige was not compromised by the arrangements to the advantage of the other king. Obviously Henry and François would have to be attended by an agreed and equal number of nobles, prelates, gentlemen, servants and soldiers; but where should the meeting take place? This presented a difficulty, for it was always the practice for the inferior to visit the superior. Wolsey wished the meeting to take place at Guisnes in English territory; the French suggested Ardres, ten miles away, on French soil. The arrangements for the meeting were thrashed out in lengthy negotiations between the kings' ministers and their resident ambassadors. On the English side, all the proposals were inspired by Wolsey, who thought that, as it was the French who had suggested the meeting and had the greatest interest in having it take place, they could be forced to agree to his conditions. He was determined that the meeting should be arranged in such a way as would glorify not only Henry but also himself.

After the bickering between the French and the English had gone on for several months, Wolsey proposed to François that both the kings should appoint him as their proctor to make all the arrangements for the meeting on their behalf, not in his capacity as Henry's minister but as the impartial Papal Legate. François realised that he had no alternative but to agree if he wished the meeting to take place, and on 23 February 1520 he appointed Wolsey as his proctor. He told him that he was sure that he could safely entrust his honour to Wolsey's keeping; and Wolsey, having gained this striking diplomatic success, was careful to make arrangements which were in no way offensive to François. These were finally settled at a meeting near Calais between high-ranking counsellors on both sides – the Count of Châtillon, the Marshal of France, on the one side, and the Earl of Worcester, the Lord Chamberlain, for Henry – though the arrangements for this meeting to arrange the meeting, in their turn, involved lengthy arguments about procedure and prestige.

It was agreed that the two kings should meet between Guisnes and Ardres, precisely on the frontier. Each king, with his retinue, would halt thirty yards apart on their side of the border, and Henry and François would ride forward and embrace without dismounting; then they would dismount and embrace again. The festivities and tournaments would take place in the fields between Guisnes and Ardres, in both kings' territories; the banquets in specially constructed banqueting halls; and mass in a specially erected chapel. At night each king would retire to sleep in his own kingdom, Henry to Guisnes and François to Ardres. On the next day after the first meeting, François would enter English territory to visit Queen Catherine at Guisnes, and simultaneously Henry, taking a different route to avoid meeting François on the journey, would enter French territory and visit the Queen of France at Ardres. Afterwards the kings would meet informally whenever they wished on both sides of the frontier.

On the question as to which king should have the place of honour on the right when they rode together side by side, it was agreed that when they were in English territory Henry would yield the place of honour to François, who would ride on the right, and François would reciprocate by allowing Henry to ride on the right when they were in France. There remained the knotty problem as to which king's shield should hang on the right-hand side above the tournament ground; but this was finally settled. There would be a tournament near Guisnes where Henry's shield would be placed on the right; but François's would be on the right at another tournament to be held near Ardres. After much argument, the date of the meeting was fixed, Henry promising to be at Calais, ready to proceed to the meeting, by 31 May 1520 at the latest.[9]

Charles was intending to sail from Spain to the Netherlands in the spring of 1520, and as he was unable to prevent the meeting between Henry and François, he proposed that he himself should meet Henry first. As time was short, and the emperor's sea voyage might be delayed by the winds and weather, Wolsey asked François to postpone his meeting with Henry for a month, to the end of June. But now it was François's turn to be difficult. He absolutely refused to agree to a further postponement, giving as his excuse that his queen was pregnant and that by the end of June her pregnancy would be too far advanced for her to be able to attend the meeting.[10] So Wolsey had to tell the emperor that his meeting with Henry could not be held until July, after the meeting with François, when Charles and Henry could meet on the frontier between Calais and Gravelines. Charles was so eager to meet Henry before François did that he proposed that he should land in England on his way from Spain to the Netherlands, as well as having the longer second meeting in July, though this involved waiving his precedence as emperor by being the visiting monarch. It was agreed that Charles should sail up the Channel and land at Sandwich on 15 May, where Henry would meet him and escort him to Canterbury. The emperor and the king would spend a few days there with Charles's aunt, Queen Catherine, before Henry and Catherine sailed for Calais for the meeting with François.[11]

Charles was worried about what Henry and François were up to, and though Henry and Wolsey assured him that nothing would be agreed at the meeting of Henry and François which would compromise his interests, he decided to try to make sure of this by winning Wolsey's goodwill. Before he left Spain in March 1520 he appointed Wolsey Bishop of Badajoz, undertaking to obtain the dispensations for pluralities and non-residence from the Pope. The revenues of the bishopric of Badajoz amounted to 5,000 ducats a year. Charles also arranged with the Bishop of Palencia to pay Wolsey an annuity of 2,000 ducats a year out of the revenues of this other Spanish see. Apart from this, he offered Wolsey another annuity of 3,000 ducats. Wolsey refused the offer of the bishopric of Badajoz, which he suggested should be given to Charles's ambassador in England, the Bishop of Elna, and asked Charles to give him an additional annuity instead. He seems to have thought that he might be compromised with the French if he held a Spanish bishopric, and that resentment might be caused among the cardinals in Rome if he appropriated too many of the European sees.

Wolsey did not forget his able subordinates, and suggested to Charles's ministers that the emperor might pay annuities to Ruthall, the Bishop of Durham, to Pace, and to Henry's efficient secretary, Brian Tuke. Charles agreed to pay an annuity of 1,000 florins to Ruthall, one of 800 florins to Pace, and one of 300 florins to Tuke, but stipulated that these would have to come out of the annuity of 3,000 florins which he had offered Wolsey. Wolsey could afford to be generous, and agreed.[12]

The plan for the meeting at Sandwich nearly fell through, for adverse winds detained Charles at Corunna. Wolsey told him that Henry could not wait for him after 26 May; but on that very day Charles landed at Dover, and spent three days with Henry and Catherine at Canterbury, where they banqueted, went to mass in the cathedral, and gave their offerings at Becket's tomb. Charles then sailed to Flushing, and Henry crossed to Calais on 31 May, the last possible day if he was to fulfil his promise to François. He was accompanied by a retinue of 3,997 persons and 2,087 horses. Eleven hundred and seventy-five persons and 778 horses accompanied Queen Catherine.[13]

Thomas More went with the king and court to Canterbury for the meeting with the emperor, and to Calais for the meeting with François. Like the other members of the Privy Council, he had been ordered to come with 12 servants in his retinue. The king's Almoner and chaplains and 70 knights had also been instructed to bring 12 servants with them. The 20 barons were each to bring 22 servants; the 10 earls were each to bring 42; and 4 bishops were to come with 44 servants each. The Marquess of Dorset and old Foxe, the Bishop of Winchester, were both to have 56 servants. The Archbishop of Canterbury and the Dukes of Suffolk and Buckingham were each to have 70. The Earl of Essex, as Earl Marshal, was to have the special privilege of bringing 130 servants; but all were eclipsed by the Lord Legate, the Cardinal of York, with his 300 servants.[14]

The fields where the meeting was to take place were covered with 2,800 tents; but for the kings and their chief attendants more substantial buildings had been erected. A palace had been built with foundations of stone, walls of brick, and the rest made of wood. A visitor from Milan thought it was so beautiful that even Leonardo da Vinci of Florence could not have done better. The great chamber was 124 feet long, 42 feet wide, and 30 feet high. The dining room was 80 feet long, and the drawing room 60 feet long. All these rooms were larger than any room in Henry's palaces in England. They were elaborately and richly decorated with cloth-of-gold, which caused the meeting to become known as 'the Field of Cloth-of-gold'. There were also cellars containing 3,000 butts of the most expensive wines.[15]

Wolsey's part in it was well publicised. On the day after Henry and his retinue landed at Calais, Wolsey rode in state from Calais to Ardres to inform François that Henry had arrived. He was preceded by a hundred archers of the king's guard, dressed in crimson velvet with scarlet cloaks. Then came fifty gentlemen ushers of his household, riding bareheaded and with great gold maces in their hands. Then came the bearer of the double cross of gold which was always borne before Wolsey on state occasions, one cross for him as Archbishop of York and the other as Cardinal, the cross-bearer riding bareheaded in robes of crimson velvet; then four lackeys in cloth-of-gold. Then came Wolsey's immediate bodyguard of four young men who surrounded him as he rode on a mule, rather than on a horse, in imitation of Christ's humility in riding on an ass; but Wolsey's mule was most gorgeously decked in gold and crimson velvet. Wolsey wore a rich velvet robe covering his lower garment of crimson velvet, and a red hat on his head with large hanging tassels. Six bishops rode behind him along with the Grand Prior of St John of Jerusalem – the head of the Order of the Knights of St John who held the island of Rhodes in the Eastern Mediterranean as an outpost of Christendom a few miles from the mainland of Turkey. Another hundred archers of the king's guard made up the rear of the procession.

At the French frontier Wolsey was met by Marshal Châtillon, who escorted him to Ardres. In Ardres the French king's guards lined the streets to receive him, and artillery was fired as he entered the town. He rode to François's lodging, and dismounted. The king was waiting to greet him, bareheaded with his cap in his hand, and embraced him. After a banquet, Wolsey rode back in state to Calais.[16]

François and Henry met on 7 June in the fields on the frontier, in the manner which had been so carefully arranged. The tournaments, banquets and festivities continued for nearly three weeks, and the kings did not bid each other farewell till 24 June. On the previous day, St John's Eve, there was a great religious ceremony in the chapel which had been built in the fields and gorgeously adorned, with a gold crucifix studded with jewels on the altar, and statues of six saints in solid gold. Wolsey celebrated mass – something which he hardly ever did – with the French Cardinal de Bourbon assisting him, after Wolsey had washed his hands in a bowl of water brought to him by the Dukes of Buckingham and Suffolk, and after some bishops had put a pair of jewelled sandals on his feet. Pace preached a sermon on the blessings of peace, and reminded the audience that everyone present would have full remission of all his sins, because the Pope had granted Wolsey, as his Legate, the special privilege that whenever he celebrated mass in his pontificals there should be a plenary remission of sins.[17] When the kings finally separated, there was a general exchange of gifts. François gave Wolsey gold vases worth 20,000 crowns. His mother, the Duchess of Angoulême, gave him a jewelled crucifix worth 6,000 crowns.[18]

Henry and Wolsey kept their word to Charles not to plot anything with François to his detriment, though Wolsey had several discussions about international affairs with François during the festivities. The French attempt to raise the possibility of the Duke of Albany's return to Scotland was unsuccessful, as Wolsey made it clear that England would never agree to this; but the project to marry Henry's daughter, Princess Mary, to the Dauphin was taken a step further by the signature of a formal engagement.[19]

Henry's second meeting with the emperor took place at the beginning of July. After the great expense of the Field of Cloth-of-gold, it was a cheaper and smaller affair. The barons and Privy Councillors were limited to two horsemen each in their retinue; the earls and bishops to six horsemen; the Dukes of Buckingham and Suffolk to ten horsemen; Archbishop Warham to ten horsemen and ten men on foot; and Wolsey to fifty horsemen and fifty men on foot.[20] After the two sovereigns had met on the frontier between Calais and Gravelines, Henry granted Charles the honour of being host first. He went with Charles to Gravelines, and after staying there for two nights escorted him to Calais to entertain him there, with Henry riding on the right as long as they were in the Netherlands, but giving Charles the place of honour after they crossed the frontier into English territory.[21]

Erasmus came to Gravelines with the emperor and met More there and in Calais. He had written to More that he would attend the meeting of the sovereigns in order to say goodbye to all his old English friends, for at the age of fifty he was conscious, like other sixteenth-century men of the same age, that his end might not be far off. He had another motive for going to Gravelines and Calais: he hoped to persuade Henry and Wolsey to use their influence to prevent the final break between the Church and Luther. He was quite unsuccessful; Henry and Wolsey were very friendly, and listened to what he had to say; but he made no impression on them with his arguments that it was essential to prevent Luther being sent to perdition and taking most of Germany with him.[22]

In any case, it was too late. On 15 June the Pope had issued a bull excommunicating Luther unless he recanted his opinions within sixty days. On 22 September the Papal Nuncios, Aleander and Caraccioli, published the bull in Cologne. On 28 September Aleander met the emperor in Antwerp, and Charles immediately issued a decree suppressing Lutheranism in the Netherlands. On 8 October Aleander published the bull at a great ceremony in Louvain, at which Luther's books were publicly burned. Aleander took the occasion to make a strong attack on Erasmus, who, he claimed, had paved the way for Luther by his Greek New Testament and his jibes at the Church. Next day, Erasmus was expelled from the theological faculty by the University of Louvain.[23].

Luther had meanwhile issued his three great tracts, *On the Liberty of a Christian Man*, his *Address to the Nobility of the German Nation*, and *On the Babylonian Captivity of the Church of God*, in which he directly attacked the Pope and the Church of Rome. On 10 December he burned the Pope's bull at Wittenberg in the presence of a cheering crowd. In April 1521 he appeared before the emperor at the Diet of Worms and was condemned and put under the ban of the Empire. The Duke of Saxony sent soldiers to escort him into safety in his territories.

The emperor had taken stern measures against the Lutheran heretics, and the universities in his dominions had burned Luther's books. The Pope, and many other people, expected Henry and Wolsey to take similar action in England. But when Wolsey knew that a foreign potentate wanted him to do something, his first reaction was to wonder how he could use the situation to get some benefit for his king and himself. His term as Legate expired in the summer of 1521, and he asked the Pope to renew it for another two years, if not for life; until the Pope had done so, he would do nothing that the Pope wanted him to do. When the Pope urged him to organise a ceremonial burning of Luther's books in London, and to suppress the Lutheran heresy in England, he issued a decree banning the importation into England of Lutheran publications; but he told the Pope that he did not think that his powers as Legate were sufficiently extensive to allow him lawfully to burn the books. If the Pope wished him to do this, he would not only have to extend his term of office as Legate, but to issue a bull which made it clear that his power as Legate was unlimited.

On 6 January 1521 Leo extended Wolsey's term as Legate for a further two years, giving him power to order a visitation of monasteries and granting a plenary indulgence to all persons who were present when he celebrated mass in the presence of the king and queen. He wrote to Wolsey, thanking him for the zeal that he had shown for the Church in banning the importation of Lutheran books into England. But some weeks later, he instructed his secretary, Cardinal dei Medici, to write to Wolsey that the Pope could not believe that the powers which he had already given him as Legate were insufficient to allow him to burn Luther's books, and expressing the hope that he would take the necessary action without further delay. Wolsey was under internal pressure, as well as pressure from Rome, to burn the books. The University of Oxford warned their Chancellor, Archbishop Warham, of the danger of Lutheran heresy; and in April Warham wrote to Wolsey urging him to organise a public condemnation of Luther and a burning of his books.[24]

With his legatine powers extended, Wolsey was quite willing to comply, and a great burning ceremony was held at Paul's Cross in London on 12 May 1521. Wolsey went in state to the cathedral, walking to the altar under a golden canopy borne over him by four doctors of divinity. After mass, they all went out into the churchyard at Paul's Cross, where a crowd of thirty thousand spectators awaited them. Wolsey took his seat on a raised platform under a canopy of state. Four great dignitaries sat at his feet, the Archbishop of Canterbury and the Papal Nuncio on his right, and the Bishop of Durham and the emperor's ambassador on his left. Fisher preached the sermon, paying tribute to Luther's learning and the apparent purity of his life, but denouncing him for his pride, the sin of Lucifer, which vitiated all his virtues, and had led him to set up his own personal opinions against the weight of the authority of the Pope, the Church, and all learned Catholic doctors. Then Luther's books were burned, and the decree was read out condemning him as an excommunicated heretic and prohibiting everyone from reading his works.[25]

The king himself took a hand in the campaign against Luther. He wrote a book, *The Assertion of the Seven Sacraments*, denouncing Luther's works. During the summer of 1521 it was known throughout Europe that he was writing the book, for Wolsey wished to make the maximum propaganda out of it, and to ensure that Henry was rewarded for it by being granted an honorific title by the Pope. For some time, Henry had been irked that, as king of England, he had no title to compete with the king of France's title of 'the Most Christian King' and the king of Castile's of 'the King Catholic'. During the war against France in 1513, when Julius II denounced Louis XII as a schismatic and proclaimed it a war for the defence of the Church, Henry suggested to Julius that Louis's title of 'the Most Christian King' should be taken away from him and given to Henry; but Julius was not prepared to go so far.

A superbly bound copy of Henry's book, decorated with gold and jewels, was presented to the Pope in Consistory by John Clerk, the English Ambassador in Rome, at a ceremony on 4 October 1521. The Pope rewarded Henry by granting to him and his successors the title 'Defender of the Faith'. The book won tributes from all the orthodox doctors. Henry was praised for his learning and his piety; having previously defended the Church with his sword – in the war of 1513 – he now defended her, equally valiantly and effectively, with his pen.[26]

It is not surprising that most scholars and courtiers were sure that Henry had not written the book himself. They found it difficult to believe that the virile young king, who spent most of the day in the saddle and in pursuit of pleasure, and could only be induced with great difficulty to read and write diplomatic despatches, should have the learning and the patience to write a theological treatise of fifty thousand words. Some thought that Wolsey had written it. Others, after Fisher's sermon against Luther at Paul's Cross, believed that he was the real author. Luther himself was convinced that Lee had written it, remembering his polemic against Erasmus's New Testament. But most people thought that it had been written by More. The evidence of all those with inside knowledge, including More himself, strongly indicates that, though Henry consulted Wolsey, Fisher, More and other learned men, he wrote the book himself. He found state papers boring, but he was not bored by theological controversy, and took many hours off from hunting to sit in his closet, researching and writing the book. He was much more likely to undertake such a task than Wolsey. We know that Wolsey drafted the dedicatory epistle to the Pope, but this was something which came much more naturally to him than the theological arguments about dispensations, penance, and the administration of the sacrament of the altar to the laity in both kinds, which Henry expounded so clearly and fluently in *The Assertion of the Seven Sacraments*.[27]

Henry, whose accession had been hailed with universal joy after the oppressions of his father's ministers, began the thirteenth year of his reign in April 1521. He had so far fulfilled the hopes of his subjects, for if they had grumbled about the taxation imposed to pay for his war with France, there had been no tyranny, no rebellion, no execution of prominent nobles. Dudley and Empson had most deservedly been executed for their misgovernment under Henry VII; the Yorkist

Pretender, Edmund de la Pole, had been unjustly but discreetly beheaded to prevent him from causing trouble during the war of 1513; and an example had been made of fifteen rioters after Evil May Day. This was so far the total of political executions during his reign.

Then suddenly, without warning, the Duke of Buckingham was arrested on a charge of high treason in April 1521. The son of the Duke of Buckingham executed by Richard III, he was descended from Edward III and John of Gaunt. After Princess Mary, Henry VIII's sisters, and some Plantagenet descendants whose line had been attainted, he was the nearest in succession to the crown, and could therefore claim, despite his remote connection with the Tudors, to be Henry's nearest male heir. He hated the French and disliked Wolsey and his pro-French policy, and had expressed his anti-French feelings at the time of the Field of Cloth-of-gold. He had often written letters to Wolsey asking for favours in suitably respectful language, but had been heard to say rude things about him in private. He was arrogant, and had antagonised several members of his household, who were only too ready to make allegations and give evidence against him.

On the depositions of his chaplain and his Chancellor and other servants, he was arrested and charged with plotting to usurp the throne from Princess Mary after the king's death. A court of his peers was hastily set up under the presidency of the Duke of Norfolk, and within a month of his arrest he had been tried, convicted and sentenced to death, and beheaded on Tower Hill. The evidence of his servants incriminated two of his friends, Lord Abergavenny and Lord Montague; but Wolsey was a good friend to both of them. After they had made their submission, denounced Buckingham, and given some gifts of land and money to Henry and Wolsey, they were pardoned, set free, and allowed to keep the bulk of their lands. Buckingham's lands in twenty-four counties of England and Wales, as well as his houses in London and Calais, were seized by the king.[28]

Buckingham's execution seems to have aroused more excitement abroad than in England, for Charles V and François I both believed that a revolution had broken out against Henry, and competed to win his goodwill by offering to send troops to help him suppress it. Wolsey hastened to assure them that the situation was completely under control, that Buckingham was Henry's only disloyal nobleman, and that Abergavenny and Montague had been foolish rather than wicked.[29] In England, many people believed that Wolsey was responsible for the duke's fall; but it was probably only because of the subsequent writings of Wolsey's enemy, the Italian Polydore Vergil, who was imprisoned in England for criticising Wolsey and for forging dispensations, that the historical myth has arisen that Wolsey was solely responsible for Buckingham's unjust conviction and death. The truth appears to be that both Henry and Wolsey thought that he was a potential threat to Mary's succession to the throne, and decided to seize the opportunity of getting rid of him with which they had been provided by his indiscreet utterances and the malice of his servants.

We have no record of what More thought of Buckingham's execution. It occurred at a time when More had been in the king's service for three years, and had just been knighted and appointed Under-Treasurer, under the Lord High Treasurer, the Duke of Norfolk. He had, to all appearances, completely committed himself to leading the life of a courtier and a counsellor to his prince; and it was the duty of a loyal counsellor to give good advice to his king in private, not to criticise him in public or even in letters to his friends. The only passage in More's writings which could perhaps be construed as a reference to it is in the religious book *The Four Last Things* which he wrote a year later, not intending it to be published or to become known beyond a small circle of his friends. He refers, in this tract, to a hypothetical case in which the arrest and execution of a powerful duke for high treason would be a striking illustration of the transient nature of worldly glory.[30]

There is no reason to believe that More questioned the propriety of Buckingham's arrest and execution, either in the Privy Council or in private with Henry or Wolsey; nor is there any indication that he ever protested to them against any of their actions during the first nine years of his service as a Privy Councillor. He received his share of the pickings after Buckingham's death, when Henry granted parts of the traitor's forfeited lands to various courtiers. More was given the manor of South, near Tonbridge in Kent, with the rights which Buckingham had in Queen Catherine's park at Southfrith.[31] The prospect of receiving forfeited lands, after the execution of a powerful nobleman for high treason, was one of the incentives which induced men to enter the king's service without receiving a regular salary.

When More first entered the king's service, Henry told him that he expected him to be his loyal servant, but God's first.[32] More evidently did not believe that his service to God was incompatible with supporting every Machiavellian act of political expediency, every diplomatic deception, and every violation of international law and the accepted canons of conduct in Christendom, in which Henry and Wolsey engaged between 1518 and 1527. Nor did he hesitate to do all in his power to ingratiate himself with Wolsey. His friend Ammonio, Henry's Italian secretary, was amused as he watched More's daily efforts to win the cardinal's favour; he wrote to Erasmus that More was always the first of all the courtiers to say 'Good morning' to Wolsey.[33] There is no reason to believe that he ever made the slightest criticism of Wolsey, or addressed him in other than the most flattering terms, until the day came when Wolsey fell from power and More could safely denounce and insult him.

CHAPTER 8

THE CALAIS CONFERENCE

No subject in Europe could equal, or even approach, the power, wealth and status of Thomas Wolsey. It was not merely that as Lord Chancellor he was the highest officer in the state, and that as Papal Legate *a latere* he ruled the English Church; not only did his archiepiscopal see of York, his diocese of Bath and Wells, and his annuities from foreign sovereigns, bring him in large annual revenues, to say nothing of the casual gifts that he received; but, most extraordinary of all, his king allowed him to attain a status which was not granted to the most powerful minister of any other prince. Foreign ambassadors described him as being 'another king'; as '*ipse rex*' – the king himself; as 'King, author of everything'; as 'the beginning, middle and end' of all the achievements of English policy.[1]

It was not surprising that English ambassadors abroad wrote their letters and despatches to him as well as to the king; but it was unprecedented that Charles V and Margaret of Austria, François I and his mother Louise d'Angoulême, hardly ever wrote to Henry VIII without at the same time writing another letter along the same lines to Wolsey, which was not dictated to a secretary but written in their own hand. They worded their letters as if they were writing to an equal, and expressed their respect and love for him in the warmest terms. All over Europe, rulers, statesmen and political observers discussed what 'the emperor' would do, what 'the Most Christian King' (of France) would do, and what 'the King and the Cardinal of England' would do.

On 6 October 1519 Sebastian Giustiniani returned to Venice after serving for four years as ambassador in England. Four days later, in accordance with the usual practice, he rose in the Senate and delivered a very lengthy report on his mission, describing the geography of England, the social habits of the English, and the character, as well as the policy, of King Henry and his ministers, with a frankness which was possible only in the privacy of the Senate, with no one present except the Doge and Senators. He told them that the Cardinal of York was of low origin, and had two brothers who held benefices and other perks which he had obtained for them. Wolsey ruled both the king and the whole kingdom. When Giustiniani first arrived in England, Wolsey used to say: 'His Majesty will do so and so.' Some years later he would say: 'We shall do so and so.' By 1519 he was saying: 'I shall do so and so.'

Wolsey was about forty-six years old. He was very handsome, learned, and eloquent as a speaker. He was very able, and worked very hard. He himself carried out all the work which in Venice was performed by all the magistrates, officers and councils of the city, in criminal and civil jurisdiction and in every aspect of state affairs. He had the reputation of being very just as a judge. He was always favourable to the common people, especially to the poor. He heard their suits rapidly, and made the lawyers plead for poor men without charging any fee.

Giustiniani said that Wolsey lived in a very fine palace. This was Hampton Court, which Wolsey had acquired in 1514 on a long lease from the Prior of St John of Jerusalem, and had enlarged into a magnificent building. It was right out in the country, but only a day's ride from both London and Windsor, and it could be reached more quickly from London, in a few hours, by water, for it was on the north bank of the Thames. It had 280 rooms, and was manned by a staff of five hundred servants. Giustiniani told the Senate that when he was received by Wolsey at Hampton Court, he walked through eight rooms before reaching Wolsey's presence chamber, and that all these rooms were hung with tapestries which were changed once a week. Wolsey's sideboard at all times contained plate worth 25,000 ducats, and his silver was said to be valued at 150,000 ducats. His revenues from the archbishopric of York brought him 14,000 ducats a year, and from the bishopric of Bath and Wells 8,000 ducats; his share of the fees of the court of Chancery was 5,000 ducats a year; and every year he received gifts worth about 15,000 ducats on New Year's Day. When Giustiniani left London he was engaged in delicate negotiations with Wolsey about the grant of a licence to Venetian merchants to import Candian wines into England. Wolsey told Giustiniani that he would be very grateful if the Doge and Senate would send him a hundred Damascene carpets as a gift. Giustiniani was sure that the Venetian merchants in London would be willing to bear the expense of buying the carpets, which would settle all the difficulties about the Candian wines.

Giustiniani told the Senators about the difficulties which he had had in gaining access to Wolsey. The cardinal never granted an audience to anyone, neither to English noblemen nor to foreign ambassadors, until they had asked for it three or four times; sometimes Giustiniani had to ask six or seven times. When he first went to London in 1515, he sometimes dined with Wolsey at his table; but by 1519, when he went to dinner at Hampton Court, he sat with other notables at a lower table while Wolsey dined alone, and no one else was served until Wolsey had finished the course. In his report to the Senate, Giustiniani did not mention what he and other Venetian ambassadors in England had sometimes written in their letters to the Doge – that Wolsey could be very unpleasant to deal with. When he was angry, he became very excited and abusive; but at other times he could be very affable.[2]

According to More – or perhaps we should say, according to Harpsfield – Wolsey was very vain, and loved to hear things said in his own praise. When More was in the Tower in 1534, he wrote a religious book, *A Dialogue of Comfort against Tribulation*, in the form of a dialogue between two imaginary characters, Antony and Vincent. At one point in the book, Vincent describes an occasion when he attended a ceremonial event in Germany, at which 'a great man of the Church . . . one of the greatest in all that country' made a speech. The speech was followed by a banquet, at which the great churchman invited all those present to say what they thought of the speech; and he listened with undisguised satisfaction as all the guests, including Vincent, vied with each other in praising the speech and flattering the great churchman; for 'never was he satiate of hearing his own praise'. Harpsfield says that More was referring, in this story, not to a great man of the Church in Germany, but to Wolsey in England. In view of Wolsey's unpopularity, both when More wrote in 1534 and when Harpsfield wrote twenty years later, we cannot rely on the accuracy of the story or on the assertion that More was referring to Wolsey; but it is easy to believe that Wolsey enjoyed being flattered. If the incident really occurred at a banquet given by Wolsey, was More the Vincent who competed with the others in flattering him?[3]

In the autumn of 1521 Wolsey was involved in the most subtle and unscrupulous of all his diplomatic manoeuvres. The universal peace of 1518 proved to be short-lived. At a time when Christendom was threatened from within by the Lutheran heresy, as well as from without by the Turk, Charles V and François I plunged Western Europe into a major war which raged, with only brief intervals of peace, for nearly forty years and played a vital part in facilitating the triumphs of the Protestant Reformation.

The trouble began with a border incident on the southern frontier of the Netherlands. Robert de La Marck, the Count of Sedan and Bouillon, who was a satellite of France, made a raid into the Netherlands, and Charles V sent his general, the Count of Nassau, to drive him out and pursue him into his own territory. After La Marck had complained to François I that Nassau had invaded Sedan, François sent troops to help La Marck. Charles protested, and appealed to Henry and Wolsey for diplomatic support. Henry and Wolsey offered to mediate. Both Charles and François accepted this mediation, but

François's soldiers continued to operate against Nassau.

The trouble between Sedan and the Netherlands, though potentially dangerous, was hardly of sufficient importance to cause a major European war; but at this juncture François greatly exacerbated the situation by invading Navarre, which had formerly been ruled by his protégé, the French Comte d'Albret, but had been conquered by Ferdinand of Spain in 1512 and had been recognised by François, in the peace treaties of 1518, as being part of Charles V's Spanish kingdom. At first, François suggested that his intervention in Navarre was merely a counter-move in reply to Nassau's attacks on Sedan; but as his troops easily overran Navarre and reached the gates of the capital, Pamplona, it became clear that he intended to reconquer the country for d'Albret. The Spanish garrison at Pamplona put up a stout defence before the French captured it in an assault which is chiefly remembered today because a Spanish officer, Ignatius de Loyola, received a severe leg wound, and during his illness and convalescence decided to reform his life and found the Society of Jesus.

Charles prepared for war with François, and called on Henry for assistance under the Treaty of London of 1518 by which all the signatories had undertaken to assist the victim of aggression against the aggressor. He was justified in claiming that France was the aggressor, because, whatever the rights and wrongs of the Sedan-Nassau incident, it could have been settled peacefully through the mediation of Henry and Wolsey, whereas the invasion of Navarre was a deliberate attempt to overthrow the peace settlement of 1518. But Wolsey never gave anything for nothing, and as always saw the situation as a chance to extract advantage for Henry, for his countrymen, and for himself. He believed that England could now pursue one of two alternative policies. One policy, the obvious one, was to remain neutral and to offer aid, or minor advantages, to the highest bidder. The other policy was more daring, with long-term advantages – to join in a permanent alliance with the emperor to completely crush France.

In contemplating this second possibility, Wolsey was influenced chiefly by the problem of the succession. Henry and Catherine of Aragon had been married for twelve years in 1521. They had had six children, but only one of them had survived for more than a few weeks; of the two sons of the marriage, one had died at seven weeks and the other after a few days. Only Princess Mary, born in February 1516, was still living. As Catherine was now thirty-five, it seemed unlikely that she would give birth to a son. Henry was beginning to believe that their marriage was cursed, and that God was punishing him because he had sinned in marrying his brother's widow in defiance of the Biblical texts, even though he had been granted a Papal dispensation to marry

Catherine. If he had no male heir, his dominions would pass to his daughter Mary, and the prince whom she married would become ruler of England. Mary was engaged to marry the Dauphin, but the English nobility and people, with their hatred of the French, would not wish to see a French prince as King of England. They would prefer to have Charles, a scion of the house of Burgundy, England's traditional ally.

Wolsey therefore put forward an ambitious proposal to the emperor. England would repudiate the marriage contract between Mary and the Dauphin, and make a new contract by which Mary should marry the emperor. Mary's age was a minor problem, for she was five, whereas Charles was twenty-one; but though Mary could not legally marry Charles until she was twelve, this had the advantage that it provided Henry and Wolsey with an excuse for not sending her to live in Charles's territories until she was a little older, thereby retaining their hold over her person and their freedom of action where she was concerned. Wolsey proposed that Henry and Charles should wage war against François, with Henry reviving his old claim to the crown of France, until the French were completely defeated. After driving them out of Navarre, Charles would annex Guienne and Languedoc and the provinces of the old duchy of Burgundy around Dijon which France had seized in 1482 after the death of Charles the Bold. Henry would reign as king over the rest of France, and at his death his daughter Mary, Charles's empress, would rule over them and over England together with her husband.

When Wolsey first put these proposals to Charles through the emperor's ambassador in London and the English ambassador in Brussels in the spring of 1521, it was too late to prepare an invasion of France that year. Wolsey therefore proposed that this should be postponed at least until the beginning of the next summer, and preferably until the spring of 1523. When the time came, Henry or his deputy would land at Calais with a large army, and would be joined by a force of German mercenaries enrolled in the Netherlands by Charles's Regent, his aunt Margaret of Austria, at Charles's expense; though as Charles was in financial difficulties, after the great cost of his election as emperor and his campaigns against François I, Henry would lend him the money to pay the mercenaries. With these mercenaries and his own men, Henry would invade northern France. Charles's Spanish subjects would drive the French from Navarre and invade Guienne and Languedoc; the Count of Nassau would attack eastern France near Sedan; the Cardinal of Sion would stir up the Swiss to invade France from Savoy; and Charles's Spanish soldiers in his kingdom of Naples would fight the French in Italy.

Meanwhile, until the great operation began, Henry would not declare war on François or give any indication that he was intending to do so. This would prevent François from taking steps to meet the invasion. It would also mean that François would continue to pay the instalments of the money that he had agreed to pay for Tournai under the peace treaty of 1518 and the pensions which he was paying to Wolsey and other members of Henry's council. In the meantime Charles would either have to carry on the war against France by himself, without help from Henry, or he could pursue the course which Wolsey advised him to take and agree to a truce until Henry was ready to launch the joint attack on France.

Wolsey suggested that, in order more effectively to lull French suspicions, Henry should offer his services as an impartial mediator between Charles and François and invite them both to send envoys to Calais to meet Wolsey in an attempt to settle their disputes by peaceful negotiation. Wolsey would propose to both parties that they should agree to a truce while negotiations took place. If the French agreed, he would urge Charles to agree too. The joint attack on France would then be postponed till the truce expired in the spring of 1523, which would give Charles and Henry more time to prepare it thoroughly and to find the money to pay the mercenaries.

Charles was annoyed at Wolsey's proposals, for he felt that under the Treaty of London he was entitled to Henry's aid against the French aggressor without any prior conditions being imposed by Wolsey. He was also unwilling to make a truce with France or to compromise his honour by sending envoys to negotiate with the French on English soil at Calais, especially as he was already enrolling and paying mercenaries whom he intended to employ against France that summer. François was more willing to send negotiators to Calais, for he was already in occupation of Navarre, and was happy to sit tight and avoid all military action in Flanders and northern France while negotiations were carried on at Calais on the basis of the *status quo*. Henry and Wolsey were anxious for the world to see the emperor and the king of France, the two most powerful monarchs in Christendom, sending their envoys to seek peace from Wolsey's hands in Calais. They persuaded Charles to agree to send his envoys to Calais by telling him that the negotiations there were only a ruse to deceive the French; they persuaded François to send his representatives there by assuring him of their friendship, but saying that it would be difficult for them to refuse Charles's call to them to give him assistance under the Treaty of London if François refused their offer of mediation.

Despite his annoyance with Wolsey, Charles needed English help against France. He stalled on Wolsey's offer, and suggested that England should immediately send him aid under the Treaty of London and declare against France; then, out of their alliance and wartime collaboration, they might more easily proceed to the permanent alliance that Wolsey proposed. Wolsey turned down this suggestion, and told Charles that it was all or nothing. Henry would not get involved in war with France unless it was a war to gain the crown of France, with the succession settled by Princess Mary's marriage to the emperor. If Charles refused to agree, Henry would pursue a policy of neutrality, and Wolsey would really act as a fair and neutral mediator at Calais.[4]

Charles decided to accept Wolsey's terms and to hide the resentment which he felt. But there were many details to be agreed, not least the financial arrangements for Mary's dowry if she married him, and he felt that these could not be settled by negotiations at long range. He therefore suggested that Wolsey should visit him in the Netherlands to discuss the alliance with him personally.

Wolsey crossed to Calais on 2 August 1521 in stormy weather at the head of a large delegation of secretaries and assistants, which included Ruthall, Tunstal and More.[5] Ruthall was the only one of them who knew about the secret offer to the emperor. A few days later, the powerful French and imperial delegations arrived. Charles's envoys were headed by his Chancellor, Gattinara, and François's by the Chancellor of France, Duprat. Gattinara was one of a very small number of Charles's advisers who had been told about the secret plan for the alliance with England. The Pope, who was egging Charles on against the French, and the Venetians, who were François's allies, sent their ambassadors to attend the conference as observers.

The first session of the conference was held on 7 August, after a lengthy wrangle between the French and imperial delegates about precedence and the seating arrangements. On the same day, Charles wrote to Wolsey, asking him to meet him as soon as possible to settle the terms of the secret treaty. He had come to Bruges to be nearer to Calais, and urged Wolsey to be there by the following Sunday in four days' time. He explained that he could not wait very long in Bruges, because he had an army of mercenaries ready to invade France, and he did not wish to waste time while he paid their wages and the good campaigning weather of the late summer slipped away. If Wolsey could not be at Bruges soon, he would have to follow Charles to his camp on the French frontier.[6]

Wolsey was eager to visit Charles and conclude the alliance, but he thought it would do no harm if the emperor were kept waiting a little. He was also conscious that the French would fear the worst, and might even guess the truth, if he suddenly left Calais in the middle of the peace negotiations and went to see the emperor in Bruges. So he worked out a clever plot with Gattinara. At the opening session in Calais, Gattinara was to say that the emperor had sent him and his colleagues there only to announce that Charles refused to negotiate with the French as long as their troops were in occupation of Navarre, and then to walk out of the conference as he had instructions to refuse even to listen to the French envoys. Wolsey would then express his dismay at the breakdown of his mediation efforts, after Henry had gone to such trouble to send so many of his ministers to Calais, and at the affront that this would cause the Pope and his nuncio, after which Wolsey would adjourn the conference while he tried to persuade Gattinara to return to the negotiating table.

Gattinara would attend the second session and declare that out of his respect for Henry, the Pope and Wolsey, he had agreed to go beyond his instructions and to be present on this occasion, but could not take any further part in the negotiations without going to Bruges to consult the emperor. Wolsey, in his great anxiety to prevent the breakdown of the conference, would suggest that he himself should go with Gattinara to Bruges to persuade the emperor not to wreck the peace talks before they had even started. In due course he would return from Bruges with Gattinara, and when the conference resumed, Gattinara would attend and announce that the emperor had changed his mind and had ordered him to negotiate with the French at Calais with Wolsey as mediator.[7]

The plan worked exactly as Wolsey had hoped. When François I heard about Wolsey's visit to Bruges he was suspicious, but Duprat wrote to him from Calais explaining the reason which Wolsey had given for it, and stating that he was inclined, on the whole, to trust in Wolsey's good faith.[8] Meanwhile Charles was waiting for Wolsey in Bruges. The English agent in Bruges, Spinelly, wrote to Wolsey, stressing the impatience with which Charles was awaiting him, because for the emperor one hour at this time meant more than a hundred hours in ordinary circumstances.[9] But Wolsey was not going to hurry. Thirteen years before, he had travelled along this same road from Calais into Flanders at the greatest speed, and had impressed Henry VII by covering the journey from Richmond and back again in four days; now he would travel as slowly as the dignity of a Papal Legate and of the cardinal of England required, and impress the world by keeping the emperor waiting. He did not leave Calais till 12 August, the day after the latest day on which Charles had asked him to be in Bruges, and then took three days over the sixty-mile journey, reaching Bruges on the evening of 14 August.[10]

Charles concealed his resentment from the public, and received Wolsey with great honour in Bruges. He went with his whole court to meet Wolsey at the city gates, where he waited for nearly an hour and a half till Wolsey arrived, riding on his mule and escorted by his retinue of 1,050 horsemen, resplendent in their red satin garments. Wolsey did not dismount when he met the emperor, but raised his hat. Charles likewise raised his hat, and he and Wolsey then embraced, as equals, from saddle to saddle. Wolsey's only concession was to give the emperor the place of honour on the right as they rode side by side to the lodgings which had been reserved for Wolsey. To be escorted by the emperor to the door of his apartments was a quite unprecedented honour for the subject of a foreign ruler. Next day Charles and Wolsey went to mass in the cathedral, where they shared the same kneeling-desk under the emperor's canopy of state.[11]

Charles appointed Margaret of Austria and his minister, Berghes, to carry on the negotiations, but took part personally in the talks. None of his other counsellors, except Gattinara, knew what was going on. Wolsey took with him to Bruges several members of the English delegation in Calais, including Ruthall and More. Most of them knew nothing about the secret plan; More, though a member of the Privy Council, was not informed. Wolsey confided the secret only to Ruthall, his former patron and protector who now acted as his subordinate and secretary and wrote the letters which he sent to Henry containing his reports on his activities at Calais and Bruges.

There was tough bargaining at Bruges, chiefly about money. What dowry was Henry to provide for Mary if she married the emperor? Charles asked for a million ducats, and told Wolsey that the king of Portugal had offered this sum if Charles married his daughter; but Wolsey would not agree, and finally persuaded Charles to be content with £80,000,* after Wolsey had endured what he described to Henry as much criticism from Charles and much loss of sleep.[12] There were also disagreements about the date when England was to declare war on France. Wolsey urged Charles to agree to a truce with François, if the French could be persuaded to offer terms which he could reasonably accept; they could then put off the campaign against France to the summer of 1523. But Charles was already fighting the French – his troops had just captured Bouillon – and he wished Henry to declare war as soon as possible. It was eventually agreed that Wolsey would continue his efforts at Calais to arrange a reasonable truce, but if Charles was not prepared to agree to a truce on the terms which Wolsey could obtain from the French, Henry would declare war in November. He would not immediately engage in military operations, but would be in Calais with an army of 40,000 men, commanded by himself in person, no later than 15 May 1523.[13]

King Christian II of Denmark was on a visit to the emperor, and went with Charles to Bruges. He was an ally of the king of Scots, and was

---

* The rate of exchange of the ducat for the £ was subject to great fluctuations, but averaged approximately six ducats to the £.

anxious that this should not involve him in difficulties with England, especially at a time when he was confronted with a rebellion of his Swedish subjects. While Wolsey was in Bruges, Christian sent three of his courtiers, one of them an archbishop, to Wolsey's apartments to tell him that the king very much wished to speak to him, and inviting Wolsey to visit him in his rooms in the palace. Wolsey told them that if the king wished to speak to him, he would be delighted to receive Christian in his apartments. The archbishop was shocked, and said that it was out of the question for the king to be humiliated in this way. Wolsey then relented, and told the archbishop that he would walk through the palace garden on his way to visit the emperor; if the king of Denmark were in the garden at the same time, he and Wolsey could talk together. The king was there in the garden, and spoke to Wolsey. After a while, Wolsey said he must go to the emperor, and suggested that the king and he should continue their conversation next day in Wolsey's rooms. The king agreed, and duly came to Wolsey's rooms. When he left, Wolsey accompanied him only as far as the bottom of the stairs. Wolsey wrote and told Henry about this incident, informing him that he had made the king of Denmark come to him in order to enhance Henry's prestige.[14]

Wolsey raised another matter with Charles in Bruges. The Pope was ill, and it was generally realised that he might not live long. Wolsey asked Charles to support his candidature for the Papacy when Leo died. A majority of the members of the College of Cardinals had either been appointed as the nominees of the house of Habsburg or had been bribed by Charles's agents in Rome, though the king of France's cardinals were also numerous. The decision as to who should be the next Pope would therefore depend more on Charles than on anyone else. Charles had intended to support the election of Leo's cousin, Cardinal Medici, the Archbishop of Florence, who was Leo's Secretary of State; but he promised Wolsey in Bruges that he would tell his cardinals to vote for him in the conclave after Leo's death.[15] He probably never intended to keep his promise.

In Bruges, Wolsey developed a friendship with Margaret of Austria which, to some estent at least, was probably sincere on both sides, for it survived the political alliance between England and the Empire. Wolsey told Margaret that he regarded her as a mother, though she was in fact a few years younger than he.

Erasmus came to Bruges from his home at Ardelach near Brussels when he heard that More was there with Wolsey.[16] It was the last time that they were ever to meet. We do not know what they said to each other on this occasion; but for the first time an issue had arisen on which they were adopting very different attitudes. They must both have realised that to a considerable extent they disagreed about Luther and

Lutheranism; but they seem to have avoided entering into controversy on the subject, and by tacit consent to have agreed to differ. Soon after this meeting in Bruges, Erasmus moved from the Netherlands to Switzerland, largely to avoid the witch-hunt against Lutheranism at Louvain; and both the geographical and the doctrinal distance between him and More caused their friendship to peter out, though it was never ruptured.

Wolsey and Margaret of Austria signed a secret treaty on 25 August, embodying the proposals which Wolsey had made to Charles for the military alliance for the destruction of France. It contained a clause that Henry and Charles would suppress Lutheranism in their realms and in any territory that they conquered in the course of the war; and it provided that after the defeat of France they would lead a crusade against the Turk.[17] No one expected this last provision to be taken seriously. The treaty was to be formally ratified by Charles as soon as the Pope had given his consent to it; and the Papal nuncio in Brussels, who had come to Bruges with Charles, was now let into the secret. Charles and Margaret told none of their ministers except Gattinara and Berghes. On the English side, only Henry, Wolsey, Ruthall and Pace knew.

Contarini, the Venetian ambassador at Charles's court, tried to find out what was happening, so that his government could inform their French allies. He followed the emperor to Bruges, but could discover nothing. He became suspicious when he heard that only Charles, Margaret, Gattinara and Wolsey were taking part in the negotiations. He asked several times for an interview with Wolsey, but Wolsey always sent word that he was too busy to see him. He then tried More, whom he invited to dinner,* in the hopes of being able to find out something. If More suspected what Wolsey was up to, he revealed nothing to Contarini. The ambassador was impressed by More's learning, but wrote to the Doge and Senate that More did not drop the slightest hint that Wolsey had come for any other reason except to facilitate the negotiations at Calais. Contarini heard something more from the emperor's confessor, who told him that Charles had just heard that Sultan Soleiman the Magnificent was besieging Belgrade, and hoped to use Wolsey's presence in Bruges as an opportunity for planning a crusade against the Turk.

On 22 August Gattinara invited Contarini to dinner and told him a pretty story. He said that Charles had invited Wolsey to Bruges because

---

* 'Dinner', in the sixteenth century, was the main meal of the day, which was normally begun at 11 a.m. or midday.

he hoped to persuade him that Henry was morally bound to come to his assistance against the French aggressor under the terms of the Treaty of London, but that unfortunately Wolsey had not been impressed by the emperor's arguments and had refused to agree to any proposals for an alliance. Contarini said that many people thought it strange that so great a personage as Wolsey, after negotiating for some time at Calais, should come to Bruges merely in order to refuse to agree to Charles's proposals. Gattinara then said that he would take Contarini into his confidence and reveal the fact that Wolsey had thought that Charles was so young and inexperienced that if he came to Bruges he would be able to talk Charles into agreeing to anything he wanted. But Wolsey had learned his mistake, for Charles had proved far too shrewd for him; so Wolsey was returning to Calais in high dudgeon, having achieved nothing in Bruges. Contarini learned nothing more from an informant in the house of the Papal nuncio, who told him that no agreement had been reached between Charles and Wolsey during their talks.

At last, on 22 August, Contarini succeeded in gaining admission to Wolsey's presence; but Wolsey merely apologised for being too busy to speak to him at length, and said he would send for Contarini as soon as he had a free moment. But Contarini heard nothing more.[18]

The day after he had signed the treaty with Margaret, Wolsey left Bruges on 26 August for Calais. The emperor escorted him through the gates of Bruges, and then embraced him and bade him farewell. Contarini decided to escort him a little further in the hopes of discovering some information. He managed to get to Wolsey's side, and as he rode beside him he asked him point blank why he had come to Bruges. Wolsey said that when the Calais conference began, he had discovered for the first time, to his consternation, that the emperor's envoys had no commission from the emperor to pursue negotiations with the French. Realising that it would be a great disgrace for his king and for himself if he had to return to England without achieving anything, he had gone to Bruges to persuade the emperor to allow his envoys at least to negotiate, and he had with much difficulty persuaded the emperor to agree to this. He then urged Contarini to use his influence with his government to persuade Venice to remain neutral in the hostilities between Charles and François in Italy, after which he very firmly said goodbye to Contarini, who went back to Bruges.[19]

Having made the emperor wait for him in Bruges, he now made the impatient Duprat wait even longer for him in Calais. He took four days over the journey and reached Calais on 29 August. He announced that his visit to Bruges had been most successful, as he had persuaded the Emperor to instruct his envoys to take part in the peace negotiations; but he found that the visit had aroused the suspicions of the French.

Rumours were circulating in Europe that Henry was about to enter the war on the emperor's side. The French spies in England reported that the people there were preparing for war; and English students at Paris University were hurriedly preparing to leave France before they were interned.[20]

But Wolsey succeeded in dispelling the fears of Duprat and his colleagues. He sent More* and Sir Thomas Boleyn to tell Duprat that the armaments which were being prepared in England were merely routine measures of national defence which were taken every year in August and September. A day or two later, he himself spoke in private to Duprat. He said that though Henry thought it best to preserve an official neutrality, he was more sympathetic to François than to Charles, and then proceeded to give a detailed and completely fictitious account of his negotiations in Bruges. He had done nothing there which in any way harmed François's interests; he had told Charles that Henry would never permit him to invade the duchy of Milan; he had refused a large sum of money which Charles had offered him, and had accepted only two small bars of silver which could not be worth more than 2,000 francs, and which he could hardly have refused.[21]

The French were completely taken in. 'We have thanked him very much,' they wrote to François on 8 September

for the goodwill which we see more and more he bears towards you, and we asked him to continue it, and said that you would not be ungrateful to him. He spoke more openly than usual, and by his words and manner made it plain to us that he is very displeased with the King Catholic's [Charles's] Council and also with the Chancellor [Gattinara], not having found them as tractable as he had expected. . . . We have discovered from various sources what the Cardinal did in Flanders, and we find that what he told us was true, and that there is no doubt that he came away very dissatisfied.[22]

On 11 September Duprat dined alone with Wolsey in Wolsey's private apartments. Wolsey told him, in strict confidence, some secret intelligence about the emperor's military preparations in Italy, Flanders and Navarre, and said that he would do his utmost to maintain the indissoluble friendship of England and France. He said that he did not wish to be Pope, or to gain any other personal advantage for himself, for he already had more worldly goods than a churchman ought to have. He

---

* Duprat wrote that he was visited by the Treasurer of England and Sir Thomas Boleyn. As the Treasurer, Norfolk, was not in Calais, it is clear that Duprat meant the Under-Treasurer, More.

explained that there was a good deal of anti-French feeling in England, and that he had proposed holding the conference at Calais as the only way to avoid the pressure to give military aid to the emperor. He said that he knew there were rumours that he had made some agreement at Bruges which harmed France, but it was not true, for he knew that if he had done so, he would have forfeited Henry's favour for ever. On the contrary, he would prefer to lose his head than see the destruction of the friendship with France that he had built up. He then said that the real reason for the Duke of Buckingham's execution was that Buckingham had opposed his pro-French policy.[23]

While the conference was in session, fighting was going on all around Calais, on the frontier between France and the Netherlands, which impeded the trade of the merchants in Calais. Wolsey asked Duprat to allow corn to be brought to Calais through the battle zone. When Duprat agreed, Wolsey called in More and the other members of the English delegation, and told them that Duprat, unlike the emperor's ministers, had agreed to let the corn come to Calais. 'In our need they have supplied us with corn,' said Wolsey, 'and those who we were so sure were our friends have refused to do this.'[24]

The conference met regularly several times a week, and continued in session for three months.[25] Though Wolsey's main purpose was to fool the French into believing that he and Henry would continue to pursue a friendly neutrality towards them and were working for a peaceful settlement, he was sincere in his efforts to persuade both François and Charles to agree to a long truce which would enable him to postpone the English declaration of war and the great attack on France until the summer of 1523, as well as bringing credit to Henry and to himself in the short run by enabling them to pose as successful peacemakers. He therefore tried, like a good mediator, to persuade both sides to make concessions, while at the same time he was secretly passing on military intelligence to Gattinara. When fifty of the emperor's soldiers made a successful raid on Ardres during the temporary absence of the French garrison, Wolsey urged Gattinara to order them to demolish the walls or burn the town before they withdrew.[26]

It was not easy to reach agreement at Calais, for Charles knew that if he refused to agree to a truce, England would enter the war on his side in November. The French offered to agree to a truce north of the Alps, but not in Italy, on the basis of the *status quo*. Charles at first refused to agree to any truce unless the French withdrew their troops from Navarre. Wolsey persuaded him to modify his stand and to agree to a truce if the French surrendered Fuentarrabia, which they had captured after conquering Navarre; but the French refused to surrender Fuentarrabia or anything that they held. Wolsey's health, which had been troubling him before he left England, broke down under the heavy strain of work. He fell ill with a fever, and had to miss several sessions of the conference in September, leaving Ruthall to deputise for him.[27]

Charles's troops were having the best of the fighting, and won two important successes, capturing Tournai in October and Milan in November. On 16 November the emperor instructed Gattinara to break off negotiations in Calais. Wolsey's public expressions of regret at the break-up of the conference and his failure to achieve a truce were nothing less than the truth. Despite what had been agreed in the Treaty of Bruges, he and Henry had no intention of declaring war in November. He managed to persuade Gattinara that in view of the emperor's military victories, nothing would be lost if Henry delayed the declaration of war until he was ready to begin operations. Before he left Calais he signed a secret treaty with Gattinara pledging England to declare war on France at the latest by March 1523, and renewing the agreement of Charles and Henry to extirpate heresy and uphold and restore the authority of the Pope in any territory in their possession or occupation. On the same day, François wrote to his envoys in Calais instructing them to tell Wolsey, before they left, of the great affection that he felt for him, and that the treaty for the marriage of Princess Mary to the Dauphin remained in force.[28]

While persuading Charles to agree to a postponement of the date of the English declaration of war, Wolsey encouraged him to believe that both the declaration and the invasion of France might come a good deal sooner than March 1523. Charles was planning to return from the Netherlands to Spain by sea in the spring. He agreed with Wolsey that he would land in England on his way, and pay Henry a second visit – thus for the second time giving Henry the precedence of being the host – and that during his stay in England Henry would send a herald to François's court to declare war. He would then send an army to Calais before the end of the summer of 1522.

Wolsey sailed for England on 28 November. Henry, who had been very worried about his health and feared that he had been working too hard in Calais, was delighted to see him, and expressed his deepest gratitude for all that he had done in Calais and Bruges.[29]

Leo X died on 1 December. The ambassadors in Rome immediately sent messengers riding 'in post' to tell the news to their princes. It would take at least a fortnight for the news to reach London, and nearly as long for it to reach Ghent, where the emperor was in residence, and another fortnight would be needed for the messengers to return to Rome with instructions from Ghent and London. But the cardinals in Rome wished to choose the new Pope with the minimum of outside pressure, and, despite the protests of the ambassadors, fixed the beginning of the conclave for 26 December. The ambassadors urged them to wait at least until after the end of the Twelve Days of Christmas on 6 January, which with luck would allow just enough time for the ambassadors to receive their orders from the emperor and from Henry; but the cardinals granted only forty-eight hours' postponement, and the conclave began on 28 December.[30]

Wolsey was relying on the support of the emperor's cardinals, thinking that Charles would have instructed them in advance to vote for him. When the news of Leo's death reached him on 16 December, he immediately told Charles's ambassador, the Bishop of Elna, that Henry wanted him to be chosen as Pope, but would accept Cardinal Medici as second best. The ambassador thought that Wolsey was not very hopeful about his chances, but was far from despairing. Charles wrote to Henry, to Wolsey, and to the Bishop of Elna, telling them that he would support Wolsey for the Papacy, as he had promised Wolsey in Bruges.[31] He wrote to Henry that Wolsey's 'prudence, doctrine, integrity, experience, and other virtues and good habits make him eminently worthy to hold this see,' and added that he would use all means to achieve this, including, if necessary, 'the army which I have in Italy, which is not small.'[32] Margaret of Austria also wrote to Wolsey assuring him that Charles would fulfil his promise. She reminded Wolsey that he had told her that he regarded her as a mother, and she wrote that she hoped that her son would soon be her father – her Holy Father.[33]

But what did Charles really think, and what did he do to help Wolsey? Although many of his letters to his ambassador in Rome have been preserved, in only one of them does he instruct the ambassador to canvass support for Wolsey; and this undated letter was probably written in December 1521 – much too late. Throughout the autumn, he had been receiving letters from the ambassador which were highly critical of Wolsey; and at about this time he told Margaret, to her distress, that he was angry at Wolsey's arrogant attitude, complaining that Wolsey tried to dictate terms to him about Princess Mary's dowry as if he were a prisoner. But whatever Charles may or may not have done for Wolsey, it is clear that his supporters among the cardinals in Rome believed, rightly or wrongly, that he wished them to vote for Cardinal de Medici, not for Wolsey.[34]

In Rome, Wolsey's candidature was energetically canvassed by Clerk, Henry's ambassador; by the cardinal of Sion; and by Cardinal Campeggio, who, as well as holding several other bishoprics in various parts of Europe, was Bishop of Salisbury. They found a good deal of opposition to Wolsey among the cardinals. Many objected because he was too young, for they preferred to choose an old Pope who would die soon, so that they themselves might have another chance to be chosen at the next election. Wolsey was in fact aged forty-nine, or possibly less, in December 1521, but Campeggio assured the cardinals that he was nearer sixty than fifty. There was also a feeling that he was too powerful, and so great that he would be unapproachable. Others said that he could not be trusted to be loyal to the emperor's interests.

With thirty-nine cardinals in the conclave, the winner would need to get at least twenty-six votes. Cardinal Medici, who was the favourite to win, had fifteen promises of support in advance; but when it came to the actual voting, the cardinals went back on all their promises, and in the secrecy of the conclave ignored the wishes of the princes and pleased themselves and their personal friends. Cardinal Medici received only three votes on the first ballot, and did no better later on. As the voting continued, support grew for Cardinal Farnese, but he never managed to get more than twenty-two votes. Then on the ninth ballot Medici, seeing that he could not win, proposed his friend, the Flemish Cardinal Adrian, bishop of the Spanish diocese of Tortosa, who had not been thought to have a chance. Both his Flemish nationality and his Spanish see indicated that he could be trusted to favour the emperor. Support for Adrian grew, and on 9 January he was elected on the fourteenth ballot, and was proclaimed as Pope Adrian VI. It was the last time that a non-Italian was chosen as Pope until a Polish Pope was elected in 1978.

Wolsey received contradictory reports as to the votes that he received. Clerk told him that he received nine votes on the first ballot, twelve on the second, and nineteen on the third, but that afterwards his support fell away. Campeggio, who was in the conclave, wrote that Wolsey received a few votes in every ballot, and sometimes as many as eight or nine. The official record states that he was proposed only once, on the fifth ballot, when he received seven votes.[35]

The new Pope was in Spain at the time of his election, and to the annoyance of the Roman people and of the Vatican officials showed no great hurry to come to Rome. Six months after his election he sailed from Barcelona in the summer of 1522 and caused the emperor some anxiety by landing at Villefranche and staying for a few days in the south of France before proceeding to Genoa and Ostia, and arriving in Rome on 29 August. He was more sympathetic to the French, and more neutral between François and Charles, than Charles or Wolsey had expected; and instead of vigorously supporting the war against France, as Julius II had done, he several times appealed to Charles and François to stop fighting and unite against the Turk and the Lutherans. Before he left Spain, he granted a request from Henry VIII to appoint Wolsey as Abbot of St Albans, the third richest monastery in England, in addition to all his other benefices, with the usual dispensations for pluralities and non-residence.[36]

Henry entered the war as he had promised, for he had no longer any reason to delay. The French envoys at Calais had been fooled by Wolsey during the conference, but their spies' reports of the military and naval preparations in England opened their eyes to what was happening. Henry and Wolsey had one of their rare disagreements when Henry wished to warn the English merchants not to make their usual autumn voyage to Bordeaux to buy wine, lest the French, realising that war was imminent, should detain and intern the ships and their crews. Wolsey succeeded in dissuading Henry from warning the merchants, arguing that if they did not go to Bordeaux the French would interpret it as a sign that England was about to declare war, while he was sure that if they went there in the usual way, the French would not intern them for fear of annoying Henry and driving him to abandon his position of friendly neutrality to France. But François refused to pay the instalments due in November 1521 of the money owing to Henry for the cession of Tournai, arguing that as the emperor had captured Tournai he was no longer obliged to pay Henry for it.[37]

When Charles left Brussels on 23 May 1522 on his journey to Spain, Henry had already sent his herald to declare war on François. Charles reached Calais on 26 May, and next day crossed to Dover, escorted by an English fleet manned by 10,000 men.[38] At Dover, Wolsey was rowed out in a barge to meet the emperor as his ship entered the harbour, and afterwards Henry received him in Dover Castle. The king and the emperor rode by Canterbury and Sittingbourne to Greenwich, where Queen Catherine and the little Princess Mary were in residence. Charles was accompanied by his retinue of 2,044 noblemen, gentlemen and servants, and Henry by most of the English notables, including the Under-Treasurer, Sir Thomas More.

While they were at Greenwich, the herald arrived on 5 June to report to Henry that he had issued the 'defiance' – the declaration of war – to François at Lyons on 29 May. Henry gave, as his reasons for declaring war, François's breach of the Treaty of London by assisting Robert de La Marck; his invasion of Navarre; his action in sending Albany to Scotland; and several other minor actions of an unfriendly character, culminating in his failure to pay the last instalment of the money due to Henry. François denied that his actions constituted a breach of the treaty, claimed that he had withheld payment of the money because he had known for two years that Henry was planning to attack him, and declared his eagerness to meet Henry in battle.[39]

On 6 June Charles and Henry went from Greenwich to London. They were met by the Lord Mayor and corporation a mile from St George's Bar, where More welcomed them in a speech in which he praised both sovereigns and acclaimed their friendship and alliance. They rode through London amid the cheers of the people, and a few days later went to Windsor, where they signed two new treaties, one providing for military action against France, and the other for Mary's marriage to the emperor. The Treaty of Windsor declared that Henry and Charles were unable to proceed with a crusade against the Turk until they had established peace in Christendom by curbing the ambition of the French king. They agreed not to make a separate peace with France, and to call on Pope Adrian VI, whom they had so highly esteemed when he was in a lower position than that which he now occupied, to join their league as the common father of Christendom. Henry then accompanied Charles to Southampton, where Charles embarked for Spain on 6 July. On the way, at Bishop's Waltham on 2 July, they signed another treaty by which Henry agreed to have an army ready at Calais before 1 August and to maintain it in the field until 31 October, and Charles agreed to have forces available there to help Henry within six days of the landing of the English army.[40]

While he was in London, Charles granted Wolsey another annuity of 9,000 'crowns of the sun' (the highly-valued German *Sonnenkronen*), payable in half-yearly instalments in London or Calais beginning on 1 November 1522. This was to compensate Wolsey for the loss of the pension which François had paid him in return for his surrender of his bishopric of Tournai, as François had now stopped paying the pension because of Wolsey's devotion to the emperor's cause. At Bishop's Waltham, Charles signed letters patent by which he promised to obtain from the Pope a further pension of 2,500 ducats a year for Wolsey, to be paid from the revenues of vacant benefices in Spain, to compensate him for his refusal of the bishopric of Badajoz. Charles, on his side, asked Henry to lend him 200,000 ducats to pay his mercenaries. Henry agreed to lend him 50,000 ducats, repayable after one year.[41]

Preparations were now vigorously undertaken for war against the French and their Scots allies. The clergy were asked to contribute voluntary gifts of money. Warham gave £1,000, and Foxe £2,000. Tunstal, who had just been appointed Bishop of London, gave £333, as did several other bishops. Wolsey headed the list with a gift of £3,000.[42]

The command of the army to invade France was given to Thomas Howard, Earl of Surrey, the son of the victor of Flodden. He and his men landed at Calais only a few weeks later than the date which had been fixed in the treaty with the emperor, and they crossed the French frontier and linked up with Charles's mercenaries from the Netherlands near Ardres on 2 September. It was late in the summer to begin a campaign, but there was time to do some damage to the French before winter set in. During the war of 1513 Wolsey had been responsible for the organisation of money and supplies, but now he took over the

Henry VIII, about 1520, by an unknown artist

Charles Brandon, Duke of Suffolk, by an unknown artist

supreme direction of the military strategy of the war. On 9 September he sent instructions to Surrey from Hampton Court. As this was a joint operation with the emperor, Surrey must avoid any disagreements with Charles's generals, and must comply with their wishes as far as possible. He was to do all the damage to the French that the time of year would allow, and if possible try to provoke them to battle; but he was not to waste time besieging any strong place unless he was sure that he could capture it within twelve or fifteen days.[43]

The English and imperial forces advanced into the Boulonnais, ravaging the country, burning towns, villages and farms, and in one case a church which had been fortified and looked 'more like a house of war than the house of God'.[44] Around Lottinghen they burned everything in an area five miles long and eight miles wide. Advancing south into the country near the French headquarters at Montreuil, they burned the castle of the Duke of Vendôme, the commander of the French army. Vendôme protested to Surrey against his policy of wholesale burnings, and complained that he was waging very foul war;[45] but he did not allow himself to be provoked into fighting a pitched battle, as Surrey hoped he would. Despite his indignation, he agreed to Surrey's proposal for an exchange of prisoners-of-war. When the English prisoners were released, they told Surrey that their French captors in Montreuil had laid all the blame for the war and the devastation on Wolsey.

By the middle of September the invaders had advanced more than fifty miles into France and were burning the country around Doulance. They turned north-west, and besieged Hesdin. By now, Charles's commanders were becoming anxious that the French would carry out reprisals for the devastation by invading and burning the border regions in the Netherlands, which, unlike England, were not beyond their reach. Hesdin did not surrender as quickly as Surrey expected; at the end of September the rain set in; and the supplies which were supposed to come from the Netherlands had not arrived. The emperor's general suggested that they should raise the siege and end the campaign. Surrey wrote to Wolsey for instructions. Wolsey told him that he must carry on operations until the end of October, as Henry had promised to do under the Treaty of Bishop's Waltham; but the emperor's commanders marched home to the Netherlands, and after burning a few more villages and farms Surrey led his troops back to Calais.[46]

In the war against the Scots, things had turned out differently. Henry and Wolsey appointed the Earl of Shrewsbury to command the army in the north; but while he was carrying out Wolsey's instructions for mustering men in the Border counties and transporting supplies and soldiers to Berwick and Norham, the Scots struck first. Albany called on the whole Scottish host – all men between the ages 'of sixty and sixteen' –

to meet him outside Edinburgh, and quickly led 4,000 of them over the Border and marched on Carlisle. As Carlisle was defenceless, and the army which Wolsey was raising had not yet arrived, Lord Dacre, the Warden of the Western Marches, offered Albany a truce for one month. Albany was unwise enough to accept it, perhaps because the Scots were conscious that basically the English were stronger than they, and were therefore always anxious to keep the peace and appease Henry if this was possible.[47]

Henry's first reaction was anger that Dacre, without any authority from him, should have compromised his honour by asking the Scots for a truce; but Wolsey told him that this was a very satisfactory arrangement. He explained that if Dacre had not made the truce, Carlisle would have fallen to the Scots; and as Dacre had acted without authority, Henry could disclaim responsibility for the truce and violate it when this became expedient. As skirmishes on the Border still continued, Albany protested to Wolsey that he and Henry's sister Queen Margaret wished to be friends with England, but that the English had tricked him into agreeing to a truce and had then gone back on their word.[48]

He received a stinging reply from Wolsey, who wrote to him in French, knowing that Albany could speak hardly a word of English. Wolsey praised Queen Margaret's efforts for peace, but informed Albany that Henry wished to vindicate his honour by arms, and not trust to uncertain promises. Albany's servant who brought his letter to Wolsey had gossiped about Albany's intention to take vengeance on the English for the injuries that they had done to Scotland; but Albany should remember that vengeance falls on the necks of those who seek it. As for Albany's suggestion that the English had been guilty of dissimulation about the truce, Albany had perhaps had experience of deception in the other countries where he had lived, and therefore wrongly believed that it was also the manner of England. So wrote the Cardinal of York, a year after his conduct at Calais and Bruges.[49]

CHAPTER 9

MORE VERSUS LUTHER

IN the years after 1517, More underwent a profound intellectual and emotional transformation. Two events took place at about the same time which changed his way of life and his outlook on the world. One was his appointment to be a member of the Privy Council; the other was the rise of Lutheranism in Europe. The first made him, for the time being, an instrument of Henry VIII's tyranny; the second transformed him into a religious fanatic. While Wolsey reacted to the Lutheran threat, and to the Pope's appeal for Christian unity to confront it, by deliberately instigating a war to make Henry king of France at the price of tearing Chistendom apart; while Erasmus, with increasing pessimism, tried hopelessly to prevent a final break between Catholics and Protestants; while many men who had read and admired the works of More and his fellow-humanists enthusiastically followed Luther's call for a Reformation; and while the conservatives said that Erasmus and the humanists had laid the eggs which Luther hatched, More became a savage persecutor of heretics, equalling the worst of his fellow-persecutors in effectiveness and outdoing them all in malice.

More and the humanists had been as conscious as Luther of the disgraceful corruption which had gripped the Church. Although we have no record of More's views on the subject in the first months after All-Hallows' Eve 1517, he must have felt, like Erasmus, that Luther's denunciation of the activities of Albert of Brandenburg and Tetzel was entirely justified, and that the thousands of students and ordinary people who read or listened to Luther's *Ninety-five Theses* with such enthusiasm were expressing the feelings of any sincere Christian about the shameful practices of the ecclesiastical hierarchy. But from the beginning there was a fundamental difference between Erasmus and Luther, between the humanists and the Lutherans. The humanists wished to remove the corruptions and to reform the Church in order to strengthen it; the Lutherans, almost from the beginning, wished to overthrow the Church, believing that it had become incurably wicked and was not the Church of Christ on earth. Erasmus and More thought that the reformation should be carried out by Popes and princes; Luther believed that it should be accomplished by a popular revolution under the leadership of princes – or, more accurately, of German dukes who ruled as princes in their territories, but who, it could be argued, were not really 'princes' in the sense in which the word was used by sixteenth-century theologians, meaning independent sovereign rulers, but were subjects defying *their* 'prince', the emperor Charles V.

Erasmus reacted to the inevitable conflict with great sadness. He thought that his Lutheran friends were right on the issue in dispute, but were disrupting the Church and the social fabric by encouraging anarchy and inciting popular movements of men who could not understand Greek or even Latin, and who would never respect the position of the intellectuals as the cultured popes and kings would do; while on the other hand, he thought that the supporters of the corruption were defending the unity of the Church, law and order, and the society in which humanist intellectuals could live and write with the help of pluralities and dispensations.

He decided to opt out, not primarily from fear, but from a genuine neutralism. His friend, the painter Dürer, called on him to choose the martyr's crown; but he declared that he might be prepared, if necessary, to suffer martyrdom for Christ, but not for Luther.[1] But he would not condemn Luther. When he complained to the Pope and his other friends in the hierarchy that he was unjustly suspected of Lutheranism, they called on him to prove his orthodoxy by issuing a public denunciation of Lutheranism. This he refused to do, although the Church, realising that a condemnation of Luther by Erasmus would have a powerful propaganda effect, repeatedly pressed him to do so. At considerable risk to himself, he refused to line up with the persecutors of well-meaning, if misguided, reformers. Eventually he succumbed to the pressure, chiefly because he had been touched on his weakest point – his sensitivity to any kind of personal criticism – by a hostile tract of Ulrich von Hutten, who denounced him for not supporting the Lutherans.[2]

More reacted very differently. He had none of Erasmus's hesitations. On the contrary, Lutheranism removed all the contradictions in his character, and produced a new Thomas More, into which all his conflicting personalities merged. Thomas More the barrister, Thomas More the humanist, Thomas More the would-be monk, Thomas More the author of *Utopia*, and Thomas More the Privy Councillor, all gave way to an amalgam of them all, Thomas More the anti-Lutheran, the persecutor of heretics. For there was one thing that all the Thomas Mores had in common: their hatred of anarchy, the mob, revolution. The barrister who administered the law of England and enforced judicial authority in London; the Greek scholar who relied on the patronage of princes and bishops; the man who yearned for the austerities and discipline of the strictest monastery; the visionary who conceived of a perfect society in which it was a capital crime to discuss politics outside the Senate; and Henry VIII's minister, who with his fellow-Privy Councillors enforced censorship of books, forbade un-licensed preaching, and ordered the arrest and imprisonment without trial of any husbandman who had been overheard criticising the king or Wolsey in an inn – all united to denounce, insult, torture and burn any Lutheran or sacramentary who was so impregnated by Pride, the sin of Lucifer, that he dared to disrupt the social order by putting forward his own personal beliefs, his own idea of right and wrong, his own conscience, against the official pronouncements of the Church.

Nearly all the humanists were moved, one way or another, by the accusation that they had fostered the Lutherans. Some of them agreed with the conservatives that Lutheranism was the logical consequence of humanism, and became Lutherans; others set out to prove that they and the Lutherans were not identical, but complete opposites. Fisher became a zealous anti-Lutheran and persecutor; it was probably at his own request that he was selected to preach the sermon against Lutheranism when Luther's books were burned at Paul's Cross. But while Fisher persecuted with dignity, and without sacrificing his intellectual integrity, More attacked the Lutherans hysterically and meanly, in a way which degraded him both intellectually and morally.

His chief motive was not fear for his own safety or position, but a sense of guilt for what he had done. He felt responsible, as a humanist, for Lutheranism. He believed that the humanists' jokes about the corrup-tions of the Church had been responsible for the Lutherans' war against the Church. He could not deny the accusation that he and his friends had laid the eggs which the heretics had hatched. He had to atone for this, and would not shrink from any means that were necessary to undo the harm that he had caused. As an intellectual and moralist, he could not make a greater sacrifice than to write what he knew were lies and cheap, vulgar abuse. He was prepared to make this sacrifice, and eagerly sought the opportunity to do so.

The publication by Lupset of *Julius at the Gates of Heaven* had given the conservatives a splendid handle with which to attack Erasmus and the humanists. They no longer needed to find questionable words in his translation of the New Testament, or small omissions in his Greek text; they could denounce him for frivolously and sacrilegiously suggesting that the deceased Holy Father would be refused admission to Heaven and would thereupon summon soldiers to force the gates by storm. More deeply resented the attacks on Erasmus, not only because they were directed against his friend, but because, by implication, they were aimed at himself and all the humanists. He wrote an indignant letter to a monk, an Augustinian canon, who had claimed to recognise Erasmus, by his style, as the author of *Julius at the Gates of Heaven*, and had castigated him for writing it. We do not know who the monk was, but it was almost certainly John Batmanson, who in 1520 made a series of attacks on Erasmus and his books, and afterwards, by an ironic coincidence, became the Prior of the London Charterhouse where More had once lived. The only other monk who publicly attacked Erasmus in England was Henry Standish, the Bishop of St Asaph, who preached a vigorous sermon against him at Paul's Cross. Although it has been suggested that Standish was the monk to whom More wrote, this is certainly wrong, because Standish was a Franciscan, not a member of a contemplative order; nor would More have addressed the Bishop of St Asaph in the harsh and haughty language in which he wrote to the monk.

More asked the monk how he dared to criticise Erasmus, a man far more learned than he. As for *Julius at the Gates of Heaven*, 'I have never been very interested in discovering the name of the author, or the type of work it is, although I have heard different views on both points.' He then condemned the monk for deducing that Erasmus was the author because of similarities of style between *Julius at the Gates of Heaven* and Erasmus's books.

> When you base your argument on the style which you maintain is Erasmus's own peculiar style, I cannot hold back a laugh as I recall that you, utterly incapable of telling what style or language is, deny to Erasmus, universally known to be thoroughly conversant with all the niceties of speech, the right to make any criticism with regard to style in Jerome's works [the Vulgate]; yet you take it upon yourself to determine what is typical of Erasmus's style, although a huge throng of writers are doing their best to imitate Erasmus's manner of writing.

> It was absurd of the monk to compare Erasmus to Luther.

> It is strange how you are always trying to appear a little clever. I am surprised at the unusual amount of time you have to spend on schismatical and heretical books – that is, if you are telling the truth. . . . But if the books are good, why do you condemn them? If bad, why read them? You have no chance of becoming proficient in refuting errors and warning the world, since you gave up interest in the world by shutting yourself up in the cloister. Then what else do you accomplish in reading what is evil, except to learn about it?[3]

This was cool, brazen lying. When More wrote this letter, he knew very well that Erasmus was the author of *Julius at the Gates of Heaven*.

More's letter is undated, but it was obviously written after Lupset first published the book in April 1517, and probably in 1520, after Batmanson's attacks on it. Yet Erasmus had sent a copy of his manuscript to More before it was published; and More had written to Erasmus on 15 December 1516 telling him that the manuscript had safely arrived and thanking him for sending it.[4] More's clear implication, in his letter to the monk, that he had not read *Julius at the Gates of Heaven* was as untrue as his denial of Erasmus's authorship, though this, too, was implied, for nowhere in the letter does More directly state that Erasmus was not the author.

The two events which changed More's life – the rise of Lutheranism and his appointment to the Privy Council – were followed a few years later by a change in his personal surroundings. In about 1522 or 1523 he moved house, leaving London and settling in the country. He left his London house in Bucklersbury and moved to the village of Chelsea, four miles south-west of London and separated by three miles of fields and woodlands from the edge of the built-up area at Westminster and Charing Cross. More lived in the manor house at Chelsea, of which no trace remains today. It was surrounded by a few acres of garden and grounds. It was not a large and ostentatious dwelling, but a simple gentleman's house.

Chambers, in his great biography of More, writes that 'we are so accustomed to think of the household of Sir Thomas More at Chelsea that we are apt to follow Froude in his mistake of localizing there the description of More and his household which Erasmus wrote.'[5] Chambers then points out that at the time when Erasmus stayed with More, and afterwards when he wrote about it to Ulrich von Hutten, More was still living in Bucklersbury. But Chambers, who denied the suggestion that there was any difference in outlook and character between the earlier and the later More, did not appreciate the difference between the More of Bucklersbury and the More of Chelsea. Not only did Erasmus never visit More in Chelsea, but he never met him again after he moved there, and probably never realised that his friend had become a different person. The More who lived in Chelsea was the More described, not by Erasmus, but by his son-in-law Roper, and afterwards by relatives and friends who had heard about More from Roper, and carried on the Roper family tradition.

Another change occurred about the time of the move to Chelsea: More's children became adults, and married. Like many sixteenth-century women, his daughters married when they were, by our standards, very young. His eldest daughter, Margaret, was married on 2 July 1521, shortly before they left Bucklersbury, when she was sixteen; her bridegroom, William Roper, was a twenty-two-year-old barrister, with strong sympathies to Lutheranism which were to cause More much anxiety. More's two other daughters were both married on 29 September 1525 in the same private chapel at Willesden. Elizabeth, who was probably aged nineteen, married William Dauncey; Cecily, aged about eighteen, married Giles Heron. Both their fathers-in-law were knights holding offices at the King's court. Apart from his own children, he adopted a little girl, Margaret Gigs, who married his former page, the court physician, John Clement. Margaret Clement was an exceptionally devout Catholic.

More's son John was probably about twenty when he married in 1529 Anne Cresacre, the daughter and heiress of a Yorkshire gentleman.[6] Holbein's portrait of Anne confirms what Roper and the other biographers write about her, and indicates that she was gayer and more attracted by worldly pleasures than the other members of her husband's family; but she never caused a scandal, or outraged the strict decorum on which her father-in-law insisted. On one occasion she annoyed More by hinting that she would like to be given a pearl necklace, and by persisting in her demands after he had brushed aside her requests. He therefore decided to play on her a variation of the trick that he had played on his first bride twenty-five years before, though this time his motive was not to indulge in the pleasure of deceiving his wife but to perform the duty of mortifying his daughter-in-law. He had a necklace made with peas instead of pearls, and, putting it in an impressive box, presented it to Anne, telling her that it was the necklace which she had wanted for so long. When she opened the box and saw the peas, 'she almost wept for very grief'. We are told that, after this, she caused no further trouble.[7]

There is no doubt that More was a kind father to his children. His relationship with his eldest daughter, Meg, was particularly close. We do not have to rely on the book written by Meg's husband, for some of her letters to More, and his to her, have survived, and have moved modern readers by the picture they reveal of the mutual love of father and daughter. But his attitude towards the other children seems to have been more ambivalent. Here, too, this complex and contradictory man fluctuated between a sincere love and the hostility and revulsion that he displayed in his book *The Four Last Things* and which surely went beyond the occasional irritation which the most devoted parent sometimes feels.

Roper tells the story of how More saved Meg's life when she was dying of the sweating sickness. The 'sweat' was first brought to England by Henry VII's Breton soldiers in 1485, and returned once or twice in most decades until its last appearance in 1551. It came in summer, and raged for a few months. The victims were suddenly attacked by it without warning, sometimes when walking in the street. The symptoms were a high temperature and a violent sweating. In many cases it proved fatal within a few hours; those who survived recovered completely within a day or two. The best chance of survival was to lie still in bed in a moderately warm room; extreme heat, cold, and movement of any kind made things worse. It was very infectious. Henry VIII took extraordinary precautions to avoid meeting any person who had been in contact with the sweat, or visiting any place where it had broken out. The common people were not able to escape so easily, and those who lived together in the towns, especially in London, suffered worse than those in the countryside.[8]

Meg fell ill with the sweat, and became unconscious during the dangerous first few hours. The best physicians were called to her bedside, but could do nothing for her. Then More went to his oratory to pray, asking God, if it was His will, to spare her life. While he was praying, the inspiration came to More that she might be given an enema. He returned at once to the physicians, who said that the idea had not occurred to them, but that it might be a useful suggestion. She was given the enema; she immediately recovered consciousness; and, like other survivors, was soon well again. Roper, who tells this story to show More's saintliness and God's special favour to him, adds a revealing detail: when Meg had recovered, More said that if she had died he would have retired to a monastery and abandoned all interest in worldly affairs.[9] This seems to confirm, not only his great love for Meg, but his lack of affection for his wife and his other children.

More was in advance of most, if not all, of his contemporaries in his attitude towards the education of women. He not only advocated it in *Utopia*, but applied it in practice with his daughters, providing them with an education which was given to few women except royal princesses. He arranged for them to be taught to read and write, to speak and write Latin and Greek, and to be learned in the classics and the humanities as well as in divinity. He always wrote to them, and they replied, in Latin. He set them tasks in writing Latin, requiring them to express their opinion on some classical book or religious text or commentary. Meg wrote Latin essays and epistles which impressed Erasmus, and translated his *Treatise on the Pater Noster* into English.[10] But More was a sixteenth-century father, just as his daughters were sixteenth-century daughters. Those passages in his letters in which he praises his daughter's piety and learning show clearly that he took the contemporary view that if God endowed a woman with virtues and intellectual gifts, this was in order to bring credit to her father and husband.

More's relationship with his second wife was less happy than with his children. Mrs Alice Middleton – 'Dame Alice', as she was known in

More's household – was a widow, probably aged about thirty, when she married More. She was less docile than More's first wife, Jane. He tried to educate her, but did not succeed in teaching her anything except how to sing and accompany herself on the lute and virginals.[11] Even more than many of his contemporaries, he often indulged in humorous, or perhaps half-serious, banter about what husbands had to endure from their wives, particularly from wives who gossiped and talked a great deal. This was a family tradition. His father, Sir John More, who married three wives, often complained of the evils of matrimony and of what a curse a talkative wife was; and Thomas More eclipsed him in his frequent and witty remarks on this subject.

Alice was not only uneducated and lacking in skills and social graces; she was also very ugly, with a large hooked nose. More often made jokes about her looks and her ignorance to his guests at the dinner table, in her presence, perhaps in order to draw their attention to the fact that he had married an ugly and uneducated wife instead of lusting after a beautiful and cultured woman. Fortunately, Alice did not usually understand the jokes which More was making at her expense, because, to her annoyance, he usually spoke Latin with his guests at dinner, which was a language she did not understand. But the worst examples of his humour seem to date from stories told by his great-grandson, Cresacre More, a hundred years after his death. The famous remark by More, when he mockingly referred, in front of Alice and the children, to the ugliness of her nose, was told by Cresacre More in 1631 and afterwards inserted in an eighteenth-century edition of Roper's life of More; but it is not found in any of the sixteenth-century manuscripts or in the earlier printed editions of Roper, and has been rejected by modern scholars as a forgery.[12]

For More, the object of family life was not love, affection and happiness in a twentieth-century sense, but duty, service to God, and the subjugation of the lusts of the flesh by discipline, atonement and self-mortification. Like most sixteenth-century families, it was not the modern 'nuclear family', but the large unit, with the old judge and his third wife, Thomas More and his second wife, three daughters, one son, three sons-in-law, one daughter-in-law, one adopted daughter, her husband, eleven grandchildren, a secretary, a jester, and a considerable number of servants. They were all united in devotion and obedience to their master, Sir Thomas More, who was the head of the house, though he gave precedence in all matters to his venerable father. More saw to it that the household worked and prayed, and did not waste their time in idle amusements. There was compulsory attendance at common prayers, both in the morning and in the evening; and on holy days he made them get up in the middle of the night for an hour's prayer at midnight.

Games were forbidden much more strictly than in most households. The law forbade the working classes to play cards or dice except during the Twelve Days of Christmas; only the aristocracy could indulge in these recreations all the year round. More forbade all the members of his household, even noblemen's sons who were there as pages or guests, to play cards or dice at any time of the year, even during the Twelve Days of Christmas. His chief object was to prevent the slightest risk of sexual misconduct. He took rigid steps to segregate the sexes. The men and women servants not only lived apart in separate parts of the building, but were even forbidden to speak to each other, except in very special cases when this was absolutely necessary.[13] This segregation and discipline was unknown in the ordinary sixteenth-century household.

More subjected himself to a sterner ordeal than any which he inflicted on others. Going to bed at nine o'clock, he rose at two and prayed and worked in his study on his literary labours till seven, when he breakfasted and began his legal, official, and private business duties. He normally limited himself to only one dish at dinner. Every Friday and fast day – the Ember Days and the eve of the major saints' days – he withdrew to a special building which had been erected in the grounds of his garden a little way from the house. It was known as the New Building. Here he stayed all day, praying and flogging himself with a whip and a cord which had been twisted into hard, painful knots. Already as a young man in the Charterhouse of London he submitted to rigorous austerities, and he was flogging himself by the time that he married Alice; but most of the information that we have about these flagellations refers to the years when he lived in Chelsea, and he probably increased their severity in the years after the rise of Lutheranism and his entry into the king's service.

He nearly always wore a hairshirt to irritate his skin and mortify his flesh; as Under-Sheriff of London, Speaker of the House of Commons, Chancellor of the Duchy of Lancaster and Lord Chancellor he wore it under his splendid robes of office. He did not wish to boast of his self-mortification, and told only two people about it – his confessor in Bucklersbury, the parish priest, Father Bouge, and Meg, who washed it for him and cleaned up the blood with which it was covered from the whippings. Dame Alice wondered why he never gave her his shirt to wash; she became suspicious, and asked Father Bouge about the hairshirt.

The whole family found out one summer evening, when More, supping informally at home on a warm day, removed his ruff and loosened his tunic, revealing the hairshirt underneath. His daughter-in-law, Anne, noticed the shirt, and laughed, to Meg's distress. Before he died, he bequeathed the hairshirt to Meg, and after her death it passed to Margaret Clement. Many years later, when Margaret Clement was a refugee in Flanders in Elizabeth I's reign, she showed it to More's biographer, Stapleton, who was surprised and impressed to see that it was far rougher and more uncomfortable than any ordinary hairshirt.[14]

In 1522, about the time when he moved to Chelsea, More wrote a religious treatise, *The Four Last Things*, which he obviously did not intend for publication, and never finished. It was first published by More's nephew, William Rastell, in 1557, more than twenty years after More's death. More probably intended it to be read by the members of his family and household, for he wrote it in English and not in Latin, as he probably would have done if he had not intended anyone to read it except himself and Meg. It was the first time that he had written on a religious subject since his translation of the biography of Pico della Mirandola in 1504, and it was his first original religious work. It was certainly no coincidence that he wrote it after he had been a member of the Privy Council for four years, when he was rising in influence at court, and when he had discovered, what he may well have suspected earlier, that the diplomatic mission to Calais and Bruges, in which he had served under Wolsey, had been an almost unparalleled piece of diplomatic trickery designed to plunge Christendom into a cruel war at a time when the Pope, and even Henry and Wolsey themselves, were ostensibly calling for Christian unity to defeat the external threat from the Turk and the internal threat from Luther.

'The four last things' were death, the Day of Judgment, the pains of Purgatory, and the eternal joys of Heaven. More's treatise began by bringing home to the reader the horror of death, for if men realised the dreadful agony that was in store for them on their deathbed, they would not so thoughtlessly savour the joys of life and concern themselves with worldly advantage. What man, asks More, would be happy if he had been sentenced to death and was awaiting execution? Nor would he be any happier if he knew that a fellow-convict was being taken to his place of execution one mile away, while he himself would be carted for twenty or even for a hundred miles before reaching the place where he was to suffer death. Yet young men do not worry at all about the prospect of dying, and assume that it is the oldest man in the town, and not they, who will die. Consider the case of a lusty young man aged twenty, and an old man of ninety. 'Both must ye die, both be ye in the cart carrying forward. His gallows and death standeth within ten miles at the farthest, and yours within eighty. I see not why ye should reckon much less of your death than he, though your way be longer, since ye be sure ye shall never cease riding till ye come at it.'[15]

More was sure that death was always a very painful experience, so

painful that 'a stroke of a staff, a cut of a knife, the flesh singed with fire'
would be far preferable; for 'if thou die no worse death, yet at the
leastwise lying in thy bed, thy head shooting, thy back aching, thy veins
beating, thine heart panting, thy throat rattling, thy flesh trembling, thy
mouth gaping, thy nose sharping, thy legs cooling, thy fingers fumbling,
thy breath shortening, all thy strength fainting, thy life vanishing, and
thy death drawing on.'[16] Even in the sixteenth century, with its
primitive medicine, people sometimes died peacefully in their sleep; but
More ignored this possibility. He was convinced that, apart from all the
other pains of death, the moment of dying, when the soul left the body,
was one of unbearable torture; for Christ Himself, who had endured
without a murmur the pain of his scourging, of the crown of thorns, and
of the nails which fixed Him to the cross, had emitted a great cry of pain
at the moment of death.[17]

More then pointed out another horrible feature of death – that when a
man dies, his wife and children, and his friends, would be at his bedside,
and he would have to spend his last moments on earth looking at their
faces. Would it be pleasant, for a dying man, to have his friends standing
around his bed pestering him to leave them something in his will? 'Then
shall come thy children and cry for their parts. Then shall come thy
sweet wife, and where in thine health haply she spake thee not one sweet
word in six weeks, now shall she call thee sweet husband and weep with
much work and ask thee what shall she have.'[18] A strange deathbed
horror to haunt the imagination of that devoted father and family man,
Saint Thomas More.

He proceeded to examine the Seven Deadly Sins. He began with
Pride, the mother of all sins, which was found not only in rulers and those
who revel in the gifts of God of power, wealth, beauty, physical strength
and learning, but also in hypocrites who pride themselves on being more
pious than their fellow-men. He then dealt with Envy, Wrath and
Covetousness, and turned to Gluttony. Thinking no doubt of the many
kings and nobles who died in their fifties after a life of heavy eating and
drinking, he wrote that he wished physicians would not, in such cases,
give the immediate cause of death, but would more accurately ascribe it
to gluttony. Gluttony was not only a sin in itself, but led to two other sins,
Sloth and Lust; for after over-eating and drinking, men fall into a
drunken stupor, and More had been informed that it was easier to
seduce a woman when she was drunk.[19]

In discussing gluttony, he digressed into that favourite theme of
medieval theologians, that sin begins with the eye. Many men did not
wish to indulge in gluttony until they saw the meat on the sideboard;
and

the eye is also the bawd to bring the heart to the desire of the foul beastly pleasure beneath the belly. For when the eye immoderately de-lighteth in long looking of the beauteous face, with the white neck and round paps, and so forth as far as it findeth no let, the Devil helpeth the heart to frame and form in the fantasy, by foul imaginations, all that ever the clothes cover.

The Devil is so successful in this that 'the mind is more kindled in the feigned figure of his own device than it should haply be if the eye saw the body belly naked such as it is indeed'.[20]

More wrote a few lines about Sloth, and then stopped. It is not merely that the rest of his manuscript has been lost, because Rastell notes at this place in the treatise: 'Sir Thomas More wrote no farther of this work.'[21] There remained one sin that he had not yet dealt with – Lust. Perhaps he could not bring himself to write on this subject.

More was one of the learned men who helped Henry VIII write his book *The Assertion of the Seven Sacraments* in 1521; but like others who were in a position to know, he always maintained that Henry had written the book himself.[22] Luther made a reply to the book. His friends urged him not to publish it, for they knew the danger involved in attacking the king of England; but Luther was not the man to be dissuaded from answering a critic. His *Martin Luther's Answer in German to King Henry of England's Book* was published at Wittenberg in August 1522, and a Latin translation appeared seven weeks later. It shocked everyone except his ardent supporters by the language in which he criticised the king. It was, on the whole, no more hostile than the usual sixteenth-century theological polemic, and less abusive than many; but public opinion in 1522 felt that a king should be criticised, if at all, only in the most respectful language. Luther called him 'Lord Henry by God's ungrace King of England'; the 'lying King of England'; 'King Heinz'; 'dear Junker'; and 'Heinz of England'. Moreover, the book contained one outrageous sentence, in which Luther declared that since Henry 'knowingly and consciously fabricates lies against the Majesty of my King in Heaven, this damnable rottenness and worm, I will have the right, on behalf of my King, to bespatter his English Majesty with muck and shit and to trample underfoot that crown of his which blasphemes against Christ'.[23]

Henry himself did not deign to reply to Luther, but treated him with a contemptuous silence. Instead, in January 1523 he wrote to the Duke of Saxony, drawing his attention to Luther's attack upon him, and stating that although he personally did not care what Luther said about him, he thought that the duke should realise that this seditious Luther, by attacking a king in this way, was threatening the social fabric of Christendom. The Duke of Saxony replied that he had no responsibility for what Luther wrote. Henry's letter and the duke's reply were published in May 1523.

Though Henry could not lower himself by entering into controversy with Luther, he was eager that his supporters should do so. A reply to Luther was written very hurriedly by the German orthodox theologian, Thomas Murner, who had spent the summer at Henry's court, and was published in Strasbourg in November 1522 under the title *Whether it is the King of England who is a Liar, or this Luther*. Fisher followed with his *Confutation of Lutheran Assertions*, which was published early in 1523. Eck, who had disputed against Luther before the emperor at the Diet of Worms, wrote another defence of 'the invincible King of England' against 'the calumnies of the impious Luther' which was published in May 1523. In October came a book by Queen Catherine's Spanish confessor, Alphonso de Villa Sancta, and in December two more, one by Edward Powell and one by More. Meanwhile Fisher was writing a longer work, *The Defence of the King's Assertion against Babylonian Captivity*, which appeared soon afterwards. All these books were in Latin.

The erudite editors of Yale University's edition of More's works are almost certainly right in their opinion that More was asked by Henry to write this book as part of a three-level reply to Luther. At the highest level, the king would maintain a dignified silence and write only to the Duke of Saxony; at the second level, the Bishop of Rochester would reply with a learned treatise against Luther; and at the lowest level More would write a book consisting of nothing but vulgar abuse. They are also probably right in thinking that publication of More's book, which he wrote during the winter of 1522-3, was delayed by official decision until after Henry's letter to the Duke of Saxony had been published in May 1523, and that the further delay was due to the fact that Henry and his counsellors were hoping that Erasmus would write an answer to Luther, and thought that More's book should be held up until he could read Erasmus's manuscript. Erasmus had in fact been stung by Hutten's criticism into coming out at last against Luther, and on 4 September 1523 he wrote to More telling him that he was intending to write a book attacking Luther; but as it was clear that Erasmus had not yet begun work on the book, it was decided that the publication of More's book should be no longer delayed. More wrote a new preface, which he dated 17 September, and the book was published in December.[24] To twentieth-century readers, it is an incredible publication.

While it is no doubt true that the king ordered More to write an obscene book against Luther, this in no way absolves More from personal responsibility for writing it. He was certainly not forced to write the book. It would seem, from what More wrote in later years, when he was discussing his attitude, as Lord Chancellor, towards Henry's divorce from Catherine of Aragon, that Henry did not compel his counsellors to undertake a task which they were unwilling to perform; if Henry discovered that his counsellor's heart was not in a job, he switched him to other work and gave the unwelcome job to someone else.[25] It is painfully obvious that in this case More's heart was very much in the job, for no reluctant author could have written with the passion, the gusto and the venom which More displayed in the *Answer to Luther*. It would not be surprising if he volunteered for the job which he knew that someone was expected to perform.

If it is surprising, to our minds, that the book could have been written at all, it is even more extraordinary that More should have written it in Latin, and have intended it, not for the popular masses in England, but for educated readers. It was almost certainly the intention that, after being read by orthodox priests and doctors in Europe, it should be translated into the vernacular languages, especially into German; but, surprisingly, it was not translated. It is too much to hope that this was because it was thought to be so disgusting that it would antagonise the readers.

The *Answer to Luther* must of course be judged by the standards of More's contemporaries, and not by ours. We today in 1982 discuss sex with complete freedom, but we do not usually talk or write about excrement. In More's day, excrement was discussed more freely than sex. Luther made several references to it in his letters and in some of his books, including one passage in his *Answer to King Henry of England*; and More, in *Utopia*, had no qualms in mentioning shitting as one of the sensual pleasures which the Utopians enjoyed. To this extent, his *Answer to Luther* was certainly less shocking to his readers than it is to us; and it did not, in fact, arouse any widespread condemnation or embarrassment among the Catholic doctors who read it. The Lutherans and reformers were of course indignant; it laid the foundations for the intense hatred which they came to feel for More as their most cruel persecutor. Some of his friends, and the more moderate Catholics, mildly deplored it. Murner warned More that one could not throw dirt at Luther without getting dirty oneself. Erasmus, typically, wrote to More congratulating him on the book, but told his other friends that he thought it was too bitter.[26] But it won the giggling approval of Catholic Europe, and in later years it was praised by leading orthodox theologians and churchmen like Cochlaeus and Nicholas Harpsfield.

When these excuses have been made, and rightly made, for More, it must be pointed out that the *Answer to Luther* went far beyond the accepted standards of sixteenth-century abuse and vulgarity. It is grossly misleading to say, as most of More's modern biographers have done, that More replied to Luther's abuse in the same hard-hitting tone, and wrote in the accepted style of his time. Not only is the *Answer to Luther* more obscene than anything that Luther ever wrote, but no other sixteenth-century polemicist, either on the Catholic or the Protestant side, sank to the depths which More reached in this work. Compared with the didactic censoriousness of Cranmer, the bitter invective of Gardiner, the magisterial denunciations of Pole, the biting sarcasm of Knox, and even the broad and occasionally coarse humour of Luther, More's *Answer to Luther* reads like the scribblings of a dirty-minded schoolboy on a lavatory wall.

More's admiring Catholic biographer, Stapleton, who was a close friend of More's family, wrote in 1588 that More wrote *Answer to Luther* because he thought that Luther should be 'overwhelmed with filth'.[27] He set about this pious task with enthusiasm. He calls Luther a 'scoundrel*'; a 'dolt'; a man who 'blasphemes with his polluted lips' against the Church; a 'lousy little friar'; 'filthier than a pig and more foolish than an ass'; a supporter of the Turks, 'deserving the applause of Jews, Turks and heathens'; a drunkard, 'Father Tosspot'; a 'toadying buffoon who was once a friar, later a pimp', who wins the laughter of his supporters 'by the filthiest gestures and the most obscene words'. He 'has nothing in his mouth but privies, filth, and dung'; he 'would cast into his mouth the dung which other men would spit out into a basin'; a 'privy-minded rascal . . . . shitting and beshitted'. He is fit only 'to lick with his anterior the very posterior of a pissing she-mule'. More tells Luther that 'Orcus [Hades] vomited you as a most horrible plague onto the earth'; he calls on him to 'swallow down his filth and lick up the dung with which he has so foully defiled his tongue and his pen'; and he calls on his readers to throw back into Luther's 'shitty mouth, truly the shit-pool of all shit, all the muck and shit which your damnable rottenness has vomited up, and to empty out all the sewers and privies' over his head.[28]

More is just as abusive about Luther's supporters. He not only calls them rude names, but repeatedly makes libellous accusations against them. He was perhaps being merely abusive when he alleged that Luther derived his ideas from his followers who 'scatter among all the carts, carriages, boats, baths, brothels, barber shops, taverns, whore-houses, mills, privies and stews', where they 'diligently observe and set down in their notebooks' what a servant says insolently, a whore wantonly, a pimp indecently, and 'a shitter obscenely'. He was perhaps merely expressing an opinion when he wrote that 'the most absurd race of heretics, the dregs of impiety, of crimes and filth, shall be called

---

* More's Latin is given here in the English translation made by Sister Scholastica Mandeville in the Yale University Press edition of *More's Works*.

Lutherans'. But he was making factual statements, which he expected his readers to believe, when he stated that all the Protestant women who had married former priests and monks were 'foul prostitutes' and 'public strumpets', and that Lutherans publicly copulated in their churches, defiled the images of the saints and the crucifix, and 'bespatter the most holy image of Christ crucified with the most foul excrement of their bodies destined to be burned'.[29] Did he believe these wildly exaggerated stories of the excesses of the image-breaking Lutheran mobs? Or was he deliberately lying, as he had lied when he wrote to the monk about *Julius at the Gates of Heaven*?

A few years earlier, More had been as conscious as Erasmus and all his other humanist colleagues of the corruption of the Church; but he asserted in the *Answer to Luther* that all was perfect until Luther arrived. This, at least, is the clear implication, though More, with what was surely the chicanery of a brilliant lawyer, avoids saying this directly.

> What was once held to be more religious than fasting? What was more exactly observed than Lent? Yet now these men . . . . dedicate every day to bacchanalian orgies. Who does not know how continence was once prized? How strictly conjugal fidelity was commended, how esteemed by the ancients the chastity of widows, how zealously, how rightly, virginity was praised? And all these things by the authority of Christ Himself. Now this Antichrist has taken away almost completely all sense of modesty. Priests, monks, virgins, dedicated to God, now by the favour of the Devil, in the Church of the wicked, under the title of lawful spouses, with great pomp of demons, celebrate nefarious nuptials.[30]

While claiming only that this virtuous state of affairs 'once' existed – not necessarily in 1517 – More states that it is 'this Antichrist', Luther, who has taken it all away, though even Fisher and Pace, and other Catholic polemicists, admitted that the Lutheran heretics led very virtuous private lives. More goes on to accuse the Lutherans of indulging in adultery and bigamy with Luther's approval. There is no hint, of course, of what More knew very well, that both the invincible King Henry VIII and the Cardinal of York, Papal Legate, had a mistress and a bastard son.

It is interesting that More, in several places in the book, should have thought it necessary to justify himself for writing so scurrilous a work. He wrote that he was conscious that he who touches pitch will be wholly defiled by it, and that 'while I clean out this fellow's shit-filled mouth, I see my own fingers covered with shit'.[31] He apologised, too, for using obscene words which might offend some of his readers. But how could anyone refrain from writing like this against Luther, 'when he reads everywhere the most filthy insolence of a most stupid scoundrel against a most prudent prince', in view of the contrast 'between the goodness of the prince and the malice of the buffoon'?[32]

Not only was More himself embarrassed by the book, but so were the king and the cardinal, for it was almost certainly at their insistence that More published it anonymously under the name of William Rosse. He also went to considerable trouble to deceive his readers into believing that Rosse really existed and was indeed the author, though all his friends, and many of his more informed readers, knew that he had written it. Fisher actually revealed the truth, presumably by a slip of the tongue, when he named More as the author in a sermon in London in 1526; and More admitted the truth to Eck, when Eck visited England in 1525, giving Eck a copy of the book in which the author's name, 'Gullielmi Rossei', was underlined, and 'Thomae More' written in the margin.[33]

In his later English writings More kept up the pretence that the book was written, not by him, but by Rosse, and many of his readers were taken in. He had done the same thing in *Utopia*, inventing a fictitious person, Raphael Hythlodeus, the visitor to Utopia whom he pretended he had met. It was perhaps the fact that some of the readers of *Utopia* had believed in the existence of Hythlodeus and the island of the Utopians that gave More the idea of doing the same thing again. But what was a harmless joke in *Utopia* was a very serious and deliberate lie in *Answer to Luther* – a lie designed to protect More's reputation and the reputation of King Henry's Council by concealing the fact that he had lowered himself by writing a coarse and libellous book.

To make the readers believe in Rosse's existence and authorship, More invented three other fictitious characters, John Carcelius, Ferdinand Baravellus, and Hermann of Prague. In a preface by Carcelius, and a number of fictitious letters between Carcelius and Rosse, it is revealed that Rosse read Henry VIII's book a year before, in Venice, and was most favourably impressed by it, and that he afterwards moved to Rome, but because of the plague withdrew twenty miles from Rome, where he met Carcelius, who persuaded him to write a book in defence of the king against Luther.[34]

There is also a letter from 'Ferdinand Baravellus of the Ancient Nobility' who is 'a man very outstanding in theology' and 'a Spaniard remarkably learned in every branch of learning'. In a letter dated 'From our University, February 11', Baravellus defends Rosse from the accusation that he should not have written such an abusive and coarse book, saying that no learned man would censure Rosse for using coarse language against a 'completely mad buffoon' who 'raves wildly against the most illustrious king who is fully adorned with all noble qualities of body and mind'.[35] Hermann of Prague, a young man studying in England, is introduced in a letter from Rosse to Carcelius in a complicated story which explains the delay in publishing Rosse's book. Thus More, whom Chambers, following Dean Swift, calls the 'most virtuous Englishman who ever lived',[36] forged a letter from a fictitious Spanish theologian, praising and justifying his book which he knew might be regarded as obscene and which he was ashamed to publish under his own name.

Yet among the abuse and the lies there are one or two passages in *Answer to Luther* in which More reveals his deepest beliefs and which explain why he wrote the book and why he did all that he did during the rest of his life. He wrote that he was 'moved to obedient submission' to the see of Rome, not only by the arguments in favour of it, but because he had noticed that everyone who had declared himself an enemy of the see of Rome had soon afterwards declared himself also to be a notorious enemy and traitor to Christ and to our religion.

> I am also much moved by the consideration that if the faults of men should be imputed to their offices in this manner, not only will the Papacy not endure but also royal power, and supreme magistracy, and the consulate and every administrative office whatever will fall into ruin and the people will be without a ruler, without law and order. If this should ever happen, and it seems to threaten in several places of Germany, then men will finally realise, at great loss, what a profound difference there is in human affairs between having even bad rulers and having no rulers.[37]

He warned the German princes, only two years before the Peasant War of 1525, that though they might hope to benefit from Luther's attacks on the Pope by seizing Church property, so, too, 'the people look to the time when they may shake off in turn the yoke of the princes and strip them of their possessions'. Having accomplished this, then, 'drunk with the blood of princes and revelling in the gore of nobles . . . . with the laws trampled underfoot, according to Luther's doctrine, rulerless and lawless', they would exterminate each other.[38] The prospect of the princes in Germany being stripped of their possessions shocked the man who had once written *Utopia*.

While More was denouncing the wickedness of Luther and Lutherans, he was confronted with a Lutheran in his own home. His son-in-law, William Roper, had become a Lutheran. Roper was a very sincere and religious man who embraced any cause in which he believed with unreserved enthusiasm and a passionate readiness for self-sacrifice.

He began as a devoted Catholic, submitting himself to rigorous fasting and mortification of the flesh far in excess of what was imposed by the laws of the Church. He was obviously receptive to any propaganda which attacked the corruption of the worldly clergy, and was converted to Lutheranism when he read Luther's *Babylonian Captivity*. As the book was published in 1520, Roper must have converted to Lutheranism about the time when he married Margaret More in July 1521; and Harpsfield states that he was a 'marvellous zealous Protestant' when he married her. He became as ardent a Lutheran as he had formerly been an ascetic Catholic; 'neither was he content to whisper it hugger-mugger, but he thirsted very sore to publish his new doctrine and divulge it'.

Roper made contact with the Hansa Lutherans, and was caught in the drive against the heretics of the Steelyard. He was brought before Wolsey; but More intervened on his behalf, and though the other Lutherans were forced to recant at Paul's Cross, Roper was let off with a warning. More was naturally very perturbed at having a Lutheran son-in-law, and spent many hours in argument with Roper in unsuccessful attempts to convert him.

Eventually, Roper abandoned his heresy and became once again an exceptionally zealous Catholic. He described the circumstances of his conversion to Harpsfield, who wrote about it in his life of More. After trying in vain to influence Roper by his arguments, More said to Meg one day, when they were talking in the garden at Chelsea:

'Meg, I have borne a long time with thy husband; I have reasoned and argued with him in those points of religion, and still given to him my poor fatherly counsel; but I perceive none of all this able to call him home; and therefore, Meg, I will no longer argue nor dispute with him, but will clean give him over, and get me another while to God and pray for him'. And soon after, as he [Roper] verily believed, through the great mercy of God, at the devout prayer of Sir Thomas More, he perceived his own ignorance, oversight, malice and folly, and turned him again to the Catholic faith.[39]

A twentieth-century biographer can find other explanations for Roper's conversion. His love for his devoutly Catholic wife; his affection and respect for More; the disillusionment felt by so many Lutherans at the disagreements between the various Protestant sects; and the fear and horror of the revolutionary violence in Germany, could have combined to persuade him to adopt a course which would enable him, with a clear conscience, to avoid incurring the danger of the stake. As for More, his patience with Roper had at last borne fruit. His fanatical hatred of heresy had stopped short of his own threshold. He had used his influence with Wolsey on Roper's behalf, and had not pressed for his son-in-law to be punished and burned. He was prepared to lie, slander and persecute for the cause of the Church against Lutheranism; but he would not make Meg a widow.

CHAPTER 10

WITH THE EMPEROR
AGAINST FRANCE

In the spring of 1523 Wolsey's renewed two-year term as Legate *a latere* again expired; and the Bishop of Durham, Ruthall, who had once been Wolsey's patron and later his secretary, died on 4 February. Wolsey thereupon wrote to Clerk, the English ambassador in Rome, and instructed him to ask the Pope to appoint him Legate for life and Bishop of Durham in Ruthall's place; he would then resign his bishopric of Bath and Wells in favour of Clerk. There was a good deal of opposition among the cardinals at the Papal Court, particularly to the request for a legacy for life in place of the usual two years' extension, for it was obvious that Wolsey wanted this so that he would be freed from the necessity of asking the Holy See for a favour every two years. The Pope was reluctant to give up this bargaining weapon.

Eventually, after much argument and gifts to cardinals, the Pope agreed to appoint Wolsey as Legate for another five years; to create him Bishop of Durham; to create Clerk Bishop of Bath and Wells, with a dispensation for non-residence so that he could continue as the ambassador in Rome; and to waive the whole of the annates payable both on Durham and on Bath and Wells. Cardinal Medici wrote to Henry and Wolsey apologising for his failure to obtain the legacy for life, but protesting that he had done his best and had got everything that was possible.[1]

But the Papal Legate the Cardinal Archbishop of York, Bishop of Durham, Abbot of St Albans and Lord Chancellor of England, was largely preoccupied with diplomatic and military affairs in the spring of 1523. He was methodically and relentlessly proceeding with his plans for the total destruction of François I and an independent France by a great campaign in the summer which was to dwarf the destructive raids of the previous autumn. An English army of 15,000 men, under the command of the Duke of Suffolk, would land at Calais, where they would be joined by 6,000 German mercenaries sent from the Netherlands by Margaret of Austria, and paid for by Margaret with money lent to her by Henry VIII. At the same time, the emperor would invade Guienne from Spain with 15,000 Spanish troops, whom he would equip and victual with the money that he had already borrowed from Henry. With the help of the Cardinal of Sion and English money, Swiss mercenaries would be raised and sent to join the emperor's armies in Italy, where they had already captured Milan, though there were no immediate plans for an invasion of France from Italy in 1523.[2]

Wolsey was meanwhile working to separate France from her only two allies, Scotland and Venice. The Scots were to be terrorised into banishing the Duke of Albany and repudiating the alliance with France by a series of destructive raids across the Border. Wolsey could not deal so easily with Venice, but here, too, he had means of pressure available to him. The Venetians were allied to France because they were the enemies of the emperor owing to their quarrel about the ownership of the frontier town of Verona; but while remaining allied to the emperor's enemy, they hoped to preserve a friendly neutrality towards the emperor's ally, England. They had done this successfully for the past fifteen years owing to the mutual interest of England and Venice in continuing their trade relations.

Henry and Wolsey had for long been urging the Venetians to break with France, but in 1522 they began to apply the pressure much more seriously. They invited Venice to join the anti-French alliance and offered to mediate in the Venetians' disputes with the emperor. The Venetians agreed to allow Pace to come to Venice to mediate and to negotiate an alliance; but they were hoping to play for time, and not to repudiate their alliance with France, or at least not until it was clearer which side was going to win.

When Charles V visited England on his way to Spain in May 1522, Wolsey requisitioned all the Venetian merchant ships at Southampton, telling the Venetian ambassador that they were needed to help transport the emperor and his large retinue to Spain. The Venetians reluctantly agreed, realising that they were hardly in a position to refuse, although they protested that their merchants would suffer considerable inconvenience and loss of profits if their ships had to sail to Spain. But Gattinara, at Winchester, told Contarini, the Venetian ambassador at Charles's court who accompanied Charles on his journey, that the emperor had not asked to have the use of the Venetian ships for his voyage to Spain, and did not need them. The ships remained at Southampton, but Wolsey did not release them from the requisition and allow them to sail home to Venice with their merchandise.

When the Venetian ambassador in London tried to obtain the release of the ships, Wolsey made it clear that they would not be allowed to sail unless Venice repudiated her alliance with France, settled her dispute with the emperor, and joined the anti-French alliance. He adopted a very aggressive attitude towards the Venetian ambassador, saying that the Venetians were not to be trusted and that Venice was the lowest of all the powers of Christendom. Gattinara in Valladolid also applied the pressure, telling Contarini that he knew that if the Venetians did not reach an agreement with the emperor, Wolsey would make this an excuse to confiscate all the Venetian ships and merchandise in England. While the Doge and Senate tried to spin out the negotiations with Pace in Venice, and rejected Wolsey's suggestion that they should pay the emperor 500,000 ducats for Verona, Henry and Wolsey told the Venetian ambassador in London on New Year's Day that they would allow the Venetian ships to sail if the Venetians gave security for 100,000 ducats that they would not help France in the war.

In February 1523 there were momentary hopes that the ships would be released; but Wolsey then said that they would first have to be repaired. Afterwards he said that they could sail with their merchandise, but that they would have to leave their guns behind, as Henry needed them for the coming campaign against France. This would have meant that the ships would be defenceless on their journey against pirates in the Gulf of Genoa and the Turkish navy in the Mediterranean.

Eventually the Venetians, impressed by the strength of the anti-French alliance and unable to resist the pressure from Wolsey, reached an agreement with the emperor by which they paid him 200,000 ducats for Verona in instalments over eight years. On 4 July 1523 the Venetian ships sailed from Southampton after having been detained for more than thirteen months; and on 29 July Venice joined the anti-French alliance. Wolsey made the most of this diplomatic success. He ordered the Lord Mayor of London to celebrate Venice's adhesion to the alliance in the traditional way with bonfires in the streets and the fountains running wine, as if it had been a great military victory.[3]

Wolsey's next target was Scotland. Hearing that François I was sending Albany back to Scotland to attack England from the north, Wolsey sent Thomas Howard, Earl of Surrey, to Newcastle to subject Scotland to the same destruction which he had inflicted on the Boulonnais in the previous autumn. As usual, Wolsey dealt with every detail of the campaign himself. Writing to Lord Dacre, the Warden of the Western Marches, he informed him of his plan for Dacre and Surrey to invade Scotland with 25,000 men carrying with them victuals for eight days, while a fleet manned by 2,000 men would be sent to Leith with more victuals for another eight to ten days. This army could in sixteen or eighteen days destroy Edinburgh or do some other feat which would make the Scots realise what they suffered for the Frenchmen's sake. He told Dacre that he was arranging for nine or ten thousand ten-gallon castrells of beer to be sent to Berwick, which would provide a gallon a day for the 25,000 men. Wolsey's tenants in his diocese of

Durham would be sent to the Border at a wage of eightpence a day with 120 carts and wains, with two horses to carry each castrel. He wrote that the king would not grudge spending thirty or forty thousand pounds for his honour and safety, to protect his ten-year-old nephew, King James V of Scotland, from Albany, and perhaps to sever France and Scotland for ever.[4]

He decided, however, that it was impossible to send this large force to Scotland at the same time as he was sending Suffolk to invade France with the most formidable army 'as hath passed out of this realm at any time this 100 years'.[5] He consoled himself with the destruction of Haddington and Jedburgh, and the devastation of Teviotdale and the Merse and the harvest which should have fed the local inhabitants in the coming months. On 30 August he wrote to Sampson, the Dean of the Chapel Royal, and to Sir Richard Jerningham, who had been sent as ambassadors to the emperor's court at Valladolid. He told them that all Teviotdale and the Merse had been so destroyed

> that there is left neither house, fortress, village, tree, cattle, corn, or other succour for man, insomuch as some of the people which fled from the same and afterward returned, finding no sustentation, were compelled to come into England begging bread, which oftentimes when they eat, they die incontinently for the hunger passed, and with no imprisonment, cutting of their ears, burning them in the face or otherwise, can be kept away. Such is the punishment of Almighty God to those that be the disturbers of good peace, rest and quiet in Christendom.[6]

Albany landed in Scotland, and raised an army to revenge the injuries that the Scots had suffered. But when he sent them to attack Wark Castle, the English Border fortress, on 2 November, they were driven back into Scotland. Surrey boasted to Henry that Albany had not done ten shillings' worth of damage in England.[7]

François I, defeated in Scotland, deserted by the Venetians, and threatened with invasion on three sides, was about to suffer an even heavier blow, which Henry, Wolsey and the emperor hoped would be the knock-out blow. In the spring of 1523 the Duke of Bourbon, High Constable of France, made secret approaches to Charles and offered to betray François, to come over to Charles's side, bringing with him several powerful nobles and 10,000 soldiers, and to start a rebellion against François in France. In return, he asked Charles to give him his sister in marriage with a dowry of 100,000 crowns. When Charles received this very secret proposal from Bourbon, he encouraged him with a favourable reply without definitely committing himself. He decided not to tell Henry and Wolsey anything about it. But Bourbon told them, without telling Charles that he had done so. Charles's ambassador in England, who had been let into the secret but had been told not to tell Wolsey, was taken aback when Wolsey began to discuss the matter with him.

Bourbon, who ought to have been the Allies' trump card, was to be the cause of much dissension and suspicion between them. He was expecting to be rewarded for his treason by Charles; but the Allies had agreed to make Henry king of France after the defeat of François, and Bourbon would therefore become Henry's subject, not Charles's. Henry and Wolsey suspected from the beginning that Charles planned to use Bourbon for his own advantage, and not to benefit Henry. They insisted that before Bourbon's services were accepted, he must swear allegiance to Henry as king of France. They sent Sir John Russell, a gentleman from Dorset who had won Henry's favour and thirty years later became the first Earl of Bedford, to contact Bourbon in his province of the Bourbonnais. Bourbon agreed to become Henry's subject as part of his deal with Charles, while Henry promised to include him as a party in any peace treaty that he made with François. But Henry and Wolsey were still suspicious, especially after Dr Knight, their ambassador to the Netherlands, passed on to them the report of a spy who revealed that Bourbon was in fact planning, after François's overthrow, to double-cross Henry and make himself king of France.[8]

Henry and Wolsey were in a good bargaining position about Bourbon, because they knew that both Bourbon and Charles relied on them for money. Apart from the immensely wealthy king of Portugal, who remained neutral and avoided the expense of wars while he accumulated the treasure which he obtained from the East Indies, Henry was the richest king in Europe. He was also the only one of the allied sovereigns whose system of government made it possible for him to fight wars with armies raised from his own subjects without engaging foreign mercenaries. The emperor, Margaret of Austria and the Italian dukes relied on him for money to pay their mercenaries and in other ways to finance their wars.

This money had to be raised by taxing the English people. The English, with their hatred of foreigners, especially of the French, could be relied on to give enthusiastic support for the war; but the merchants and property-owning classes were reluctant to pay too high taxes. A great deal of money would be eagerly given; but a demand for too much would provoke resistance. Wolsey was conscious of this when Parliament was summoned to meet at Westminster in April 1523 for the purpose of voting money for the war.

If the MPs were to be persuaded to vote the money, it was more than usually important to have a reliable man as Speaker of the House of

Commons. Henry and Wolsey chose More for the post. The Speaker, then as now, presided as chairman over the debates in the House, but this was not his most important duty. His office, as the name implied, was to be the spokesman of the MPs in their negotiations with the king. He was always elected by the MPs from one of their number, but it was a long-established rule that the king had to approve of the member who was chosen as Speaker. Recently it had become the practice for the king to choose the man he wanted as Speaker, and virtually to force the MPs to elect him. A generation that had seen the hated Dudley elected as Speaker and acting in the office as the mouthpiece of Henry VII's oppressive government, did not expect the Speaker to stand up for the liberties of the House of Commons against the Crown, and it was not until nearly a hundred years after More's death that any Speaker ventured to do this.

It was arranged that More should be elected as an MP – he was probably returned unopposed for the City of London – and he was duly chosen as Speaker after he had made the conventional speech saying that he considered himself unworthy to hold the office, but eventually yielding to the wishes of the MPs and the king and agreeing to accept it. Everyone knew that this was play-acting, but a more serious deception was about to be practised on the MPs. The session was opened by Henry's speech from the throne in the House of Lords, after which Tunstal, now Bishop of London and Master of the Rolls, told the Lords that Parliament had been convened to vote money for the war. Wolsey then spoke about the war at greater length. 'His Highness is comen unto the wars', he said,

> not by any will or appetite which His Grace hath thereto, but only by extreme constraint, enforce and necessity; as well for the guarding of his honour and the reputation of this his realm as also for the conservation of his oath and promise made to the Emperor, his good brother, nephew and ancient ally, and for the revenging of such injuries, breaches of amities and promises, with non paying of his annual tribute and detaining of his rights from him, by his ancient enemy, the French King; and semblably, for violation of the peace which was concluded with the Scots.[9]

Having assured them that His Grace was confident that with the help of Almighty God and the prayers of the MPs he would win a great victory over the enemy, he proceeded to ask them for money.

The MPs in the House of Commons made patriotic speeches about the age-old duplicity of Frenchmen and Scots and the need to teach them both a lesson; but they were reluctant to vote all the money that

Wolsey asked for. Speeches against the tax demands were made in the House. At that time, and for many years afterwards, the public were not admitted to hear the debates, and no report of the proceedings was allowed to be published; but news of the opposition in the House of Commons leaked out, and was spoken of in the streets and taverns. This annoyed Henry and Wolsey even more than the reluctance of the MPs to vote the money. Wolsey decided to apply some pressure. Both as Lord Chancellor, Archbishop of York, Bishop of Durham and Abbot of St Albans he was entitled to sit and speak in the House of Lords, but he had no right to enter the House of Commons. He nevertheless went down to the House of Commons with his usual escort of retainers and armed guards and demanded admission. This angered the MPs. Some of them insisted that while they would admit Wolsey and listen to what he had to say, they would not allow him to enter escorted by his armed retinue.

What part did the Speaker, Sir Thomas More, play in this conflict? It seems clear from the conflicting versions given by Roper and in Wolsey's letters to Henry that it was a subtle and devious one. According to Roper, he persuaded the MPs to admit Wolsey's armed escort by pointing out that if they were compelled to agree to Wolsey's demands, the presence of the escort would give them a good excuse if their constituents criticised them for their compliance. Roper then proceeds to tell how Wolsey scolded the MPs for their reluctance to vote the money and for having leaked news of their opposition to the public outside the House, but that his harsh words failed to overawe More or the MPs, and in the end Wolsey was compelled to accept a lesser sum than his original demand.

Roper is certainly right on this point. In view of the initial opposition in the House of Commons to the demand for money, Parliament was prorogued in April after a few days and did not reassemble until 31 July. In the meantime, negotiations took place behind the scenes in which the Speaker was active. When Parliament reassembled, the House of Commons agreed to a bill imposing a tax of one shilling in the pound on all English subjects and two shillings in the pound on all aliens resident in the kingdom. The bill became law, and Parliament was dissolved a few days later without having voted the full sum that Wolsey wanted.

Roper says that Wolsey blamed More for this, and was very angry with him. He summoned More to his new house in York Place, which later became known as Whitehall, and said to More that he wished that More had been in Rome instead of thwarting him in London. More commented that he, too, would have preferred to have been in Rome, and changed the subject, saying that he preferred the gallery there in York Place to Wolsey's gallery at Hampton Court. Wolsey, says Roper, then proceeded to revenge himself on More by persuading the king to appoint him as ambassador to Spain, knowing that More did not wish to leave his home and family; but More appealed to Henry, who excused him from going to Spain.[10]

Roper's account of this incident is the foundation of the oft-repeated story which was the subject of a picture by Vivian Forbes that since 1927 has adorned the walls of St Stephen's Hall in the Houses of Parliament and was used as the MPs' official Christmas card in 1979. In this story, More is seen as the hero who maintains the rights of the House against Wolsey and the Crown; but Wolsey's letters tell a different tale. They strongly suggest that More collaborated with Wolsey in a clever piece of trickery; that Wolsey, like a shrewd negotiator, asked for more than he wanted; and that More, after a suitable delay, persuaded the MPs to vote the sum that Wolsey really needed.

On 24 August, after the dissolution of Parliament, Wolsey invited More to Hampton Court and gave him a letter to take to Henry, who was at his house at Easthampstead in Berkshire. In the letter, Wolsey reminded Henry that it was usual, when Parliament was dissolved, to give the Speaker a gift of £100 as a reward for his services, but that in view of the 'faithful diligence' which More had shown in the recent Parliament in obtaining the grant of the money, he suggested that on this occasion More should be given an additional gift of £100, making £200 in all. 'I am the rather moved to put Your Highness in remembrance thereof,' he wrote, 'because he is not the most ready to speak and solicit his own cause.' More was one of the few courtiers who was not out to line his own pockets. Unlike the others, he did not make suit for himself. He aimed, not at his own profit, but to be the king's servant, though God's first; and on this occasion he had served the king well. Henry agreed to Wolsey's suggestion, and More received the £200, which was of course worth about £100,000 in terms of 1982 prices.[11]

In view of this letter, Roper's story of More persuading the MPs to admit Wolsey's armed guards must be seen in a different light. As was to be expected, More's role as Speaker was to help, not hinder, the aims of Henry and Wolsey and to get the MPs to admit Wolsey and his retinue and vote the money. It is more difficult to accept the rest of Roper's story, with his account of Wolsey's resentment against More. Some of More's biographers have believed it, and thought that Wolsey, overcoming his initial irritation, afterwards changed his mind and urged Henry to pay More the £200; but everything we know about both Wolsey and More makes this unlikely. There seems little doubt that Roper, writing twenty-five years after Wolsey's death and twenty years after More's, when Wolsey's reputation was low with both Catholics and Protestants, imagined the story about Wolsey's resentment, perhaps confusing it with More's earlier resistance in Parliament to the royal demand for taxation in Henry VII's reign.

With Ruthall dead and Pace in Venice, Wolsey had lost his two most important assistants, for Ruthall had acted as his secretary and Pace as Henry's. He and Henry appointed Brian Tuke and More to take their place. More had shown, during the last few months, as the author of *Answer to Luther* and as the Speaker, his ability and his readiness to resort to any means, however questionable, in the king's service. He was given his new position a fortnight after the dissolution of Parliament, at the same time as he received his reward of £200. He became the most important instrument of English foreign policy after the king and the cardinal, though he was never more than a top-level executive of the decisions which Henry and Wolsey took.

In the late summer of 1523 Henry went on his usual progress through Surrey, Berkshire and Oxfordshire, while Wolsey stayed nearer London at his country houses at Hampton Court and The Moor near Rickmansworth. More went with the king and acted as his secretary at Easthampstead, Woking, Guildford, Abingdon and Woodstock, being the only man, apart from Henry, Wolsey and Tuke, the cardinal's secretary, who saw the confidential communications between the king and Wolsey. His daily duties were to read Wolsey's letters aloud to Henry in the evenings after Henry returned from hunting, either before or after supper, according to the king's inclination, and then to write to Wolsey next day, while Henry was hunting, telling him Henry's wishes and his reaction to Wolsey's letters. More was therefore one of the very few men who was informed at every stage of the secret negotiations with Bourbon and the other military preparations. We can only guess what he thought about the moral aspect of these transactions.

In February 1523 news reached Rome that the Christian Knights of Rhodes had surrendered the island to Soleiman the Magnificent after a long siege, and that Belgrade had fallen to the Turkish army in the Balkans. The Pope was very alarmed at the loss of these two bastions of Christendom in the East, and appealed to all Christian princes to end their internecine quarrels and to unite against the Turk. He proposed that they agree to a three-year truce during which they would go on a crusade against the Turk; if they had not defeated the Turks within three years, the truce would be prolonged until six months after the end of the crusade.[12]

The emperor replied that he could not agree to a truce without Henry's consent; and Henry and Wolsey refused. Their official line was that the quarrels of Christendom were caused solely by the ambition of the French king. A truce would leave him in a strong position to start a new war in Christendom in the future; the proper course was to defeat France first, after which a peaceful and united Christendom could launch the crusade against the Turks.[13] Twelve years later, when More was a prisoner in the Tower, he devoted part of his book *A Dialogue of Comfort against Tribulation* to dealing with the plight of the Christians under Turkish domination in Hungary and the wicked selfishness of the Christian powers who pursued their quarrels and ambitions instead of uniting against the Turk.[14] But in 1523 he played his part in furthering these quarrels, with all their cruelty and deceit, as a true servant of his prince. No wonder that he consoled himself with the thought which he adopted as his text in *The Four Last Things*: 'Remember the last things and thou shalt never sin.'[15]

Wolsey, in his communications with the emperor and his ministers, and in his appeals to Parliament for money, always referred to the preparations to send an 'army royal' to invade France, to be commanded by the king in person or by his Lieutenant. This emphasized the importance of the intended operation, and stirred the enthusiasm of Henry's subjects by conjuring up visions of a more glorious repetition of the campaign of 1513 and of Henry V's triumphs a hundred years earlier. But for Henry and Wolsey the important words in this undertaking were 'or his Lieutenant',[16] for they never intended that Henry himself should command the army. They were too apprehensive of the possible set-backs to risk involving Henry in an operation which might turn out to be a fiasco.

They went ahead with the preparations to send an army to Calais under the command of the Duke of Suffolk; but the delays in the preparations and in consultations between the allies, with the time taken for letters to pass between Henry and Wolsey in London and Charles in Spain, again delayed the beginning of the campaign until the autumn. On 2 July 1523 Sampson and Jerningham signed a new treaty with Gattinara at Charles's court at Valladolid. An English army of 15,000, with Margaret of Austria's 6,000 soldiers from the Netherlands, would invade France and besiege Boulogne before 16 August, while the emperor would invade Guienne from Spain with 20,000 troops. No date was fixed in the treaty for Charles's entry into Guienne, but Gattinara made a verbal promise that it would be before 20 August. Both invasions would be continued at least until 31 October. An even bigger invasion of both Picardy and Guienne under the personal commands of Henry and Charles would take place before 31 May 1524, or, if both princes agreed to postpone it, in the spring of 1525.[17]

Bourbon urged Henry and Charles to pursue a bolder plan. He revealed to them that François was assembling his army at Lyons with the object of invading Italy, and would not be in a position to meet an attack from the north. Henry's army should not waste time besieging Boulogne, but should march straight for Paris by the shortest route.

Bourbon would declare himself for Henry and launch his rebellion against François on the day that Henry's army crossed the French frontier near Calais. Henry's troops should not repeat the burnings and lootings of September 1522, but should proclaim that they came as liberators to free Henry's loving French subjects from François's tyranny.[18]

The plan appealed to Charles and his general in the Netherlands, the Count of Buren, but not to Henry and Wolsey. On purely military grounds, Wolsey believed in the traditional strategy of not leaving a fortified enemy stronghold unsubdued in the rear of an advancing army; and, with his personal experience of the supply problem in 1513, he was conscious of the difficulties of victualling the army if it advanced rapidly to Paris, especially if they were to follow Bourbon's advice and not pillage from the local inhabitants. He was also very suspicious of Bourbon, and feared that the English soldiers would be used to make Bourbon, not Henry, king of France, and to gain advantages for Charles in the south. It would be much wiser to besiege and capture Boulogne, which would then be incorporated into Henry's realm, and one day, perhaps, sold back to François for good money, like Tournai after 1513.

Henry agreed with Wolsey's point of view. On 12 September More wrote to Wolsey from Woking that despite all the arguments of the emperor and Margaret of Austria and their ministers, Henry was determined to follow his advice. He was not prepared to abandon the plan to besiege Boulogne and instead to send his army, for Charles's benefit, into a distant land where it would be difficult to obtain provisions. 'His Grace saith that Your Grace hit the nail on the head', wrote More, 'where ye write that the Burgundians would be upon their own frontiers to the end our money should be spent among them, and their frontiers defended, and themselves resort to their houses'.[19]

But Suffolk and Buren found that Boulogne was better defended than they had expected, and that the weather prevented the English navy from carrying out the planned attack on the town from the sea. Buren therefore pressed Suffolk to abandon the siege and march on Paris, and Charles and Margaret of Austria renewed their pressure on Henry and Wolsey to permit this.[20] They persuaded Wolsey to agree to try out Bourbon's plan, but Henry was more reluctant. On 20 September More wrote to Wolsey from Abingdon that Henry was doubtful if the march on Paris would be as easy as was suggested, because of the victualling problem. Nor did he think that François would linger in the south and plan an invasion of Italy while Suffolk and the allies were advancing in the north. 'His Grace thinketh that the French King is not unlikely to do as His Highness would himself if he were in (as our Lord keep him out of) the like case; then would he appease his own realm ere he would invade another', and would turn and crush Bourbon first. Henry was also sceptical about the feasibility of following Bourbon's advice and ordering the soldiers to refrain from burning and looting, for if they were not to be allowed any spoil, Henry thought it would be hard to keep them from crying 'Home, home!'[21]

But Henry eventually agreed, and at last, on 19 September – late in the year to start a campaign – Suffolk crossed the French frontier near Ardres, and three days later linked up with Count Isselstein, the commander of Margaret of Austria's forces. Within a month they had advanced over a hundred miles into France, passing to the east of Amiens and capturing the towns in the neighbourhood of St Quentin. Henry was delighted when he heard the news at Woodstock. On 30 October More wrote to Wolsey, telling him of Henry's pleasure at the unresisted entry of his armies into the bowels of France and the likelihood of his obtaining his ancient rights to the French crown. He attributed the success to Wolsey's planning and preparations of money and supplies, which had brought results which he would not have thought possible. After taking Braye and Montdidier, Suffolk and Isselstein crossed the Somme near Bouvain on 4 November and were within sixty miles of Paris.

Contrary to his promise, Charles had not moved into Guienne, but had kept his Spanish armies camped on the frontier at Narbonne. Bourbon's rebellion had also gone wrong. A few days after Bourbon's secret meeting with Russell, just before Suffolk's army left Calais, one of Bourbon's pages betrayed his plans to François I. François, who was at Grenoble, summoned Bourbon to come to him; but Bourbon, realising that the plot had been betrayed, escaped in disguise to the emperor's territories in northern Italy. This was very unsatisfactory for Henry and Wolsey; if Bourbon was with Charles's armies in Genoa, he would more than ever be Charles's man, not Henry's.

In Paris, the people prepared to defend the city against the attack by Suffolk's army. On 31 October the Duke of Vendôme entered Paris with his forces, proclaimed Bourbon a traitor, and fortified the defences. But Suffolk's army found that they had no supplies beyond the Somme. As the winter set in, the carts carrying provisions from the Netherlands were bogged down on the road; and the authorities in the Netherlands refused to send money along the dangerous and unguarded roads so far from their frontier. There was a heavy frost in the middle of November, and there was no adequate shelter. Over a hundred of Suffolk's soldiers died of cold and sickness in two days. The frost was soon followed by a thaw which made the roads impassable for the artillery and the supply carts. Isselstein insisted on re-crossing the Somme, capturing Guise and a few French towns further east for effect, and then retreating for the winter to Valenciennes on the frontier of the Netherlands. Suffolk led his army back to Calais.[22]

Henry and Wolsey had another disappointment in store for them. On 30 September, when the good news of Suffolk's advance was coming in, a courier from Rome reached Wolsey at The Moor and informed him that the Pope had died on 14 September. Adrian VI had been a disappointment to Charles, Henry and Wolsey, for he had been a far less zealous supporter of the anti-French alliance than his predecessors, and had repeatedly issued rather annoying appeals to them to make a truce with France and go on a crusade against the Turks. Within an hour of receiving the news of Adrian's death, Wolsey wrote to Henry at Woodstock, telling him that though he thought he was unworthy to fill the Papal chair, and would prefer to continue in Henry's service rather than to be ten popes, yet, knowing Henry's eagerness for him to obtain the Papacy, he was writing to the ambassador and to his friends in Rome and would spare no effort to make sure he was elected. He instructed Clerk and Pace, who was still in Italy, to urge the cardinals to vote for him, or, as a second-best, failing him, for Cardinal Medici, who would be a reliable supporter of Charles against François. Next day, Wolsey sent Henry a draft of a letter to the emperor, which he asked Henry to copy out in his own hand, requesting Charles to order his ambassador and his cardinals in Rome to work for Wolsey's election.[23]

On 4 October, Wolsey wrote from Hampton Court to Clerk and Pace. He told them that as both the king and the emperor were determined that he should be Pope, he had agreed to comply with their wishes. Clerk and Pace were to point out to the cardinals the great experience which he had in dealing with the problems which confronted Christendom; the great favour in which he stood with the emperor and other princes; his generosity; his frank, pleasant and courteous inclinations; his freedom from all ties of family and party faction; and the number of wealthy benefices which he held and which would become vacant and available for his supporters if he were elected Pope. If he were Pope, he would launch a great crusade against the Turk, for in that case Henry would come to Rome and proceed from there to the crusade; he was sure that, in view of his international influence, many more princes would be likely to join the crusade than if anyone else were Pope. Knowing the resentment which had been caused by Adrian's delay in leaving Spain after his election in the previous year, he promised that if he were chosen he would be in Rome within three months. He ended by instructing Clerk and Pace to be liberal in their promises, and not to refrain from any reasonable offers, especially to the younger men, who were usually the most needy.[24]

But the cardinals in Rome again hurried on the conclave before there was time for the foreign sovereigns to bring their influence to bear. It began on 1 October, the day after Wolsey received the news of Adrian's death. Although Charles told Henry and Wolsey that he had ordered his ambassador in Rome to work for Wolsey, he held up his letter to the ambassador until it was too late to influence the result, and the ambassador's influence was used in Cardinal Medici's favour. The cardinals were in conclave for forty-nine days before they reached a decision. Medici had strong support from the beginning, and though the determined opposition to him seemed to make his election impossible, his main rival, Cardinal Colonna, the French nominee, aroused equally strong opposition. Colonna, realising that he could not win, tried to persuade the pro-French cardinals to choose Cardinal Jacobizzi as a compromise candidate; but they rejected his proposal. Cardinal Monte at one time came near to success, but he, too, failed. Eventually, after the cardinals' diet had been reduced to bread and water and the population of Rome had made violent demonstrations of protest against the delay, Cardinal Medici was elected on 18 November and took the name of Clement VII.[25]

No one in the conclave had even proposed Wolsey as a candidate. On 2 December Clerk and Pace wrote to Wolsey, telling him that though his friends had tried to propose him, the cardinals would not hear of it, and insulted those who ventured to mention the possibility.[26] Thus Wolsey lost what was to be his last chance of becoming Pope and of reaching a position where he would have been safe out of the reach of Henry's power in 1529 and 1530. We may be sure that this was a factor which did not occur to him in 1523. He comforted himself, and Henry, with the thought that the new Pope was their second choice, and a staunch friend of the emperor and the anti-French alliance.[27] The election of Clement VII was yet another diplomatic set-back for François I.

But there was no sign that the final defeat of France was imminent. Nearly two and a half years after the signature of the Treaty of Bruges, and eighteen months after the declaration of war, Henry was no nearer to regaining his French kingdom. In January 1524 Wolsey sent new instructions to Sampson and Jerningham at the emperor's court at Vittoria. They were to propose to Charles that he should invade Guienne by May at the latest; if he did so, Henry would again send an army to Calais in June which would march on Paris. Henry would also pay for Bourbon's mercenaries. But Wolsey insisted that Bourbon should invade France from 'this side', and not at the head of Charles's armies from Italy or Spain. He suggested that Bourbon should be placed in command of Margaret of Austria's forces in the Netherlands, as he would be the ideal general to lead the march on Paris in June. In any case, he argued that Bourbon should be sent on a visit to England to discuss future operations with Henry and with him. If Charles would not agree to these proposals, Wolsey suggested that it might be better to make a truce with France rather than to continue incurring the expense of an unprofitable war.[28]

Charles gave no definite reply to these proposals. Instead, he appointed Bourbon commander-in-chief of his armies in Italy. When Henry and Wolsey invited Bourbon to visit England, Bourbon replied that he would like to come, but could not leave his post as the emperor's general in Italy.[29]

It is not surprising that English historians and Wolsey's biographers have excused Wolsey's foreign policy at this time by pointing out the bad faith and broken promises of Charles V. On the other hand, the emperor's biographers have justified his conduct by accusing Wolsey of duplicity and treachery. In fact both Charles and Wolsey were suspicious of each other, and almost from the beginning of the alliance they were both waiting for the opportunity to double-cross their ally.

In February 1524 François I's mother, Louise d'Angoulême, who was much more aware than he was of the great dangers which faced him, made a secret peace approach to Wolsey. She asked him for a safe-conduct for a monk, John Joachim de Vaulx, to visit England to put certain proposals to him. Wolsey granted the safe-conduct, and met the monk. His tactic was to show great reluctance to negotiate and to force the French to commit themselves. He informed the emperor that the French had made proposals without giving him any details of how the negotiations were progressing. He soon sent Vaulx back to France, on the grounds that he had not sufficient authority from Louise d'Angoulême, and that if she wished to negotiate she must send a more highly-placed negotiator with concrete proposals. As a result, Vaulx returned to London in April 1524 with Jean de Brinon, Seigneur of Vienne, who was President of Normandy and Chancellor of Alençon.

Brinon and Vaulx offered large sums of money, but no territory. They offered to pay all the arrears of pensions due during the war to Henry and to Wolsey himself, and to pay new and larger annuities; but they said that François would never agree to cede an inch of French soil. When they asked Wolsey what were Henry's minimum demands, Wolsey replied that they were the whole realm and crown of France, with Normandy, Gascony and Guienne and its dependencies, which were Henry's rightful inheritance. There seemed little room for compromise; but Brinon and Vaulx stayed on in London for a year, lodging in the house of Mr Lark, the brother of Wolsey's mistress, and having periodical meetings with Wolsey at York Place and Hampton Court.[30]

Meanwhile Wolsey was continuing his preparations for the war. On 25 May his representative Docwra, the Prior of the Knights of St John of

Jerusalem, signed an agreement with Praet, the emperor's ambassador in London, by which it was agreed that Bourbon should invade France as soon as possible from Italy, and that the emperor and Henry would each pay 100,000 gold crowns towards Bourbon's costs. The agreement then went on to provide for the supply of 4,000 soldiers by Margaret of Austria and to make other arrangements about money which were to apply if Henry invaded France that summer. These provisions, which did not definitely commit Henry to invade but clearly implied that he would, were inserted by Wolsey in order to deceive Charles; for three days later, Wolsey wrote to Pace in Italy that Henry did not intend to invade France that year, either in person or by his Lieutenant.[31]

In April Bourbon, at the head of an army of Charles's Spanish soldiers and Swiss mercenaries, defeated the French in a campaign in northern Italy in the course of which the heroic French captain, the famous Bayard, was killed. Following this victory, Bourbon crossed the Alps and invaded Provence. Pace was attached to Bourbon's headquarters as Henry's representative. He formed a high opinion of Bourbon's ability and was convinced of his sincerity. But though Henry and Wolsey sent Russell to Bourbon with £20,000 which he needed for his campaign, they remained cool to Pace's appeals to them to help Bourbon by invading northern France while he was engaging François's armies in Provence. While Russell waited in Antwerp, making his arrangements with the bankers, and then travelled slowly through Germany and Switzerland to Italy, Pace, advancing with Bourbon and his army through Provence, wrote to Wolsey telling him that this was the best opportunity that Henry would ever have to regain the crown of France, and urging the king to go at once to Calais with an army; even if Henry did not engage the enemy, his mere presence with an army at Calais would force François to withdraw some of his forces from Provence to meet the threat from the north.[32]

Wolsey wrote him a long reply on 17 July. He told him that the king and council appreciated his zeal and thanked him for his advice, but that, after discussing the matter, Henry and he had decided not to follow it. They thought that Pace had a blinkered view of affairs from Bourbon's headquarters; for their reports from other agents did not confirm Pace's account of the enthusiasm with which Bourbon had been received by the French people. It might help the emperor if Bourbon captured a few towns in Provence, but this would not win the crown of France for Henry; and they would not send an army to Calais until Bourbon ended his coastal operations and marched on Lyons. This brilliant analysis of the military and diplomatic situation as seen from the English point of view reveals the clarity of Wolsey's thoughts, his lucidity in expressing them, and his basic attitude towards Bourbon. He told Pace that there was reason to suppose that Bourbon had offered the emperor Provence, Languedoc and Marseilles, as well as the Bourbonnais and Auvergne; if this were true, Henry's crossing into France would be as profitable for the emperor as for himself. Six weeks later, Wolsey wrote again to Pace: no English army would be sent to invade France till Bourbon had crossed the Rhône and penetrated into the bowels of France.[33]

Bourbon's successes in Provence were checked when he besieged Marseilles and was repulsed, suffering a heavy defeat which sent him back into Italy more quickly than he had advanced. François, convinced that there would be no invasion of France from the north that year, pursued Bourbon into Italy, recaptured Milan, and struck fear in the hearts of the Pope and the Italian dukes. While François himself besieged Pavia, the Duke of Albany, who had left Scotland and had accompanied the king into Italy, led a French army against the Spaniards in the kingdom of Naples.

The emperor's ambassador in London, Praet, became increasingly suspicious of Wolsey during 1524. He did not believe that the king and the cardinal had any intention of invading the north of France, and was worried by the prolonged stay in London of the two envoys from France.[34] On 3 January 1525 he wrote to Charles about his anxieties. He wrote that Wolsey's influence with Henry and his power in England had never been greater, and he urged Charles to make sure that there was no delay in paying the pensions which Wolsey had been granted from the Spanish bishoprics. He suggested that it might also be advisable to give pensions to two or three other counsellors who were now high in Wolsey's favour, particularly Tuke and Sir Thomas More.[35]

Praet wrote again to the emperor on 19 January, strongly criticising Wolsey's vanity and ambition, and stating that there was good reason to believe that he had been in secret communication with Louise d'Angoulême throughout the war.[36] Praet gave his letter, as usual, to Tuke, who always arranged to send his despatches to Margaret of Austria in the Netherlands and to Charles in Spain by the diplomatic couriers.

But Praet was not sure that he could trust Tuke to transmit the letters to Charles. On 10 February, hearing that one of the Fuggers' banking agents was travelling from England to Spain, he gave him some letters that he had written to the emperor and to several of his ministers, and asked the agent to take them with him when he sailed from Plymouth to Spain. Next day another of the Fuggers' agents left London for Plymouth, and Praet gave him more letters for the emperor and his ministers.

The Fugger man left London that evening on the road to the west. But the Privy Council had ordered that one of the periodical patrols by the watch should be held that night, to intercept any persons who were out on the streets, to inquire as to their business, and to arrest them if they could not give a satisfactory explanation. The Fuggers' agent was stopped on the road near Brentford. He protested that he was travelling on the emperor's business, but was searched, and Praet's letters to Charles were found on him. The captain of the watch could not read, but called a local clerk, who could read enough to see that the letters were in French and addressed to the emperor. The captain of the watch decided that the matter was beyond his competence, and that he had to refer it to higher authority. He took the indignant Fugger agent, with his letters, to Sir Thomas More's house in Chelsea.

More was in bed asleep, but was awakened to deal with the problem. He questioned the Fugger agent, who told him that the letters were diplomatic despatches from the emperor's ambassador to the emperor. Despite the agent's protests, More opened the letters and read them. He ordered that the agent should be detained at his house, and early next morning sent the letters to Wolsey. The cardinal was sitting that morning in the Court of Chancery conducting judicial business, but More thought the matter sufficiently urgent to send the letters to him as he sat on the bench. As it was clear, from the letters, that another Fugger agent had left London on the previous day carrying other letters from Praet to the emperor, Wolsey sent officers riding to the west to intercept him at Plymouth or Bristol or at whatever port he intended to embark, to stop him from sailing, and to seize Praet's letters to the emperor.

Next day Praet was summoned to appear before the Privy Council, where he was confronted with Wolsey, the Duke of Norfolk (the former Earl of Surrey, who had recently succeeded to his father's title), the Marquess of Dorset, Tunstal, More and Tuke. Wolsey did all the talking. He accused Praet of writing lying reports to the emperor which were designed to cause ill will between the emperor and Henry, and said that in doing this, Praet had contravened his duty as an ambassador and had committed offences against the laws of England for which he deserved to be punished. Wolsey added that, despite this provocation, he and Henry would not abandon their friendship with the emperor, but that he would inform the emperor of Praet's misconduct and would ask for him to be recalled. Praet protested that the seizure and opening of his letters to the emperor was a violation of his diplomatic immunity, and stated that it was his duty to report to the emperor whatever he thought best, for which he was not answerable to the English government. Wolsey then ordered him to remain in his house, and forbade him to ask for an audience with Henry or himself or to communicate with the emperor or Margaret of Austria. Praet nevertheless succeeded in smuggling out a letter to Charles on 25 February, in which he told him what had happened. He warned the emperor that his prestige would suffer greatly if he allowed Wolsey to insult his ambassadors in this way, and urged him to hold Sampson and Jerningham as hostages at his court until Praet had been allowed to leave England.

In the meantime Wolsey, thinking that he had prevented Praet from writing his account of the incident to Charles or Margaret, wrote to the English ambassadors in Spain and the Netherlands, telling them that by a lucky chance the officers of the watch had intercepted letters from Praet which gave Charles a totally untrue account of Wolsey's negotiations with the French envoys and made unfounded accusations against him. Margaret of Austria, who liked Wolsey and was conscious above all of the need to preserve the trade between England and the Netherlands, wrote to Henry and Wolsey apologising for Praet's conduct and promising that he would be recalled and punished. Charles took a very different attitude. He was indignant at Wolsey's action. He wrote a letter to Praet, which he smuggled to him by a secret courier, telling him that he approved of his conduct and deplored Wolsey's, but that he would have to dissemble for the moment and postpone his revenge. He was therefore recalling Praet, as much for his own safety and comfort as for any other reason, and was sending a new ambassador to England. He added that he wished it were possible to punish Wolsey.

Wolsey sent Sampson and Jerningham a report on the interception of Praet's letters. It was more or less the same as the story that the Fugger agent told Praet, except that, according to the official English version, More was not in bed asleep when the letters were seized, but was out with the watch in the vicinity, and was called by the officer who had stopped the Fugger agent when he realised that he was carrying letters written in French. This detail perhaps reflects the different interpretations of the incident by Wolsey and Praet. While Wolsey claimed that Praet's courier had been intercepted by a lucky chance, Praet believed that Tuke had opened and read his earlier correspondence with the emperor, and that Wolsey, knowing that Praet was writing hostile reports about him, planted the watch on the road to the west with express instructions to intercept Praet's courier. This is almost certainly wrong, for we know that on 8 February the Privy Council had ordered that one of the periodical watches should patrol the roads on the night of 11 February.[37]

Wolsey would probably not have ventured to affront the emperor by seizing his ambassador's despatches if he had not known that the tide of war had suddenly turned against Charles, and that François I, after driving back Bourbon from Marseilles and recapturing Milan, was threatening to overrun all Italy. But the fortunes of war changed again.

On 6 March 1525 news reached London that on 24 February Bourbon had defeated and annihilated the French army at Pavia, and had taken the French king prisoner. Wolsey heard the news when he was on the point of holding another meeting with the French envoys in London. When he met them, he told them that their king had been captured at Pavia, and immediately stiffened his attitude in the negotiations. He said that unless they agreed at once to pay all the indemnity and arrears of pensions which he was demanding, Henry would cut off the heads of the French hostages in England and send them to France in a bag. Brinon and Vaulx were severely shaken by the news, but refused to be stampeded into agreeing to Wolsey's demands.[38]

Henry and Wolsey could not openly show how annoyed they were to hear of Bourbon's victory at Pavia. They both wrote to congratulate Charles on the victory that God had given him, and ordered great celebrations to be held all over England, with bonfires, the fountains running wine, processions, the ringing of the bells in the parish churches, and a Te Deum in St Paul's attended by the king and queen, with Wolsey celebrating a mass which automatically absolved all who were present from their sins. There were additional celebrations of the fact that Richard de la Pole – 'White Rose', the Yorkist pretender to the throne – had been killed fighting for the French at Pavia.[39] But after Pavia, Charles held the whip hand, and knew it. Bourbon kept François a prisoner for three months at Pizzighettone near Piacenza, and then sent him by sea to Spain. Charles imprisoned him in Madrid. With François his prisoner, Charles no longer bothered to plan any future military campaigns or to make any effort to please his English ally who had failed to support him in the campaign of 1524 and had intercepted his ambassador's letters. He treated François with honour, but made it clear that he would not release him until he agreed to cede to Charles the old provinces of Burgundy which France had acquired in 1482, as well as castles and territory in Flanders and Artois on the frontier of the Netherlands. He did not insist that François should surrender the crown of France to Henry or give any concessions to England.

In March, Henry and Wolsey made what was almost a routine proposal to the emperor's ambassador for a joint campaign by Henry and Margaret of Austria's mercenaries in the north, and of Charles in the south, against France in the summer of 1525, while the French king was a prisoner in Spain, and to put Henry on the throne of France in his place; but Charles replied that he did not wage war against a prisoner. Privately, Gattinara told Contarini that Charles cared very little for Henry and did not mind if Henry gained no advantages from the peace treaty. In May Charles complained to the English ambassadors that he had heard that Wolsey had spoken abusive words about him to Praet, though he was prepared to believe that Wolsey had spoken only in anger, as he had heard that he had a fiery temper.[40] Charles had not repaid any of the money that he had borrowed from Henry in 1522, and the pensions payable to Wolsey from the Spanish sees were in arrears.

While Charles was bargaining with his royal prisoner in Madrid, Wolsey was bargaining with Louise d'Angoulême's envoys in London. Eventually Charles and Wolsey, who for nearly four years had been waiting for the opportunity to stab each other in the back, did so almost simultaneously in the summer of 1525. Charles decided to break his engagement to marry Princess Mary, and instead to marry the king of Portugal's sister, Princess Isabel; for the king of Portugal was offering him a dowry of 900,000 Castilian gold doubles, more than twice the dowry which Henry had agreed to give with Mary. On 3 June the Spanish Parliament, the Cortes in Madrid, formally petitioned Charles to marry the king of Portugal's sister, and offered to vote him money if he agreed.

On 7 June Charles's new ambassadors in London, whose instructions must have been sent off from Charles's court at Toledo at least a fortnight before, asked Henry to expedite the date of Mary's marriage to Charles, to send her to his territories without delay, and to pay immediately a first instalment of 200,000 ducats of her dowry, and a further 400,000 ducats in four months' time, with which Charles would be able to finance an invasion of France from both Spain and Italy. Henry and Wolsey had no intention of paying another 600,000 ducats to a debtor who had defaulted in his previous repayments. They offered to release him from his obligation to marry Mary, and leave him free to marry Isabel of Portugal, if he repaid the money that he owed, released Henry from the obligation to make war on France under the Treaty of Windsor, and obtained from the captive François advantageous peace terms for Henry. On 16 August Charles told the English ambassadors that he could not give any firm date for the payment of his debt to Henry, and that it was premature to rescind the Treaty of Windsor while he was still negotiating with François, but that he nevertheless hoped that Henry would release him from his contract to marry Mary so that he could marry Isabel of Portugal.[41]

Meanwhile Wolsey had at last reached agreement with Louise d'Angoulême's envoys. On 27 July Brinon and Vaulx had a long bargaining session with Wolsey at Richmond, where Wolsey had gone to escape the plague in London. They agreed to pay an additional 2,000,000 crowns to Henry to be added to all the other payments due from France to England under the peace treaties of 1475, 1514 and 1518, with all the arrears due under the earlier treaties, which had not been paid since the outbreak of war. The French would pay 50,000 crowns as soon as the peace treaty was signed, and 100,000 crowns per annum, payable on 1 May and 1 November each year, until the whole sum was paid. Wolsey insisted that, in addition to the treaty being signed by Louise d'Angoulême as Regent for her son, it should also be guaranteed by the leading French nobles and by the *Parlements* of Paris, Rouen, Bordeaux and Toulouse, who would undertake to be liable for the payment of the money. Louise d'Angoulême thought that the terms were outrageous, but was sure that she had no alternative but to accept them, and wrote to Wolsey, who had deceived François in 1521 and was the most hated man in France, thanking him for his efforts for peace, and expressing the undying gratitude of the king and herself. She did not limit her gratitude to words, but agreed to pay Wolsey all the arrears due on the pensions paid to him as compensation for his resignation of the bishopric of Tournai, amounting to 121,898 crowns of the sun, payable in seven annual instalments.[42]

The terms were embodied in a peace treaty which was signed at The Moor on 30 August 1525, with Brinon and Vaulx signing for France, and Warham, Norfolk, the Marquess of Exeter, the Earl of Worcester, the Bishop of Ely and More for England. The French ceded no territory, but undertook to pay the enormous indemnity which had been agreed in their meeting with Wolsey on 27 July. On his side, Henry agreed to do all in his power to persuade Charles to release François from captivity. Apart from the payments to Wolsey, several of Henry's other counsellors received annuities under the treaty. More received a pension of 150 crowns of the sun. He had just been appointed Chancellor of the Duchy of Lancaster and High Steward of Cambridge University on the death of Sir Richard Wingfield, who had held both these offices.

The peace treaty was not popular in France, but Louise d'Angoulême managed with considerable difficulty to persuade the four *Parlements* to ratify it. For Henry and Wolsey, it was the beginning of a complete switch in their foreign policy. In the struggle between France and the Empire, England had changed sides.[43]

CHAPTER 11

WITH FRANCE
AGAINST THE EMPEROR

WOLSEY probably devoted more time and more mental and nervous energy to directing English foreign policy than to any of his other duties; but he was also very active in performing the varied functions of the Lord Chancellor. As Lord Chancellor he was the leading member of the Privy Council, and regularly attended the meetings, which were normally held several times a week; he was the chief executive officer of the government, as the king's prime minister; and he also sat every Sunday as a judge in the court of Chancery. He introduced no innovations into the working of the court of Chancery, but because of his energy, his dominating personality, and his great power, the court was much more active in his time than it had been under his predecessors.

The Chancellor's jurisdiction, and his system of equity, had developed as a result of appeals to the king by dissatisfied litigants who petitioned him to remedy the injustices caused by the common law that the king's common law judges had established. The king had ordered his Lord Chancellor to do equity in these cases, and the Chancellor did so by an arbitrary, if beneficial, exercise of royal power. Equity, as the saying went, was 'as long as the Chancellor's foot' – that is to say, it varied with every Chancellor's idea of what was just. This was still true in Wolsey's day. It was not until the end of the seventeenth century that the court of Chancery began to follow settled principles and judicial precedents which in due course made equity as inflexible, and sometimes as unjust, as the common law. So much was the jurisdiction of the court of Chancery regarded as a personal intervention of the Lord Chancellor that for nearly three hundred years after Wolsey the Lord Chancellor was the only judge of the court and heard every case himself. This was a heavy burden for a Lord Chancellor who was also an archbishop, a bishop and an abbot, who as Papal Legate supervised the entire government of the Church throughout England, and who personally directed every detail of his king's internal and foreign policy.

It is not surprising that, despite Wolsey's phenomenal energy and the speed with which he handled business, there were complaints from litigants about the time that they had to wait before he dealt with their cases. He worked incessantly, and the strain affected his health. After 1520, as he approached and passed the age of fifty, he suffered from longer bouts of illness. Once he caught, and survived, the sweating sickness, and there are several references to his being ill with a flux or a fever.[1] He also became increasingly irritable, and more liable to lose his temper with ambassadors. These outbursts of anger were often calculated for diplomatic effect, but strain may have played a part. He sometimes worked himself up into a fury, went red in the face, and so frightened ambassadors that they hardly dared to confront him. But he quickly forgot his resentment, and sometimes congratulated an ambassador who had stood up to him. He once urged the Count of Montmorency, the Great Master of France, to follow the advice which he, as an older man, could give him – that if he had an angry altercation with an ambassador, he should make friends with him as quickly as possible.[2]

In view of the arbitrary nature of the Lord Chancellor's equity, there was no clear distinction between his judicial and his executive acts. This was especially true of a Chancellor as powerful as Wolsey, and so prone to take shortcuts which ignored the legal technicalities. Sometimes he settled disputes by giving judgment sitting in the court of Chancery; but on other occasions he merely dictated a letter to a secretary in his closet at York Place or Hampton Court, ordering a litigant to do what he commanded.

Wolsey's most important decision, as Lord Chancellor, was to use the power of the law and the state against the illegal enclosures of common land which had caused so much resentment among the poorer classes in the countryside. It would be interesting to know whether Wolsey read *Utopia*, with its attacks on enclosures, and if so, how he reacted to it; for on 28 May 1517, five months after *Utopia* was published, he appointed a commission to investigate all enclosures which had taken place since 1485. Next year he ordered a further inquiry to be held, and on 12 July 1518 he issued a decree annulling all enclosures which had taken place illegally, and directing that the land was to be returned to common use. Several wealthy landowners and influential courtiers and dignitaries were fined for having illegally enclosed lands; and Wolsey's first protector, Foxe, the Bishop of Winchester, only escaped a fine by a humble submission to Wolsey. But Wolsey did not succeed in dealing with the evil, and surreptitious illegal enclosures continued.[3]

In the Star Chamber in Westminster, Wolsey exercised the judicial powers of the king's Council, dealing with cases where the gravity of the offence, the importance and position of the defendants, the need for speedy justice, or merely administrative convenience, made it advisable that the council, rather than the ordinary common law judges, should try the case.[4] The energy and efficiency of Wolsey and his subordinates succeeded in enforcing the king's peace throughout most of the realm. Wolsey boasted, with justice, that law and order prevailed in England, where the royal authority was much more firmly established than in many other countries and than it had been in England in earlier times. Only the lawless Border regions in Northumberland continued to be largely outside the king's peace, though from time to time the Wardens of the Marches, at Wolsey's insistence, sent men to seize and hang a few of the worst offenders.[5]

The ecclesiastical courts dealt with offences against the canon law, with wills, and with matrimonial causes. As Archbishop of York, and Bishop of Bath and Wells and later of Durham, Wolsey had a court which dealt with these matters in his dioceses. Ordinarily, the Archbishop of Canterbury's court of Arches was a court of appeal in ecclesiastical causes; but as Legate *a latere*, Wolsey had a legatine court which was above the archbishop's court. This sometimes led to clashes with Warham; but though Warham protested more than once against the encroachments by Wolsey's officers on the jurisdiction of his court of Arches, he always submitted in the end without making too much difficulty, and Wolsey was prepared to offer reasonable compromises to pander to Warham's feelings. Here again, Wolsey did not clearly distinguish between his judicial and executive acts. He dealt with the long-standing dispute between the Earl of Oxford and his wife, who was the Duke of Norfolk's sister, by peremptory orders in letters to both of them to refrain from pestering each other or interfering with each other's property. Both the earl and the countess reacted to these letters by promising, in the most humble and submissive language, to do everything that Wolsey commanded.[6]

The most serious crime which came before the ecclesiastical courts was heresy, which was dealt with by the bishop and his chancellor and ordinary in every diocese, though in Henry VIII's reign the more important heretics were usually tried before special commissioners appointed *ad hoc* to try the case. If, after a hearing and long disputations in the bishop's court or before the commissioners, the defendant was convicted of heresy, the court, in its judicial discretion, could impose some penance and grant the heretic absolution, or it could excommunicate him and deliver him to the civil power for punishment. The punishment was regulated by three Acts of Parliament of the reigns of Richard II, Henry IV and Henry V, of which the Act for the Burning of Heretics of 1401 was the most important. It enacted that when a man or woman was condemned as a heretic and excommunicated by the bishop's court, the sheriff and the JPs of the shire were to burn the heretic alive in some public place in the district.

The usual practice of the ecclesiastical courts, in the first half of the sixteenth century, was to grant absolution to a heretic who had recanted and repented, either before or during his trial, and to order him to 'carry his faggot'. A public ceremony was held at which the heretic appeared, barefoot and dressed in penitential garb, and carrying a faggot of wood on his shoulder, as a reminder of the fire in which he deserved to be burned. He confessed his sin and repudiated his heresy, and a leading churchman preached a sermon against heresy. Sometimes some further penance was imposed, such as a term of imprisonment, or confinement in a monastery. If the heretic refused to recant, he was excommunicated and delivered to the secular arm to suffer death by burning. This sentence was also imposed in the case of a relapsed heretic who had again been guilty of heresy after recanting and carrying his faggot. He was not given a second chance and allowed to carry his faggot again; even if he recanted, he was normally burned.

This combined operation of Church and State against heresy, like so many other aspects of ecclesiastical and secular government, was concentrated in the person of Wolsey. As Archbishop of York and Bishop of Durham, he had jurisdiction over all cases of heresy in his two dioceses; as Legate *a latere*, his supreme ecclesiastical jurisdiction entitled him to try cases of heresy in every part of England; and as Lord Chancellor, he was the head of the secular arm of government responsible for the arrest of suspected heretics and the burning of those convicted and excommunicated in the ecclesiastical courts. Being in absolute control, under Henry, of government policy, it rested with him to decide what attitude would be pursued towards heretics. His policy towards heretics was relatively tolerant. He may have been responsible for the deaths of many soldiers killed in wars and of women and children left to starve to death in their devastated villages in the Boulonnais and in Teviotdale; but he was not responsible for the deaths of heretics.

Ten heretics were burned in Henry VII's reign, and four during the first six years of Henry VIII's. After Wolsey became Lord Chancellor in December 1515, eight heretics were burned between 1517 and 1521 after having been excommunicated by the courts of the bishops of London, Lincoln, and Coventry and Litchfield.[7] No other heretics were burned until after Wolsey fell from power in 1529 and was succeeded as Lord Chancellor by More, after which five heretics were burned during More's two and a half years in office. It is not surprising that no heretics were condemned by Wolsey's ordinaries in his episcopal courts in York and Durham, because heresy never secured a foothold in the north until the end of the sixteenth century, and there is not a single case of a heretic being condemned to be burned in these two dioceses during the whole of the Reformation period; but Wolsey could have used his power as legate to persecute all over the districts in south-east England where heresy was rife, and his power as Lord Chancellor to egg on the secular officers to arrest, and the bishops to condemn, the heretics. He did not intervene to save the martyrs who were burned in London, Amersham and Coventry during his period in office; but he was a restraining influence on the more savage persecutors.

Within a few years of Luther's appearance in Germany, his ideas had taken root in Cambridge among the young priests and students of divinity. These Lutheran sympathisers met secretly at the White Horse Inn in Cambridge. The leader of the group was Robert Barnes, the prior of the monastery of Barnwell in Cambridge. Barnes was closely connected with another prominent Lutheran, Richard Bilney, a Bachelor of Divinity of Trinity Hall in Cambridge, who was actively propagating Lutheran doctrines in Norfolk. There were also many Lutherans among the foreigners of the Steelyard, the organisation in London of merchants from the Netherlands, Scandinavia and the German Hansa towns. But after Wolsey had authorised and participated in the burning of Luther's books in May 1521, and had issued his order banning the importation of Lutheran books into England, he took no further action against Lutherans for nearly five years.

He was more irritated by the personal attacks which the Lutherans launched against him, for his relative tolerance did not prevent them from denouncing his lack of Christian humility, his pluralism and his nepotism, and in singling him out as the supreme example of the corruption of the Church. In 1525 a young barrister of Gray's Inn, Simon Fish, produced a play in the Inn written by William Roy. It was a farce about Wolsey, and Fish acted the part of the cardinal, burlesquing him and ridiculing his pomp and worldliness. Both Roy and Fish thought it wiser to go abroad after the performance. They went to the Netherlands, where Roy met William Tyndale, and helped him print an English translation of the New Testament. Many copies were smuggled into England. In 1526 Roy wrote a poem, *Read me and do not grudge, for I say nothing but the truth*, which was published in Worms but was intended to be read in England, and was read there. In it, he attacked the persecutors of Lutherans, especially Standish, the Bishop of St Asaph, whom he called 'Judas'. He compared Wolsey to Pilate, who found no fault in Jesus but acquiesced while the persecutors persecuted.[8]

On Christmas Eve 1525 Barnes preached a provocative sermon in Cambridge, in which he denounced holy days and the great feasts of the Church. He was arrested and sent to Wolsey in London. Wolsey examined him on twenty-five articles which were charged against him, passing quickly over his denial of the value of prayers to the saints and of holy days and his doctrine of justification by faith, and then referred to an accusation which he took more seriously. Barnes had attacked the pomp of cardinals and bishops, and had called on them to spend their money, not on ostentatious display, but on alms for the poor. Wolsey asked Barnes whether he expected him to disband his retinue of armed guards and spend the money thus saved on alms for the poor, because this would make it impossible for him to provide any government for the commonwealth. Barnes replied that he thought that Wolsey would be a better Christian if he gave the money to the poor, and that he was not capable of judging what was necessary for the government of the commonwealth. Wolsey seems to have been amused by the reply and to have reacted to it not unsympathetically. He told Barnes that he was sending his case to be tried by the bishops, and wished him luck.[9]

Proceedings were taken at the same time against three German merchants from the Hansa towns. On Friday 26 January 1526 More and other members of the Privy Council, accompanied by a substantial bodyguard, forced their way into the headquarters of the Steelyard as the Hansa merchants were sitting down to supper. While his officers stationed themselves at the door and prevented anyone from leaving, More told the merchants not to be alarmed, but said that he and his escort had come because one of the Hansa merchants had recently been imprisoned for clipping the king's gold. The king would not have taken so serious a view of the business were it not for the fact that some of the Hansa merchants in London had been bringing heretical books by Martin Luther and others into the king's realm, 'causing great error in the Christian faith amongst His Majesty the King's subjects, which first arose in the Steelyard'. He interrogated the merchants, seized the keys of the building, and eventually left at midnight, taking with him three of the merchants, who were placed under arrest. He returned next day in the afternoon, and searched every room in the building for heretical books. He then ordered nine of the merchants' chief officers to appear before Wolsey in Westminster and to bring with them a merchant who was suspected of heresy.

The nine leading merchants duly found the wanted culprit, and brought him before Wolsey, who sent him to prison and ordered the nine leaders to give security for £2,000 that no Hansa merchant would leave England for twenty days.[10] The men who had been arrested were examined on 8 February by two bishops (Clerk and Standish), the Abbot of Westminster, and seven canon lawyers, including Stephen Gardiner and Wolsey's solicitor, John Allen, the future Archbishop of Dublin. The defendants were asked whether they acknowledged the jurisdiction of the Legate's court, whether they believed the Pope to be the head of the Church, what they believed about the Real Presence, and whether they had ever eaten meat on prohibited days. Wolsey was not present at their trial, but he attended the examination on the same day of Henry Prickness, the Vicar of All Hallows the Great in London, who had been caught with one of Luther's books. Prickness said that it had been accidentally dropped in his room by a ship's purser at Michaelmas; that the book was in Latin, and that he could not understand Latin; and that he did not know that Luther's books had been burned and banned until after he was arrested.[11]

Barnes and all these heretics recanted, and carried their faggots at a ceremony at St Paul's on 16 February. Wolsey attended with thirty-six bishops and abbots. It had been intended to hold the proceedings, as usual, at Paul's Cross in the churchyard, but as it was raining they took place in the cathedral. Wolsey sat in state on a platform while Fisher preached a sermon against Lutheranism. Barnes was sent back to the Fleet prison, from which he succeeded in escaping six months later. The others were released.[12].

The order which prohibited the Hansa merchants from leaving England caused them inconvenience and disrupted their trade. At the end of the twenty days they had heard nothing further from the authorities, so they asked for an audience with Wolsey, who admitted them to his presence after another eight days had passed. It was obviously not heresy which was chiefly worrying Wolsey, for he reprimanded them for exceeding their privileges by importing into England commodities which were not covered by their licences, and with evading payment of the full customs duties; but after he himself had dealt with these matters, two Chancery lawyers spoke about heresy, and required each merchant to give an undertaking not to deal in Lutheran books. Wolsey then released the chief merchants from their £2,000 bond and removed the restrictions on leaving England. On 3 March the leaders of the Hansa merchants wrote a report of what had happened to the Mayor and Council of Cologne and asked for advice as to what they should do. 'For what the Lord Cardinal said is His Majesty the King's will. Even in case the merchants try to ask the King for some help, still the Lord Cardinal's word will remain supreme.'[13]

Soon afterwards Bilney was arrested and brought before Wolsey. He agreed to recant, and Wolsey did not even send him for trial, but released him after he had sworn an oath not to preach or otherwise advocate Luther's doctrines, but to repudiate them whenever they were discussed in his presence.[14]

The English ambassadors and agents in the Netherlands reported to Wolsey that Tyndale and Roy were printing English Bibles there and smuggling them into England. Tyndale stated that his object in translating the Bible into English was to make it possible for every ploughboy to be as knowledgeable in Scripture as the most learned clerk;[15] but translating the Bible had been officially condemned as heretical by the Church, because it encouraged the discussion and questioning of Catholic doctrine. Wolsey fully accepted the necessity of suppressing Bible-reading as a dangerous and potentially seditious practice, and instructed Hacket, the English agent at Antwerp, to warn the authorities there about Tyndale's activities and to request them to arrest and extradite any English subject who was guilty of heresy.

Tyndale and Roy and their printer were alerted as to what was afoot; and hurriedly left Antwerp on a barge which took them up the Rhine to Cologne, where they continued their printing of illegal English Bibles. Warham bought up the complete stock from the printer, and burned all the copies. As this cost him £66.9s.4d., he asked his fellow-bishops to contribute to the expense of buying them. Tyndale spent the money which Warham paid for the Bibles on printing new ones.[16]

Hacket pursued the English heretics in the Netherlands with great enthusiasm, but found Wolsey less zealous. On several occasions Hacket unearthed a number of heretics among the English merchants in Antwerp and Bergen-op-Zoom, but could not persuade Margaret of Austria's ministers to extradite them. The government of the Netherlands was persecuting Lutherans, but adopted a strictly legalistic attitude to Hacket's demands. They insisted that heresy was not an extraditable offence under the Extradition Treaty of 1505 between England and the Netherlands. If English residents in the Netherlands had been guilty of treason or sedition against the king of England, they would be extradited; if they were guilty of heresy, they would be tried and burned in the Netherlands. The government in Malines therefore asked Hacket to prove that the Englishmen he denounced were guilty of the one offence or the other, and on several occasions Hacket asked Wolsey to send the evidence from England. Wolsey never replied until Hacket had written several times, and then failed to supply him with all the documents that he required. If it had been a question of gaining some diplomatic or military advantage, Wolsey would have dealt with the matter with his usual speed and energy; but extraditing obscure heretics from Antwerp did not interest him very much.[17]

He was much more eager to pursue a great project which appealed to several aspects of his character – his vanity and desire for posthumous glory, his encouragement of culture, and his wish to help the poorer sections of the population. He decided to found a new college at his University of Oxford. With his large revenues, he could have afforded to found the college from his own resources, supplemented perhaps by contributions from wealthy benefactors who would have been willing to pay to win his favour; but he chose a more arbitrary method, which involved no cost to himself. He suppressed a number of monasteries and seized their property in order to give it to the college. He obtained from the Pope the necessary bulls enabling him to suppress any monastery in England, and he set about carrying out his scheme for his college in 1524. The monastery of St Frideswide in Oxford was suppressed; the site of the monastery was taken for the erection of his Cardinal's College, and the monastery's lands and manors were given to the college.

Wolsey's commissioners suppressed twenty-one other monasteries in Staffordshire, Northamptonshire, Oxfordshire, Berkshire, Buckinghamshire, Suffolk, Essex, Kent and Sussex, and gave their revenues to Cardinal's College. In some cases the commissioners found that acts of immorality, or less serious irregularities, had been committed in the monasteries, and this was used as an excuse to suppress them; in other cases, the prior was induced, by promises of favours or veiled threats, to agree voluntarily to dissolve the monastery and to surrender the property to Wolsey for the use of Cardinal's College. The suppressed monasteries between them held 242 manors in seventeen counties, which brought in the income of £2,000 a year which Wolsey wished Cardinal's College to have.[18]

One of the most active of Wolsey's commissioners in the suppression of the monasteries was Thomas Cromwell, an able solicitor and land agent in Wolsey's service. Ten years later, after he had replaced Wolsey as Henry's chief minister, he adopted the same procedure when he set about suppressing all the monasteries in England. He was completing the work which he had begun on the orders of a cardinal and Papal Legate under the authority of the Pope's Bull.

Apart from suppressing monasteries, Wolsey raised money for his college by extracting donations from persons who wished to gain his favour. Priests and other suitors who asked for benefices and favours were told that their requests would be favourably considered if they gave donations to the college. Bishops, abbots and noblemen were asked for contributions, and few of them ventured to annoy the cardinal by refusing. The Abbot of Peterborough was one of the few who did. Wolsey told Longland, the Bishop of Lincoln, that he thought that £400 would be a suitable donation for the abbot to give; but the abbot would not oblige. When Longland pressed him, and hinted that his resignation might be required, the abbot offered 400 marks (£266.13s.4d.) instead of £400. Under further pressure, the abbot agreed to pay 500 marks, but as this was still £66.13s.4d. short of the £400 which Wolsey wanted, Longland forced the abbot to resign.[19]

The suppression of the monasteries caused a good deal of resentment among the monks who found themselves without a home, though in some cases they were given other employment, or compensated by small pensions. At Tonbridge, and at Bayham nearby, the suppression caused disturbances among the people of the district, who were not appeased by Warham's attempts to persuade them that part of the property of the monasteries might be used to found schools in the district, where their sons could be educated.[20] But far more widespread discontent was aroused by the imposition in 1525 of new taxation for the war. This time Henry and Wolsey did not call a Parliament to vote them money, but appealed to the people to contribute to a loan to the king, an 'Amicable Grant' to enable him to sail for France and regain the French kingdom which his ancestors had held. After the news of the French king's capture at Pavia had been celebrated all over England, Wolsey shamelessly ordered the sheriffs and JPs to tell the people that the king and his ally the emperor would invade France in person in the summer to win Henry's French kingdom, although he had in fact decided that no army would be sent to France that year and was making good progress in his secret negotiations with Brinon and Vaulx.[21]

During the summer of 1525 Wolsey received reports from Warham at Otford, from the Duke of Suffolk at Eye, and from the Duke of Norfolk at Norwich, telling him of the opposition in their districts to payment of the Amicable Grant, of the refusal of the local representatives to attend the meetings which had been fixed for them to discuss the grant with the king's commissioners, and, in some cases, of flat refusal to pay any money. Warham found strong opposition in West Kent, although he tried to get the people to contribute by reminding them that the king had been born in Kent, at Greenwich. At Levenham in Suffolk and at Cranbrook in Kent the local inhabitants assembled and agreed amongst themselves that they would not pay. In both places, some of the ringleaders were arrested and charged with conspiracy and sedition; but were released with a warning.[22]

In the disaffected districts, the people blamed Wolsey for the taxes, for the discontent was directed against him personally. It was perhaps with the object of appeasing the unrest and of lessening his personal unpopularity that he issued a new proclamation against illegal enclosures on 14 July 1527. In November he summoned a number of offenders to appear before him in the court of Chancery. In February 1528 he issued another proclamation against enclosures, and in 1529 some enclosures were demolished in Northamptonshire and Kent at his orders.[23]

This did not quench the people's hostility. His power and wealth aroused envy, and seemed to many critics to symbolise the worldly selfishness of the clergy and the evils of pluralism, non-residence and nepotism in their worst aspects. By 1522 the old poet, John Skelton, was writing thinly-veiled attacks on him which circulated in the country, despite Wolsey's attempts to prevent this. Everyone recognised the identity of 'Hough ho', who 'ruleth the ring'; and Skelton wrote quite openly, in his poem *Why come ye not to Court?* asking:

> Why come ye not to court?
> To which court?
> To the King's court,
> Or to Hampton Court?
> Nay, to the King's court;
> The King's court
> Should have the excellence;
> But Hampton Court
> Hath the preeminence.

Skelton denounced the 'base progeny' and 'greasy genealogy' of the 'bragging butcher' who 'carrieth a King in his sleeve'. Wolsey made no serious attempt to suppress these verses which were secretly circulating in manuscripts in the court and elsewhere; instead, he bribed Skelton, by gifts and patronage, to write several poems in which he praised Wolsey in the most fulsome style.[24]

Hampton Court was only one of Wolsey's four splendid residences. By 1525 he also had York Place in Westminster, near Charing Cross, where he built an impressive palace. He had two country houses in Hertfordshire, The Moor and Tyttenhanger, which he held on long leases from his own abbey of St Albans. In the spring of 1525 he assigned his lease of Hampton Court as a gift to the king, but under an agreement whereby he continued to live there; and in exchange the king granted him the use of Richmond Palace. He had his suite of rooms in all the king's palaces, and lived in his rooms at Hampton Court both when the king was and was not in residence there.

It was probably about 1510, when Wolsey was nearly forty and was rising in the king's service, that he began living with the woman who was his concubine, and perhaps his only mistress, for many years. We know very little about her, and not even her Christian name, for she is referred to, in the few surviving documents, as 'the daughter of one Lark', who was probably an innkeeper at Thetford in Norfolk. She had two brothers who entered the Church and obtained several benefices, thanks to Wolsey's influence. One of them, Thomas Lark, became Master of Trinity Hall at Cambridge.

Wolsey and Mistress Lark had an illegitimate son and daughter. The son took the name 'Thomas Winter', and was referred to as 'the Lord Cardinal's nephew'. Wolsey provided him with an excellent education. After spending his childhood at Willesden, he was sent to the Universities of Louvain, Padua and Paris, where several English and foreign notables, including Erasmus, bestirred themselves to help him. The daughter became a nun.

As Wolsey grew too old, too ill and too busy to need the services of Mistress Lark as a concubine, he arranged for her to marry Master Lee, a gentleman and landowner of Adlington in Cheshire. Wolsey was determined to give a good dowry with her, and found a convenient way of doing this. According to his enemies, he summoned Sir John Stanley, the illegitimate son of the former Bishop of Ely, who had been knighted for his valour on the battlefield of Flodden, and ordered him to give some of his lands to Lee as part of Mistress Lark's dowry. When Stanley refused to comply, Wolsey imprisoned him in the Fleet prison for a year, and did not release him until he agreed to grant the lands to Lee. Stanley was so shaken by the experience that he became a monk in Westminster Abbey, and died there soon afterwards.[25]

Thomas Winter must have been about sixteen in 1525 when Wolsey thought it was time to make suitable provision for him. The king had just done the same for his own bastard, the son of his mistress Elizabeth Blount, the daughter of Lord Mountjoy. Henry created him Duke of Richmond and appointed him, at the age of six, to be President of the Council of the North, which exercised the jurisdiction of the Privy Council north of the Trent. The boy was given a miniature royal court, with officials as well as his tutors, at various houses in Yorkshire.

In December 1525, Winter was appointed Dean of Wells, and by March 1526 he had also become Provost of Beverley Abbey, Archdeacon of York, Archdeacon of Richmond, Chancellor of the diocese of Salisbury, a canon of York, Salisbury, and Lincoln cathedrals and of Southwell Abbey, and Rector of Rudby in Yorkshire and of St Matthew's parish in Ipswich. He was under the canonical age at which he was eligible to hold any of these offices; but Wolsey obtained dispensations for him from the Pope for age, pluralities and non-residence. The English ambassador in Rome tactfully reminded Wolsey that it would be necessary for him also to obtain a dispensation on account of his illegitimate birth, and this, too, was duly granted by the Pope.[26]

Wolsey's power and wealth had never been greater, but one source of his income was not coming in as he had expected. Charles V not only defaulted in repaying his debts to Henry, but after the summer of 1525 fell into arrears with the pensions that he had granted to Wolsey from the revenues of the bishoprics of Badajoz, Palencia and Toledo. Charles was very angry with Wolsey. Not only had Wolsey intercepted his ambassador's despatches and made a separate peace with France, but it was becoming clear that he was instigating Louise d'Angoulême to pursue a hostile policy against Charles and to renew the war against him as soon as possible. Charles thought that this was solely due to Wolsey's spite because he had not used his influence to get him elected Pope; but the emperor's repudiation of his marriage contract with Mary was a more important factor. If Mary was not to marry Charles, another match must be found for her, and the obvious solution was to revive the original plan for her to marry into François I's family by a match with François's second son, the Duke of Orleans, or even with François himself, whose queen had recently died. A marriage with France entailed a fundamental revision of English foreign policy, especially as Mary was the heiress to the throne of England and there was less and less likelihood of Catherine of Aragon producing a son.

Wolsey had no intention of waging war against the emperor, and did not wish to take any step which would interfere with the trade between England and the Netherlands which was so essential to both countries; but subject to these limitations, he wished to do all he could to injure Charles and weaken his power. The only place where he could hope to do this was in Italy; and knowing that many of the Italian rulers, including the Pope, were alarmed at the emperor's power in Italy after his victory at Pavia, Wolsey set about forming an alliance of France and the Italian states against the emperor.

Henry and Wolsey now put pressure on the Venetians to do precisely the opposite of what they had bullied them into doing in 1522–3: they urged Venice to make an alliance with France against the emperor. After the Venetians had recovered from their initial surprise at Wolsey's suggestion, they accepted it and made an agreement with Louise d'Angoulême which suited Henry and Wolsey perfectly. France and Venice formed a league for the defence of Italy, and invited other Italian states to join it. France would pay two and two-thirds, and Venice one and one-third, of the costs of any military operations in which the League engaged. Henry would be named as Protector of the League, but this would not be announced until Henry decided that the time had come when it was propitious to do so. To Wolsey's disappointment, the Pope refused to join the League and reaffirmed his friendship with Charles.[27]

There was little that Louise d'Angoulême could do against Charles, despite all Wolsey's encouragement, as long as François was a prisoner in Madrid; but a peace treaty between Charles and François was eventually signed in January 1526, after François had been a prisoner for nearly a year. François agreed to cede to Charles the provinces of Burgundy which France had acquired in 1482, as well as Tournai, Charleroi and other towns on the frontier with the Netherlands. He abandoned his claim to Milan and all territory in Northern Italy, recognising the title to Milan of Charles's protégés, the Sforza family. He engaged to marry Charles's sister, the widowed Queen of Portugal. He agreed to pardon Bourbon for his treason, to reinstate him in his lands in France, and to pay him all the revenues from these lands which had been withheld after his desertion. François was to be immediately released from captivity, but his two sons, the Dauphin and the Duke of Orleans, aged nine and six, were to be sent to Spain to be held there as hostages until François had carried out the terms of the peace treaty. François crossed the Spanish frontier into France, and his children were delivered to the Spanish authorities, on the bridge across the Hendaye River near Fuentarrabia on 17 March. François immediately wrote to Wolsey, thanking him for his efforts to persuade the emperor to release him, and stating that he knew that he owed his freedom entirely to Wolsey. He told the English ambassador that he would honour Wolsey as a father all his life.[28]

Wolsey received similar assurances of devotion from Charles, who, after criticising Wolsey to Sampson and Jerningham, the English ambassadors, in the summer of 1525, decided to dissemble. In January 1526 he told Edward Lee, who had joined Sampson and Jerningham in Toledo, that he had always loved and honoured Wolsey as a father, and that although he had been temporarily alienated from him by certain reports which he had received, he now had no doubts as to his friendship. Wolsey, on his side, wrote to Charles deploring that Praet's misleading reports had caused Charles to doubt his respectful affection for him; but as soon as Henry and Wolsey heard that François had returned to France, they sent Taylor, the Deputy Master of the Rolls, to tell François, speaking not as an ambassador but in his personal capacity as a lawyer, that François was not legally bound to observe his treaty with Charles because he had been a prisoner when he signed it, and because he had been forced to deliver his sons as hostages for the observation of the treaty.[29]

Wolsey's great anxiety was that François would be deterred from acting vigorously against the emperor by his fears for the safety of his sons in Spain. Vaulx came to London to calm Wolsey's fears. Thomas More carried on the negotiations with Vaulx, and on 8 August 1526 More and Vaulx signed a treaty at Hampton Court by which François agreed that he would not secure the release of his sons in Spain by making any agreement with Charles which contravened his treaties with Henry.[30]

In the spring of 1526 Soleiman invaded Hungary with an army of 150,000 men; but Henry and Wolsey remained quite unmoved by the Pope's appeals to them to save Christendom from the Turk. They promised to send financial aid to Hungary, but they refused to take the Turkish menace seriously, and believed that though the Turk might threaten the Habsburg territories, he was no threat to England. In August 1526 Charles's brother-in-law, King Ladislaus of Bohemia and Hungary, was defeated by the Turks at Mohacz, and was drowned in the Danube while escaping from the battlefield. His Hungarian kingdom was overrun by the Turks. Charles's brother Ferdinand succeeded him as king of Bohemia and Hungary; but though he established his authority in Bohemia, power in Hungary was seized by a prominent Hungarian noble, John Zapolya, who proclaimed himself Vaivode of Hungary and established friendly relations with the Turks. Henry and Wolsey supported Zapolya against Ferdinand in order to annoy Charles. They sent Sir John Wallop as an ambassador to Zapolya, and though Wallop was stopped at Wroclaw on Ferdinand's orders and not allowed to proceed to Hungary, Henry and Wolsey succeeded in establishing contact with the Vaivode and encouraged him to do all he could to harm Ferdinand and Charles.[31]

But Italy was the main scene of Wolsey's anti-imperial machinations. Egged on by the English ambassador and by Henry's agents in the college of cardinals, the Pope's Secretary of State, Gilberti, Bishop of Verona, persuaded Francesco Sforza, the Duke of Milan, to break his alliance with Charles V and to unite with the other Italian states to drive the emperor's Spanish troops from Italy and seize Charles's kingdom of Naples, which was to be given to Sforza. In May 1526 a Holy League for the defence of the Papacy between the Pope, Venice, Sforza and François I was signed at the French court at Cognac. Charles was invited to join the League on condition that he released François's sons from captivity; but he had no intention of doing this, as François had taken no steps since his release to perform the terms of the Treaty of Madrid and surrender Burgundy and the towns of Artois and Picardy. In August the Pope issued a bull proclaiming Henry as Protector of the League; but Henry and Wolsey had no wish to be embroiled, and publicly refused to join the League on the grounds that Henry's treaties of friendship with the emperor made this impossible. Privately, Wolsey told the Pope and the Venetians that Henry would join the League as soon as the emperor gave him some excuse to do so; and he promised to send £20,000 to pay the mercenaries employed by the League to fight against the emperor's troops.[32]

The League assembled an army of 20,000 Venetian and Papal soldiers, and, relying on Wolsey's promise of the £20,000, took steps to hire 10,000 Swiss mercenaries. In July the army of the League defeated the emperor's troops at Lodi and captured Milan. But Charles's Viceroy in Italy enrolled the support of the powerful Colonna family and marched on Rome, calling on the Pope to abandon his allies in the League. Although Wolsey urged the Pope and Gilberti to refuse the emperor's peace offers, the £20,000 that he had promised for the mercenaries did not come. As the emperor's troops approached Rome, Giberti wrote desperate letters to Wolsey, appealing for help. In a letter to the Papal Protonotary, Gambara, in September 1526, he complained bitterly of being deserted by Wolsey, and wrote that the king and the cardinal of England would incur everlasting shame if they abandoned the Apostolic See in its hour of need.[33] A few days later, the emperor's troops, supported by the Colonna faction, entered Rome and looted in the city. The Pope retired to his Castle of San Angelo, and signed a four-months' truce with the emperor's viceroy, leaving his allies in the League to continue operations by themselves.

Henry and Wolsey, realising that the League would collapse unless something was done, sent Sir John Russell to Italy with the £20,000 that they had promised. When Russell reached Rome on 6 February 1527, Cardinal Campeggio wrote to Wolsey that Henry, by sending the money, had shown that he was God's blessing to the Holy See. Giberti wrote to Wolsey that Russell's arrival had saved the Church from the worst tempest in which it had been tossed, and pleased the loving parent by enclosing a renewal of the dispensations for the Dean of Wells.[34]

In these circumstances, it is not surprising that Wolsey had difficulties in obtaining his pensions from Spain. He had received nothing since midsummer 1525, as neither of the instalments due at Christmas 1525 and at midsummer 1526 had been paid; and he had never been paid any of the pension due to him for the surrender of his bishopric of Tournai, which Charles had undertaken to pay in 1522 after François stopped paying it on the declaration of war. Edward Lee, the ambassador in Spain, told Wolsey that his best chance of getting the money was to enlist the services of a German who lived at Charles's court, and was known as John of Almain. Almain offered, for a consideration, to persuade the ecclesiastical and royal officials to pay Wolsey. Wolsey agreed that if Almain succeeded in recovering the 7,500 ducats which were due from the Spanish bishoprics for Christmas 1525 and midsummer 1526, he could retain 500 ducats as his commission. On 19 September 1526 he wrote to Lee from The Moor, telling him to increase his offer to Almain. If Almain obtained the four years' arrears of the 9,000 ducats per annum due for Tournai, Wolsey would pay him 2,000 ducats and a further 1,000 ducats a year out of the 9,000-ducat pension if it was paid in future. Wolsey threatened to sue for the money in the Papal court in Rome if there was any further delay.[35]

Almain's efforts produced welcome results. On 31 January 1527 Lee was able to write to Wolsey from Valladolid telling him that the pensions from the Spanish bishoprics for Christmas 1525 and midsummer 1526 had been paid to him, and that he was retaining 600 ducats to cover his expenses as ambassador in Spain and was sending the balance to Wolsey by merchants who were travelling to England. Although the pension due at Christmas 1526 had not yet been paid, Lee expected to receive it before the end of February. Lee told Wolsey that both the Archbishop of Toledo and the Bishop of Palencia had offered to redeem the pension by paying a lump sum of 8,000 ducats and 22,000 ducats, which in each case was the equivalent of four years' pension; but he had turned down the offer, telling them that he was sure that Wolsey had many more than ten years of life remaining to him.[36]

While Wolsey was using the services of the English ambassador to obtain the pensions which Charles had granted him, he was negotiating an alliance with France against Charles. On 26 February 1527 an important delegation from France arrived at Dover; it consisted of the Bishop of Tarbes, the Vicomte de Turenne, and the president and a councillor of the *Parlement* of Paris.[37] They joined Vaulx, the resident ambassador in London, and spent two months in top-level negotiations with the English government. At the first meeting, Turenne informed Wolsey that François considered that he owed his freedom from captivity to him. Wolsey replied that when he met François at Ardres at the Field of Cloth-of-gold, he had at once become his devoted servant because of his nobleness and his virtues, and that nothing had happened since that time to destroy his affection for François, which was the greater because of the close resemblance between François and Henry in their dress and personal appearance.

The English delegation at the formal negotiating sessions consisted of Norfolk, Suffolk, Tunstal, Thomas Boleyn, Fitzwilliam, Bishop West of Ely, and More. They met the Bishop of Tarbes and his colleagues at York Place. The more tricky and important negotiations were conducted informally by Wolsey himself. On several occasions he extracted concessions from the French by telling them that several members of the Council, and some of the English representatives at the talks, were hostile to the French alliance and criticised him for being so friendly to France; it was therefore essential for the French to give way on the point at issue, or his English colleagues would insist on breaking off the negotiations. He fell ill during the talks, but this reduced him to inactivity only for a few days.

Wolsey and the English negotiators tried to persuade the French envoys that François should break off his engagement to marry Charles's sister and should agree to marry Princess Mary; only at the end of the negotiations did Wolsey suggest, as a second-best, that Mary should marry the Duke of Orleans. The English and French also agreed that they should send their ambassadors to Spain to ask Charles to release François's sons and to pay his debts to Henry. They were to propose to

Charles that the Treaty of Madrid should be rescinded and new terms substituted. François would surrender Hesdin to Charles in exchange for Charles returning Tournai to him; but otherwise François would make no territorial cessions. Instead, he would pay Charles an indemnity of 2,000,000 crowns for the release of his sons. François would pay Charles 600,000 of these 2,000,000 crowns immediately, and another 600,000 crowns in three years' time; the balance of 800,000 crowns would be paid by François, not to Charles, but to Henry in satisfaction of Charles's debts to Henry. If the emperor refused to agree to these proposals, or did not reply within a reasonable time, the English and French ambassadors would present him with an ultimatum demanding that he accede to their demands within thirty days, after which they would declare war. If it came to war, the costs of the war would be borne by François. Henry and François would cement their alliance by a meeting at Calais; in the meantime, Wolsey would meet François at Amiens to consolidate their preparations for war against the emperor.

The French envoys had strongly objected to the stipulation that François should pay the whole cost of the war, especially as Wolsey insisted that the money be paid even if war did not break out and if the negotiations for Mary's marriage fell through; but Wolsey held all the cards, for if the French did not accept his terms they would have to face the emperor on their own. The terms were embodied in a treaty which was signed on 30 April 1527 at York Place by the Bishop of Tarbes and the president of the *Parlement* of Paris for France, and by Norfolk, Suffolk, Boleyn, Fitzwilliam and More for England. A supplementary treaty was signed on 29 May by the Bishop of Tarbes and Vaulx for France, and for England by More and Stephen Gardiner, the Archdeacon of Taunton, a brilliant young canon lawyer who had recently become Wolsey's secretary. It provided that England and France would maintain an army of 31,000 men in Italy to fight the common enemy.[38] Wolsey also told the French envoys that François would have to provide an army of 33,000 men, and Henry 19,500 men, for a joint invasion of the Netherlands from Calais in May 1528. He promised that Henry would be ready with his contingent before François was.[39] Henry and Wolsey had not the least intention of fulfilling this promise.

Wolsey sent Sir Francis Poyntz as ambassador to Charles in Spain to carry out the steps agreed in the treaty, culminating in the declaration of war if Charles would not give way. But Henry and Wolsey did not wish to go to war with Charles, and regarded the declaration of war only as a last resort. They hoped to persuade François to make further concessions, and to offer to pay the full 1,200,000 crowns to Charles at once, keeping their offer back for the moment in order to produce it later as a concession. Wolsey was confident that his prestige and diplomatic skill would eventually induce Charles to agree to an acceptable compromise which the mediation of the Cardinal of England alone could achieve.

This reluctance to declare war, but the necessity of considering it as an ultimate step, presented a difficulty. War could only be declared by a herald going to Charles, accompanied by his pursuivants, and issuing Henry's 'defiance' to the emperor and his challenge to war. As Wolsey did not wish Charles and his ministers to know, during the earlier stages of Poyntz's negotiations, that a declaration of war was contemplated, he sent the herald and his pursuivants to Valladolid disguised as servants in Poyntz's retinue, with their herald's uniforms carefully concealed among their baggage.[40]

In the spring of 1527 the Pope, encouraged by Wolsey and by Russell's arrival with the money, resumed the war; and, as the truce had expired, the Papal forces joined the Venetians in a new campaign against the emperor. Charles sent the Duke of Bourbon to crush them with an army composed partly of Spanish troops and partly of German mercenaries. Mercenaries never behaved well towards the civilian population, and, according to the Papal authorities, many of Bourbon's German mercenaries were Lutherans who hated the Pope and the Catholic faith. As Bourbon approached Rome, Russell sent horrifying reports to Wolsey of the sacrilegious atrocities which were being committed by the soldiers of the general to whom he had taken money three years before, on the occasion of his last visit to Italy. He and Sir Gregory di Casale, one of the Italian agents in Henry's employ, wrote to Wolsey that Bourbon's Spanish and Swabian soldiers had desecrated the Host in the churches, throwing it into the river or into the vilest places, even on Easter Day, when they should have been receiving it in church. They burned every town and village through which they passed, even if there was no resistance; they abducted and raped both girls and boys; they forced monks and nuns to copulate together. Russell and Casale thought that if God did not punish such cruelty and wickedness, it would show that He did not trouble Himself about the affairs of this world.[41]

On 4 May Bourbon and his troops reached the gates of Rome. He asked the Pope to allow them to pass through the city on their march to Naples, offering to pay for all provisions. The Pope refused to admit them into Rome, and on 6 May Bourbon launched the assault. He himself was killed in the fighting, but his men entered Rome, slaughtering every man, woman and child that they met in the streets, though some of the civilian population saved their lives by jumping into the Tiber. The Pope and his cardinals fled to the Castle of St Angelo, and the emperor's troops looted Rome for twelve days. Then the Pope agreed to the viceroy's terms. The Pope paid an indemnity of 300,000 ducats to the emperor's army; every cardinal paid 200,000 ducats; and a number of rich merchants of Rome paid 100,000 ducats each. Clement and eight of the cardinals were detained in the Castle of St Angelo.[42]

The sack of Rome shocked Sir Thomas More. It was to have a decisive effect on the fortunes of the Cardinal of York.

François I, by Joos van Cleve, about 1530

The battle of Pavia, by an unknown artist

CHAPTER 12

THE KING'S SECRET MATTER

Sir Thomas Boleyn, of Hever in Kent, had been serving Henry VII and Henry VIII as a courtier and diplomat for nearly thirty years, and had been sent by Wolsey on important embassies to France and Spain. In 1525 he was created Viscount Rochford. He had two daughters, Mary and Anne, whom he brought to court when they reached a suitable age. Mary married Sir William Carey, and became Henry VIII's mistress. At a later date, perhaps about 1525, Henry fell in love with her sister Anne, who was aged about eighteen in that year. All the people who met Anne agreed that she was not beautiful, and her enemies may have been speaking the truth when they alleged that she had six fingers on one hand; but men were always falling in love with her, for her natural gaiety had been enhanced by the polish and daring which she had acquired during her residence at the French court.

Her father, the king and Wolsey all agreed that she would be a suitable wife for Sir James Butler, whose father, the Earl of Ormonde, was sufficiently influential in Ireland to make it desirable to link him to a prominent English courtier; but Boleyn and Ormonde could not agree about the dowry, and the match fell through. Anne remained at court, engaging in innocent flirtations with the king, Sir Thomas Wyatt and other young gentlemen. The Earl of Northumberland's son, Lord Percy, fell in love with her, and apparently she was in love with him. Percy was one of a number of young noblemen and gentlemen who were completing their social education, and furthering their future careers, by living in Wolsey's household as gentlemen-in-waiting on the cardinal. He wished to marry Anne, but was already bound by a precontract of marriage to Mary Talbot, the Earl of Shrewsbury's daughter. By the canon law, a precontract prevented the parties from contracting another marriage unless the precontract was invalidated or a dispensation was obtained, although the precontract did not in itself constitute a marriage until it was consummated by sexual intercourse.

Wolsey told Percy to cease pursuing Anne Boleyn, as she was an unsuitable match for him; and when Percy persisted in his courtship, Wolsey scolded him publicly in front of other gentlemen of his household. Even this did not deter Percy; so Wolsey summoned his father, the Earl of Northumberland, who travelled up from Alnwick, upbraided Percy before Wolsey's gentlemen, and took him back to Northumberland and married him to Mary Talbot. According to George Cavendish, who was present when both Wolsey and Northumberland rebuked Percy, Wolsey had acted on orders from the king, who told him to prevent Percy from marrying Anne because he himself was in love with her; but if this is so, Henry must have fallen seriously in love with Anne at an earlier date than the other evidence suggests. Cavendish writes that Anne bitterly resented Wolsey's conduct towards Percy, and never forgave him, with disastrous consequences for Wolsey.[1]

Charles V, Catherine of Aragon, Nicholas Harpsfield, and all the Catholic writers believed that it was Wolsey who first suggested to Henry that his marriage to Catherine was unlawful by divine law, despite Pope Julius II's dispensation of 1503, and that he was living in sin with his brother Arthur's widow. Wolsey and Henry always denied that Wolsey was responsible. Henry stated that it was his confessor, Longland, the Bishop of Lincoln, who first raised the matter with him. Longland said that he had discussed the question with Henry, but that Henry, not he, had mentioned it first.[2] There had in fact been doubts among Henry VII's advisers about the legality of the dispensation when it was originally granted, and Henry VIII, who was a little worried about it when he contracted to marry Catherine in 1505, became increasingly doubtful as all Catherine's children died except Mary, and as she failed to give birth to a surviving son. He pondered on the text from Leviticus: 'If a man shall take his brother's wife . . . they shall be childless', even though there was a directly conflicting text in Deuteronomy.

Whatever doubts Henry had, there could be no question of nullifying his marriage to Catherine and repudiating the wife with whom he had lived for fifteen years, as long as he was allied to her nephew Charles; but the rupture of the alliance with the emperor in 1525, and the *rapprochement* with France, changed the situation just at the time when Henry was falling in love with Anne Boleyn. By the spring of 1527, when the Bishop of Tarbes and his colleages were in London negotiating the treaty of alliance against the emperor, Henry and Wolsey were taking steps to nullify the marriage with Catherine. Wolsey was considering the possibility of negotiating a marriage between Henry and François I's sister-in-law, Madame Renée, the daughter of Louis XII. He knew that Henry was in love with Anne Boleyn, but imagined that he merely wished to make her his mistress, though she had so far resisted his advances. Wolsey did not know that Henry wished to marry Anne, believing that she was capable of bearing him a son who would be England's future king.

Henry and Wolsey stated on several occasions that the Bishop of Tarbes raised the question of Mary's legitimacy during his negotiations in London about her marriage to François or to the Duke of Orleans.[3] There are good reasons for believing that this was untrue; but if Henry and Wolsey were thinking of the possibility of divorcing Catherine, the question of Mary's legitimacy would have to be cleared up, and was therefore probably mentioned to the Bishop of Tarbes.

By April 1527 Wolsey was collecting evidence for the divorce. He sent his agent, Wolman, to Winchester to see Foxe, who was nearly eighty and blind, and had retired from court to his diocese a few years before.[4] Wolsey hoped that Foxe would swear a deposition about the doubts which had been felt by Henry VII and his advisers in 1504 as to the validity of the dispensation, and about the pressure that Henry VII had exerted to force his son Henry to enter, against his will, into the precontract with Catherine. Foxe did not say what was expected of him; but Wolsey devised a plan by which the need for evidence could be ignored, the divorce rushed through secretly, and the world confronted with a *fait accompli*. Instead of Henry adopting the obvious course of bringing a nullity suit against Catherine in the ecclesiastical courts, Wolsey would summon him to appear before his legatine court to answer a charge of living in unlawful cohabitation with Catherine. It would then not be necessary for Catherine to be a party to the proceedings, and she would not be represented, or even informed that the trial was taking place. Wolsey invited Warham to sit with him as a judge in his court, knowing that Warham in 1504 had been one of the most doubtful of Henry VII's counsellors about the validity of the dispensation.

Wolsey put the plan into operation nine days after the Bishop of Tarbes and the French envoys left London. On 18 May he and Warham opened the court in Wolsey's house at York Place. Henry and five canon lawyers were the only other persons present. The proceedings were adjourned till 20 May, when two more lawyers appeared as advocates for Henry and for the court, and there were two further sessions on 27 and 31 May.[5] But Wolsey had miscalculated. He found that by the canon law, Catherine was, after all, entitled to intervene in the proceedings as an interested party, and could appeal to the Papal Court in Rome to invalidate any decision of Wolsey's legatine court if she had not been given notice of the trial. Wolsey pointed out the difficulties to Henry in a discussion at which Norfolk and Suffolk were also present, and advised him not to try to force through the divorce until they had discovered the attitude which the Pope and the French king would adopt. Henry was not too pleased at this, and thought that Wolsey was lukewarm about the divorce.[6]

Wolsey also thought that it would be advisable to gain the support of the bishops, who were invited to express an opinion on the validity of the dispensation of 1503. The bishops knew what was expected of them, and all except one stated that they thought that the dispensation did not validate the marriage of a man to his brother's widow. The exception was Fisher. He wrote an opinion in which he stated that there was nothing in Scripture which invalidated the marriage of a childless widow to her deceased husband's brother; that if there was any doubt as to the meaning of conflicting Biblical texts, it was for the Pope to resolve it, and a Papal dispensation automatically did this; and that it would be wrong to invalidate a marriage which had been publicly recognised as valid for eighteen years.[7]

The day after the last session of Wolsey's court, news reached London on 1 June of the capture and sack of Rome by Bòurbon's troops. Wolsey wrote to Henry, telling him of the 'lamentable spoils' and 'cruel murders' committed by the emperor's soldiers at Rome, who had 'spared neither the sacred, age, sex nor religion'; but it was typical of Wolsey that he immediately thought out ways of deriving some advantage from the situation. It provided an important argument against making peace in Christendom and embarking on a crusade against the Turks, for the cruelty and tyranny of those who claimed to be Christian princes was worse than that of the Turks, 'who, if they had entered Rome, would not have perpetrated greater nor so many abominations, to the hindrance of Christ's name and religion, as these have done'.[8] He noted that the conduct of the emperor's army could be used as an excuse for declaring war on Charles; in the meantime, he sent a formal protest to the emperor against the sacrilegious conduct of his soldiers. He asked Charles to state whether the soldiers had acted with or without his authority when they sacked Rome; and if they had contravened his orders, would he punish those responsible? Wolsey also arranged for the English clergy to send a protest to the Spanish clergy against the outrage committed against the Pope and the Church.[9]

When Wolsey heard that the Pope was being held a virtual prisoner by the emperor's viceroy in the castle of St Angelo, he saw a way by which he might use the situation to facilitate Henry's divorce from Catherine. He would send an agent to Rome who would secretly visit the Pope in St Angelo, and persuade him to delegate all his Papal authority to Wolsey, who would act as his Sub-Pope while he was held as a prisoner and was incapable of acting freely. If the Pope would not agree to this, Wolsey hoped that the pro-French cardinals could be persuaded to go to Avignon, where they would hold a synod and appoint Wolsey as the Pope's deputy during his imprisonment.[10]

Rumours of the proceedings in Wolsey's legatine court had somehow leaked out. The emperor's ambassador in London, Inigo de Mendoza, had heard about the plan to divorce Catherine by 18 May, the day on which Wolsey held the first session of the court, and he wrote and informed Charles. It was perhaps Mendoza who told Catherine. She raised the matter with Henry, who said that he was reluctantly taking steps to dissolve their marriage, as he was sure that it was sinful. She burst into tears. Henry and Wolsey had hoped that when Catherine heard about the divorce, she would not oppose it, but would retire to a nunnery; but she made it clear that she would strongly contest any divorce proceedings.[11]

Wolsey had no forebodings of troubles ahead when he set out on his journey to meet François I at Amiens. He left York Place on 3 July, accompanied by the Papal Nuncio, the Earl of Derby, Tunstal, More, the Bishop of Ely, three other peers, seven knights, his secretaries Gardiner and Vannes, his legal advisers, thirty-nine other gentlemen and an escort of nine hundred horsemen.[12] He told Henry that he was well received by the crowds as he rode through London, and he was sure that the realm had never been in better order, despite the rumours to the contrary. He stayed the first night at Sir John Wiltshire's house at Dartford, where Warham was staying. Wolsey told Warham about the Queen's bitter opposition to the divorce, and they wondered how she had got to hear of it.

Next day Wolsey and his retinue moved on to Rochester, where Wolsey stayed in Fisher's palace. He had a long talk with Fisher about 'the king's secret matter', and tried to persuade Fisher to change his mind and deny the validity of Henry's marriage to Catherine. He told Fisher that the Bishop of Tarbes had expressed his doubts about the validity of the dispensation of 1503, and asked him if he had been in touch with Catherine about the divorce proceedings. Fisher said that she had asked him to advise her about it, but that he had told her that he could not act for her without the king's permission. According to the letter that Wolsey wrote to Henry next day from Faversham, he persuaded Fisher that it was essential, in this hour when the Church was in danger and the Pope a prisoner, for the queen to consent to the divorce; but Wolsey was almost certainly exaggerating his success with Fisher.[13]

He continued his journey, and between Sittingbourne and Faversham he met the Hungarian ambassador, who had been sent by John Zapolya to ask Henry for help against Ferdinand of Bohemia. They had a brief discussion on the highway about the situation in Eastern Europe. Wolsey stayed the night at Faversham, and next day reached Canterbury. He spent four days there, staying with the Abbot of St Augustine's. He embarked at Dover at 3.30 a.m. on 11 July, and reached Calais five and a half hours later.[14]

The summer of 1527 was one of the worst ever known in England and northern France, with almost continuous rain and high winds. The weather was so bad that Wolsey stayed in Calais for eleven days before beginning his journey to Amiens. He had taken the Great Seal of England with him, as he had done when he went to Calais and Bruges in 1521, and he wrote to Henry from Calais about various aspects of internal and foreign policy, and about the divorce. He found many things which displeased him in the administration at Calais; the town was in great decay and disorder, and the soldiers were unpaid. He set about putting things right, and repairing the defences of Calais.[15]

He was in excellent spirits, joking happily with the gentlemen of his retine. He told them that the French would be very friendly, but would speak to them in French and would assume that they understood the language. He advised them, if they did not understand what the French said, to reply in English, for then the French would not understand *them*, which would not matter at all. He urged a Welsh gentleman in his escort to speak Welsh to the French and see what they made of it.[16]

While he was in Calais he heard disconcerting news from England. Henry was very annoyed with him because he had appointed a priest to a benefice in Calais which Henry had intended for his nominee. Wolsey maintained that the Lord Chancellor had the right of presentation to the benefice, but Henry was informed that the right belonged to the king. Wolsey agreed to find another benefice for his priest and to give the Calais benefice to Henry's man, without acknowledging that the right of presentation belonged to the king; and Henry caustically commented that if Wolsey was right in this contention, which he did not accept, he was grateful to him for complying with his wishes. It was a little worrying, coming so soon after Henry had expressed his doubts as to whether Wolsey was really keen on the divorce; but Wolsey was not seriously alarmed, especially as Henry sent him a red deer for his table.[17]

Wolsey set out from Calais on 22 July. François had ordered that he was to be received with unprecedented honours, and had granted him the right to pardon convicted French criminals in any town through which he passed. He was received on the frontier by the Duke of Vendôme with a thousand horsemen and escorted to Boulogne. As he entered the town, three pageants were performed in the streets to welcome him. He could not observe them as closely as he would have wished, because his mule was being difficult and he had to concentrate to prevent the mule from throwing him; but he noticed that the pageants showed François and Henry liberating the imprisoned Pope from the tyranny of the emperor. He spent the second night at Montreuil and the third at Abbeville, where he was received with similar honours. He wrote to Henry that he noticed that there was great dearth in France, and that the lodgings provided for him and his retinue were far inferior to those in England.[18]

At Abbeville he heard that François had injured his leg while hunting, and would therefore travel slowly, taking six days to cover the ninety miles from Paris to Amiens. Wolsey was determined not to wait in Amiens for the king to arrive, but to make the king wait for him. He therefore waited for ten days at Abbeville. He wrote a letter from Abbeville to Cardinal Ghinucci and Lee, the English ambassadors in Spain. He told them that they might hear of a rumour which was circulating in England that the king was taking steps to divorce the queen, but that there was not a word of truth in the story.[19]

He heard that François would reach Amiens on Saturday 3 August. On that day he rode to Péquigny Castle, where he stayed the night before entering Amiens on Sunday afternoon.[20] The mayor and town council of Amiens received him two miles outside the town, and half a mile further on, François himself was waiting with Louise d'Angoulême, his sister the Queen of Navarre (who some years later wrote the *Heptameron*), Madame Renée, his courtiers, and an escort of five thousand horsemen. When Wolsey saw François, he galloped forward to greet him, cap in hand. The king removed his cap and embraced Wolsey, and then presented him to the king of Navarre before greeting Tunstal, Lord Sandys, Sir Henry Guildford and More. François and Wolsey spoke for a little while, with Wolsey holding his cap in his hand but eventually agreeing to replace it on his head at François's insistence.

They rode together into Amiens, entering the town by a wide street, with François and Wolsey side by side in the centre, flanked by Cardinal Salviati, the Papal Legate in France, and Cardinal de Bourbon. François insisted on escorting Wolsey to his lodgings, which had been splendidly decorated in cloth-of-gold; but when the king left him, Wolsey accompanied him, so that it would be he who would escort the king. François stopped his horse, and would not leave till Wolsey had left him. Wolsey thereupon dismounted, and spoke to François for a moment, cap in hand, before ending this competition in courtesy and riding back to his lodgings.

Wolsey and François stayed in Amiens for three weeks, engaging in great festivities and negotiating a strengthening of the alliance. At mass in the cathedral, François and Wolsey knelt together side by side. François invited Wolsey to a great banquet, at which François, Wolsey and Louise d'Angoulême sat together at one table, with the king and queen of Navarre, Madame Renée, the Papal Legate, the other cardinals, and the Great Master Montmorency sitting at a lower table. When Wolsey invited François to dine at his lodgings, he sat with François, Louise d'Angoulême, the king of Navarre, Renée and nine other ladies at the same table. The Venetian ambassador, who attended the banquet, wrote that the quantity of meats served was tremendous. He also noted that Wolsey's servants, who waited on him at the table, were bareheaded, and knelt as they presented the dishes to him, whereas François's servants wore their caps and stood as they served the king.[21]

There were a number of matters to be negotiated at Amiens, and François conducted many of the talks lying down on a couch, as his leg was troubling him; and he insisted that Wolsey should sit in his presence. Wolsey's main objective was to persuade François to make more concessions to Charles in the negotiations at Valladolid, for he and Henry were very anxious to avoid having to declare war on the emperor. He suggested that he and Louise d'Angoulême should invite Charles to meet them at Perpignan, on the Spanish frontier, for he was confident that he would be able to settle the differences between Charles and François at a personal meeting with the emperor. But François was hardening his attitude and complaining of Charles's unreasonable demands; he said that only his affection for Henry and Wolsey prevented him from declaring war on Charles. He was ready to consider sympathetically the idea of breaking off his engagement to Charles's sister and marrying Princess Mary instead.[22]

Wolsey tried hard to win the support of the other cardinals and the Papal nuncios at Amiens for his plan to convene a meeting of all the anti-imperial cardinals at Avignon, where they would declare that as the Pope was a prisoner in the emperor's hands, and not a free agent, they would appoint Wolsey as the Pope's vicar to act for him and exercise all the Papal powers during his imprisonment; but the cardinals at Amiens pointed out the difficulties. Wolsey had meanwhile instructed the English agents in Rome to try to gain access to the Pope in St Angelo and persuade him to agree to the divorce of Henry and Catherine. On 11 August, after he had been eight days with François at Amiens, he wrote to Henry that though he had found much affection in the French king, he had not yet mentioned 'your private matter' to him, as he thought it best to dispose of the other questions first; but he assured Henry that he was using all his efforts to accelerate the divorce.[23]

On 18 August François confirmed the treaty with England at a ceremony in Amiens, and next day left on a pilgrimage to some shrines in the neighbourhood, having invited Wolsey to meet him for further discussions at Compiègne. The negotiations were resumed at Compiègne on 1 September. There were more festivities, and a great boar hunt in the Forest of Compiègne, where Wolsey and Renée watched François, whose leg had healed, perform feats of horseman-ship.[24] Wolsey persuaded François to make a further concession to Charles, but François told him that this was his final offer. He agreed to cede Charleroi and the neighbouring districts with the salt granaries to the Netherlands, and to pay Charles 2,000,000 crowns of the sun, 1,200,000 crowns to be paid immediately to Charles, and the balance of 800,000 crowns to Henry in satisfaction of Charles's debts; Charles would thereupon immediately release François's sons. Wolsey wrote to Lee and Poyntz at Valladolid that he was sure this was the furthest that François would go. Charles declared that the proposal was quite unacceptable. He would be willing to waive his demand for Burgundy, but François must relinquish his claim to Milan; and Charles insisted that the whole of the 2,000,000 crowns should be paid to him, and none of it to Henry.[25]

Wolsey was entertained as lavishly at Compiègne as at Amiens, but he was irritated to discover that books and tracts attacking him personally were still being published in France, and he protested to François's ministers at the failure of the French authorities to suppress them. He was also annoyed that his lodgings at Compiègne were broken into and a valuable silver dish stolen. Wolsey's servants caught the thief, who was a twelve-year-old boy, and after Wolsey had complained to the French authorities, the boy was put in the pillory. Wolsey had been robbed in nearly every place where he stayed in France. Some other unauthorised person broke into his lodgings at Compiègne and drew a picture on the wall of a figure wearing a cardinal's hat being hanged on a gallows.[26]

But Wolsey had more serious cause for anxiety at Compiègne. On 5 September he received a letter from Henry's secretary, Dr Knight, written from Beaulieu in Hampshire on 29 August, telling him that Knight would shortly be arriving in Compiègne on his way to Rome, where he was being sent by Henry to see the Pope about Henry's divorce. Henry had not consulted Wolsey about sending Knight to Rome, and Wolsey was displeased; he did not like things to be done without his knowledge. He wrote at once to Henry, suggesting that it would be better not to send Knight to Rome, because Ghinucci, with his experience and personal knowledge of the Pope, would be able to handle 'your secret matter' much better than Knight. 'If Your Grace will take a little patience', he wrote, 'your intent shall honourably and lawfully take the desired effect.'[27]

On 10 September Knight arrived at Compiègne, and showed Wolsey his instructions from Henry. He was to gain access to the Pope and ask him to grant Henry a dispensation which would enable him, if his marriage to Catherine was dissolved, to marry a woman whose sister had been his mistress. Wolsey had had no idea that Henry wished to obtain such a dispensation from the Pope. He must now have realised, for the first time, that Henry intended to divorce Catherine in order to marry Anne Boleyn.

Wolsey told Knight that he had written to the king suggesting that Knight should not go to Rome, and he ordered Knight not to proceed on his journey, but to stay at Compiègne until further instructions had been received from Henry. Three days later, Wolsey received Henry's reply to his letter. It was very friendly in tone, but stated that after considering Wolsey's advice, Henry was still determined that Knight should go to Rome. Wolsey then told Knight to go to Venice, where he would find the money that he needed for his journey to Rome, and wrote to Henry, thanking him for his letter; it had made him very happy, confirming 'the assured trust of your gracious love and favour'. He assured Henry that he had done everything in his power to facilitate Knight's journey to Rome; but he was clearly worried that Henry, without consulting him, was taking steps on his own to enable him to marry Anne Boleyn.[28]

Wolsey decided to return to England at once. On 17 September he left Compiègne, having received gifts of a golden chalice and silk tapestries from François worth 30,000 crowns.[29]

In later years, it was said that the Boleyns were Lutheran sympathisers, and that Rochford, with his relative the Duke of Norfolk, was the head of a party which was scheming to overthrow Wolsey. There is no real evidence that the Boleyns were sympathetic to Lutheranism before the time when Anne's marriage to Henry became associated with opposition to the Papacy; and it is unlikely that there was any planned conspiracy to overthrow Wolsey in the autumn of 1527. But Wolsey was becoming increasingly unpopular in England, both with the nobility and with the people, and it was obviously potentially dangerous for him if someone else was exercising strong influence over Henry. He was confident that he could deflect the danger, and had a simple plan for doing so: he must convince Henry that it was impossible to divorce Catherine without the Pope's consent, and that he was the only person with sufficient influence in Rome to obtain this consent.

Charles had been shocked to hear, from Inigo de Mendoza and from Catherine, that Henry was seeking to divorce her. He wrote what he called a 'very moderate' warning to Henry to desist from a step which would be a scandal to Christendom, and instructed his ambassador in Rome to prevent the Pope from granting the divorce. He sent the General of the Franciscans, the future Cardinal Quignones, to Rome to reinforce his ambassador's arguments and persuade the Pope that Catherine would never obtain justice if her case was tried in Henry's realm. It must therefore be transferred to the Papal Court in Rome.[30]

The divorce was another reason for Charles to condemn Wolsey, for he was sure that it was Wolsey who had put the idea into Henry's head. Wolsey found that his Spanish pensions were again falling into arrears. Mendoza was worried about this. After the Anglo-French treaty was signed in May 1527, he wrote to Charles that the alliance with France was very unpopular in England, and that everyone blamed Wolsey for it. He reported that Norfolk and Tunstal were the leaders of a party in the Council that was working to overthrow Wolsey, who would shortly be replaced as Lord Chancellor by Tunstal. But by the autumn Mendoza was taking a different attitude. It now appeared to him that Wolsey, after his return from Compiègne, was as much in favour with Henry as ever, and he feared that England would declare war on the emperor if Wolsey did not receive his pensions from Spain. He wrote repeatedly to Charles, urging him to pay the pensions quickly.[31]

Charles swallowed his hatred of Wolsey, and made a last attempt to win him over. On 30 September 1527 he wrote to Mendoza and instructed him to do all in his power to bring Wolsey into his service. He promised to pay all the arrears of Wolsey's pensions, at the rate of 9,000 ducats per annum, which would amount to a considerable sum, as the pensions were now five years in arrears. He offered him a new, additional pension of 6,000 ducats a year until there was a vacant Spanish bishopric which could be given to him. He would also arrange for whatever duke obtained Milan to make Wolsey a marquis of some territory in the duchy of Milan with an income of 12,000 ducats a year, or 15,000 ducats a year if Wolsey felt that 12,000 ducats was not enough. Wolsey would hold this Milanese marquisate for life, and after his death it would descend to anyone whom Wolsey nominated. All that Charles required from Wolsey in return was that he should continue to pursue his former policy of friendship.[32]

But Wolsey was no longer in a position to accept these offers, even if he had wished to do so. He needed one thing above all – to obtain the divorce for Henry, which precluded friendship with Charles. He told Henry about Charles's offers, and said that the lavishness of them showed the weakness of Charles's position.[33]

Wolsey staged another great trial of heretics. It cannot have been coincidence that this show trial, like the trial of Barnes and the Hansa heretics, occurred at a time when Wolsey wished to obtain an important favour from the Pope and the Papal court. In February 1526 he wanted the Pope to join the Holy League against the emperor in Italy; now he wanted authority to try the divorce case in England. Bilney was again arrested and brought before Wolsey, who also examined Bilney's Cambridge friend, Thomas Arthur. Bilney was accused of more than forty offences of heresy – of denouncing images and crucifixes, of advocating the holding of church services in English, and of supporting

Luther's heresies. Very similar charges were brought against Arthur.

On 27 November 1527 Bilney and Arthur were put on trial in the Chapter House of Westminster before Wolsey, Warham, seven bishops and other canon lawyers. Wolsey asked them a few questions, and reminded Bilney that when he had examined him in the previous year, he had sworn an oath not to propagate Lutheran doctrines. Wolsey then appointed Tunstal, Fisher and the Bishop of Ely to deal with the case, and after a number of hearings they persuaded both Bilney and Arthur to recant. As Bilney had not been sent for trial on the previous occasion, but had merely sworn an oath to Wolsey, he was not classified as a relapsed heretic, and was therefore allowed, like Arthur, to carry his faggot after his recantation. He returned to Norfolk crushed and ashamed, to confide his grief to his friend Hugh Latimer, who had so far escaped being charged with heresy.[34]

On 5 December Wolsey and the bishops examined a London heretic, Richard Foster, who was charged with expressing doubts about the Real Presence; he, too, recanted. Wolsey's demonstration against heresy culminated in a great ceremony on 5 January. He went by barge from York Place to Blackfriars, where he landed, and proceeded with a large escort to St Paul's. He walked to the high altar with the emperor's ambassador on his right and the French ambassador on his left, accompanied by four bishops, two abbots, and four priors. Dr Capon preached a sermon on the great misery which the Church had suffered from Lutheranism and the shameful injuries inflicted upon the Pope. The emperor's ambassador, who listened in silence to this implied attack upon Charles, was afterwards invited, with the French ambassador, to a great banquet given by Wolsey which was particularly lavish, although England was suffering from a serious food shortage after the disastrous harvest.[35]

Relations with Charles had reached breaking point. As Charles refused what François insisted was his final offer, the French and English ambassadors at Burgos decided to follow their instructions and declare war. On 22 January 1528 Clarencieux Herald put on his hidden uniform and went with the Guienne Herald of France to issue the defiance of Henry and François to Charles. Clarencieux stated that as Charles's troops had desecrated Rome and held the Pope a prisoner, Henry was joining with François to make war on Charles in order to force him to liberate the Pope and the French king's sons and to pay his debts to Henry.[36]

Charles gave his reply in writing five days later. He stated that he had already sent orders to release the Pope from captivity, and that he would free the French princes when François had performed the Treaty of Madrid. He had never refused to repay his debts to Henry, but there was a dispute about the amount, and Henry, by demanding too much, had forfeited his right to any of the money under the usury laws. Charles then referred to Henry's plans to divorce his aunt, Queen Catherine, which would be a scandal to Christendom; and it was an insult to him for Henry to attempt to bastardise his daughter Mary, whom he had offered to Charles as a bride. Charles stated that he was sure that Henry would not have embarked on such disgraceful proceedings had it not been for the machinations of the Cardinal of York, who had persuaded Henry to begin the divorce out of spite because Charles had refused to use his army in Italy to force the cardinals to elect Wolsey as Pope, which Wolsey had asked him to do. This attack by Charles on a minister of a foreign sovereign in a diplomatic note was quite without precedent. Soon afterwards, Charles told Margaret of Austria to arrange for printed tracts attacking Wolsey to be smuggled into England to convince the people that Wolsey alone was responsible for the war.[37]

Henry and Wolsey were not pleased when they heard that their ambassadors had instructed Clarencieux to declare war. They had never intended to go to war with the emperor, and Wolsey had been confident that he would be able to induce Charles and François to agree on terms. They wrote to Ghinucci and Poyntz, whom Charles was detaining in Spain until Inigo de Mendoza was allowed to leave England, and accused them of exceeding their powers by allowing their French colleagues to persuade them to declare war without referring back to Henry and Wolsey for further instructions.[38]

Henry and Wolsey sent Windsor Herald to Margaret of Austria's court at Malines. All the people who saw him ride by in his herald's uniform assumed that he had come to declare war; but his instructions were to ask Margaret to allow trade between England and the Netherlands to continue for six weeks, notwithstanding the state of war between his king and the emperor. She willingly agreed, and within the six weeks sent an envoy to England to ask for the period to be extended indefinitely. Wolsey persuaded Henry to put the navy on alert in case English ships were attacked at sea; but this was the only military action that was taken. Wolsey and the French discussed impressive schemes for a joint Anglo-French invasion of the Netherlands from Calais and Picardy; but Henry and Wolsey never meant to put this into practice, for they intended to leave their French ally to do the fighting.[39]

François sent an army to invade Italy. At first the French were successful, and seemed to be on the point of capturing Naples; but by the end of 1528 Charles's army had gained the upper hand. Wolsey had meanwhile persuaded François to agree that the war should be confined to Italy. On 15 June 1528 a truce for eight months was signed at Hampton Court between England, France and the emperor, which was only to apply on 'this side of the mountains', that is to say, north of the Alps.[40]

The alliance between England and France meant that war in Europe had not, as usual, been accompanied by fighting on the Border between English and Scots and the destruction of Teviotdale and the Merse. But the ending of French intrigues in Scotland and of their attempts to regain power for Albany had not put an end to Henry's troubles there. As James V approached the age when he would be old enough to rule, the opportunities for Henry and Wolsey to exercise their influence through his mother Queen Margaret, Henry's sister, were disappearing; and Margaret herself was causing anxiety to her brother.

Margaret had retained her affection for Henry and England, and had a healthy respect for his power. She had always represented the English influence at the Scottish court; but her position was made difficult by the attitude of Henry and Wolsey, who believed that the Scottish lords, bishops and abbots would be more likely to pursue a pro-English policy if their castles and abbeys were periodically burned as a demonstration of English power. She had quarrelled with her husband, the Earl of Angus. This was annoying for Henry and Wolsey, because Angus and his brother, Sir George Douglas, were the most devoted English collaborators among the Scottish nobility. In June 1526 Angus carried out a *coup d'état* in Scotland, and took control of the young king's person, keeping the fourteen-year-old boy a virtual prisoner.

Angus claimed that he was a devoted husband, and assured Henry and Wolsey that he wished to be reconciled with the queen; but she had taken a violent dislike to him, refused to meet him, and became friendly with her former enemy, Albany. She fell in love with a young nobleman, Henry Stewart, and asked Albany, who was now François's ambassador in Rome, to arrange with the Pope for her to obtain a divorce. Clement obliged her, and granted her a divorce in March 1527.

Both Henry and Wolsey wrote repeatedly to Margaret, urging her to be reconciled to Angus. In April 1528 Wolsey took time off from his labours to obtain Henry's divorce, and wrote to Margaret. He informed her that the king her brother was motivated by his concern for the welfare of her soul, and for her reputation, in urging her to be guided by the 'undeceivable Spirit of God' and to turn 'to God's Word, the lively doctrine of Jesus Christ, the only ground of salvation'. He was shocked that she had been seduced by flatterers into an unlawful divorce from the right noble Earl of Angus, and urged her to remember 'the divine ordinance of inseparable matrimony first instituted in Paradise.'[41]

The plans of Henry and Wolsey received a set-back in July 1528 when James V escaped from Angus's custody, joined with his mother and Henry Stewart and their partisans, and drove Angus and the Douglases over the Border. Henry granted them asylum in England, and refused James's demands to surrender them. Although the English ambassadors in Edinburgh reported that Margaret would never agree to be reconciled to Angus, and that Angus was very unpopular with the Scottish lords, Henry and Wolsey would not withdraw their support for him, and accepted his offer to lead raids over the Border into Scotland whenever this was required of him.[42]

Wolsey was meanwhile making every effort to obtain from the Pope the necessary authority to annul Henry's marriage to Catherine. He thought up an ingenious scheme. The obvious procedure would be for the Pope to grant Wolsey, as Legate, authority to try the divorce case under the usual 'general commission'; but Wolsey asked him to revive the antiquated practice of granting a 'decretal commission' which, after laying down a binding rule of law, authorised the commissioner merely to ascertain the facts without being free to decide the point of law. Wolsey drafted a form of decretal commission for Clement to grant him. It stated that as the validity of Henry's marriage to Catherine depended on the validity of the Papal dispensation of 1503, Wolsey was to determine the issue as to whether there was any defect in the dispensation. If he held that there was, this would automatically annul the marriage without permitting any argument or appeal on the question of law.

On 5 December 1527 Wolsey wrote to Sir Gregory di Casale* and ordered him to gain access to the Pope. He was to tell him that Henry was a most devoted son of the Church and would do everything possible to liberate him and defend the Church against her enemies, if the Pope obliged him in the matter of the divorce. Casale was to impress on the Pope that the whole English nation and nobility, without any exception, wanted Henry to have a male heir, and that it was the duty of the Pope, as the Father of Christendom, to prevent the civil war that would arise in England if there was no heir. The Pope must therefore grant a decretal commission to Wolsey to try the divorce case in England. Wolsey told Casale that he was paying 10,000 ducats into Casale's bank in Venice to enable him to bribe the cardinals in Rome to use their influence to obtain this commission.[43]

He wrote again to Casale next day. Casale must make the Pope realise that if he refused to gratify Henry in the divorce case, it would never be possible for Wolsey to serve the Papal interests again. If the Pope granted the decretal commission, it would be agreeable to God. Wolsey then resorted to what was almost certainly a deliberate lie, and

* Sir Gregory's brother, John Casale, was also employed by Henry as an agent in Italy. All the references in the text to 'Casale' are to Sir Gregory.

told Casale to inform the Pope that there were secret reasons why the divorce should be granted which could not be put into writing, as Queen Catherine was suffering from certain incurable diseases which made it impossible for Henry and her ever to live together as husband and wife. While the king's friendship was of the utmost importance to the Pope, his enmity would have terrible consequences; if the Pope did not comply, Wolsey's life would be shortened, and he dreaded to think what would happen.[44]

It had occurred to Wolsey that it would cause adverse comment and accusations of bias if he were appointed to be the sole judge in a divorce case in which Henry was one of the parties. He therefore wrote to Casale on 27 December and suggested that the Pope should appoint another cardinal to sit as a judge under the decretal commission. But this judge must be a cardinal who could be trusted, and preferably Campeggio, the Bishop of Salisbury, or, failing him, one of a number of cardinals whose names Wolsey put forward; on no account must it be a pro-imperial cardinal. He impressed on Casale the need to act with great urgency, for delays would be dangerous.[45]

Wolsey did not know, when he wrote these letters, that the Pope had escaped from St Angelo in disguise and was now safe from Charles's soldiers at Orvieto. On 1 January 1528 Clement gave Knight the dispensation, for which Henry had asked, to marry the sister of his former mistress if his marriage to Catherine was annulled; but this in no way implied that the marriage of Henry and Catherine was invalid, and Clement made objections to granting a decretal commission.[46] Wolsey therefore sent his very able secretary, Gardiner, and another skilful young diplomat, Edward Fox, to visit the Pope at Orvieto and press him for the decretal commission.

Their instructions from Wolsey were to impress on the Pope that Henry would be satisfied with nothing less than a decretal commission in the terms in which the English agents at the Papal court had drafted it. Wolsey stated that he realised, from the reports of these agents, that the Pope had been labouring under the misapprehension that the king had set on foot this cause, not from anxieties about the succession but out of 'a vain affection or undue love for a gentlewoman of not so excellent qualities as she is here esteemed'. They must tell the Pope that Wolsey was prepared to guarantee his soul that Henry loved and honoured the widow of his dearest brother, and would always treat her as a sister, and acted solely from the dictates of his conscience. The king was also very conscious of 'the approved, excellent, virtuous [qualities] of the said gentlewoman, the purity of her life, her constant virginity, her maidenly and womanly pudicity, her soberness, chasteness, meekness, humility, wisdom, descent of right noble blood, education in all good and laudable [qualities] and manners, apparent aptness to procreation of children, with her other infinite good qualities'.[47]

On their way to Orvieto, Gardiner and Fox were to visit the French court and secure François's co-operation in putting pressure on the Pope. Wolsey told them that it was important that François's general, Lautrec, should accomplish some feat in Italy which would make it easier for the Pope to help Henry's cause.[48] He expected François to shed French blood and risk a military defeat in Italy in order to persuade the Pope that it was safe for him to offend the emperor by granting Henry a divorce.

Gardiner and Fox left London at the beginning of February, and after being held up at Dover by wind and storms, and nearly shipwrecked during the crossing to Calais, they visited François at St Germain-en-Laye, and travelled on by Lyons, Genoa and Lucca to Orvieto at the greatest possible speed. They always began their day's journey before daybreak, and never stayed two nights in the same place. They reached Orvieto on 21 March, seventeen days after leaving Lyons. They stayed at Orvieto for three weeks, and together with Casale saw the Pope nearly every day, spending four or five hours a day arguing with him and the cardinals of his secretariat. Gardiner, who played the leading part in the discussions, formed a low opinion of the Pope. He wrote contemptuously that the Pope was sitting on a couch which was covered with a rug not worth twenty shillings, and complained that no man was so slow to give an answer to any request as the Pope.[49]

Gardiner adopted an increasingly threatening attitude. He wrote to Wolsey that he was following the lines that Wolsey had laid down in his talk to him and Fox in his closet at York Place on the Friday before their departure. On 4 April, Gardiner warned the Pope that if he and his cardinals would not show the way to the wanderer (a task entrusted to them by God), and especially to a prince to whom they were so much indebted, the king and the lords of England would be driven to think that God had taken away the key of knowledge from the Holy See, and would begin to adopt the opinion of those who thought that if pontifical laws were not clear to the Pope himself, they might well be committed to the flames. Gardiner's tactics had some effect, for three days later, on the Tuesday in Holy Week, the Pope summoned Gardiner and Casale and showed them a commission which he had drafted, giving Wolsey power to hear the divorce suit in England and give any judgment which he pleased; but Gardiner was not satisfied, for it was not a decretal commission. He told the Pope that he thought it was God's will that when he reported what sort of men be here, the favour of that prince who was their only friend would be taken away, and that the Apostolic See would fall to pieces with the consent and applause of everyone.[50]

Gardiner had made the position very clear to Clement; but the General of the Franciscans and the emperor's ambassador had made Charles's attitude equally clear. If Clement refused to take the necessary steps to grant Henry his divorce, England would follow Germany into schism and heresy; if he granted the divorce, the emperor, whose troops controlled Italy, might again imprison him, perhaps depose him from the Papacy, and again put Rome to the sack. Clement's solution was to gain time by promising both sides that he would do what they wanted, and then stall, and if necessary break his promise. But Gardiner could not move him on the decretal commission, and had to be satisfied with two alternative general commissions. One of them appointed Wolsey as the sole judge of the divorce case; the other appointed him jointly with Campeggio, naming Wolsey as the senior of the two Legates, and stipulating that either of them would be free to act, if necessary, without the assistance of the other. This left Wolsey free to use whichever commission he thought best.[51]

Fox returned to England with the commissions, leaving Gardiner at Orvieto. He reached Greenwich on Sunday 3 May at 5 p.m., and asked to see Wolsey; but as Wolsey had left court two hours before, Fox went to the king. Henry ordered him to make his report to Anne Boleyn, and soon afterwards joined Anne and Fox in Anne's chamber. Fox told them that he and Gardiner had obtained the commissions, and stressed that this was due entirely to Wolsey, as they would never have succeeded had it not been for Wolsey's letter to the Pope. Henry was very pleased with the commissions. Fox then went to Durham Place in the Strand, which was the Bishop of Durham's London residence. It now belonged to Wolsey as Bishop of Durham, and he was living there while York Place was being repaired and furnished in a manner which Fox described as 'most sumptuously and gorgeously'.

It was 10 p.m. when Fox reached Durham Place, and Wolsey had gone to bed; but he rose and heard Fox's report. Unlike Henry, Wolsey was far from satisfied with the commissions which Fox had brought; however extensive the powers which he had been granted under the commissions, he had not obtained a decretal commission.[52] Rightly or wrongly, he believed that the decretal commission was necessary; and, what was more important, he had asked for it, and did not wish Henry to know that he could not obtain everything he wanted from the Pope.

He therefore wrote to Casale on 10 May, and told him that it was essential that he and Gardiner obtain a decretal commission; they could promise the Pope that it would be kept absolutely secret, so Clement need not fear that he would suffer any adverse consequences by granting it. He also wrote to Campeggio, urging him to come to England as soon as possible, and promising him that he would not lack money for his journey or rewards for his efforts.[53]

Gardiner and Casale obtained a decretal commission in the middle of June; but the Pope granted it so reluctantly that Casale was afraid that he might revoke it. On 20 July the emperor's ambassador demanded in Charles's name that the Pope should not grant any commission which would allow the divorce to be tried in England, as Catherine could not obtain impartial justice in Henry's realm. He also demanded that the Pope should issue a decree forbidding Henry to proceed with the divorce. Clement hedged, and gave no reply to the emperor's ambassador. Hearing of this development, Casale returned to the Pope and asked him for a formal promise that he would not revoke the grant of the decretal commission. Clement complied, and on 23 July gave Casale a 'pollicitation' in which he stated that 'we vow and promise on the word of a Roman Pontiff' that he would never be persuaded by anyone to revoke the decretal commission.[54] Wolsey had, after all, obtained everything he wanted from the Pope.

CHAPTER 13

CAMBRAI AND BLACKFRIARS

MANY contemporary observers, as well as historians writing with
hindsight, thought that the situation was very dangerous for Wolsey in
the summer of 1528; but if Wolsey himself had any fears, he did not let it
affect his usual optimism. He seems to have been quite confident that he
would ride the storm; and though he was fully aware of the dangers, he
was sure that he could overcome them. He was happily planning for the
future. He was not only 'most sumptuously and gorgeously' repairing
and furnishing York Place and going ahead with his plans for his new
Cardinal's College at Oxford, but he planned to erect another
Cardinal's College as a school for the children of his home town of
Ipswich. He had always retained an affection for Ipswich and East
Anglia. Although he normally never travelled throughout England,
going no further from London than his country houses of Tyttenhanger,
The Moor and Hampton Court, he occasionally went on a pilgrimage to
the shrine of Our Lady of Walsingham in Norfolk, although this was
further from London than that other great place of pilgrimage, Becket's
tomb at Canterbury.[1]

He realised that at a time when the Pope was so reluctant to grant
facilities for Henry's divorce he would be especially likely to oblige
Wolsey in less important matters. In May 1528 he obtained from the
Pope authority to suppress monasteries and seize their property to
endow his Ipswich College as he had done with Cardinal's College at
Oxford.[2]

He ordered the authorities of Cardinal's College, Oxford, to transfer
to the Ipswich college some of the lands that he had obtained for them,
and set about acquiring additional funds for the Ipswich college by the
same methods which he had used for the Oxford college.[3] His fund-
raising activities for Ipswich caused even more resentment than his
similar efforts for his Oxford college. His Cardinal's College at Oxford
might be designed for his own glorification, but it was an established
tradition to found an Oxford college. Ipswich's only claim to distinction
was that Wolsey's father had been a butcher there, and that it was the
cardinal's birthplace, and the foundation of a college at Ipswich was

seen as a more blatant piece of vainglory. Wolsey's demands for donations fell on the wealthier classes, both among the clergy and the laity, and they resented it. The opposition to the cardinal among the nobility had never been stronger.

The poorer classes were also angry with him in the summer of 1528 because of the war with the emperor and the food shortage. The clothiers and their workmen in East Anglia, in South-east England, and in the West country feared that the war would lead to an embargo on the import of English cloth into the Netherlands, and consequent bankrupt-cies of English clothiers and unemployment among their employees. A series of droughts in the past three or four years, followed by the continuous rain in the summer of 1527, had led to a shortage of corn all over England. Many farmers hoarded what corn they had. Wolsey sent commissioners all over the realm to examine the farmers' corn stocks. They allowed the farmers to keep enough for themselves and their households for the year, but requisitioned the rest for sale at reasonable prices. This did not prevent the price of wheat from rising from eighteen pence a bushel to seven groats and twopence (thirty pence or 2s.6d.) by June 1528.[4]

It was unfair to blame Wolsey for the weather; but as he had been responsible for the government of England for the previous fifteen years, and had been at pains to let everyone know this, it was natural for the people to hold him responsible for all their ills. They remembered also the taxation of 1525, the Amicable Grant, which was supposed to be a loan; and there were demands for the repayment of the loan.

The discontent was most serious in the Tonbridge area of West Kent, where there had been disorders at the time of the suppression of the monasteries by Wolsey in 1524 and the demand for the Amicable Grant in 1525. On 13 February 1528 Wolsey sat in the court of Star Chamber and issued an order to the judges of the Court of King's Bench and the Commissioners of Assize instructing them to deal severely at the next Kent Assizes with any troublemakers in the county. But other districts were affected. At Westbury in Wiltshire the clothworkers assembled in February and demonstrated in protest against the threat of unemploy-ment; in March there were riots at Taunton and Bridgwater; and in April there was a demonstration against unemployment by the clothworkers at Colchester. There were rumours that the clothworkers of Suffolk would rise and march through Essex to link up with the malcontents of Kent.[5]

Wolsey believed that the clothiers were unnecessarily dismissing their employees in order to stir up discontent with the war against the emperor and to force the government to make peace and preserve the threatened trade with the Netherlands. He issued a decree forbidding any clothier from dismissing any of his workmen. He also summoned some of the leading clothiers of Suffolk and Essex to York Place, and warned them that he knew who were the ringleaders among them and would send them to the Tower.[6]

In Holy Week, in April, the villagers of Tonbridge, Penshurst, Bidborough, Speldhurst and Sevenoaks assembled, contacted each other, and decided to present a petition to Warham, asking for the repayment to them of their loans to the king. On the Tuesday after Easter a hundred of them went to the archbishop's palace at Knole and gave him the petition. Warham said that this was not a good time to ask for the repayment of the loan, when the king needed money for the war against the emperor; but that if they would disperse and refrain from unlawful associations, he would present their petition to the king and speak in their favour. When Wolsey heard about Warham's reply to the petitioners, he was angry and worried, for he thought it would encourage opposition. He gave orders that all news of it was to be suppressed, and warned the authorities in Essex to be on the watch for men coming from Kent who might spread the news in Essex.[7]

The knights and gentlemen of Kent had been alerted by Wolsey as to the dangers that threatened, and in May they discovered a conspiracy which they believed could have developed into a serious revolt of the inhabitants of Goudhurst and Cranbrook. It began when three clothworkers and a cutler at Goudhurst met at the house of one of them, and discussed the rumour that there would soon be a revolt in London. One of them said: 'We, with other good fellows, will rise for [to get] the Cardinal.' Another man, Robert Milner, said that they must not kill the cardinal, for if they did, the Pope would put the realm under an interdict; but they should take him to the sea-side, put him in a little boat, make four holes in the boat, and plug the holes with pins. They would then embark in another boat, tug Wolsey's boat out to sea, and there remove the pins, leaving Wolsey to sink and drown. When they mentioned their plan to a fuller from Cranbrook, he told them that there were at least fifty persons at Cranbrook who would rise and help them carry it out; and they were promised the support of a hundred men of Frittenden. At other meetings in Bedgebury Forest and at Goudhurst, they decided to seize corn from the rich and give it to the poor. They thought that Jack Straw's revolt in 1381, and Robert of Redesdale's, would not have failed if they had taken prominent gentlemen as hostages; so they decided to seize Sir Alexander Culpepper at his house at Bedgebury, Sir Edward Guildford at Halden, and Mr Darrell at Scotney Castle, and to send fifty men to capture the ordnance at the Block House at Rye.

Seventeen of the plotters were arrested. They were induced to make full confessions, and when they were tried for high treason and misprision of treason at the assizes at Rochester in June, they pleaded guilty and were sentenced to death. Two other plotters, who had escaped, were charged in their absence; but Robert Milner, who had suggested taking Wolsey out to sea, and had played the most prominent part in their discussions, was not arrested or charged. He was possibly an *agent provocateur* employed by Wolsey.[8]

The sweating sickness returned in the summer of 1528, and Henry again took steps to avoid contact with any person from whom he might catch it, or to visit any place where a case of the sweat had been reported. But one of Anne Boleyn's servants caught the sweat. With great regret, Henry sent Anne away from court to prevent her from infecting him, and she went to her father's house at Hever, where she fell ill with the sweat, but soon recovered. The sweat also appeared in Wolsey's household, which made it impossible for Wolsey to come to court. Henry retired to Wolsey's house at Tyttenhanger, where he saw no one except a handful of his personal servants and Hennege, who acted as his secretary, for his chief secretary, Tuke, had fallen ill with the sweat in London. Henry wrote letters regularly to Wolsey, urging him to face the risk of catching the sweat with the same courage which he himself was displaying, and expressing his anxiety for Wolsey's health. He also wrote emotional letters to Anne at Hever, telling her of his fears for her and his grief at their enforced separation. Wolsey remained at Hampton Court, where he allowed only four of his servants to approach him.[9]

In April 1528 the Abbess of Wilton died, and her office became vacant. In theory, the monks and nuns of an abbey were entitled to elect a new abbot or abbess; but in practice they could usually be persuaded without difficulty to elect the nominee of some powerful patron. When the headships of religious houses fell vacant, Wolsey often sent commissioners to put pressure on the monks or nuns to remit to him the duty of choosing the new head. In this case he decided to appoint the Prioress of Wilton, Lady Isabel Jordan, who had been the abbess's deputy, to succeed her as the new abbess.

But Anne Boleyn wanted her brother-in-law's sister, Dame Elinor Carey, who was an elderly nun of Wilton Abbey, to be promoted to be abbess over the prioress's head. She persuaded Henry to write to Wolsey instructing him to ensure that Dame Elinor was elected. Wolsey was not prepared to see his nominee ousted by Anne's. He sent his agents to examine the nuns at Wilton, and they forced Dame Elinor to admit that she had had illegitimate children by two priests, and had more recently been the mistress of one of Lord Broke's servants. When Wolsey reported this to Henry, the king wrote to Anne and explained that it was impossible to appoint Dame Elinor as abbess; nor could they appoint

Carey's other sister, who had also been guilty of immorality. But Wolsey's prioress, too, had had lovers in her youth, and Henry promised Anne that he would not allow Wolsey to score over her by obtaining the post for the prioress. He wrote to Wolsey that although he thought that both Dame Elinor's sister and the prioress were now too old to commit acts of immorality, neither of them was suitable, in view of their past misconduct, to be Abbess of Wilton, and Wolsey should therefore find a fourth person and arrange for the nuns to elect her as their abbess.

Wolsey was not willing to agree to this compromise, and persisted in appointing the prioress. When he heard that Henry was annoyed at his attitude, he wrote to Henry expressing his regret at having offended him, and saying that he had not realised that Henry objected to the prioress. This was a brazen excuse, for Henry had made his views on the subject quite clear to him.[10]

On 14 July Henry wrote to him from Ampthill. Considering what had happened, it was a surprisingly friendly letter; but after assuring Wolsey that he was writing as a friend, and asking him to accept his letter in this spirit, he told him how annoyed he was at his persistence, and at the excuse of ignorance which he had put forward.[11]

Henry also proceeded to deal with another matter. He wrote that there was a great deal of resentment in the country over the way in which Wolsey was forcing the religious houses to contribute to the cost of his college at Ipswich. He asked Wolsey 'as a master and friend' to accept his comments in a friendly spirit. On the same day, Hennege wrote to Wolsey that he should not be too upset by Henry's letter, because immediately after writing it, Henry had read it aloud to him and Russell and had told them what a high regard he had for Wolsey.[12]

Wolsey replied in a letter in which he expressed his deep regret for having offended the king. Henry wrote back that the matter of the prioress was not very serious, and in view of the humbleness of Wolsey's submission he was content to overlook it. As for the contributions of the religious houses to Wolsey's college at Ipswich, 'I would it were more, so it be lawfully'; but 'surely there is great murmuring of it throughout all the realm, both [among the] good and bad'.[13] Wolsey wrote back, saying that Henry's 'gracious loving letters' showed that 'no spark of displeasure remaineth in your noble heart towards me', which had so comforted him that he had been restored to life. He assured the king that the money that he had received from religious houses was considerably less than had been reported, but that in future he would not accept any gifts for his college, however freely offered, from any religious person, even if he had to sell all he possessed in order to pay for his college.[14]

At the very time when he was carrying on this correspondence with Henry, Wolsey sent his agent, Bell, to Wilton to force the nuns to accept the prioress as their abbess. Bell found that they were most unwilling to do this; but after he had prevented anyone from entering or leaving the abbey, and had incarcerated three or four of the nuns in their cells, he was able to browbeat the others into electing the prioress.[15]

Wolsey likewise continued to demand donations for his college at Ipswich. On 2 July 1528 he wrote to Norfolk's sister, the Countess of Oxford, and asked her to allow his master of works at Ipswich to take some stone and cullions for the college from the cliff in the countess's village of Harwich. She wrote to him on 8 July, explaining that although she would have liked to grant his request, when her receiver and Wolsey's chaplains met on the cliff, they realised that if any appreciable quantity of stone was removed, the cliff would be washed away and collapse on to the town. Wolsey replied on 15 July, which must have been the day on which he received Henry's letter complaining about his methods of obtaining contributions to the college. We do not know what Wolsey wrote to Lady Oxford, but in her reply of 22 July she stated that she regretted that he believed that her story about the danger to the cliff was only an excuse for refusing to let him have the stone, and invited him to take his pleasure in her haven of Harwich, whether it was harmful to the town or no.[16]

He was confident that he had no serious cause for worry as long as Henry believed that he, and he alone, could induce the Pope to grant the divorce. During the summer he wrote repeatedly to Campeggio and to the English agents in Italy, urging Campeggio to begin his journey to England as soon as possible.[17] Campeggio was taking his time. Apart from the fact that everyone connected with the Papal court was notoriously slow, he had the excuse of ill-health, and knew that the Pope would welcome any delay which would enable him to postpone the decision as to whether he preferred to see England in schism or a second sack of Rome.

During the war of the Holy League against the emperor in 1526, the Pope's Venetian allies had sent troops to garrison Ravenna and Cervia in the Papal States to prevent them from falling into the hands of the emperor's troops. When the Pope made his truce with the emperor, the Venetians refused to evacuate the two towns, which had belonged to Venice for a hundred years before Pope Julius II seized them in 1508. As Clement VII could not persuade Venice to surrender them to him, he made a strong protest to the king of France; but François thought that Venice was a more reliable ally than the Pope, and declined to intervene in the quarrel.

Wolsey saw his opportunity. On more than one occasion he had persuaded and bullied the Venetians into doing what he wanted. Now he would make them surrender Ravenna and Cervia to the Pope on condition that the Pope gave Henry his divorce. But despite all the efforts of the English agents in Venice, the arguments of Wolsey with the Venetian and French ambassadors in London, and an indignant letter from Henry to the Doge, the Venetians refused to surrender Ravenna and Cervia.[18] They realised that Wolsey's position was weaker than it had been in earlier years, and they did not believe that he would again seize their ships and disrupt English trade with Venice at a time when there was already so much dissatisfaction in England at the loss of the markets in the Netherlands. The failure to obtain Ravenna and Cervia for the Pope was a diplomatic defeat for Wolsey, and was noted as such in Rome and elsewhere.

On 5 October 1528 Richard Foxe died at the age of eighty-one, and his see of Winchester, the richest in England, became vacant for the first time for twenty-seven years. Wolsey wrote to Henry next day, asking for Winchester. On becoming Bishop of Winchester, he would resign as Bishop of Durham; and he asked Henry to appoint his son Thomas Winter – 'my poor scholar, the Dean of Wells' – as Bishop of Durham, which Henry had previously indicated that he would be prepared to do. He pointed out to Henry that if Winter became Bishop of Durham, Winter's other benefices, which were worth £2,000 a year, would become vacant.[19]

A few months earlier, Wolsey had arranged for Winter to be appointed Archdeacon of Oxfordshire, of Norfolk and of Suffolk, and Rector of St Leonard's in York, in addition to his other benefices. All this time, Winter was studying at the University of Paris, where he had Lupset and several other eminent humanists as his tutors; and the French authorities, at the suggestion of the ambassador in London, had given him the lease of a house in Paris. Despite this gift and his income of £2,000 a year, 'my poor Dean of Wells', as Wolsey usually called him, was often short of money; for he had all his father's love of the good things of life, and much more time on his hands. Wolsey therefore granted him a lease of all the minerals of the bishopric of Durham, which brought him in another £185 a year.[20]

Henry agreed to appoint Wolsey as Bishop of Winchester, but refused to make Winter Bishop of Durham. He kept Durham vacant, with the idea of offering it as a bribe to Campeggio if Campeggio gave judgement for him in the divorce case.[21] In the meantime, Wolsey continued to draw the revenues of the see of Durham, in addition to those of York and Winchester.

Campeggio was not hurrying. He sailed from Corneto on 25 July, but he did not land at Dover till 29 September, and he was so troubled by gout that he had to be carried in a litter when he entered London eight days later. He lodged at the Duke of Suffolk's house in the Strand, and spent most of his time in bed, where he held long bedside talks with Wolsey, and was also visited by Henry and Catherine.

Wolsey was perturbed to discover that Campeggio's object was to avoid, if possible, giving any decision in the divorce case, and to prevent the case ever coming to trial. If he could achieve this by persuading Catherine to enter a convent and submit to a divorce, as Henry and Wolsey wanted, he would be satisfied; if not, he hoped to persuade Henry to be reconciled with Catherine and to withdraw his attempts to obtain the divorce. At his first meeting with Wolsey, he said that the Pope hoped that Wolsey would, if necessary, help him to persuade Henry to abandon the divorce. He suggested, as an alternative to the divorce, that the Pope should grant a dispensation to allow Princess Mary to marry her illegitimate half-brother, the Duke of Richmond, in the hopes that this would safeguard the succession; but Wolsey explained that he and Henry had already considered and rejected this suggestion. Although Campeggio had brought the decretal commission with him, he said that he had orders from the Pope not to let it out of his possession or allow anyone except Henry and Wolsey to see it. Wolsey argued that it was essential for his credibility and prestige that he should be allowed to show it at least to the members of the council; but Campeggio would not agree, and insisted on holding Wolsey to the promise that he had given to the Pope, that no one but he and Henry should know that the decretal commission had been granted. Wolsey was particularly shocked when Campeggio told him that he had orders from the Pope not to give judgment in the divorce case until he had received further instructions from Rome.

On 27 October Wolsey and Campeggio visited the queen in order to ask her to enter a nunnery and not defend the divorce case. Wolsey went on his knees to her, and begged her to agree, in order to avoid the grave dangers to the realm which would result from her refusal and from Henry's failure to have a male heir; but she firmly refused, and declared her love for Henry and her resolve to remain his loyal and obedient wife. Wolsey promised her that if she agreed to enter a nunnery, he would obtain from the Pope a dispensation for her to break every rule of the nunnery except for the requirement that she should remain sexually chaste; but she was unmoved. Campeggio thought that her attitude was very unreasonable, as he could not see why any woman who was approaching fifty – Catherine was in fact not yet forty-three – could object to entering a nunnery; but as she was so inflexible, he told Wolsey that the Pope expected him to join Campeggio in persuading Henry to abandon the divorce. Wolsey said that this was out of the question; he told Campeggio that if the king's desire was not granted, supported as it was by all the learned men of the kingdom who feared God, it would lead to the speedy and total ruin of the kingdom, of himself, and of the Church's influence in England.[22]

On 1 November Wolsey wrote to Casale, expressing his anxieties about Campeggio's attitude, and telling him to urge the Pope to send Campeggio new instructions. If the Pope refused to grant this favour to Henry, who had done so much for the Church, 'I see permanent ruin, infamy, and subversion of the position, the authority, the dignity and the reputation of the Apostolic See'. Unless the Pope complied with Henry's wishes, it would be impossible to prevent him from taking those measures which he was constantly being urged to take. Wolsey thought that the Devil was inspiring the Pope to resist Henry's desires, knowing that this would lead to the alienation of the devotion felt to the see of Rome.[23]

While Campeggio recovered from his illness, and played for time, and Henry and Wolsey became increasingly exasperated by the delay, a new difficulty arose. The Papal dispensation of 1503 had been contained in a bull the words of which could be interpreted – though this was arguable – as meaning that the dispensation for Henry to marry Catherine was granted on the assumption that her previous marriage to Prince Arthur had not been consummated. Wolsey and his lawyers were therefore accumulating evidence to prove that Arthur and Catherine had consummated the marriage, though Catherine strongly denied this; for, according to their interpretation of the words of the bull, this would invalidate the dispensation. But the emperor's advisers now discovered a Papal brief which had been issued in 1503 along with the bull, in which the wording of the dispensation was slightly different, and clearly stipulated that the dispensation was to apply even if the marriage of Arthur and Catherine had been consummated. Wolsey and his agents denounced this brief as a forgery; the lawyers in Spain asserted that it was genuine.

Henry asked Catherine to request Charles to send the brief to England, so that its authenticity could be established and the brief produced in evidence at the trial of the divorce. Catherine sent a request for the brief to Charles; but she smuggled a letter to him, telling him that she had been compelled to ask him to send it, and that on no account should he comply with the request, because she was sure that Wolsey would destroy this vital document if he got his hands on it. Wolsey was unsuccessful in his attempts to persuade the Pope to order Charles to send the brief to England, and Charles sent only a certified copy. When it arrived, Wolsey was delighted to find that the date of the brief gave him an excuse for alleging that it was a forgery. The brief was dated 27 December 1503, in accordance with the calendar ordinarily used in Rome – and in Spain – by which the year began on 1 January; but official Papal documents were always dated according to the ecclesiastical calendar with the year beginning on Christmas Day. The brief should therefore have been dated, like the bull, 27 December 1504. There were other minor inaccuracies in the brief. Wolsey decided to keep quiet about them, so that he could raise the point for the first time at the trial; for otherwise the emperor and his lawyers in Spain would forge another brief with the errors corrected.[24]

In January 1529 the Pope fell ill, and a rumour reached England that he had died. Wolsey was greatly perturbed by the news, because a new Pope might claim that he was not bound by Clement's promise not to revoke the decretal commission; and with the emperor's armies dominating Italy, it was likely that one of Charles's nominees would be elected to succeed Clement. But as usual he soon took an optimistic view of the situation, and saw how he could turn it to his own advantage. He and Henry urged their agents in Italy to work to get him elected Pope.

Never before had Henry intervened so strongly in Wolsey's favour at a Papal election. The instructions sent in the king's name at the beginning of February to Gardiner, Casale and his other agents in Rome were signed by Henry at the beginning and the end; but they were probably suggested by Wolsey himself. They stated that the king would be reluctant to seek a remedy for his matrimonial problem from any source other than the authority of the Apostolic See, and this made it essential that the new Pope should be favourable to his cause. The only Pope who would be acceptable to him was Wolsey. Wolsey's qualities, if fairly judged, should of themselves be sufficient to win him the election; but as human frailty unfortunately played a part in elections, Gardiner and the others must offer large bribes to the cardinals to vote for Wolsey. Henry would also pay for two or three thousand mercenaries to attend the conclave to protect Wolsey's supporters and overawe their opponents. If Wolsey were not elected, the cardinals should withdraw from the conclave and announce their intention of electing another Pope at a rival conclave. But having said this, Henry ended his instructions by stating that if it proved impossible to secure Wolsey's election, he would accept Campeggio as Pope.[25]

On 7 February Wolsey wrote a personal letter to Gardiner. He said that although he felt that he was too old to take on the duties of being Pope, he was willing to accept the office because he knew that no other cardinal could gain the confidence of Henry and François and restore the Church and the Apostolic See to its former dignity. So Gardiner was to spare no effort and expense to get him elected Pope.[26]

Soon afterwards news reached England that the Pope had recovered from his illness, and Wolsey resumed his badgering of Clement. He also urged François to help with the divorce by forcing the Venetians to surrender Ravenna and Cervia to the Pope.[27]

The trial of the divorce case began at last on 31 May 1529 in the hall of the Blackfriars church near Ludgate in the city of London. Wolsey and Campeggio sat as judges in the presence of fourteen bishops and abbots, and both Henry and Catherine were represented by counsel. After the opening formalities the proceedings were adjourned, for Wolsey was unable to persuade Campeggio to proceed at a faster pace than the slow stages by which cases moved in the courts in Rome.

At the session on 18 June there was a sensational development, which was still remembered by the people of London more than seventy years later when Shakespeare included it in his play *Henry VIII*. Catherine appeared before the court in person, and, dispensing with the services of her counsel, addressed the court herself. Turning to Henry, who was present, she asked him to do justice to her, a poor friendless alien in his realm; to take her back as his loving wife; and to admit to the court that she had come to his bed a virgin on their wedding night. She then told Wolsey and Campeggio that she refused to submit to their jurisdiction, and appealed to the Pope to hear the case in his court in Rome. Her action took Wolsey, Campeggio and Henry completely by surprise. Henry reacted by declaring the high regard which he had for her, and said that only the dictates of his conscience could have driven him, most reluctantly, to forsake her and bring divorce proceedings. Wolsey said that he was widely suspected of having instigated Henry to begin the divorce case, and asked Henry to deny the truth of the rumours. Henry said that they were indeed untrue; it had been his confessor, the Bishop of Lincoln, who had first raised doubts in his mind about the legality of his marriage to Catherine, whereas Wolsey had tried to dissuade, rather than to encourage, him from repudiating it.[28]

Wolsey and Campeggio had another shock ten days later, when Fisher intervened in the proceedings at Blackfriars. He stated that when the king began the divorce proceedings, he had invited all his bishops to speak their minds freely. Fisher therefore felt obliged to do so now. He declared that he believed that the marriage of Henry and Catherine was valid, and that no court had power to dissolve it. His intervention was unexpected, and had a great effect on the public.[29]

Wolsey and Campeggio overruled Catherine's objection to their jurisdiction, and proceeded for several weeks to hear evidence from aged noblemen, gentlemen, ladies and servants which was supposed to prove that Arthur and Catherine had consummated their marriage after their wedding in November 1501. The court heard how Prince Arthur had looked pale and tired on the morning after the wedding, no doubt because of his exertions on the wedding night, and of how he had told his gentlemen in the morning, after his first night with his Spanish bride, that he had been 'in the midst of Spain' last night.[30] There was enough evidence for Wolsey to give the decision which he wanted to give on the consummation issue; but he had other worries. His agents in Rome reported to him that the Pope was under pressure from the emperor's ambassador and the pro-Spanish cardinals to revoke the commission to Wolsey and Campeggio and to 'advoke' the case to his court in Rome; and they believed that he was considering doing so, despite his promise in the pollicitation of 23 July 1528. As the trial at Blackfriars continued, Wolsey became increasingly alarmed at the prospect of the advocation of the case to Rome, particularly after Catherine's appeal to the Pope in court on 18 June. On 22 June he wrote to Casale that he must at all costs stop the advocation to Rome. 'For you may constantly affirm unto his holiness that if he should at any prince's suit grant the said advocation he should not only thereby lose the King and devotion of this Realm from him and the see apostolic but also utterly destroy me for ever.'[31]

François and Charles had begun secret negotiations during the winter without telling Henry and Wolsey. By April 1529 they had agreed to hold peace talks at Cambrai, on the Netherlands' side of the frontier with France, at which François would be represented by Louise d'Angoulême and Charles by Margaret of Austria, who was the widow of Louise's brother, the Duke of Savoy. They invited Henry to send envoys to the talks at Cambrai. Wolsey was sure that he would be able to use the peace negotiations for his own advantage. He himself would go to Cambrai at the head of an impressive delegation, and deal with the two royal ladies with whom he had established such friendly relations at Bruges, Amiens and Compiègne. They would be unable to agree amongst themselves, but he would mediate, and would ultimately persuade them both to accept a compromise which would include some benefits for Henry and new pensions for himself from bishoprics in France and in the emperor's territories. The only difficulty was how to arrange his own time-table, for the divorce case was due to be heard in London at the end of May.

In the middle of May, he sent Suffolk and Fitzwilliam to François's court at Orleans to consult with the French on their peace negotiations with Charles. A few days after Suffolk and Fitzwilliam left, he had a talk with the French ambassador in London, Jean du Bellay, the Bishop of Bayonne, in his rooms at Richmond Palace. He adopted his usual tactic of stressing how most of the Council, the nobility and the people opposed the French alliance, and that only he favoured it. He said that he hoped to tie England and France so closely together that it would be impossible for England ever again to be the ally of the emperor. He told du Bellay that Norfolk and Suffolk had been suggesting to Henry that Wolsey had not done all he could to promote Henry's marriage to Anne Boleyn, and said that he would be grateful if François and Louise d'Angoulême would let Suffolk know, while he was at their court, that Wolsey had repeatedly urged them to put pressure on the Pope to grant the divorce. He also urged François to use all his influence in Rome in favour of the divorce, for otherwise he would be the cause of Wolsey's utter ruin, and Wolsey would never again be in a position to do François a service.[32]

When du Bellay saw Wolsey a week later on 25 May, Wolsey put forward a number of other suggestions. Louise d'Angoulême should drag out the peace talks with Margaret of Austria and keep them going throughout September and October, and, in the meantime, the French armies should try to capture Milan, Parma and Piacenza; for as Charles would not be expecting them to launch an offensive in Italy during the peace negotiations, he would be caught napping, and would be unable to put an army in the field to face the French. This would be so harmful to Charles's prestige that he would be compelled to accept less advantageous terms in the peace negotiations.[33] What Wolsey really meant was that Louise should not reach an agreement with Margaret until Wolsey, having given judgment in the divorce case in London, could join them at Cambrai and negotiate the peace that they had been unable to make by themselves; and that the French, by their successful offensive in Italy, would encourage the Pope to risk Charles's anger and give Henry his divorce.

On 4 June Suffolk wrote to Henry from Orleans describing a conversation that he had had with François. This talk almost certainly took place after François had been informed of Wolsey's request to du Bellay that François and Louise should tell Suffolk how eager Wolsey had been for the divorce. But François hated Wolsey. He remembered how Wolsey had tricked him during the Calais conference of 1521; how he had sent armies to invade and ravage France in 1522 and 1523; how he had extracted an outrageous indemnity from France in 1525; and how he had left the French to do the fighting in the present war. Yet François had been forced to dissemble, to write flattering letters to him, to treat him as an equal and a beloved brother at Amiens and Compiègne. But now, cold calculating statecraft coincided with his personal resentment; why should he help a king who had often been his enemy to retain the services of a very able minister?

At his meeting with François, Suffolk asked the king, after promising never to reveal it, what he thought was Wolsey's attitude towards the divorce. François gave a cunning answer. He said that when Wolsey was at Amiens and Compiègne he seemed to favour the divorce, for he did not like Queen Catherine.

Charles V, about 1527, by an unknown artist

ANNA BOLINA VXOR HENRI: OCTA

Anne Boleyn, by an unknown artist

'But I will speak frankly unto you. . . . Mine advice shall be to my good brother, that he shall have good regard, and not to put so much trust in no man, whereby he may be deceived, as nigh as he can. And the best remedy for the defence thereof is to look substantially upon his matters himself' . . . Further saying unto me, that my Lord Cardinal of England had a marvellous intelligence with the Pope, and in Rome, and also with the Cardinal Campegius. Wherefore, seeing that he hath such intelligence with them, which have not minded to advance your matter, he thinketh it shall be the more need for Your Grace to have the better regard to your said affair.[34]

François told du Bellay about his talk with Suffolk, and du Bellay told Wolsey. When Suffolk returned to England, Wolsey confronted him in Henry's presence, and accused him of denigrating him to the French king. Suffolk was taken aback; he admitted discussing Wolsey with François, but said that Wolsey had received an incorrect report of what he had said. Suffolk complained to du Bellay about this breach of confidence, and du Bellay complained to Wolsey, whose disclosure to Henry and Suffolk caused him embarrassment.[35] This may well have been a blunder on Wolsey's part; it showed Henry and Suffolk that he was scheming with the French ambassador.

As the trial at Blackfriars continued, it became increasingly clear that Wolsey would not be able to lead the English delegation at the peace talks. In the middle of June he was still determined to go, and was confident that only he could negotiate the peace. Suffolk reported that François had told him that Louise and Margaret would make peace after two days' talks at Cambrai. This caused great anxiety in Henry's Council, who did not wish to see England left out of the negotiations; but Wolsey continued to assure everyone that no peace could be made without him. He declared that if he did not take part in the talks at Cambrai, it would be an insult to the Holy See, of which Henry was the ally and protector. He wrote to Casale, instructing him to tell the Pope that he would meet Margaret of Austria and Louise d'Angoulême at Cambrai, and that unless he was there, no peace would be concluded. He promised the Pope that he would see that nothing was agreed at Cambrai to the detriment of the Apostolic See, provided that the Pope did nothing to hinder the divorce by advoking the cause to Rome. He demanded that Campeggio agree that they should give judgment for Henry in the divorce case within twenty days, so that he could leave for Cambrai. But by the end of the month he realised that it would be impossible for him to go, and on 30 June Tunstal, More, Knight and Hacket were appointed as the English envoys to Cambrai.[36]

Wolsey was right in thinking that he was the only man who possessed the necessary status to hold his own with Louise and Margaret at the peace talks. Tunstal and More were important members of the council, and More was famous throughout Europe as an intellectual; but they could not compete with the royal ladies, especially as England had played no part at all in the war. When Tunstal and More reached Cambrai, they found that Louise and Margaret had already made peace, and the English delegation were for a time unable even to obtain a copy of the peace treaty.[37]

From the English point of view, the terms were very unsatisfactory. François agreed to pay Charles 2,000,000 crowns, to cede Tournai, Charleroi, and the disputed frontier regions to the Netherlands, and to resign his claim to Milan. Charles agreed to free François's sons from captivity, and to allow François to keep the provinces of Burgundy, though Charles reserved his right to them. François was to keep the forfeited lands of the dead Duke of Bourbon, but abandoned his protection of the Duke of Guelders and Robert de La Marck. He was to marry Charles's sister. The whole of the 2,000,000 crowns was to be paid to Charles, and none of it to Henry in satisfaction of Charles's debts; and François also agreed to take upon himself the liability to pay Charles's debts to Henry, from which Charles was to be released. Henry and Wolsey had no alternative but to agree to these terms, unless they wished to be excluded from the peace and left to carry on the war against Charles by themselves; and Tunstal and More signed the peace treaty at Cambrai on 5 August. They had the slight consolation of also signing a favourable trade agreement with the Netherlands.[38]

Worse was to come for Wolsey. After two years of shilly-shallying the Pope had at last decided, at whatever cost, to come down on Charles's side. He sent envoys to Spain to negotiate with Charles, and on 29 June 1529 they signed a treaty of alliance at Barcelona by which the Pope's nephew was to marry Charles's illegitimate daughter. The negotiators at Barcelona had not yet heard the news from Italy that on 21 June Charles's armies had routed the French at Landriano. After Landriano, the arguments of the English and French agents in Rome carried no weight. On 6 July the Pope told Casale and his colleagues that he had decided to allow Catherine's appeal and advoke the case to Rome. On 16 July the decision was formally taken in the Consistory, and letters officially notifying Wolsey, Campeggio and Henry were sent on 19 July.[39]

The report of Casale's talk with the Pope on 6 July reached Wolsey on 22 July. He still hoped that he could somehow dissuade the Pope from advoking the cause to Rome;[40] but he was undoubtedly less surprised than anyone else at the developments which took place when the court at Blackfriars reassembled next day. Everyone expected that judgment would be given for Henry that day. Henry was present, and there were many spectators in the hall. But when Gardiner, as Henry's counsel, asked the court to give judgment for the king, Campeggio said that he and Wolsey needed more time to consider the great mass of documents; and as the legal term in the Roman courts finished at the end of July, they would have to adjourn the court until after the summer vacation, and would sit again in October. This decision, which took everyone by surprise, caused consternation. Suffolk shouted out: 'It was never merry in England whilst we had Cardinals amongst us'.[41]

Within days the news was spreading throughout England and Europe: the Cardinal of York had fallen.

CHAPTER 14

THE FALLEN CARDINAL

WE do not really know why Wolsey fell from power. The people who were responsible, or were accused of being responsible, for his ruin did not leave any surviving record of their actions or motives, and we have to rely on the gossip and speculation of foreign ambassadors, Wolsey's servants, and members of the general public, none of whom, perhaps, was in a position to know the truth. They all agreed that Anne Boleyn was chiefly responsible, and this is certainly not disproved by the friendly, respectful and charming letters that she wrote to him from time to time during the two years before his downfall.

The observers also picked out Norfolk, Suffolk, and Anne's father Rochford as being Wolsey's chief enemies in the Council. There is some evidence that Suffolk was the most determined of the three. This has often been condemned as an act of base ingratitude by Suffolk, who had been protected by Wolsey in 1515 when he was in grave danger after offending Henry by his unauthorised marriage to Henry's sister, the widowed Queen of France. Suffolk was not the only ungrateful courtier in the sixteenth century who did great injury to a benefactor in order to advance his career; but this is not an explanation of why Suffolk turned so strongly against Wolsey. He was annoyed that Wolsey had unjustly deprived the Abbot of St Benet's Holme of his abbey;[1] but was there perhaps some other incident, of which no record has survived, which embittered Suffolk against Wolsey?

Whatever part the individual members of the Council may have played, the real reason for Wolsey's fall was that Henry had decided to break with Rome. The time had come for him to put into operation the threats that Wolsey and Gardiner had been making on his behalf during the past eighteen months, and take England into schism because the Pope would not grant him a divorce. This meant encouraging the numerous elements among his people who hated foreigners, priests, monks and Wolsey. The foreign ambassadors, Wolsey, More, and the Catholic writers of the next generation called these elements 'Lutherans', and believed that they were led by the Lutheran Boleyns. This was both true and untrue, according to the meaning attached to the word 'Lutheran'. If it meant the followers of Luther, who believed in his heretical doctrines, then the forces that worked against Wolsey and supported Anne Boleyn were not Lutheran; for neither the Boleyns, nor anyone in England apart from a small minority of potential martyrs, were Lutherans. But those who denounced 'Lutherans' used the term in a much wider sense to mean the large and growing body of opinion among all classes of the population who objected to the hegemony of a foreign Pope, to the delays and expense involved in lawsuits and the procurement of dispensations in Rome, to the domination of a corrupt bureaucracy of priests, to the high rents extorted from them by the monks who were their landlords, and to the proud, powerful and fabulously wealthy Cardinal of York. In this sense, the Boleyns, many of Henry's courtiers, and probably a majority of the English people were Lutherans, though they were quite happy to watch a heretic burned for repudiating transubstantiation, Purgatory, salvation by works, and images, or for translating the Bible into English.

In their drive against heretical books, the Church proscribed not only doctrinal innovation but also this more popular form of criticism. Tracts like Simon Fish's *A Supplication for the Beggars* and other works which denounced the pomp of prelates and the rapacity of monks were far more effective propaganda than the theological books of Luther and Tyndale. When, in the spring of 1529, Campeggio complained to Henry that heretical books were circulating at court, he was referring above all to the *Supplication for the Beggars*, which was apparently being read with great approval by Anne Boleyn and by Henry himself.[2] The Papal supporters were inaccurate when they condemned these anti-Papist, anti-clerical forces as 'Lutheran'; but they were right in believing that the national hatred of Rome and the churchmen would lead in due course to doctrinal heresy.

In June 1529, while Wolsey was sitting in state with Campeggio in his legatine court as the judge between the king and queen, and was to all appearances the ruler of England and the arbiter of Europe, the king's agents were already compiling a dossier against him and sending Henry's secretaries a long list of the offences and irregularities, however technical and trivial, which Wolsey had committed during the last fifteen years.[3] The adjournment of the legatine court, and Suffolk's denunciation of cardinals, at Blackfriars on 23 July were everywhere taken as a sign of Wolsey's downfall. People did not merely believe and say that the cardinal was about to fall, but spoke as if he had already fallen.

Only Wolsey himself refused to believe it. As usual, he kept his nerve, and tried to remedy the situation. On 27 July he wrote to Casale explaining that it was essential that the Pope should reverse his decision about advoking the case to Rome, and send instructions to Campeggio to give judgment for Henry when the court at Blackfriars sat again in October; for if the Pope advoked the case to Rome and summoned Henry to appear there, none of Henry's subjects would tolerate it, and if Henry appeared in Italy, it would be at the head of a formidable army.[4] This threat was not likely to impress the Pope, in view of the difficulties and delays which had occurred in recent years whenever Henry had promised to send an army even to Calais, especially as Charles did in fact have a formidable army in Italy which had thrashed Henry's French ally at Landriano.

A few days after the adjournment of the court at Blackfriars, Henry left on his usual summer progress. Wolsey stayed at Hampton Court and The Moor, and was unable to see Henry for several weeks. There was nothing unusual in this, as he was nearly always separated from Henry in August and September every year during the king's progresses; but this year it came at an unfortunate time for Wolsey. He wrote regularly to Henry, putting forward suggestions as to how to induce the Pope to rescind the advocation of the divorce case to Rome and to issue a new commission to try it in England. He received replies from Gardiner, who, after his very able handling of the divorce business in Italy and at Blackfriars, had been appointed as Henry's principal secretary. Gardiner wrote to Wolsey several times during August, thanking him, on Henry's behalf, for his letters and advice and conveying Henry's good wishes. He also wrote asking Wolsey for information about the text of the Treaty of Madrid, its legal interpretation, and about other aspects of internal and foreign policy. Henry, Gardiner, and the members of the Council were trying to learn how to govern England without Wolsey; and Wolsey had no alternative but to teach them.[5]

As the emperor had made peace with England at Cambrai, he sent a new ambassador to London. He chose a very able churchman from Franche-Comté, Eustace Chapuys, who remained at Henry's court for the next sixteen years and sent Charles, about once a week, a long report on the political situation in England, thus providing one of the chief sources of information for twentieth-century historians. He arrived in London in the last days of August 1529, and in his first dispatch to Charles on 1 September he reported that Wolsey's affairs were getting worse and worse every day. Chapuys was given to understand that Henry did not wish him, or any foreign ambassador, to visit Wolsey, and as Queen Catherine confirmed that Wolsey was finished, Chapuys took care not to call on him.[6] He wrote to Charles on 4 September that Suffolk, Norfolk and Rochford now ruled at court, and were determined to destroy Wolsey. 'Formerly no one dared say a word against the cardinal, but now the tables are turned and his name is in everybody's mouth; and, what is worse for him, libellous writings, I am told, are being circulated about him.'[7]

But du Bellay visited Wolsey on 15 and 16 September, and was surprised to find him so unperturbed.

During the two days that I was with him, he spoke to me sometimes about what was going on at this court, not showing himself as annoyed with them as I am sure he is. I have less hope of his maintaining his influence, since my talk with him, than I had before, for I see he trusts in some of his own creatures, who, I am sure, have turned their coats. I am very shaken, for I should never have believed that they would have been so wicked; and the worst of it is that he does not realise it.[8]

Wolsey was still going ahead with his plans for his college at Ipswich, and received new bulls from the Pope, allowing him to suppress monasteries for this purpose. But there were ominous signs. When he sent Rowland Phillips, the Vicar of Croydon, to press the Abbot of Wigmore in Herefordshire to surrender his monastery, offering him a pension of 40 marks a year if he complied, the abbot refused the offer. Phillips wrote to Wolsey on 31 August that not long ago the abbot would gladly have accepted the pension, but that now he relied on a great change taking place, and especially on the extinction of Wolsey's authority. On 10 September Wolsey's agent in Southampton reported that the Vicar of Southampton had appointed a chantry priest in the town without consulting Wolsey, in defiance of his authority as Bishop of Winchester.[9]

Wolsey thought that it was high time that he saw the king. At the beginning of September he wrote to Henry, asking permission to visit him, as he had things to discuss with him which he could not conveniently put into writing. He received a reply from Gardiner from Woodstock on 12 September, saying that Henry could not imagine what business Wolsey might wish to discuss which could not just as well be put into writing; would Wolsey therefore send him a very brief note stating whether the business concerned internal or foreign affairs, and if foreign affairs, what country.[10] Wolsey apparently did not pursue this line any further, but thought of another way of gaining access to Henry. Campeggio was about to return to Rome, and it would be necessary for him to pay the usual farewell courtesy visit to Henry to ask leave to depart and receive his passports for the journey. Wolsey would go to court with Campeggio, for it would be difficult for Henry to object to his being present on such an occasion. He invited Campeggio to come and stay with him at The Moor, to make it more difficult for Campeggio to go to Henry without taking him with him.

Campeggio wrote to Henry asking leave to pay his farewell visit and to bring Wolsey with him. Henry, on his progress, had now reached Grafton in Northamptonshire, some fifty-five miles from London, and Campeggio was told that he and Wolsey could both come to Grafton, but must not bring with them more than ten or twelve servants each.[11] This was a reasonable order in view of the limited accommodation available at Grafton, though it was generally interpreted as a step to abate the pride of the two Papal Legates. Wolsey and Campeggio reached Grafton on 18 September. Apart from his foreign embassies and his occasional pilgrimages to Walsingham, it was the first time during his fifteen years in high office that Wolsey had travelled so far from London.

When they reached Grafton, Campeggio was shown to his apartments in the palace; but when Wolsey asked which rooms had been assigned to him, he was informed that there was no lodging available for him. Then Sir Henry Norris, the King's Groom of the Stole, appeared, and in a most friendly manner invited Wolsey to make use of his apartments. Wolsey changed out of his riding habit in Norris's rooms, and was told that accommodation had been provided for him for the night at Mr Empson's house at Easton Neston, a few miles away. The courtiers were wondering whether Henry would agree to receive Wolsey; they were betting on it, and the odds were that he would not be admitted to the king's presence.

When the time came for Campeggio to be received by the king, Wolsey went with him to the audience chamber. The counsellors and courtiers whom Wolsey knew so well were waiting there for the king to arrive. Wolsey doffed his cap to them in salute, and they doffed theirs to him in return. When Henry entered, he embraced both Wolsey and Campeggio warmly. After the audience, he took Wolsey apart to a window seat, and had a long talk with him, during which Henry insisted that Wolsey replace his cap on his head. Cavendish, who was present among Wolsey's attendants, overheard one remark in their conversation, when Henry showed Wolsey a document and commented that it was in Wolsey's handwriting; but Cavendish is not always absolutely accurate in points of detail, and even if he correctly heard what Henry said, it gives no hint of what they were discussing. Everyone agreed that Henry had been very friendly to Wolsey. It was dark by the time that Wolsey left, and he was escorted by torchlight to Mr Empson's house at Easton Neston.

While he was having supper in Empson's house, Gardiner arrived from Grafton. He talked to Wolsey at supper about his recent journey home from Italy, and about hunting, and greyhounds as hunting dogs. But afterwards they withdrew together, and talked for a long time.

What did they discuss? Once again, the secret has died with them.

Wolsey rode over to Grafton next morning, hoping to speak to Henry again; but he found that Henry was on the point of leaving for a day's hunting. Henry told him to attend a meeting of the Council, and then to escort Campeggio on his journey from Grafton. Henry said goodbye to Wolsey in a very friendly way, and rode off to the hunt. Wolsey never saw him again.

After Henry had left, Wolsey presided at a meeting of the Council, where everyone treated him with their usual deference, and routine business was transacted. Wolsey then rode away with Campeggio to his abbey of St Albans, which he had so rarely visited during the seven years that he had been its abbot. He spent a day there before continuing his journey to The Moor. Campeggio left The Moor for Rome.[12] At Dover his luggage was thoroughly searched by the customs officials, despite his indignant protests that this was a violation of his diplomatic immunity. He heard a rumour that they had searched his luggage because they thought that he was smuggling Wolsey's valuables and secret documents out of England.[13]

Wolsey was encouraged by his reception at Grafton, and was determined to carry on as if nothing had happened. The Michaelmas law term began on 9 October, and Wolsey went to Westminster Hall to sit in the court of Chancery on the first day. The public were surprised to see him come there, with as large an escort of retainers and armed guards as ever. But while he was sitting in the court of Chancery, the Attorney-General was applying in the court of King's Bench next door for a summons ordering Wolsey to appear in the court of King's Bench to answer a charge of being guilty of a *praemunire*.[14] A *praemunire* was the equivalent of the offence which in France and other European countries was called '*lèse-majesté*' – a grave offence against the king which fell just short of high treason, and was punishable, not by death, but by imprisonment for life, with forfeiture of all the guilty man's goods to the king. The offence which was alleged to be a *praemunire* was Wolsey's exercise of his powers as Papal Legate, which was said to be a usurpation by an agent of a foreign potentate of the king's sovereign power in his realm. The Statute of Praemunire of Edward III's reign had been directed against the usurpation of power in England by the Pope; but since 1462 it had been recognised that a Papal Legate was not guilty of a *praemunire* in exercising his legatine powers.

Wolsey immediately understood the situation. Under pressure from the king's government, the common law judges of the court of King's Bench, who had always regarded the Lord Chancellor as a rival, and shared all the national prejudices against Rome, Papal Legates and Wolsey, were certain to find him guilty. This meant dismissal from all his offices, and that his personal liberty and his property would be at Henry's mercy; but there were also grounds for hope. The fact that he had been charged with a *praemunire* and not with high treason meant that he would not be put to death; and this raised the possibility, and even the probability, of a pardon, and perhaps of a return to power at some time in the future. Wolsey was apparently told privately by Gardiner or some of his friends at court that, if he pleaded guilty, Henry would pardon him and allow him to live quietly in retirement and to retain part of his property.

Despite being charged with a *praemunire*, he remained Lord Chancellor for another week. It was not until 16 October that Norfolk and Suffolk came to York Place and informed him that the king ordered him to deliver up the Great Seal to them. Wolsey asked them for their written authority from the king. As they had nothing in writing, Wolsey refused to hand over the Great Seal, claiming that, as the king had entrusted it to him, it was his duty to retain it and guard it until he had proof that the king wished him to surrender it. Wolsey had always been prepared to dispense with formalities in order to expedite business during his days of power; but now he saw things from another angle. Norfolk and Suffolk had to return to the king at Windsor to obtain his written authority. When they came again to York Place next day, and showed it to Wolsey, he delivered up the Great Seal to them.[15]

There was much speculation among the courtiers and diplomats as to who would be appointed to succeed him. The rumour spread that instead of choosing an ecclesiastic, the king would take the almost unprecedented step of appointing a layman, the Duke of Suffolk, as Lord Chancellor. But the nobility, especially Norfolk, were opposed to the aggrandisement of Suffolk, who was only a humble gentleman by birth before he rose through Henry's favour to become a duke and the king's brother-in-law. On 25 October it was announced that the king had entrusted the Great Seal to Sir Thomas More, who was appointed Lord Chancellor. His appointment caused surprise, and was seen as a compromise and stop-gap which was intended to prevent a possible split between Suffolk and Norfolk.[16]

On 22 October Wolsey signed a statement pleading guilty to the charge of a *praemunire*.[17] He did not attend his trial in the court of King's Bench eight days later, when his counsel pleaded guilty on his behalf. The court then pronounced him convicted of a *praemunire*, and sentenced him to be imprisoned during the king's pleasure and all his property to be forfeited to the king. In pleading guilty, Wolsey had done what was expected of him; but he could not cringe, because he was psychologically incapable of doing so. He never demonstrated so clearly as he did during the last year of his life, after his fall from power, his character, his self-confidence, his optimism, his fighting spirit, his shrewd calculation of a situation, his ability to drive a good bargain and to negotiate from weakness, his skill in playing a bad hand, his dignity, and the respect which his strong personality extracted from all who met him.

He was informed that he must leave York Place and take up residence at Esher, a house belonging to him as Bishop of Winchester, only a few miles from Hampton Court. He prepared to leave, and ordered his officers to make an inventory of his priceless gold plate and tapestries, and all his other goods, so as to be ready to hand them over to the king's officers. The word had spread among his servants, and among the public in London and Westminster, that he was to be taken to the Tower; but when his Treasurer, Sir William Gascoign, expressed his sympathies, Wolsey assured him that he was not going to the Tower. The river was full of boats, for more than a thousand people had come in the boats to see Wolsey taken to the Tower. But when he walked for the last time down his private stairs from York Place to the water, and entered his barge, it was rowed away, to everyone's surprise, in the opposite direction. He went up-stream to Putney, where he landed, intending to go overland to Esher.

He had just mounted his mule when Sir Henry Norris arrived, and handed Wolsey a valuable ring as a gift from the king. This was not merely a gesture of goodwill; if the king gave a man a ring, it was a sign that he did not wish the man to be arrested without the case being referred to him personally. If the council, or any other authority, gave orders to arrest Wolsey, he would only need to show them the king's ring, and he would be taken to Henry's presence and not incarcerated in the Tower or some other prison. Wolsey dismounted from his mule, and on his knees by the water's edge at Putney he thanked the king for his kindness and Norris for bringing him the news. His gentlemen had some difficulty in helping him to remount; but he was a happier man as he rode up the hill through the village to Putney Heath and westward to Esher.[18]

Before the end of October, he was visited at Esher by Norfolk, who treated him with courtesy and respect. Norfolk accepted Wolsey's invitation to dinner; but when Wolsey suggested that they should wash hands together, and that Norfolk should sit by his side at the dinner table, he declined both these honours, and insisted on sitting in a lower place. Wolsey said that now that it was illegal for him to be a Papal Legate, it was not proper for Norfolk to accept an inferior position. Norfolk replied that he had never honoured Wolsey as a Papal Legate, but as he was still a cardinal and Archbishop of York, he acknowledged that Wolsey's rank was superior to his own. This conversation was not merely a display of courtesy; both men were safeguarding themselves by refusing to allow the other to manoeuvre them into a position in which they could be accused of aspiring to a higher rank than that which the king had granted them.[19]

After dinner, Mr Justice Shelley of the Court of Common Pleas arrived, and told Wolsey that the king wanted him to give him York Place. Wolsey had a bargaining counter here. By his conviction for a *praemunire*, he had forfeited all his property to the king; but as only he, and not his successors in the sees of York and Winchester, had been guilty of the *praemunire*, the forfeiture would only be valid during his life, and the property would revert to his successors after his death. This would not apply if Wolsey voluntarily conveyed the property to the king. Wolsey told Shelley that he wished to do everything in his power to please the king, but could not injure his sees by giving away their property. After Shelley had said that in return for York Place, Henry would give back to Wolsey all the other property of the archbishopric of York which had been forfeited under the *praemunire*, Wolsey agreed to surrender York Place; but he ended the conversation by asking Shelley to remind the king that there was a Heaven and a Hell.[20]

Parliament met on 3 November; it was to sit for seven years, and carry through a revolution in the ecclesiastical and social systems of England. More, as Lord Chancellor, opened the proceedings with a denunciation of Wolsey's misdeeds, and soon afterwards More introduced a bill of attainder which passed without difficulty in both Houses. It confirmed the judicial decision of the court of King's Bench that Wolsey was guilty of a *praemunire*; it was the almost invariable practice, when prominent public figures were convicted of high treason or *praemunire*, to confirm the judgment of the court by Act of Parliament.

The bill listed, in forty-four articles, all the offences, real and false, serious and trivial, which Wolsey had committed during his years in power. After beginning with his most serious crime, the exercise of his authority as Legate, he was accused of making treaties with the Pope and the French king without Henry's authority; of authorising Sir Gregory di Casale to make a treaty with the Duke of Ferrara; of using the term 'the King and I' in his letters to foreign parts, thus showing that he 'used himself more like a fellow to your Highness than like a subject'; of having endangered the king's person, when, knowing that he had 'the foul and contagious disease of the great pox broken out upon him in divers places of his body, came daily to Your Grace, rowning in your ear and blowing upon your most noble Grace with his perilous and infective breath', while he pretended that he had merely a cold in the head; of reading the letters of English ambassadors abroad and not showing them to the king; and ordering spies to send their reports to him personally; of granting himself licences to export grain, to his own profit, at times when the export of grain was prohibited; of suppressing monasteries, with the result that vagabonds, beggars and thieves increased; of not allowing the members of the council, except for one or two great personages, to express their opinions in the discussions at the council meetings; of making litigants in the court of Chancery come to his house to conduct their business; of interfering, by his judgments as Chancellor, with the decisions of the common law judges (an accusation which the judges made against every Lord Chancellor); of granting *ex parte* injunctions to plaintiffs in the defendant's absence; of forcing the religious houses to remit to him the right to elect their head; of appropriating to his own use the greater part of the revenues which his son Winter drew from his ecclesiastical benefices; of imprisoning Sir John Stanley and not releasing him until he had given his land to Mr Lee of Adlington, who married Lark's daughter, 'which Woman the said Lord Cardinal kept, and had with her two Children'. The last charge was that he had stopped the bishops from taking steps to prevent the spread of Lutheran heresies at Cambridge University.

In view of these offences, the House of Lords begged the king to make an example of the cardinal. Thomas More headed the list of the signatories of the bill, followed by Norfolk and Suffolk and fourteen other peers, including the Earl of Dorset, who had been a pupil of Wolsey's at Oxford thirty years before.[21]

But Wolsey knew that his fate depended, not on the lies that More and the peers told about him in the House of Lords, but on Henry's decisions and on the influence that could be brought to bear for and against him at court. He knew that it was necessary to negotiate the best possible bargains and to give bribes in the right places. He gave pensions of £200 a year from the bishopric of Winchester and 200 marks a year from the abbey of St Albans to Anne Boleyn's brother, Viscount Rochford – their father had been created Earl of Wiltshire in December 1529; and Winter had to surrender many of his benefices and lands to various clerics and courtiers.[22]

It was necessary for Wolsey to employ a skilful agent in these transactions. He chose Thomas Cromwell, who had acted for him in connection with the suppression of the monasteries and in other matters. Cromwell did useful work for Wolsey. He also took the opportunity to turn the situation to his own advantage. He expected, and received, gifts from Wolsey as a reward for his services, and he made full use of the opportunities which his work for Wolsey gave him of meeting the king and impressing him by his abilities. It is not surprising that Wolsey, with his knowledge of the men with whom he had to deal, did not entirely trust Cromwell. On one occasion he suspected Cromwell of working against him with his enemies behind his back. Cromwell got to hear of

Wolsey's suspicions, and wrote and remonstrated with him. Wolsey knew that he needed Cromwell, and assured him that he trusted him.[23]

The Lord Chancellor took the opportunity to acquire something for his family. More asked Wolsey to grant him a house which he owned in Battersea for the use of More's son-in-law, William Dauncey, Elizabeth's husband. The house was occupied by Wolsey's servant, John Oxenherd, who had married one of Wolsey's relations. Wolsey agreed to give the house to More on the understanding that the Oxenherds were allowed to continue to reside there and to enjoy half the pasture of the adjoining land on payment of a fair rent. A few months later, Dauncey, taking advantage of Oxenherd's absence on Wolsey's service, ejected Mrs Oxenherd and the children from the house, although they had nowhere else to go. Wolsey wrote to Cromwell, bitterly complaining of Dauncey's breach of faith, and asking Cromwell to raise the matter with More.[24] We do not know whether his protests were successful.

At Esher, during the winter of 1529–30, Wolsey heard sometimes bad, and sometimes good, news from court. Cavendish and the members of his household, all of whom remained loyal to him, believed that his enemies at court were deliberately trying to injure his health by causing him daily annoyance. His chief anxiety was the fear, that caused so much worry to all eminent persons in the sixteenth century and particularly to Wolsey, that the number of his servants would be reduced in order to lower his status and prestige. On several occasions Sir John Russell and other emissaries from the king came to Esher and ordered him to send a number of his servants to serve Henry in some capacity, usually in connection with Wolsey's property that had been confiscated by the king. But from time to time he received messages of goodwill from Henry and tokens of Henry's regard for him. Henry sent him two more rings, one of them being a ring of great value that Wolsey had given him some years before.[25]

Shortly before Christmas, Wolsey fell ill. When Henry heard this, he sent his physician, Dr Butts, and several other doctors to attend on Wolsey. This worried Wolsey a little, no doubt because he feared that his enemies might have arranged for the doctors to poison him; but he felt happier when he discovered that one of them was a Scottish doctor whom he had once befriended. The doctors had him out of bed after four days. He took the opportunity of their visit to give Butts the impression that the best cure for his illness would be for him to receive some token of the king's affection. Butts duly reported this to Henry, who not only sent Wolsey another ring, but persuaded Anne Boleyn to send him a golden ornament from her girdle as a sign of her regard for him.[26]

Gardiner, on the king's behalf, negotiated an agreement with Wolsey. The king would grant Wolsey a formal pardon for his *praemunire*, and allow him to retain the archbishopric of York, with all its lands and revenues except York Place; in return, Wolsey would surrender York Place and all his other houses to the king, and after granting leases and pensions from the property of the see of Winchester to various courtiers, would resign as Bishop of Winchester and Abbot of St Albans and surrender all the revenues of the bishopric and the abbey to the king. Wolsey did not accept this without an argument. He said that when he agreed to plead guilty to the *praemunire*, he had been led to believe that he would be allowed to retain all his bishoprics and property. He told Cromwell to explain to Gardiner and the Council that £4,000 a year was the least – 'mine degree considered' – on which he could live, which was not a meagre sum at a time when an agricultural labourer earned just over £5 a year.[27]

He could not complain of the final arrangement. On 10 February the king granted him a general pardon, and four days later all the property of the archbishopric of York, except York Place. He was also given £3,000 in money; over 9,500 ounces of plate, worth £1,753.3s.7½d.; tapestries and beds worth £800; eighty horses with their apparel, worth £150; fifty-two oxen worth £80; seventy muttons worth £12; and other things, reaching a total value of £6,374.3s.7½d. In addition, he was granted a pension of 1,000 marks a year, and was allowed, for the time being, to live in the Bishop of Winchester's house at Esher. But towards the end of the winter, Wolsey wished to move from Esher, for it was the accepted practice at the period to air a large house by leaving it empty from time to time, to minimise the risk of disease. He therefore asked Henry's permission to move from Esher, and at the beginning of February he was allowed to take up residence in Richmond Palace. This was unquestionably a mark of Henry's favour, and it was seen as such by Wolsey's enemies at court, who thought that at Richmond, Wolsey would be too close to the court and the king.[28]

For the first time in his life Wolsey, in his hour of adversity, began to show an interest in the spiritual side of religion. At the beginning of Lent, he moved from the palace to the house of the Prior of the Charterhouse at Richmond, and spent much time with the monks. They persuaded him to seek solace in prayer and penances, and gave him two or three hairshirts, which he sometimes wore.[29] This may have been the development of real religious feelings in Wolsey. It certainly made a good impression on the gentlemen of his household, and helped to present the image which Cromwell and his friends were putting forward at court, of a new, humble Wolsey, who henceforth would think only of spiritual, and never of political, matters.

He pointed out to his gentlemen the sculpture at Richmond Palace, and drew their attention to the statues of the cow, the family emblem of

Henry VII. He told them that there used to be a prophecy spoken of at Richmond: 'When this cow rideth the bull, then, priest, beware thy skull'. Wolsey said he had never met anyone who could interpret the prophecy.[30] By the time that Cavendish wrote his book about Wolsey in 1557, everyone could interpret it: when the Tudor cow (Henry) rode the bull (Boleyn), priests would be in danger. Did Wolsey himself invent the rhyme and the prophecy?

Wolsey's enemies were afraid. They knew what he would do to them if he ever returned to power and was in a position to take his revenge. Again we do not know who were the enemies who plotted his final ruin in 1530, for everyone pretended to be friendly. Norfolk, Gardiner and More all showed an apparent readiness to help Wolsey, and responded favourably to his requests; but Norfolk was speaking against him to the emperor's ambassador, and promising that he would not permit Wolsey to return to power to damage once again the friendly relations between Henry and Charles.[31]

If Wolsey's enemies were afraid of him, he was also afraid of them. To avert the danger, he resorted, as usual, to a bold and risky course of action: he invoked the aid of François I and Louise d'Angoulême. It was less than a year since François had written loving letters to '*Monsieur le Cardinal, mon bon ami*', and Louise even warmer ones to '*Monsieur le Cardinal, mon bon père et fils*'. On 15 March the French ambassador in London, Vaulx, wrote to François that Wolsey, who was now at Richmond, 'earnestly entreats Your Majesty and Madame to help him in his need, remembering the service which he rendered to you at opportune times; adding, that if you and Madame help him, as he not only hopes but fully expects, in proportion to the greatness of his fall, this will be the greater demonstration of your bounty'.[32] On the following day, Chapuys wrote to the emperor and reported that Wolsey had sent his Venetian physician, Dr Agostini, to see him, ostensibly to inquire about Wolsey's pensions which were due to be paid to him from the bishopric of Palencia; but Agostini did not confine his conversation to the pensions, and told Chapuys that Wolsey had every hope of returning to power. Wolsey said nothing about his political aspirations to Vaulx, whom he invited to visit him, a few days later, at the Charterhouse at Richmond. He gave Vaulx the impression that he wished to lead a spiritual religious life in his retirement; but if this was really what he wanted, he would hardly have troubled to invite the French ambassador to Richmond and to inform him of the fact.[33]

Norfolk and Anne Boleyn wanted him out of Richmond, and away from court and the foreign ambassadors. He was informed that the king wished him to leave Richmond and go to his diocese of York to carry out his duties as archbishop. Wolsey did not wish to go so far away from court, and tried unsuccessfully to be allowed to live in his diocese of Winchester; but he was told that he must go to York. It was not, in the circumstances, an unreasonable arrangement, for it was a usual practice for the bishops who had served on the Council to go to their dioceses and reside there when they ended their career in the king's service.

Wolsey explained that he could not afford to go to York in the state which befitted an archbishop, and asked the king to contribute to the cost of his journey. There was some opposition in the Council to this request, but they agreed to give him 1,000 marks out of the revenues of the bishopric of Winchester for his travel expenses. Wolsey wanted more, and his agents approached Henry, who secretly paid Wolsey another £1,000 without letting his council know about it.[34]

Wolsey left Richmond on 5 April, with an escort of six hundred gentlemen and servants, and twelve carts carrying his baggage. He stayed the first night at the Abbot of Westminster's house at Hendon; the second, at Lady Parr's at Rye House; the third, at the monastery in Royston; and the fourth at Huntingdon Abbey. On the fifth day, Palm Sunday, he arrived at Peterborough Abbey. He stayed several days at Peterborough, and on Maundy Thursday performed the traditional ceremony of washing the feet of the same number of beggars as the years of his life. Wolsey washed the feet of fifty-nine beggars.* He then moved north, staying at the house near Peterborough of his old colleague on the Council, Sir William Fitzwilliam, and with various local gentlemen in Stamford, Grantham and Newark. Some of his hosts were not sure how they ought to treat him; but after More and the other members of the Council had written to them, telling them that the king wished him to be received with the honours due to an archbishop of York, they all treated him with the greatest respect. At Newark he crossed the Trent into the diocese of York, and went to Southwell. It was the first time that he had set foot in the diocese since his appointment as archbishop sixteen years before; and at Southwell, three miles over the border of the diocese, he stayed. It was the nearest he could be to London and the court while complying with the order to reside in the diocese of York.[35]

At Southwell, he found the archbishops' palace in a bad state of repair, and took up residence in the canon's house nearby, while the repairs to the palace were carried out. He lived in grand style at Southwell. He repaired the palace and began transforming it into a magnificent building; he administered justice in his archiepiscopal court; and he held open house for hundreds of beggars and petitioners. A few people, thinking that he was in disgrace, treated him in an off-hand

* This would correspond with his having been born in the year ending 24 March 1472/3. As to this, see Pollard, *Wolsey*, p. 276n.

manner, and he complained to Cromwell and his agents in London that the bargemen at Hull were remiss in delivering the additional baggage which he had sent by sea and the quails that he wanted for his table; but he crushed all signs of insolence by assuring everybody that the king wished him to be treated with deference.[36]

Reports of his activities and popularity at Southwell reached London and the court. Cromwell warned him that his splendid style of living, and especially his building work at Southwell, were being interpreted by his enemies as proof that he was as ambitious as ever. Cromwell urged him to live in a humbler style. On 18 August he wrote to Wolsey:

> Sir, some there be that doth allege that Your Grace doth keep too great a house and family, and that ye are continually building; for the love of God therefore, I eftsoons, as I often times have done, most heartily beseech Your Grace to have respect to every thing, and considering the time, to refrain yourself, for a season, from all manner buildings, more than mere necessity requireth; which I assure Your Grace shall cease, and put to silence, some persons that much speaketh of the same.[37]

Wolsey claimed that the building work at Southwell had been necessary to repair the dilapidations to the palace.

From time to time, he received letters from the Council with regard to his administrative duties as Archbishop of York. On instructions from More, he sent his servants and tenants to arrest three wanted criminals in his diocese; but he explained that in view of the feeling in the district it would be risky to try to take the men to London, as More required, and he suggested that their case should be tried by some gentlemen in the locality. In June he received a letter from Henry, asking him if he could remember details of a case in 1522 in which the ship of a Breton merchant had been seized, as the merchant was now claiming compensation.[38] He wrote to Henry that 'by reasons of my great age, great heaviness and calamity, my remembrance is not so fresh and quick as it hath been';[39] but he was able to supply the information which was required. In July the House of Lords sent a petition to the Pope, asking him to give judgment for Henry in the divorce case. Wolsey was asked to sign, and his name appeared first in the list of signatories, being placed above Warham and all the other bishops, abbots and peers. The Lord Chancellor, More, did not sign.[40]

Wolsey was anxious about the fate of his colleges. Perhaps nothing that he had done during his years of power had meant so much to him as these two great monuments to his patronage of education and culture. He had asked the cardinals in Rome and the English agents in Europe to find the most learned scholars as lecturers for the Oxford college, the most valuable books for its library, and the best musicians and singers for its chapel; and foreign rulers and prelates who wished to please him had done their best to gratify him by presenting valuable gifts to Cardinal's College. Now both the Oxford and Ipswich colleges were threatened by the forfeiture of Wolsey's property through his conviction for the *praemunire*. Wolsey urged Cromwell to use all his influence at court to save the colleges, and the heads of the colleges travelled up from Oxford and Ipswich to plead their case.

The plight of the colleges aroused a good deal of sympathy among many of the king's counsellors, especially the churchmen. Cardinal's College at Oxford had been functioning for more than three years, and the Ipswich college for fifteen months, before Wolsey's fall. The Dean, the fellows and lecturers, and two hundred undergraduates were in residence at Cardinal's College in Oxford; and at Ipswich the Dean and forty-two priests, choirboys and poor men were teaching, learning and singing masses for the souls of Wolsey's father and mother. The king sent commissioners to close down the colleges, to seize all their property and divide it between the king and the friends of the Boleyns. The tenants of the Ipswich college were refusing to pay their rents to the college, believing that they ought to pay the rents to the king.[41]

Wolsey, Cromwell and the deans of the colleges tried two alternative methods of saving the colleges. They consulted lawyers about legal ways of evading the forfeiture, and they used their influence at court to persuade Henry, if the forfeiture took effect, to allow the colleges to continue when they came into his hands. When Wolsey founded the colleges he had persuaded or forced the monasteries and the other donors to give their property to him, and he had then conveyed it to the deans and fellows of the colleges, who had become the owners several years before Wolsey had been convicted of the *praemunire* in the court of King's Bench; but the lawyers advised that the forfeiture was retrospective to the date on which the crime was committed. Wolsey had pleaded guilty to having committed the first of his many acts of *praemunire* when he exercised his power as Papal Legate by appointing John Allen (now Archbishop of Dublin) as the parish priest of Galby in Leicestershire, in the diocese of Lincoln, on 2 December 1523. Any property which Wolsey owned at that date, or had held at any time after 2 December 1523, was caught by the forfeiture.[42] So the forfeiture of all the property of the two colleges could not be invalidated, and the only remedy was to appeal to Henry's charity and his renowned love of culture; but his greed and the influence of his friends at court were on the other side.

Wolsey wrote, in the conventional language of a humble petitioner, to his 'Most gracious Sovereign and merciful Prince, prostrate at Your

Majesty's feet with weeping tears', asking him 'in most reverent and humble manner' to save 'the poor college of Oxford, which for the great zeal and affection that Your Grace bareth to good letters, virtue and nourishing of learning, and in consideration of my painful and long continued service, Your Grace was contented that I should erect, found and establish'.[43]

Throughout the summer of 1530 the fate of the colleges hung in the balance, and Wolsey's hopes rose and fell. At one time Henry told the fellows that they could rely on him to favour learning; at another, he said that the common weal made it necessary to close down Cardinal's College. Norfolk said that if they could find some legal pretext to have the forfeiture declared void, he would welcome it; but the lawyers had advised them that there was no hope here. The representatives of Cardinal's College, Oxford, went to More's house in Chelsea to ask him to issue a decree of *supersedeas* in the court of Chancery to restrain the royal officers from seizing the college property. More was very 'gentle' with them, but said that he had been ordered by the council not to issue a *supersedeas*. On another occasion they reported to Wolsey that More was always very helpful to them. Gardiner was the most helpful of all, but explained to them that he could not obtain everything that he wanted from the king and council.[44]

Eventually the Oxford college was saved, but the college at Ipswich was destroyed. The idea of an impressive educational establishment existing in Wolsey's home town, where masses were sung for Wolsey's father and mother on a much grander scale than for other butchers and their wives, was intolerable to Henry and his courtiers. On 20 July Capon, the dean of the Ipswich college, wrote to Wolsey from London, where he had been working to save the college, and told him the sad news. After long suit to the Duke of Norfolk, he had been informed by the duke on 19 July that the king was determined to dissolve the college and appropriate the property to his own use; Gardiner had intervened on its behalf, but the king would not hear him. Capon would have liked to send Wolsey the valuable books in the college chapel, but dared not do so, because the king's commissioners had already made an inventory of them. He did not know where the king would send the children of the chapel.[45] Wolsey was heartbroken when he received Capon's letter, and wrote to Cromwell:

I am in such indisposition of body and mind, by the reason of such great heaviness as I am in, being put from my sleep and meat, for such advertisements as I have had from you of the dissolution of my colleges, with the small comfort and appearance that I have to be relieved by the King's Highness in this mine extreme need, maketh me that I cannot write unto you, for weeping and sorrow.[46]

It was several weeks later before he heard that at least the Oxford college was saved. Henry decided to remove Wolsey's coat-of-arms, which adorned every gate and window of the college, and to seize part of the college property; but he allowed Cardinal's College to continue in existence, with smaller revenues, under the name of King Henry VIII's College.[47] It still exists today as Christ Church.

The greatest efforts had been needed to save Cardinal's College, because by this time the opinion of the king and court had hardened against Wolsey. Early in June, Chapuys received a letter from Wolsey's Venetian physician, Agostini. He wrote in an obscure way, but if Chapuys understood his meaning correctly, he was saying that Wolsey was willing to supply Chapuys with information which would be of help to Queen Catherine; Wolsey would be as eager to do this as to gain admission to Paradise, for he knew that his only hope of recovering power was for Catherine to return to Henry's favour. On 27 June Wolsey sent another message to Chapuys, asking how Catherine's case was progressing, and urging that strong action should be taken on her behalf, presumably by the Pope and the emperor, as soon as possible. By August he was sending messages to Chapuys nearly every day, complaining of the delay in giving judgment for Catherine, for he was sure that once the divorce case was settled he would return to power.[48]

Wolsey and Dr Agostini also got in touch with three men, and used them to carry messages to people at court who were working against Norfolk. They did not know that these men had formerly been employed by Norfolk in some shady transactions. The men betrayed Wolsey and Agostini to Norfolk. On 11 July Chapuys wrote to Charles that Norfolk had told him that these three men had brought him proof that Wolsey was plotting to regain power by a conspiracy with prominent courtiers and the French government, and that the French were scheming to put Wolsey back in power so that he could free François from the obligation to pay the pension to Henry and could pursue a pro-French and anti-imperial policy.[49]

It is impossible to know the truth about these accusations. Chapuys told Charles that he was not afraid of being compromised by any inquiries which Norfolk and the council might make, because nothing that had passed between him and Dr Agostini could possibly be held to be improper;[50] but it is clear that Wolsey was in correspondence, through Agostini, with both the imperial and the French ambassadors; that he was hoping that the actions of Clement and Charles would force Henry to get rid of Anne Boleyn, and that he would then return to power; and that he was scheming with Chapuys to achieve this. His ill-wishers could interpret this as proof that he was in treasonable communication with foreign powers. The Venetian ambassador heard that Wolsey had sent secret letters to Rome, which had been intercepted by Norfolk and the Council, in which he urged the Pope to excommunicate Henry if he did not banish Anne Boleyn from court, reconcile himself with Catherine, and respect the rights of the Church.[51] Wolsey might well have been capable of thinking and scheming along these lines; but it is just as likely that the story was a frame-up thought out by Norfolk and the Boleyns in order to ruin Wolsey.

In September the council closed the ports, and for several days did not allow anyone, not even ambassadors' servants, to leave the realm. The rumour circulated that this was to prevent Wolsey from escaping abroad, or from sending letters to France or Rome.[52] There were other plausible explanations of the order; but Wolsey was doomed.

At Southwell, Wolsey was making the best of the situation. He decided to be enthroned in his cathedral, more than sixteen years after his appointment as archbishop. He was determined that it should be a great occasion, and did not spare any expense to ensure that it was done with the greatest pomp and splendour. It was to take place on Monday 7 November, and in September he moved north to Scrooby on the Nottinghamshire-Yorkshire border, where he stayed for some weeks, visiting the nearby parish churches, sometimes celebrating mass himself and always listening to sermons preached by his chaplains, and calling at the houses of the poor. The reports of his parish work reached London, but Norfolk thought that it was a sham to cover his intrigues with the French ambassador.[53]

In October Wolsey set out for his archiepiscopal palace at Cawood, seven miles south of York. He planned to stay at Cawood until Sunday 6 November, when he would enter York in state and spend the night at the dean's house before attending the enthronement ceremony and a great banquet on the Monday. He had never been to York, except perhaps on his diplomatic mission to Scotland for Henry VII twenty-two years before. On his journey from Scrooby to Cawood he confirmed a large group of children at St Oswald's Abbey and by the stone cross on a village green near Ferrybridge. He was reasonably cheerful at Cawood; but he was upset when, at dinner on All Saints' Day, Dr Agostini caught his gown in the great crucifix at the corner of the room, which fell on the head of his chaplain, Edmund Bonner, slightly cutting Bonner's head. Wolsey took this as an evil omen.[54]

On Friday 4 November, forty-eight hours before Wolsey was due to leave for York, the Earl of Northumberland arrived at Cawood with his bodyguard. Wolsey knew him well, for before he succeeded to his father's title he had served in Wolsey's household, when Wolsey had forced him to break off his courtship of Anne Boleyn. More recently, only a few months before Wolsey fell from power, Wolsey had suspected him of intriguing behind his back with his enemies at court, and Northumberland had promised that he would never write to anyone at court without sending Wolsey a copy of the letter.[55]

Wolsey was at dinner when Northumberland arrived at Cawood, and he invited Northumberland to join him. Northumberland was so overcome by the presence of the great cardinal whom he had served and dreaded for so many years, that for a long time he could not bring himself to perform the duty for which he had been sent. At last, after Wolsey had taken him into a private room, he summoned up his courage, and in a weak and almost inaudible voice said to Wolsey: 'My Lord, I arrest you of high treason'.[56]

Wolsey demanded to see Northumberland's commission. When Northumberland told him that he had orders not to show it to him, Wolsey refused to go with him unless he did. But Northumberland had brought with him, among his escort, Mr Walsh of the king's privy chamber; and Wolsey, recognising Walsh, agreed to submit to the arrest, for officers of the king's privy chamber had the power of arrest without warrant. Northumberland treated Wolsey with the greatest respect and consideration. While Walsh arrested Dr Agostini, speaking to him harshly, and sending him off towards London with his feet tied together under his horse, Northumberland told Wolsey that he had orders to take him to London when Wolsey was ready to leave, and travelling as fast or as slowly as Wolsey preferred. Wolsey asked permission to say goodbye to his household before he left. Northumberland, who had locked up all Wolsey's gentlemen and servants in the chapel to prevent them from seeing Wolsey, explained that he had orders not to allow Wolsey to speak to the members of his household; but when Wolsey refused to leave until he had said goodbye to them, Northumberland allowed him to do so.

Next morning they rode south, and after staying the first night in Pontefract Abbey and the second at the Blackfriars monastery in Doncaster, they arrived on the third day at Sheffield Park, the house of Northumberland's father-in-law, the Earl of Shrewsbury. Here Northumberland delivered Wolsey to the custody of Sir Anthony Kingston, the Constable of the Tower of London. Both Shrewsbury and Kingston treated Wolsey with great courtesy, and Lady Shrewsbury and her ladies paid him every honour. Kingston assured Wolsey that although he was being arrested to answer certain charges, the king was still friendly to him, and had only authorised his arrest in order to give him the opportunity of clearing himself at his trial; but Wolsey was too shrewd and knowledgeable to believe this.

Kingston, like Northumberland, told Wolsey that he could travel to London at his own pace, and as Wolsey fell ill at Sheffield Park, he remained there for eighteen days. He suffered from violent diarrhoea, which was not cured by the medicine powders which Shrewsbury's physician gave him, after Cavendish and the physician himself had first tasted the medicine as a safeguard against poison. By the end of his stay at Sheffield Park the physician, noticing his constant diarrhoea and the blackness of the faeces, believed that he would be dead within five days. But on 24 November Wolsey insisted on resuming the journey, though he could hardly keep his seat on his mule. They rode to another of Shrewsbury's houses at Hardwicke-upon-Line in Nottinghamshire, and spent the next night in Nottingham Abbey. On the evening of Saturday 26 November they reached the abbey at Leicester. The abbot and all the monks were waiting to receive Wolsey with full honours, by torchlight, at the abbey gate. Wolsey said: 'Father Abbot, I am come hither to leave my bones among you'.[57]

Dr Agostini, on his arrival in London, had been taken not to prison but to Norfolk's house, where he stayed for several weeks and was then released and pardoned, after making a confession which implicated Wolsey in treasonable practices with the Pope and the French king.[58] At Blois, Henry's ambassador, Sir Francis Bryan, received instructions to assure François that although Wolsey was accused of plotting with France, this did not make Henry in any way suspicious of François's goodwill, and that Henry hoped that the affair would in no way injure the friendly relations between England and France. François could now combine his wish to maintain Henry's friendship with the pleasure of at last expressing his true feelings about the cardinal, his *bon ami*. He told Bryan that he could most readily believe the accusations against Wolsey, and thought

> that so pompous and ambitious a heart, sprung out of so vile a stock, would once show forth the baseness of his nature, and most commonly against him that hath raised him from low degree to high dignity as ye have done; and said he thought by his outrageous misbehaviours he had well merited either a life worse than death, or else of all deaths the most cruel.[59]

But Wolsey was to die a natural death. By Monday 28 November he knew the end was near. At four o'clock next morning his physician brought him some chicken broth; but after taking a few mouthfuls and recognising the taste, he refused to take any more of it, for it was St Andrew's Eve, and he would not eat meat on a fast day, though the physician assured him that it would be permitted to a sick man in his condition. After receiving absolution for his sins from his confessor, he spoke to Kingston, who told him again that he had nothing to fear from the king. 'Well, well, Mr Kingston,' said Wolsey:

I see the matter against me how it is framed. But if I had served God as diligently as I have done the king, He would not have given me over in my grey hairs. Howbeit, this is the just reward that I must receive for my worldly diligence and pains that I have had to do him service only to satisfy his vain pleasures, not regarding my godly duty.[60]

He asked Kingston to urge the king to allow his conscience to tell him whether Wolsey had offended him in the matter of the divorce, and said that Henry was

a Prince of a royal courage, and hath a princely heart. And rather than he will either miss or want any part of his will or appetite, he will put the loss of one half of his realm in danger. For I assure you I have often kneeled before him in his privy chamber on my knees the space of an hour or two, to persuade him from his will and appetite; but I could never bring to pass to dissuade him therefrom.

He told Kingston that if he ever became a member of the Council, 'I warn you to be well advised and assured what matter ye put in his head, for ye shall never pull it out again'.[61] He hoped that Henry would be vigilant in suppressing Lutheranism, and spoke of his fear of uprisings like those of Wycliffe's followers in Bohemia and the Peasant Revolt against Richard II at the time of Wycliffe's 'seditious opinions'. He ended by asking Kingston to remember what he had said, 'for when I am dead, ye shall peradventure remember my words much better'.[62]

The Abbot of Leicester gave him extreme unction, and he died at 8 a.m. on 29 November 1530. By Kingston's orders, he was buried the same day as quietly as possible, but with full honours, in the abbey. Kingston then took Cavendish to Hampton Court, where they reported to Henry how Wolsey had died; but Kingston told Cavendish, if he valued his safety, not to mention the statement that Wolsey had made on his deathbed. When Norfolk asked Cavendish whether Wolsey had said anything before he died, Cavendish answered that he had spoken many idle words, as dying men do, but that he could not remember what he had said.[63]

Many people believed that Wolsey had committed suicide by swallowing some poison provided for him by his physicians;[64] but this is very unlikely. It would not have been easy to obtain poison in Sheffield Park or in Leicester Abbey, and Wolsey, like all his contemporaries, believed that suicide was a mortal sin. But though he had always loved life, he knew when he left Cawood that the best thing that could now happen to him would be to die before he reached London. He had usually managed to find the most satisfactory solution of a difficulty in both favourable and unfavourable circumstances. Death was the most satisfactory solution for Wolsey at Leicester, and he died.

CHAPTER 15

LORD CHANCELLOR MORE
AND THE HERETICS

As Thomas More approached the age of fifty, all the conflicting trends in his strange character blended into one, and produced the savage persecutor of heretics who devoted his life to the destruction of Lutheranism. To say that he suffered from paranoia on this subject would be to resort to a glib phrase, not a serious psychiatric analysis; but it is unquestionable that More, like other persecutors throughout history, believed that the foundations of civilisation, and all that he valued as sacred, were threatened by the forces of evil, and that it was his mission to exterminate the enemy by all means, including torture and lies. The worst of all the heretics were the Anabaptists, the most extreme of all the Protestant sects, who were already causing great concern to the authorities in Germany and the Netherlands. They not only rejected infant baptism, but believed, like the inhabitants of Utopia, that goods should be held in common. In 1528 More wrote to the German theologian, Cochlaeus: 'The past centuries have not seen anything more monstrous than the Anabaptists'.[1]

For the first time in his life, he was beginning to suffer from ill-health. He was troubled by pains in his chest, which seemed to become worse when he bent forward to write at his desk; and at some time before his death he had the painful experience of losing a tooth without the benefit of the pain-reducing methods of modern dentistry.[2] At fifty, many of his contemporaries were old: Henry VIII, François I, Charles V and Wolsey all died natural deaths in their fifties after their acquaintances had thought of them for some years as old men. But a few people, chiefly ascetic churchmen, lived to be eighty, and More, despite his chest ailments, would probably have done the same if he had not been beheaded at the age of fifty-seven. He had just had his forty-ninth birthday when he and his whole family were painted in the spring of 1527 by Hans Holbein the younger, a friend of Erasmus, who spent some time with More at Chelsea during his visit to England. The fanatical eyes and mouth of the heretic-baiter peer out from under the mask of the benign father in the portrait of the happy family group.[3]

He was bitterly hated by the Protestants. His contemporary,

Tyndale, and John Foxe thirty years after his death, picked him out, with one or two others, as the most cruel of all the persecutors. Neither More himself, nor his Catholic supporters in the sixteenth century, wished to rebut this accusation which in their eyes was creditable to him, though More denied a few specific allegations made by the Protestants. In the twentieth century, his admirers have tried to defend him from the charge of being a notorious persecutor. They have adopted two main lines of argument. The first is to deny the truth of the worst accusations, especially the story that he whipped heretics in his garden; and here they are probably right in many cases. The second is to claim that More, as a layman, cannot be held responsible for the persecution of heretics, because heretics were condemned in the court of the bishop of their diocese. This argument is exactly the reverse of that which has sometimes been used by apologists for the Catholic Church, including More himself in his *Dialogue concerning Heresies* – that it was the temporal power, not the Church, which burned heretics; and it is unsound.

As Lord Chancellor, More was the highest officer of the executive government, and had a very important part to play in the campaign against heretics. Even in modern democratic states, the executive branch of government is involved in the administration of justice, and the imprisonment of criminals: it is the Home Secretary or the Chief Constable who decides how much time, money, resources and man-power are devoted to the arrest and prosecution of terrorists, drug-addicts and drunken drivers. This is even truer in the case of totalitarian régimes in both the twentieth and the sixteenth centuries. To say that More was not responsible for the burning of heretics because they were tried and excommunicated by the bishops is like saying that the chief of the KGB is not to blame for the persecution of dissidents because they are sentenced to fifteen years in a labour camp, not by him, but by a judge of the regional court. It was the duty of both Wolsey and More, when they were Lord Chancellor, to decide whether to intensify or tone down the persecution of Lutherans, whether to incite or restrain the ardour of the bishops. The Lord Chancellor had more responsibility for the persecution than any individual bishop, though less responsibility than the king, who was ultimately responsible for all major policy decisions.

For some years before he became Lord Chancellor, More had played his part in the drive against heretics. His action in raiding the headquarters of the Hansa merchants was no more than the action of a high executive officer carrying our Wolsey's orders; but he also took part in the proceedings against Bilney, when he was arrested and brought before Wolsey in 1526.[4] This was unprecedented, for a common lawyer and layman would not ordinarily have joined the bishops and canon lawyers in the examination of a heretic. It was a tribute to More's learning in theology, and to the reputation which he had established as an anti-Lutheran polemicist by his *Answer to Luther*, that he was selected, contrary to all precedent, to perform this duty.

In February 1525 the German Lutheran, Bugenhagen, published a tract, his *Letter to the Saints in England*, in which he exhorted English Lutherans to stand firm in the face of persecution. More, despite his preoccupations as a member of the council, wrote a reply, in which he blamed Luther, Bugenhagen, and their doctrine of justification by faith for the rising of the German peasants in 1525, in which seventy thousand peasants had been killed. As Bugenhagen was a married priest, More denounced him as a fornicator and his wife as a harlot. He called on Bugenhagen to desert her and to renounce his Lutheran doctrines, for in no other way could he save his soul from eternal damnation.[5]

Erasmus had at last come out against Luther. Under pressure from the Pope and his friends at the Papal court, and stung by Ulrich von Hutten's criticism of him, he had promised to write a book denouncing Luther; but the months passed and the book did not appear. Instead, he wrote another book on the sanctity of marriage at the request of Catherine of Aragon, who perhaps sensed, already in 1525, that the sanctity of marriage needed to be defended. By 1526, three years after Erasmus had denounced Luther, his book against Lutheranism had still not appeared, and rumours spread that Erasmus was trying to get out of writing it; some said that he was afraid, because he had been threatened with violence by the Lutherans.[6]

On 18 December 1526 More wrote to Erasmus in Basle, telling him how eagerly he and his friends were waiting for Erasmus to finish the book. 'You would find it hard to believe the eagerness with which all good men are looking forward to that work; there are, on the other hand, some wicked persons, either partisans of Luther or your jealous rivals, who apparently are gleeful and growing in numbers as a result of your delayed response.' He told Erasmus that he could forgive him for his delay in finishing the book if it was because he was busy writing another book on marriage for the queen, or if he was correcting and perfecting the book against Luther; but if, as some said, it was because he was terrorised and had either lost interest or was afraid to go on with it, 'then I am thoroughly bewildered and unable to restrain my grief' that you should now 'abandon the cause of God'.[7]

In May 1527 Wolsey and Warham held their secret court at York Place with a view to divorcing Henry from Catherine. More may not have heard about it immediately, but must have known what was happening a few weeks later, when Fisher and the bishops were asked to express their opinion about the validity of Henry's marriage. He wrote to Cromwell in 1534 that he did not realise at first that Henry believed that his marriage to Catherine was against God's law; he thought merely that some doubt had arisen as to the validity of the dispensation of 1503 because of an ambiguity in the wording of the bull. According to his statement, it was not until he returned from accompanying Wolsey on the embassy to Amiens and Compiègne, which was in September 1527, that Henry told him, in the garden at Hampton Court, that he was worried by the text in Leviticus condemning a man's marriage to his brother's widow. It is very difficult to believe More's story, in view of the fact that he was a member of the inner committee of the council; that his friend Fisher had been consulted, and had expressed his opinion, about the divorce in June; that More was in Wolsey's retinue at Rochester when Wolsey discussed the divorce with Fisher on 4 July; and that Roper wrote that More was one of the first advisers whom Henry consulted about the divorce.

Roper writes that when Henry asked More for his opinion about the validity of his marriage to Catherine, More said that he was not sufficiently learned in divinity to be able to express an opinion on the matter. More himself, in his letter to Cromwell in 1534, gives the impression that he expressed a provisional opinion that the marriage to Catherine was valid, and that Henry then sent him to discuss the matter with Fox, who believed that the marriage was unlawful and was actively working on Henry's behalf in the divorce case.[8] But whatever the precise nature of More's answer may have been, there is no doubt that, while not openly condemning the idea of the divorce, he made it clear to Henry that he did not favour it. He did not, like an opportunist courtier, give the opinion that Henry wanted in favour of the divorce; but he did not oppose it, as Fisher did.

It has often been pointed out that in 1527 the Chancellor of the Duchy of Lancaster was not in the position of a politician holding the office today. He could not resign and go into opposition. More's position was more comparable to that of a high civil servant in modern times, who is expected loyally to carry out whatever policy the government is pursuing at the time. Fisher, although holding an official position as Bishop of Rochester and attending from time to time at meetings of the council, was in a rather different situation from More, and it was easier for him than for More to adopt the course of open resistance. More could probably have persuaded Henry to allow him to resign from the council, either on grounds of ill-health or on some other excuse, as he eventually did in 1532; but he did not wish to resign in 1527.

More afterwards stated that he eventually explained to Henry that his conscience would not allow him to support the divorce, though it would seem, from his statements, that he did not definitely say this until two years later, after he returned from Cambrai and after the close of the trial at Blackfriars in September 1529, just before he was appointed Lord Chancellor. Henry accepted his explanation, assured him that he would not force his conscience by requiring him to do something of which he disapproved, and employed him on other work – a practice which the king adopted with all his ministers who did not agree with his divorce.[9] It was obvious for which work More would be best suited. He wished to devote himself to crushing heresy, and he had shown, by his writings and other activities, that he could perform this task with great zeal and ability. More undoubtedly remained in the king's service and a member of his council, despite his opposition to Henry's divorce, because he wished to use the opportunities which his office gave him of persecuting heretics.

He wished to do this first and foremost with his pen. On 7 March 1528 his old friend and colleague Tunstal, who as Lord Privy Seal and Bishop of London was showing exceptional energy in pursuing heretics, wrote a formal letter to More entrusting him with the task of writing books against heretics, knowing that he could castigate the enemies of the Church with the ability of a Demosthenes. Tunstal granted him a licence to read heretical books so that he could undertake this work, and sent him copies of all the illegal Lutheran tracts which had been seized.[10] More immediately began to write a book against Tyndale, and his *Dialogue concerning Heresies* was published in London in June 1529.

More asserted in the book, against the contention of Tyndale and the Protestants, that God had revealed to His Church all the doctrine that was necessary for men's salvation, and that it was therefore unnecessary for salvation to read the Bible; for both the pronouncements of the Church and the text of Scripture were the Word of God and of equal weight. Anyone who challenged the decisions of Christ's true Church on earth was therefore a heretic. Nor could there be any doubt as to which Church was Christ's true Church; it was the Church that had been founded by the apostles and had continued in existence ever since, not any sect of heretics who had broken away from that Church. It was wrong that there should be continual discussion about points of doctrine upon which the Church had already decided, for it was an accepted principle in all systems of jurisprudence that once a court of law had given final judgment in a case, no one was permitted to reopen the issue on the grounds of new evidence or for any other reason; and this should apply even more to the decisions of the Church than to those of a court of law.[11]

He then proceeded to castigate the Lutherans for their attacks on images, relics and pilgrimages, but above all for their doctrine of justification by faith and not by works. This was why the people in

Germany had flocked to join Luther; he told them that if they believed in his doctrines, they would be saved by faith alone, even if they led wicked lives, and that they were under no obligation to obey the government and the law provided that they obeyed the Bible. This state of affairs had been brought about by the weakness of rulers. In several parts of Germany and Switzerland 'this ungracious sect, by the negligence of the governors, in great cities is so forsooth grown that finally the common people have compelled the rulers to follow them, which, if they had taken heed in time, they might have ruled and led'.[12]

More asserted that the burning of heretics was 'lawful, necessary and well done'.[13] It was not the clergy who burned heretics, but Christian princes, who were right to do so, just as the clergy were right to excommunicate heretics and deliver them up to the secular arm, knowing that they would then be burned. Some people believed that Christ would not have approved of burning heretics, because he had told St Peter to put up his sword; but St Augustine, St Ambrose and other fathers of the Church had realised that Christian princes 'have been constrained to punish heretics by terrible death', not only for the sake of the faith, but also to preserve peace among their subjects. Some said that because the Christians had been persecuted by the pagans and the Jews they ought not themselves to persecute others; but 'surely though God be able against all persecution to preserve and increase His Faith among the people . . . that is no reason to look that Christian Princes should suffer the Catholic Christian people to be oppressed by Turks or by heretics worse than Turks'.[14]

More came close to saying – but did not quite say – that the ecclesiastical courts in England in recent years had been too tolerant to heretics. 'I will not say that the Judges did wrong', but there had been several cases in which they had allowed a heretic to recant and carry his faggot when More was very doubtful whether his recantation had been sincere. They had shown the heretic favour, 'and almost more than lawful, in that they admitted him to such an abjuration as they did, and that they did not rather leave him to the secular arm'. He drew the conclusion 'that in the condemnation of heretics, the clergy might lawfully do much more sharply than they do'.[15]

In many passages in the book, More denounced the excesses of the Lutherans, referring to the 'harlots' whom Luther and other Protestant leaders had married; and he repeated the allegation that he had made in his *Answer to Luther* that the Lutherans used churches as brothels. But he reserved his greatest indignation for the atrocities committed by the Lutherans in the Duke of Bourbon's army at the sack of Rome in May 1527. They had tied up old men by cords around their genitals; they had torn off the genitals and thrown them into the streets; and they had roasted children on pikes if the fathers and mothers did not pay money to them to desist.[16]

Whatever the truth about these atrocities, it was a gross distortion for More to blame the Lutherans for them. The men who sacked Rome were in the pay, and under the command of the officers, of Charles V, the King Catholic of Spain and Holy Roman Emperor, whose ambassador in a few years' time would regard More as the greatest supporter in Henry's council of the emperor's policy. The troops consisted of Spanish troops, Italian auxiliaries, and 'Swabian' merce-naries – by which was probably meant mercenaries from south-west Germany and the German-speaking cantons of Switzerland. Mercenaries usually behaved badly to the civilian population, and observers of the sack of Rome differed as to whether the Italians, the Spaniards or the 'Swabians' had behaved the worst. In an attempt to exculpate the emperor and his Catholic adherents, the story was circulated that the Swabian troops in Bourbon's army were Lutherans and that the Spaniards were Moriscoes who had remained in Spain and had been forcibly converted to Christianity after the fall of the Moorish kingdom of Granada in 1492.[17] The idea that Charles's Spanish troops who sacked Rome were secret Moslems was preposterous, and the story that the 'Swabians' were Lutherans may well have been equally untrue. If some of them were, they were certainly a minority among the total force of Spanish, Italian and German troops, and in behaving as they did during the twelve terrible days in Rome they acted as mercenaries rather than as Lutherans. Thomas More, of course, had not made the slightest effort to verify the nationality or religion of the men who tore out the genitals and roasted the children; but he countered the argument that the Lutherans as a whole should not be blamed for the crimes of some of them by saying that the atrocities followed inevitably from the Lutheran doctrine of justification by faith. When it was argued that the English Lutherans had shown no inclination to behave in this fashion, More answered that they were biding their time, and would show themselves in their true colours as soon as the opportunity presented itself.[18]

Within three months of the publication of his *Dialogue concerning Heresies*, More had published *The Supplication of Souls* in September 1529. It was a reply to Simon Fish's highly successful tract, *A Supplication for the Beggars*, which had appeared in the previous year. Fish violently attacked the clergy, and alleged that beggars and lepers, the poor and the sick, were starving because bishops, abbots, priests and monks lived in idleness and luxury on the tithes that they extorted from the people. He complained that a woman earned only threepence, and a man fourpence, a day for toiling in the fields, but the woman would be paid

Thomas Howard, Earl of Surrey, third Duke of Norfolk, by Holbein

Sir Thomas More and his family.
The 1593 copy of Richard Locky's copy of the sketch made by Holbein in 1527

twenty pence a day for sleeping for an hour with a priest, a monk or a friar, and the man would get twelvepence a day for acting as a pimp for the clergy. More's *Supplication of Souls* denounced the *Supplication for the Beggars* as an impious attack on the clergy; he argued that the welfare of souls in Purgatory, which depended on the prayers of priests and monks, was more important than the welfare of bodies on earth, and reminded Fish that souls in Purgatory pray for the welfare of beggars as well as for other people.[19]

On 25 October 1529 More was appointed to succeed Wolsey as Lord Chancellor. The appointment caused surprise; it was seen as a compromise arrangement which had been necessary because of Norfolk's opposition to the appointment of Suffolk as Lord Chancellor. It soon became clear to the foreign ambassadors that though More had replaced Wolsey as Lord Chancellor, he had not replaced him as the king's foreign minister and the head of the government. From the first day, it was Norfolk who received the ambassadors and discussed English foreign policy with them; and they were sure that in home affairs, too, he was the strong man of the government. The ambassadors commented on More's charm and on his learning and intellectual distinction, but realised that he was not a Wolsey, and was of no importance as far as they were concerned.[20]

Tunstal would have been the obvious choice to succeed Wolsey as Lord Chancellor. He was a churchman and a bishop; as Lord Privy Seal he had gained experience of the working of the council and the government administration; as a former Master of the Rolls he knew about the legal side of the Chancellor's business; and he had learned how to deal with questions of foreign policy on several diplomatic missions abroad, including his embassies to the emperor's court in Spain and to the peace conference at Cambrai. He had also won praise and hatred by the energy which he had shown in persecuting heretics as Bishop of London. But instead of giving him the Great Seal, Henry appointed him Bishop of Durham in 1530 and sent him to York to govern his diocese and all the north of England as President of the Council of the North, while Stokesley succeeded him as Bishop of London, and a layman, More, was appointed as Lord Chancellor.

The choice of a layman as Lord Chancellor was not unprecedented – a layman had been Lord Chancellor in 1409 and 1454 – but in 1529 it was rightly seen as part of the national campaign against Rome and the churchmen. The Lutheran heretics welcomed it, even though it meant having More as Chancellor: they believed that although he was sure to intensify their persecution, this was a price which they would willingly pay for the long-term benefit of weakening the Church's hold on the government. Wolsey's fall, and the way in which it was brought about by an attack on his authority as Papal Legate, showed clearly that Henry, unable to obtain a divorce from the Pope, was preparing to lead the nation into schism, if not into heresy. A powerful faction at court, including the king's mistress, and growing sections of the public were giving him every encouragement to do this.

But there were factors holding him back and opposing the forces of schism and heresy. Henry was by instinct a Catholic and a conservative. He did not like Lutheran heretics, and agreed with More in considering them to be seditious, even if they were now putting forward the ideas of royal supremacy which Tyndale expressed in his book *The Obedience of a Christian Man* in 1528, and hailed Henry as the leader who would free his people from the foreign Pope and the corrupt, rebellious priests who rivalled his royal authority. Henry would use them, if necessary, to obtain a divorce, to strengthen his royal power, and to seize part of the wealth of the Church; for, unlike More, he put his own personal interests before any principle, and he was confident that he could safely give the heretics their head and suppress them later if they went too far. But the simpler and more congenial course was to obtain the divorce from the Pope, if possible. With Wolsey gone, there was little chance of this; but the door had not been finally closed on the possibility of averting the final break with Rome.

Thomas More stood alone in the government in favour of a Catholic policy. Anne Boleyn and her father, Wiltshire, were eager to pursue the anti-clerical line. So was Cromwell, who had impressed Henry so favourably by his handling of Wolsey's business that he had been appointed one of the king's secretaries and was rapidly rising in influence. Suffolk was at least mildly sympathetic to what More and the Papists called 'Lutheranism'. Norfolk was not, but as long as Henry encouraged it, Norfolk would do nothing more than make surly comments in private about 'this new learning'. Only More, in the council, was a devoted upholder of the established order; he alone was prepared to risk the loss of Henry's favour by opposing the new revolutionary forces.

His only chance of success was to win Henry's support by exploiting his close personal friendship with Henry, and by encouraging Henry's conservatism and his opposition to seditious heretics. More knew that he could not rely on the personal friendship if it was outweighed by political advantages. Some years before, during the war with France, Henry had come to More's house in Chelsea, and had walked with him in the garden with his arm around More's neck. When Henry had gone, Roper said to More that he must be in great favour with the king, for Roper had never seen Henry walk with his arm around the neck of any man except Wolsey. More replied: 'I thank our Lord, son, I find His Grace my very good lord indeed; and I do believe he doth as singularly favour me as any subject in this realm. Howbeit, son Roper, I may tell thee I have no cause to be proud thereof, for if my head could win him a castle in France, it should not fail to go.'[21]

He cannot have been hopeful of his chances of success in 1529, but he was prepared to try, and to use flattery and deception to achieve his purpose. According to Roper, soon after Cromwell first entered Henry's service, More said to Cromwell:

Mr Cromwell, you are now entered into the service of a most noble, wise and liberal Prince; if you will follow my poor advice, you shall, in your counsel-giving unto His Grace, ever tell him what he ought to do, but never what he is able to do. So shall you show yourself a true faithful subject, and a right wise worthy counsellor. For if the lion knew his own strength, hard were it for any man to rule him.[22]

Though Roper does not seem to have realised it, More was advising Cromwell to deceive his prince about the extent of his power, and to give him misleading advice in order to further what More considered to be the interests of the Church and the struggle against heresy. Cromwell disregarded More's advice; More himself followed it in his relations with Henry. But he could not fool this lion as to his strength. Wolsey said on his deathbed that if you once put an idea into Henry's head, you could never pull it out again. The idea of destroying the power and independence of the Church and of repudiating Papal supremacy had already been put into Henry's head when More became Lord Chancellor; and it would need more than clever lies by More to succeed where Wolsey would have failed.

The Parliament which assembled at Westminster on 3 November 1529 was not dissolved, like most Parliaments, after a few weeks; it continued for nearly seven years, and during this time placed the Church under the royal authority, repudiated the Papal supremacy and all ties with Rome, recognised Henry as Supreme Head of the Church of England, dissolved most of the monasteries in the country, and passed two Acts which More was prepared to defy at the cost of his liberty and his life. It was an irony that it should have been More who, as Lord Chancellor, made the opening address at the first session of this momentous and revolutionary Parliament which was to destroy the foundations of everything that he valued in English society.

In his speech, he denounced Wolsey, without referring to him by name. No verbatim report of his speech exists, but the words which Hall published in his history a few years later are confirmed, in substance, by the contemporary reports of the foreign ambassadors. More said that the king had summoned Parliament to reform 'divers new enormities' which had sprung up among the people; that the king was the shepherd, ruler and governor of his realm, whose greatness rested not on his riches and honour, for there were other rich and honourable men, but on his relationship as a shepherd to his flock.

> As you see that amongst a great flock of sheep some be rotten and faulty which the good shepherd sendeth from the good sheep, so the great wether which is of late fallen, as you all know, so craftily, so scabbedly, yea and so untruly juggled with the King, that all men must needs guess and think that he thought in himself that they had no wit to perceive his crafty doing, or else that he presumed that the king would not see nor know his fraudulent juggling and attempts; but he was deceived, for His Grace's sight was so quick and penetrable that he saw him, yea and saw through him, both within and without, so that all thing to him was open, and according to his desert he hath had a gentle correction, which small punishment the king will not to be an example to other offenders, but clearly declareth that whosoever hereafter shall make like attempt to commit like offence, shall not escape with like punishment.[23]

Even More's most ardent admirers have condemned him for trampling on the fallen Wolsey, and vilifying the man whom he had flattered in his days of power. But by sixteenth-century standards – and by More's – his words were not outstandingly venomous; and the most notable feature of the speech was not his denunciation of Wolsey but his flattery of Henry. After praising Henry for having driven out 'the great wether' Wolsey, More proceeded to explain at some length why the benign shepherd had taken so long to see the vices of the wether, and had allowed him to rule in England for many years: it was because Henry had until recently been too busy leading his victorious armies in war.[24] This was not a very convincing explanation, as Henry had not taken personal command of his army since 1513, when Wolsey was only beginning his seventeen years of power. But the people had so often been urged to pay taxes to send an 'army royal' across the sea, under the command of the king in person, that they may have imagined that Henry had actually gone on these much talked-of expeditions; and the public did not know, as More did, that Wolsey had spent much more time than Henry in planning the military measures undertaken in wartime. More would not, of course, have ventured to refer to Henry's maintenance of Wolsey as a minister without discussing it with Henry, and probably also in the council, and this passage proves conclusively that his speech was not an expression of his individual opinion but a declaration of Henry's policy.

More's critics and admirers, while censuring and excusing him for his denunciation of Wolsey in his speech on 3 November, have usually ignored the far more disgraceful document which he signed with his fellow councillors and the peers a few weeks later, when they presented their forty-four articles against Wolsey in the form of a petition to the king, requesting him to punish Wolsey with more severity than had hitherto been shown to him. More cannot have believed the ludicrous accusation that Wolsey had breathed into Henry's face, hoping that he would infect Henry with his own syphilis, while pretending that he was suffering, not from syphilis, but only from a cold.[25] If More felt any compunction about this lie, he would have felt none in denouncing Wolsey for not permitting the persecution of heretics at Cambridge, and for having cohabited with the daughter of Lark, though More, like everyone else, had known about her during the years when they all fawned on Wolsey. The Oxford grammarian, Robert Whittinton, had described More in 1520 as being 'as time requireth, a man of marvellous mirth and pastime, and sometime of as sad gravity; a man for all seasons'.[26] The man for all seasons knew that there was a season in which to lick the boots of a cardinal and a season to spit on him.

In the council, More seems to have been completely overshadowed by Norfolk, Suffolk and Wiltshire, at least as far as foreign affairs were concerned, while Cromwell continually increased his influence in the office of Secretary. The foreign ambassadors soon realised that the Lord Chancellor was no longer the most important man in the government. When the Venetian envoy, Lodovico Falier, returned to Venice in November 1531 and reported to the Doge and Senate on the situation in England during the three years that he had resided there, he stated that Norfolk and Suffolk were the most influential ministers in the government, and referred to a number of other members of the council; but he did not even mention More. The only time that More was used to negotiate with foreign ambassadors was when he, together with Norfolk, spoke to the Venetian ambassador about a trade agreement in January 1532.[27]

More spent most of his time performing his judicial duties in the court of Chancery. His conduct as a judge caused general satisfaction. As he was much less overworked than Wolsey, he eliminated the long delays which had occurred before cases were heard. He was able to spend more time on the cases when the hearing took place, and to decide all of them after proper argument in court, instead of summarily settling the issue by letters from Hampton Court or York Place. He increased the reputation which he had first established twenty years earlier when, as Under-Sheriff of London, he sat as a judge in the city. He was absolutely incorruptible, though like all the other judges of his time, he occasionally accepted a gift from a grateful litigant. He was fair and impartial, and on one occasion, when he tried a case involving a dispute about land in which his son-in-law, Cecily's husband Giles Heron, was a party, he gave judgment for the other side against Heron.[28]

But the author of *Utopia* disappointed the victims of enclosures. He helped them much less than Wolsey had done. Wolsey had not succeeded in stopping enclosures, for he had been too busy to prevent the many evasions of his decrees; but his periodical proclamations against enclosures, and the action which he took from time to time against the powerful landlords who were prosecuted and fined in his court, had placed at least some check on the evil which More had denounced in his book. When More himself was Lord Chancellor, there were no proclamations and far fewer fines.[29] More's judicial impartiality led him to be fair to the enclosing landlords and to uphold their technical legal objections; and lacking Wolsey's power and unrivalled prestige, he could not adopt so high-handed an attitude towards rich and powerful offenders. Was he also perhaps reacting against his own doctrines? Was he emphasizing to himself and others that he was now a judge in the realm of King Henry VIII, and not a visionary writing about the imaginary island of Utopia? And did he above all react in revulsion against the ideas which he had propagated as a humanist in the days before Luther hatched the eggs which Erasmus had laid, and against the Utopian visions which in the real world had led to anarchy and revolution?

Nor was there anything Utopian about his legislative activities. In the Parliamentary session of April 1530 he introduced a bill as Lord Chancellor to deal with vagabonds and beggars. In *Utopia* he had denounced the idea of dealing with this problem by cruel punishments. The Act of 1530 enacted that unemployed workmen who were old or sick could apply for a licence to their local JP authorising them to beg. If any healthy man or woman, being able to labour, 'having no land, master, nor using any lawful merchandise, craft mystery whereby he might get his living', was found outside the parish in which he was born, or in which he had resided for the last three years, and was unable to produce his licence to beg or to give an account of how he earned his living, he was to be stripped naked, tied to a cart-tail, and whipped through the market town 'till his body be bloody by reason of such whipping'. He was then to be ordered to return at once to his native parish; if he failed to comply, he was to be whipped a second time. Anyone who gave him shelter was to be fined.[30] The author of *Utopia* was at least consistent in imposing a system of internal passports and punishing illegal travel by cruel punishments; it was the beneficial aspects of Utopia that he failed to apply in practice.

With the divorce case advoked to Rome, Henry tried a new line. An unambitious Cambridge Doctor of Divinity, Thomas Cranmer, at a casual meeting with Gardiner and Fox at Waltham in August 1529, put forward the suggestion that the validity of Henry's marriage to Catherine should be decided, not by the canon lawyers in the ecclesiastical courts, but by theologians in the universities. The English universities were consulted first.[31] More, who had been appointed High Steward of Oxford University in 1524 and of Cambridge University in 1525, took no part at all, and did not commit himself in any way, while Gardiner and Fox and the University Vice-Chancellor and Proctors argued, manoeuvred and bullied the reluctant Regents first of Cambridge and then of Oxford into giving their opinion that by the law of God a man's marriage to his brother's widow was unlawful, and that a Papal dispensation could not make it valid. François I encouraged the French universities to give a similar judgment, while Charles V saw to it that the Spanish universities decided the other way. Casale, Cranmer and other English agents tried with partial success to bribe the Italian universities to hold for Henry. In July 1530 the bishops, abbots and peers in the House of Lords signed a petition to the Pope, asking him to give judgment for Henry in the divorce case. The Lord Chancellor might have been expected to sign the document, but More did not sign.[32]

Henry did not require More to act in connection with the divorce, but had other work for him to do. While on the one hand Henry put pressure on the Pope and made tentative approaches to the German Lutheran princes, on the other he showed the Pope that he was still the Defender of the Faith who could stamp out heresy if he were not alienated over the divorce. In May 1530 he appointed a commission, on which More sat with Warham, Tunstal, Gardiner and other churchmen. The commissioners' report, which was presented to Henry in the Star Chamber on 24 May, declared that it was unnecessary for a Christian to read the Bible, as the teaching and sacraments of the Church were sufficient for salvation. It was therefore a matter for the king's discretion as to whether the Bible should be translated into English and made available for his subjects to read. Henry might well decide, at some time in the future, that the Bible should be translated into English by learned and orthodox divines; but in view of the prevalence of heresy, this was not an opportune moment to do this. In the meantime, Tyndale's erroneous translation, which contained several heresies both in the English text and in the notes, should be suppressed as a heretical book.

On 22 June Henry issued a proclamation banning the importation, the printing, the distribution and the reading of a long list of heretical books, headed by Tyndale's translation of the New Testament and including the theological works of Luther, Tyndale and other leading reformers, as well as the more popular anti-clerical tracts of Roy and Fish. Anyone who found a copy of any of these books was to hand it in to his bishop within twenty days; and sheriffs, JPs and other officers were to search for these books and punish the offenders. A number of copies of Tyndale's English New Testament were publicly burned at Paul's Cross. The Protestants denounced the burning of the Bible by the government and the bishops as a blasphemous outrage.[33]

But some of the king's advisers were in contact with Tyndale. In January 1531 Cromwell instructed his agent in Antwerp, Stephen Vaughan, to get in touch with Tyndale and urge him to return to England and to place his services as a propagandist at the king's disposal. Tyndale would not trust the safe-conduct which was half-promised to him; but Cromwell arranged for a copy of his book, *The Answer unto Sir Thomas More*, in which he had replied to More's *Dialogue concerning Heresies*, to be placed in Henry's hands. Henry read it, but decided that he could not approve of it, or make use of Tyndale's services; and in any case, Tyndale would not support his divorce. Henry gave orders to intensify the drive against heretics.[34] The leading part in this campaign was played by More and Stokesley, who had succeeded Tunstal as Bishop of London when Tunstal was translated to Durham. Stokesley had been active in supporting Henry's divorce, but agreed with More on the necessity of suppressing heresy. The Lord Chancellor and the Bishop of London worked closely together in the persecution of 1531 and 1532.

During the last eight years before More became Lord Chancellor, not one heretic had been burned in England under Wolsey; in the two years and seven months when More was Chancellor, six were burned. The first one was a priest, Thomas Hitton. More saw in his arrest the workings of Providence. Hitton had been sent to England from the Netherlands by Tyndale to contact their English supporters and arrange for the secret distribution in England of the English Bible. He was walking in the fields near Gravesend, on his way back to the Netherlands, when he met a party of people searching for a thief who had stolen some clothes which were lying on a hedge. They stopped and searched him, and though they did not find the stolen goods, they found letters from English heretics to the heretics abroad. He was taken to Warham, and examined by the archbishop and by Fisher, who excommunicated him and delivered him to the secular arm to be burned. He refused to give the names of his father and mother – not, perhaps, as More supposed, because he was ashamed that they should know that he had been condemned as a heretic, but to save them from harassment by More and his officers. He was burned at Maidstone in February 1530. 'Now the spirit of error and lying', wrote More, 'hath taken his wretched soul with him straight from the short fire to the fire everlasting. And this is lo Sir Thomas Hitton, the Devil's stinking martyr!'[35]

In August 1531 Bilney was burned as a relapsed heretic in Norwich; in December, Bayfield the monk and Tewkesbury the leather-vendor were burned at Smithfield in London; and in April 1532 James Bainham, a barrister of the Middle Temple, who was the son of a knight of Gloucestershire, and had married Simon Fish's widow, was burned at Smithfield. It would be an over-simplification to claim that these heretics were burned between October 1529 and May 1532, whereas none was burned between 1521 and 1529, because More had succeeded Wolsey as Lord Chancellor. Apart from other factors, these heretics were burned when More was Chancellor because they refused to recant, or, having recanted, relapsed into heresy, whereas in Wolsey's time all the heretics whom he examined recanted at their trial. But there is no doubt that at least part of the reason is that More was a far more zealous persecutor than Wolsey.

More found time to spend some hours at least every day with his family and household in the manor house at Chelsea, from where he could travel by barge to Westminster in an hour or so. Here he showed his benign affection for his family, loving Meg more deeply than ever, rejoicing in the Catholic zeal of her formerly heretical husband, occasionally sneering at Dame Alice but more often submitting in silence to her nagging, and still, perhaps, nurturing in his heart the hatred for his family that he concealed so well, but had expressed so poignantly in *The Four Last Things*. His father was still alive, at the age of seventy-nine. He had become a judge of the court of King's Bench, but had seen his son rise to a higher office than his own. This did not affect their family relationship. Every day when More went to Westminster Hall to take his seat in the court of Chancery, he called on his way at the court of King's Bench nearby, and knelt to his father to receive his blessing.[36]

Whenever possible, More spent Fridays in the New Building, whipping himself, like the vagabonds, till the blood ran and stained the exceptionally irritating hairshirt until Meg secretly washed away the bloodstains. His religious faith sustained him in adversity. A few days after his return from Cambrai in September 1529, one of his barns at Chelsea was accidentally burned, with the corn stored in it. He heard the news when he was at Woodstock, where he had gone to report to Henry on the talks at Cambrai. He wrote to Dame Alice that the loss of the barn and so much good corn was regrettable, but they must accept God's visitation without complaint.[37]

On Sundays he attended mass in the parish church at Chelsea, and sang in the church choir, though Erasmus had thought that he had no ear for music. He dressed in the clothes of a chorister, and took his place among them. Once Norfolk came to his house on a Sunday and attended mass in the church with More and his household. Norfolk disapproved of More's action in singing in the choir dressed in a chorister's gown, which he thought was derogatory to the dignity of More's position. Roper writes that as Norfolk and More walked arm in arm back from the church to More's house, the duke said to More: 'God's body, God's body, my Lord Chancellor a parish clerk, a parish clerk! You dishonour the king and his office.' More replied: 'Nay, Your Grace may not think that the king, your master and mine, will with me for serving of God, his master, be offended, or thereby account his office dishonoured.'[38]

The household at Chelsea continued its well-regulated existence, with no cards, dice, or conversation between the sexes. If there, as elsewhere, sin began with the eye, the lusts of the menservants were checked at this early stage by More's firm rule enforcing strict segregation. But on one occasion an element of discord, rebellion and sedition appeared in More's model establishment in the form of a young boy from a heretical home who had taken service with More. The boy's father was an acquaintance of George Joye, the notorious heretic who had escaped abroad and was writing heretical books in Antwerp. The boy had come under Joye's influence in London and had learned heresies from him. He told the other youths in More's household that he had been taught that the consecrated bread and wine in the eucharist was only in a spiritual sense the Body and Blood of Christ, and that it still remained bread and wine in substance. When this was reported to More, he ordered that the boy should be publicly flogged in the presence of all the household. 'I caused a servant of mine to stripe him like a child before mine household, for amendment of himself and example of such other.'[39]

On another occasion, More heard that a mentally deranged man was causing disturbances in various churches in the neighbourhood of Chelsea. More describes him as 'one, which after that he had fallen into the frantic heresies, fell soon after into plain open frenzy beside'. The man was confined in the lunatic asylum of Bedlam, where, according to More, 'afterward by beating and correction gathered his remembrance to him, and began to come again to himself'. But the whippings did not have as beneficial an effect as More suggests, because after he was released and 'walking about abroad, his old fancies began to fall again in his head'. He made a nuisance of himself in church, where he disturbed the worshippers during the service by 'many mad toys and trifles'. His favourite trick was to steal up behind some woman who was lowering her head in deep meditation, and at the moment of the elevation of the

Host by the priest during mass, to lift up her skirts from behind and throw them over her head. Several parishioners complained to More and asked him to take some action to stop the man from behaving in this way.

One day the man happened to stroll past More's house. Someone recognised him, and pointed him out to More, who acted swiftly. He ordered his servants to seize the man, called the local constables, and ordered them to tie him to a tree in the street, and flog him 'before the whole town', with excellent results. 'They striped him with rods therefore till he waxed weary and somewhat longer', wrote More; and after his faults had been 'beaten home' to him, he confessed his misdeeds. 'And verily God be thanked I hear none harm of him now.'[40]

A judge should not be too severely blamed for not being in advance of his time. It was generally believed in More's era, and for several centuries afterwards, that the best way to cure a sufferer from mental illness was to whip him. Many of More's contemporaries would have acted as he did in ordering the man to be flogged, even if they might not have written about it with the obvious satisfaction which More showed in his account of the incident in *The Apology of Sir Thomas More*. As the man was wandering about in Chelsea, and was presumably outside the parish where he was born or had lived for the last three years, without holding a begging licence from a JP, More was legally entitled to order him to be whipped without any trial or any inquiry as to whether he was guilty or innocent of the accusations of misconduct in church. More, of course, would have seen his action in lifting women's skirts over their heads as a sexual crime which deserved to be severely punished, though he does not suggest that it was accompanied by any indecent assault on the women, and when taken together with the man's other 'mad toys and trifles' seems to have been merely a crazy prank. One wonders whether anyone troubled to explain to the wretched lunatic that his misbehaviour in the neighbouring churches at various times in the past was the reason why he was suddenly seized when he was peaceably walking past More's house and tied to a tree and whipped before crowds of jeering bystanders till he had been reduced to a state of exhaustion and for a little longer.

According to More, this man, and the boy in his household who taught heretical doctrines about the Real Presence to the other boys, were the only two cases in which he ordered a heretic to be flogged. The Protestants told a different story. By 1533, if not earlier, the story was circulating that More had tortured and ill-treated several heretics who had been detained at his house in Chelsea before their trial, and that he had ordered them to be tied to a tree in his garden and savagely flogged. More said that this was a lie which was first spread by a Cambridge bookseller, Segar Nicholson, who had been arrested at his orders for distributing heretical books and imprisoned for four or five days in More's house. More states that though Segar was not ill-treated in any way, he said, after his release, that he had been whipped and tied round the head with cords which were tightened until he fainted. More also says that Tyndale repeated Segar's story to a friend of More's, and added the accusation that More had robbed Segar of five marks. In 1563 Segar's story was published in John Foxe's *Book of Martyrs*.[41]

More denied the accusation in his *Apology* in 1533. He stated that he had often sentenced men to be flogged for robbery, murder, 'or sacrilege in a church, with carrying away the pyx with the blessed Sacrament, or villainously casting it out', in order to subject the offenders to 'well-deserved pain'; but he never flogged heretics, 'notwithstanding also that heretics be yet much worse than all they',[42] except for the two cases of the boy in his household who denied the Real Presence and the heretic who lifted up women's skirts in church.

More's twentieth-century champions have often referred to these accusations about the floggings, and his reply to the charges, as if his defence were sufficient to dispose of the allegation that he ill-treated heretics. It is very likely that Foxe's story is inaccurate; for the victims of persecution are inclined to believe accusations of cruelty against notorious persecutors even if they are in fact untrue. Whatever may have happened to Segar, and whatever Tyndale may have believed and said about More's stealing five marks from him, we know the origin of the story of the whippings in More's garden from More's own *Apology*. He ordered a boy to be whipped because the boy had told the other boys what he had been taught, and believed, about transubstantiation. He also ordered the whipping of a mentally-deranged man who, according to More, was a heretic and had misbehaved in church, after the man had been tied to a tree in the street just outside More's garden. More also claimed, in the *Apology*, that he had often ordered whippings, not only of murderers and thieves, but of those who had sacrilegiously stolen or desecrated the consecrated Host. This was a form of protest in which Protestants often engaged, in order to show their indignation against the worship of the idol in the mass. The charge against More of whipping heretics seems to be clearly proved on his own admission.

In the autumn of 1530, More's officers arrested several men who were accused of distributing some of the books which had been banned in Henry's proclamation. As this was an offence against the proclamation, More could deal with the men himself in the Star Chamber without sending them to face a charge of heresy in the court of their bishop. He sent some of them to the Tower, and fined others. He imprisoned a London merchant, Thomas Patner, in the Fleet prison for distributing

Tyndale's English New Testament. In due course, Patner was released, but was imprisoned again on Stokesley's orders. Patner's servant then drafted a petition to Parliament asking for his master to be released from prison. More got to hear of it, and warned the servant that he would proceed against him for contempt of court as a frivolous suitor if he went ahead with his petition. Patner was not released until after More had resigned as Lord Chancellor.[43]

Early in 1531 George Constantine, who had been with Tyndale and Roy in the Netherlands, came to England to arrange for the secret distribution of the English New Testament. He was caught, and brought as a prisoner to More's house in Chelsea. More had him confined in the stocks in his house for several days, and examined him repeatedly. When More asked him where Tyndale had obtained the money to print the English New Testament, Constantine said that they had used the money that Warham paid when he bought up the copies of the first edition; and More commented that he had always thought it was a stupid idea to buy up the books. According to More, Constantine gave him information which led to the arrest of several of his fellow-heretics in London, after More had persuaded him that this was the only chance of saving their souls.

Constantine escaped from More's custody. He broke the stocks, climbed the garden wall, and disappeared without a trace, eventually making his way to Antwerp. In his *Apology*, More argued that he could not have starved or ill-treated Constantine if Constantine was strong enough, after several days in custody, to break the stocks, climb the wall, and escape.[44]

In 1531 More interrogated Tewkesbury, Bayfield and Bainham, holding Tewkesbury and Bainham in custody for a time in his house. All three recanted, but immediately resumed their heresy, and all were ultimately burned. According to Foxe, More had Bainham whipped at a tree in his garden, and afterwards sent him to the Tower, where he was tortured on the rack in More's presence.[45]

In the first edition of the *Book of Martyrs* in 1563, Foxe gave the text of the statement made by Bainham at the stake. 'I come hither, good people, accused and condemned for a heretic, Sir Thomas More being my accuser and my judge.' He declared that he was being condemned as a heretic because he believed that every man was entitled to read the Bible in his native tongue; that the Pope was Antichrist; that there was no Purgatory; and that Thomas Becket was no saint, but a traitor to the crown and realm of England. At this point, one of the officials cried out: 'Thou heretic! Set fire to him and burn him!' Bainham replied: 'God forgive thee, and show thee more mercy than thou showest to me; the Lord forgive Sir Thomas More; and pray for me, all good people'; 'and so

257

prayed he till the fire took his bowels and his head.'[46]

Foxe included another passage in his first edition of 1563, in which he described how Tewkesbury was held in the porter's lodge at More's house, 'hand, foot, and head in the stocks, six days without release', and how he was whipped at Jesu's tree in More's garden, 'and also twisted in his brows with small ropes, so that the blood started out of his eyes'. He was then let loose in More's house for a day, so that his friends thought that he would be released next day; but instead More sent him to be racked in the Tower until he was almost lame.[47]

This story about Tewkesbury, and the account of Bainham's last words at the stake, were both deleted from the second edition of the *Book of Martyrs* in 1570, and this has been cited by More's modern defenders to show that Foxe had realised by 1570 that the allegations were untrue. Although this is a possible explanation, it is not necessarily the correct one. Foxe very largely re-wrote his book for the 1570 edition, adding a great deal of new material, so that the book ran to over two thousand pages and to nearly four million words; and he cut out many passages which had been included in the first edition, sometimes perhaps for no other reason except that the new edition was so long. In any case, Foxe did not delete the other specific examples which he gave in the 1563 edition of More's ill-treatment of Protestant martyrs at his house in Chelsea. He retained his account of how Bainham was

> carried out of the Middle Temple to the Chancellor's house at Chelsea, where he continued in free prison awhile, till the time that Sir Thomas More saw he could not prevail in perverting him to his sect. Then he cast him into prison in his own house, and whipping him at the tree in his garden, called the tree of Troth, and after sent him to the Tower to be racked; and so he was, Sir Thomas More being present himself, till in a manner he had lamed him, because he would not accuse the gentlemen of the Temple of his acquaintance, nor would show where his books lay; and because his wife denied them to be at his house, she was sent to the Fleet, and their goods confiscated.[48]

More also succeeded in arresting one of the most upright and able of the younger Protestants, John Frith, a scholar of Cambridge and of Wolsey's Cardinal's College at Oxford, who had become a Zwinglian and had joined Tyndale in the Netherlands. He came to England at the beginning of 1532 to help in the distribution of Tyndale's New Testament. More received a report that he was in the vicinity of Reading, and gave orders for his arrest; but he succeeded in evading More's officers, and was on the point of embarking for the Netherlands when he was caught at Milton Shore in Essex and taken to the Tower.

He succeeded in writing a book against transubstantiation in his cell with hidden writing materials, and in smuggling it out of the Tower for secret distribution among his supporters who were at liberty; but a London tailor named William Holt, who pretended to be a Protestant but was really a spy employed by More, betrayed the secret to More and sent him a copy of Frith's treatise. More replied to the arguments of 'this young man', as he called Frith, in the form of a letter to Holt, which Rastell published in 1533 under the title of *A Letter of Sir Thomas More, Knight, impugning the erroneous writing of John Frith against the blessed Sacrament of the Altar*. According to Foxe, More gave orders that Frith was not to be allowed to see a copy of it, in an unsuccessful attempt to prevent Frith from reading it and replying to it; but by the time that More's letter was published he was no longer Lord Chancellor and in a position to impose prison regulations in the Tower. Frith was eventually burned in the summer of 1533 after he had been condemned as a sacramentary, and delivered to the secular arm for burning, by the newly-appointed Protestant Archbishop of Canterbury, Cranmer.[49]

As long as More was Lord Chancellor, he could spur on the bishops to persecute heretics and seize and burn Lutheran books; but in order to retain office, he had to compromise, and go almost further than his conscience would allow him in supporting Henry's divorce and the break with Rome. Before Parliament reassembled in February 1531, Henry, the Boleyns and Cromwell had thought out another measure which was designed to weaken the power of the Church. They claimed that every bishop and priest who had submitted to the authority which Wolsey had exercised as Papal Legate had connived at Wolsey's *praemunire*, and was therefore an accessory to it, and guilty of a *praemunire* himself. According to this argument, every churchman in England was liable to life imprisonment and the forfeiture of his property to the king; but Henry would pardon them for their *praemunire* and allow them to retain their property if they pleaded guilty to the *praemunire*, agreed to pay a fine to the king, and acknowledged him to be the head of the Church. This acknowledgement of the royal supremacy was opposed by many of the clergy; and More's two closest friends among the bishops, Tunstal and Fisher, spoke against it in the Convocations of York and Canterbury. Tunstal wrote to Henry on the subject, and drew a reply from him which was friendly in tone but insisted on his submission.[50] Eventually a compromise was agreed; the two Convocations recognised that the king was the protector of the Church 'as far as the law of God allows'.

More was deeply distressed at these developments, and in the greatest secrecy made this known to Fisher, to Catherine's supporters, and to the emperor's ambassador. On 21 February 1531 Chapuys wrote to Charles that More was so shocked by Henry's policy that he would have liked to resign, but had been told that he would be thrown into the river unless he complied with Henry's wishes. We can be sure that this was not the literal truth, but obviously More was very perturbed at what was taking place and at the part that he was forced to play. On 1 March Chapuys wrote to Charles that More had shown himself to be a great supporter of Catherine's cause and very favourable to Charles's subjects. Chapuys urged the emperor to write a letter, which he could show to More, expressing his appreciation of More's attitude. Charles duly wrote the letter; but when Chapuys sent a messenger to tell More that he would like to visit him and show him the letter, More begged Chapuys, for the honour of God, not to come, for this would arouse suspicion and would make it impossible for More to continue working in the Council in the interests of Charles and Catherine. He asked Chapuys not to send him Charles's letter, for if he did, he would have to show it to Henry. He hoped Chapuys would retain it and allow him to see it at a more propitious time.[51]

Henry now increased the pressure on More, and abandoned his policy of exempting More from the duty of serving him in connection with the divorce. On 30 March 1531, the day after Henry pardoned the clergy for the *praemunire*, More addressed the House of Lords. He said that many people believed that the king wished to divorce the queen because he was in love with some lady; but this was not true, for his only motive was to obey his conscience which told him that he had offended God's law in marrying his brother's widow. More informed the House that this view had been upheld by the opinions of the universities, which Tuke then read out. The bishops of Lincoln and London, Longland and Stokesley, spoke in favour of the divorce. At this, Standish and Clerk, the bishops of St Asaph and Bath and Wells, protested that this was not a suitable time to discuss the merits of the divorce case, as the queen's supporters had not been given notice that the matter would be raised; and the Duke of Norfolk agreed that the king wished merely to inform the House of the opinions expressed by the universities. At this point, one of the peers, who must surely have realised what he was doing, asked the Lord Chancellor what opinion he held about the divorce. More replied that he had made his opinion on the subject known to the king, and had nothing further to add.

Next day, Parliament was prorogued till October. More and Norfolk went to the House of Commons, where More repeated the statement that he had made in the Lords about Henry's motive for seeking a divorce. He said that the king hoped that when the MPs went home to their constituencies, they would tell their neighbours what More had said. More thanked the MPs, on the king's behalf, and told them that

Henry was well satisfied with them.[52]

More had gone to the very limits that his conscience could allow. He knew very well that he had lied to the House of Lords and the House of Commons; that the king was motivated at least in part by his love for a certain lady; that the most invincible King Henry, the eighth of that name, Defender of the Faith, had been affected by 'the desire of the foul beastly pleasure beneath the belly'; that he had even, perhaps, lifted up this lady's skirts, like the lunatic whom More had flogged at the tree in Chelsea. But unless More acquiesced in Henry's lechery and furthered it by his lies in Parliament, how could he remain Lord Chancellor? and if he left office, who could be trusted to burn heretics? Fisher was out of favour, and might well be restrained by a new Lord Chancellor if he acted against Lutherans; Tunstal had been sent to the north, where no heretics were to be found; Stokesley was showing commendable energy as a persecutor, but as he was also an active supporter of the divorce, could he be relied upon to continue in his anti-Lutheran zeal if the Boleyns persuaded Henry to adopt a new line on heresy?

By remaining in office, More could ensure that for the time being the persecution continued unabated; but he was apprehensive for the future. He had never minimised the danger of heresy. Already, in the days before Henry had begun divorce proceedings against Catherine, More had said to Roper that, 'high as we seem to sit upon the mountains treading heretics under our feet like ants', he prayed that the time would never come when they would be happy to see Catholics and Lutherans living side by side and tolerating each other, with Christian and heretical worship taking place legally in their different churches, because the alternative would be a situation in which a Lutheran government persecuted Catholics and prohibited the celebration of the mass.[53] But in 1531 the day when Catholics would be grateful merely for toleration had not yet arrived; and More was able to burn a few more heretics before it came.

But while More was sending a handful of brave idealists to death in the fire, Cromwell was mobilising the less spiritual but far stronger forces of lay anti-clericalism in the House of Commons. The petition against the clergy, which had first been drawn up in the exultation which followed Wolsey's fall in the autumn of 1529, was now brought forward again with the active support of one of the king's most influential secretaries. It resulted, in the spring of 1532, in the clergy being required to agree to what became known as 'the Submission of the Clergy'. They were to relinquish their right to propose any measures in Convocation without the king's consent, and to abolish the power of the bishops to deal with cases of heresy in their dioceses. Henceforth heretics would be dealt with by special commissioners acting under the king's authority.

At the same time, Parliament passed a bill abolishing the payment to the Pope of the annates – the first year's rents when a new bishop was appointed – but providing that the Act was not to come into force until the king so ordered by royal proclamation.

The Lord Chancellor duly opened the new session of Parliament in January 1532, but this was the last official duty that he performed. Chapuys reported that More and Gardiner, who had been appointed Bishop of Winchester, were opposing the plan for the submission of the clergy in the discussions that were taking place in the council, but that though they were supported by the bishops, they were fighting a losing battle. Chapuys also heard that Henry was determined to proceed with the project for the submission of the clergy and was very angry with More for opposing it. On 15 May, Convocation accepted the petition of the House of Commons and agreed to the Submission of the Clergy. Next day, More put the Great Seal into a white leather bag, which he sealed with his own seal, and delivered it to Henry in the presence of Norfolk at 3 p.m. in the garden of York Place. He had resigned as Lord Chancellor, officially on the grounds of ill-health and the heavy financial burden that the office entailed. A few days later, Henry appointed another layman and common lawyer, Sir Thomas Audley, to succeed him.[54]

Charles V, who had been receiving frequent reports from Chapuys of More's sympathy for Catherine, considered his resignation to be a set-back for the queen's cause and for his own diplomacy. He expressed his disapproval to the English ambassador, Sir Thomas Elyot, who was with him at Ratisbon. 'And this we will say, that if we had been master of such a servant, of whose doings ourself have had these many years no small experience, we would rather have lost the best city of our dominions than have lost such a worthy counsellor.'*[55]

---

* Chambers (pp. 287–90) conclusively shows that Charles must have said this to Elyot on the occasion of More's resignation as Lord Chancellor, and not, as Roper wrote, when he heard of his execution.

CHAPTER 16

THOMAS MORE THE MARTYR

TWENTY-THREE months elapsed between More's resignation as Lord Chancellor in May 1532 and his arrest and committal to the Tower in April 1534. He spent the time in Chelsea writing books against heretics. But he would make no criticism of the king or comment on the direction in which Henry was moving. He denied the rumours that he had resigned as Lord Chancellor because of his disagreements with Henry's policy. He wrote to Erasmus that the only reason for his resignation was ill-health, and told him about 'those acts of fond affection shown to me by our most noble king'.[1]

Like other gentlemen of the period, he wrote his epitaph when he felt that his health was failing. It was intended to be placed on his tomb in the parish church in Chelsea, though this became impossible in view of the circumstances in which he died. It contained a brief summary of his life, from his birth in London 'of respectable, though not distinguished, ancestry', through his years of service to the 'Unconquerable Henry VIII, who is the only king to have ever received the unique distinction of meriting the title Defender of the Faith'. He stated that he so conducted himself during his years in office 'that his Excellent Sovereign found no fault with his service, neither did he make himself odious to the nobles nor unpleasant to the populace, but he was a source of trouble to thieves, murderers and heretics'. He ended by expressing his affection for both his wives, who were to be buried in the same grave with him. He could not decide which wife he had loved best. 'O, how happily we could have lived all three together if fate and morality permitted. Well, I pray that the grave, that Heaven, will bring us together.'[2]

In a letter to Erasmus, he apologised for boasting of his antagonism to heretics.

> As to the statement in my Epitaph that I was a source of trouble for heretics, I wrote that just to show off. I find that breed of men absolutely loathsome, so much so that unless they regain their senses, I want to be as hateful to them as anyone can possibly be; for my increasing experience with these men frightens me with the thought of what the world will suffer at their hands.[3]

More knew that Erasmus's attitude to heretics was different from his own, but neither he nor Erasmus ever directly referred to it. A few weeks after More resigned as Lord Chancellor, Erasmus wrote a letter of recommendation to him in favour of the German Lutheran, Grynaeus, who was coming to England to study Plato's manuscripts in the libraries of the Oxford colleges. More disapproved of Grynaeus's heretical doctrines, but would not be discourteous to a distinguished foreign scholar who was a friend of Erasmus. He wrote to Erasmus that as he had recommended Grynaeus 'for scholarly reasons, not for religious ones', he would welcome him, but would be on his guard against him. He entertained Grynaeus at Chelsea with his usual hospitality; but he insisted on either accompanying Grynaeus himself, or sending his secretary to escort him, wherever he went, so that he would have no opportunity to corrupt anyone with his heretical doctrines. He discussed his religious disagreements with Grynaeus in private in a friendly and courteous way, and carried on their argument by correspondence after Grynaeus had returned to Germany.[4]

By June 1533 he had written the longest of all his books, his *Confutation of Tyndale's Answer*. It was nearly half a million words long, and when printed filled 493 closely printed quarto pages. It was a reply to Tyndale's *Answer unto Sir Thomas More*, in which Tyndale replied to his *Dialogue concerning Heresies*. Tyndale's *Answer* was a full-length book, but More's *Confutation* was five times as long.

Like the *Dialogue concerning Heresies*, More's *Confutation* was free of the obscenity of his *Answer to Luther*, and the violence of the language was well within the accepted traditions of the theological controversy of the period. More followed the usual practice of reprinting, section by section, the text of Tyndale's book, and then replying to the passage and demolishing Tyndale's arguments. More was obviously writing with a view to pleasing the king; for his *Confutation* not only contained lavish praise of Henry, but concentrated chiefly on proving that the doctrines of Tyndale and 'his master Luther' were seditious, and constituted a threat to royal authority and the whole fabric of the social order.

More began with a striking opening sentence:

> Our Lord send us now some years as plenteous of good corn as we have had some years of late plenteous of evil books. For they have grown so fast and sprung up so thick, full of pestilent errors and pernicious heresies, that they have infected and killed I fear me more silly simple souls than the famine of the dear years have destroyed bodies.

He then pointed out that there was a link between the shortage of corn and the abundance of heretical books, because God had sent the bad harvests to punish the nation for having allowed the heretical books to circulate. Of all the heretical books, the worst was Tyndale's translation of the New Testament, which was worse than the Koran of the Moslems. Fortunately the evil of these heretical books had been checked by 'the King's high wisdom' in banning the importation into England of any book written in English and published abroad, and in requiring the name and address of the printer to be printed in every book published in England.[5]

A large part of More's book is devoted to discrediting the Protestants, especially those who had suffered martyrdom. He claimed that the heretics whom he had examined had all been cowards who feared death and had done everything possible to avoid it. George Constantine had given him useful information before he escaped, which had enabled him to arrest several of Constantine's contacts. Tewkesbury had urged his comrade James to save his life by a feigned recantation; he had himself refused to recant only because he knew that as a relapsed heretic he would be burned even if he did. So Tewkesbury 'was delivered at last unto the secular hands and burned, as there was never wretch I ween better worthy'. Nor had Tyndale any reason to be proud of his martyr Bayfield, who, though both a monk and a priest, had two wives simultaneously, one in Brabant and one in England – a statement which the Protestants said was a lie. After recanting, Bayfield relapsed into heresy, 'like a dog returning to his vomit', but he was willing to recant again as long as he thought that there was any chance of saving his life.[6]

The most controversial of More's statements was his allegation that Bilney, who refused to recant and would in any case have been burned as a relapsed heretic, had recanted at the stake at the last moment before he was burned in the sandpit at Norwich in August 1531. More gave the text of Bilney's recantation, described how he knelt and was granted absolution by the priest before the fire was lit, and referred to the names and statements of eye-witnesses to prove it. Foxe and the Protestant writers said that More was lying, and that Bilney's so-called recantation was a forgery; and they, too, quoted statements of eye-witnesses to show that nothing of the kind had occurred.[7] This makes it difficult to discover the truth. We can say, however, on the evidence of More's statements on other occasions, that he would not have hesitated to lie and commit forgery about Bilney's recantation if he had believed that it was in the interests of the fight against heresy.

There is a good deal of the personal muck-raking which was so common in sixteenth-century polemical controversy, and in which More particularly excelled. The wives of Protestants who had been monks or priests are all 'harlots'; and when Tyndale claims that a man may sincerely repent his sins without performing penance and receiving absolution from a priest, More states that Luther repents every morning and goes to bed again that night with the nun whom he had married, who of course is his 'harlot' to More.[8]

The darkest side of More's theology and character comes out in his discussion of fasting. Tyndale argued that the fasting laws had been instituted by the Church to restrain men's gluttony and immoderate living, but that it would be better if men would eat sparingly and live moderately at all times, rather than be compelled to observe the fasting regulations on the fast days appointed by the Church. More replies that many non-Christian philosophers have urged 'abstinence to tame the flesh from intemperance and foul lusts', but God had instituted fasting among Christians 'not only for that purpose, but also for a kind of pain, affliction, and punishment of the flesh for their sins, and to put us in remembrance that we be now in the vale of tears and not in the hill of joy'.[9] Here we find the same emphasis on the gloom of life which he expressed in *The Four Last Things*.

Of all the wicked heresies which Tyndale had committed, none seemed worse to More than the translation of the New Testament. When Tyndale and the Protestants objected that More and his associates had banned and burned the Word of God, More replied that it was not the Word of God that he had burned, but Tyndale's faulty translation of it and his heretical marginal notes. Certainly the marginal notes, though far less extensive and provocative than those that John Knox and his colleagues inserted into their Geneva Bible of 1560, contained criticism of official Catholic doctrine; but More's chief objection to Tyndale's Bible was the one which the conservative churchmen had made against Erasmus's translation of the New Testament – that he had translated *ecclesia* as 'congregation'. Tyndale pointed out, in his *Answer to More*, that More's 'darling' Erasmus had translated the Greek word *ecclesia* as *congregatio*. More had two answers to this, of which the first was subtle and specious, and the second fundamental and true at least in part. More argued that when Erasmus translated the Greek New Testament into Latin, he wished to find a Latin equivalent for the Greek *ecclesia* rather than to use the Greek word in his Latin text; he therefore chose *congregatio* as the best translation. But whatever might be the best Latin translation of *ecclesia*, there was no doubt that the recognised English translation of *ecclesia* was 'Church', and for Tyndale to translate *ecclesia* as 'congregation' showed a subversive intention.[10] Thus More tried to persuade his English readers, some of whom could not understand Latin, that while *congregatio* in Latin was a reasonable translation of the Greek *ecclesia*, 'congregation' in English was seditious.

But More then fell back on his real argument: Erasmus never had a seditious intent, which Tyndale has.

I have not contended with Erasmus my darling, because I found no such malicious intent with Erasmus my darling as I find with Tyndale. For had I found with Erasmus my darling the shrewd intent and purpose that I find in Tyndale, Erasmus my darling should be no more my darling. But I find in Erasmus my darling that he detesteth and abhorreth the errors and heresies that Tyndale plainly teacheth and abideth by, and therefore Erasmus my darling shall be my dear darling still.[11]

Tyndale had not overlooked the fact that Erasmus had stated in the preface of his *Praise of Folly*, in which he had laughed at the clergy as well as at many other groups, that he had written the book in More's house. More replied that his friendship with Erasmus did not prove that he himself agreed with his book; and he then went on to make a statement which came close to repudiating the works which he had written in his youth. *Praise of Folly*, says More, merely joked about the abuses of the Church; but today, thanks to 'Luther's pestilent heresies', which Tyndale has expounded in his books, the situation is different. If anyone today were to translate *Praise of Folly* into English, 'or some works either that I have myself written ere this . . . I would not only my darling's books but mine own also help to burn them both with mine own hands', because, though they are harmless in themselves, they may be used to cause harm by ill-intentioned people.[12] Which of his own books would More wish to burn if they were translated into English? Was he thinking of *Utopia*?

The main theme of *The Confutation of Tyndale's Answer* is that Tyndale, Luther and all heretics are seditious. It was not easy for More to prove this point, because Tyndale, in his book *The Obedience of a Christian Man*, had advocated royal despotism in its most extreme form. Tyndale wrote that God had appointed kings 'in His own stead' to rule over their people, including the churchmen in their realms. To resist the king and his officers was to resist God, even if the king was the greatest tyrant on earth; for the king 'may at his lust do right and wrong, and shall give account but to God only'. These doctrines were likely to appeal to kings, not least to Henry VIII, who is said to have commented, after reading Tyndale's book, that 'this book is for me and all kings to read'.[13]

But, for More, Tyndale is seditious, despite his pretence of supporting the royal authority, because he challenges the authority of the Church, which is an essential prop of the social order. Tyndale investigates the reasons which prompted God to issue His divine commandments; but such an attitude is seditious, for the orders of superiors should be obeyed without asking the reason why. Tyndale wrote that God commanded us to love even the Turks, and to try to convert them to Christianity by peaceful means; this, says More, is seditious, because it may cause Christians to disobey their rulers when they go to war with the Turks. It was seditious, too, for Tyndale and the 'stinking martyr' Thomas Hitton to object to the death penalty for theft.[14] No wonder More would have burned an English translation of *Utopia*.

Tyndale is seditious because he objects to putting heretics to death, and especially to painful deaths; but princes are right to suppress heretics and 'to punish them according to justice by sore painful death, both for example and for infection of other'.[15] The heretics themselves have at last recognised the truth of this argument, because in those parts of Germany where the Lutherans have come to power, they have been forced to persecute and put to death Zwinglians and other heretics who criticise Lutheranism, for otherwise they could not maintain law and order. In the same way, Luther and Tyndale were forced 'a little to retreat' in their support for the revolutionary peasants in Germany. Like other Catholic writers at the time, More virtually ignored Luther's vigorous support of the suppression of the Peasant Revolt in Germany in 1525, which was to arouse the indignation of Engels and modern socialists, and referred to the revolutionary peasants as 'Lutherans', holding Luther responsible for inciting the rising. So much for Tyndale's doctrine of obedience to rulers, writes More; the German peasants, following the lead of 'Tyndale's master', rebelled against their rulers, 'and thereby disobeyed God's commandment, and brought thereby the vengeance of God upon their own heads, to the slaughter of above four score thousand of them in one summer, and the remnant the worse entreated ever since'.[16]

But More found the weakest chink in his adversary's armour. Tyndale had stated that there was one exception to the rule that a subject must obey his prince without question. If the prince ordered him to violate God's law, he must disobey and passively suffer martyrdom, though even then he must not resist the prince by force or otherwise. More, like the brilliant barrister that he was, jumped in to exploit his opponent's weakness. This exception is seditious, for it means that the individual is allowing the dictates of his own private conscience to justify disobedience to the king. More seized on a passage in Barnes's writings, in which Barnes wrote that if the king ordered a man to burn his copy of the Bible, he would be justified in disobeying. King Henry has in fact ordered the burning of Bibles, says More; will Barnes and Tyndale obey this order, or will they not? for if they refuse to obey because of the dictates of their private consciences, they are seditious.[17]

In the *Confutation of Tyndale's Answer*, More wrote that he knew, from his personal knowledge, that the king's Highness 'nothing more effectually desireth than the maintenance of the true Catholic faith whereof he is by his no more honourable than well deserved title Defensor'.[18] But while he was writing the book, Henry was moving closer to the final break with Rome. In August 1532 Warham died, and was succeeded as Archbishop of Canterbury by Anne Boleyn's chaplain, Cranmer. In January 1533 Henry secretly married Anne Boleyn, who was already pregnant by him. In April an Act of Parliament made it high treason to appeal from any court in England to the Papal court in Rome. In May, Cranmer held a special court at Dunstable and gave judgment that Henry's marriage to Catherine was unlawful. It was then announced that King Henry, being a bachelor, had married Anne Boleyn a few months earlier, and that she was now the queen. According to Roper, three of More's friends – Tunstal, Gardiner and Clerk – asked him to accompany them to Anne's coronation; and, having heard that he was in financial difficulties, they sent him £20 to buy a splendid gown for the occasion. More did not go to the coronation, but kept the money, telling Tunstal, Gardiner and Clerk that as he would not oblige them by attending the coronation, he would at least comply with their other request and accept the £20.[19] On Whit Sunday, 1 June, eighteen days before the publication of More's *Confutation of Tyndale's Answer*, Anne was crowned queen in Westminster Abbey with the greatest pomp. Her daughter Elizabeth was born on 7 September.

But More, in Chelsea, continued to write in defence of the Church. His next two books were written against a new and surprising opponent. Christopher St German, an aged common lawyer, after doing nothing remarkable for the firsts seventy years of his life, had recently published a number of books in which he glorified the English common law and criticised many aspects of the exercise of the jurisdiction of the ecclesiastical courts. His latest book, *The Division betwixt the Spiritualty and the Temporalty*, was published anonymously. It was written in very moderate language, and deplored the conflict between churchmen and laymen, arguing that there were faults and intolerance on both sides. St German called on them both to cease attacking and insulting each other.

More replied to *The Division betwixt the Spiritualty and the Temporalty* in *The Apology of Sir Thomas More, Knight*, referring sarcastically to St German as 'the Pacifier'. He argued that the Pacifier, beneath the mark of his courteous and temperate language and his pretence of impartiality, was advocating most dangerous doctrines. The Pacifier rightly stated that the laity should refrain from launching abusive attacks on the clergy, but also, quite wrongly, that the clergy should not launch abusive attacks on heretics.

More's criticisms of St German form only part of his *Apology*. He took the opportunity to defend himself from the accusations that had been made against him from all quarters – that he flogged heretics in his garden; that he used too intemperate language in his attacks on them; that he had enriched himself during his years in office; and that his books were too long. He also repeated all his previous attacks on heretics, justified the statutes which enacted that they should be burned, and the activities of the ecclesiastical courts in suppressing them, and launched his usual denunciations of Luther and other Lutherans and their 'harlots'. He condemned the Pacifier for adopting an impartial position between the clergy and heretics, and stated that if any criticisms were to be made of the clergy, they should be written in Latin, and not in English for the common people to read. He expressed his opinion that heresy was 'the worst crime that can be'.[20]

St German replied to More in *A Dialogue betwixt two Englishmen whereof one was called Salem and the other Bizance*; and More in turn replied with *The Debillation of Salem and Bizance*. By Christmas 1533 he had published another short work, *The Answer to the first part of the poisoned book which a nameless heretic hath named The Supper of the Lord*. It was far more moderate in tone than anything that More had written against heretics, and the title is almost the most vicious thing that he said about his opponent. This may have been because he realised the weakness of his position, for it was his last shot in a hopeless rearguard action. In December 1533 the Council issued a proclamation abrogating the Papal supremacy over the Church of England, and ordering that the Pope must in future be referred to as 'the Bishop of Rome'. At the same time, the conspiracy of Elizabeth Barton, the Nun of Kent, was exposed. It brought More into danger.

Elizabeth Barton had first attracted attention about 1526 by her trances at Courtopestreet near her native village of Aldington in Kent. As the villagers crowded around her, they heard a hollow voice speaking as if from out of her belly. The voice of Our Lady of Courtopestreet ordered Elizabeth Barton to enter the nunnery of St Sepulchre's in Canterbury. There she met her confessor, Dr Edward Bocking, who was a monk of Christchurch, Canterbury. Under his guidance, she began to experience revelations of a controversial character. She went to see Wolsey – probably in 1528 – and told him that she had seen a vision of him with three swords – one representing his power as Legate, the second his power as Lord Chancellor, and the third his power to grant the king a divorce.

The Lady of Courtopestreet ordered the nun to go to the king, to tell him to burn English translations of the Bible and to remain loyal to the Pope, and to warn him that if he married Anne Boleyn he would die within a month and that within six months the people would be struck down by a great plague. She gained access to Henry, and passed on the warning to him. He listened with surprising patience, and showed no irritation, but henceforth she was kept under observation.

Both Warham and Fisher were impressed by her sanctity and by her revelations. Fisher believed what she said about Our Lady of Courtopestreet's warnings, and realised the political use which could be made of them in the opposition to the divorce. More was much more cautious. He first heard about Elizabeth Barton and her visions at Courtopestreet from Warham, and, relying on the archbishop's report, he had formed a favourable opinion of her. When she became active as a prophet of the disasters which would follow if Henry married Anne Boleyn, More met several of her closest collaborators. At Christmas 1532 Father Resby, a Friar Observant of Canterbury, told him about her prophecies. Father Rich, a Friar Observant of Richmond, who was an active propagandist for Catherine of Aragon, told him more about her prophecies at Shrovetide in February 1533, and invited him to meet her.

A meeting between More and the nun was arranged in the little chapel in the monastery of Sion, on the north bank of the Thames near Brentford, some time in the summer of 1533; but More, if we are to believe the account of the meeting which he gave to Cromwell, was very careful what he said to her. They discussed the case of a young woman of Tottenham, of whom More had heard, who was persuaded by the nun that her visions were illusions planted by the Devil; but More assured Cromwell that 'we talked no word of the King's Grace or any great personage else'.[21]

Soon afterwards he wrote to the nun, impressing on her the need for caution. He reminded her of how the Duke of Buckingham had been executed largely because he spoke incautiously to a monk.

> It sufficeth me, good Madam, to put you in remembrance of such thing as I nothing doubt your wisdom and the spirit of God shall keep you from talking with any persons, specially with lay persons, of any such manner things as pertain to princes' affairs, or the state of the realm, but only to common and talk with any person, high and low, of such manner things as may to the soul be profitable for you to show and for them to know.[22]

More had been cautious, but not cautious enough. The nun, Bocking, Resby, Rich and her other associates were convicted of high treason and executed after they had recanted at Paul's Cross. Fisher and More were accused of misprision of treason – of failing to inform the authorities when they knew that high treason had been committed. Both their names were included in a bill of attainder which was introduced in Parliament pronouncing them guilty and sentencing them to the usual punishment of imprisonment for life and forfeiture of their property.

Like Wolsey, four years earlier, More faced the prospect of being sentenced to imprisonment for life, or until the king chose to release him; and like Wolsey, he relied entirely on the king's pardon. But in other respects, the two fallen favourites reacted differently to the same situation. Whereas Wolsey preserved his dignity, and petitioned in the language of a humble suppliant only to save his college, not himself, More pleaded in the most abject fashion for his pardon. Most other courtiers would have done the same in his predicament, though Fisher, like Wolsey, did not. Fisher disclaimed any intention to commit misprision of treason. He said that he knew that Elizabeth Barton had told the king that he would die within a month if he married Anne Boleyn; but he had no idea that she had said this to anyone else, and he could not see how she could be held to have committed high treason if she made this prophecy only to the king himself.[23]

More repudiated the nun, dissociated himself from the opposition to Henry's divorce, and expressed his support for Henry's policy and the marriage to Anne Boleyn. He could not justify this, like his earlier compromises of conscience, by claiming that it enabled him to remain in the government and to influence Henry's policy in the right direction. Did he act simply out of the same cowardice of which he had accused Tewkesbury, Bayfield and Bainham, when they recanted to avoid a far more terrible ordeal than More faced in 1534? Or was he influenced by his respect for authority, by the duty to submit to the higher powers and avoid any action which could encourage sedition, and by his instinctive and reasoned disapproval of anything which could be interpreted as putting the dictates of an individual's conscience above his duty to obey the state?

On 1 February 1534 he wrote to Cromwell. He had not yet heard that his name was to be included in the bill of attainder in connection with Elizabeth Barton, but he had been told by his nephew and printer, William Rastell, that Cromwell had accused him of writing a book against the council's declaration abolishing Papal supremacy over the Church of England. More assured Cromwell that this was untrue. The last book which he had written was his reply to the nameless heretic's book against the Lord's Supper, which, though erroneously dated 1534 by the printer, had in fact been written and published before Christmas. If the king asked him for his opinion on any matter, it would be his duty to God and the king's grace to truly say his mind and discharge his conscience.

Yet surely if it should happen any book to come abroad in the name of His Grace or his honourable Council, if the book to me seemed such as myself would not have given mine own advice to the making, yet I know my bounden duty to bear more honour to my Prince and more reverence to his honourable Council, than that it could become me for many causes, to make an answer unto such a book or to counsel and advise any man else to do it.[24]

When he heard that his name had been included in the bill of attainder, he wrote two letters to Cromwell,[25] describing all that had taken place when he met Elizabeth Barton and her accomplices. But explanations and excuses were not enough, and on 5 March he wrote letters of complete submission to both Henry and Cromwell. After thanking Henry for having 'of your incomparable goodness' appointed him as Lord Chancellor, he assured him that he had revealed to Cromwell all that he had done in the case of 'the wicked woman of Canterbury'. He begged the king to delete his name from the bill of attainder that had been introduced in Parliament. 'Most gracious Sovereign, I neither will, nor well it can become me, with Your Highness to reason and argue the matter, but in my most humble manner, prostrate at your gracious feet, I only beseech Your Majesty with your own high prudence and your accustomed goodness consider and weigh the matter.' He wrote that his only remaining ambition was that after his short life and Henry's long one, 'I should once meet with Your Grace again in Heaven and there be merry with you'.[26]

His letter to Cromwell was much longer. He protested that he had never done anything to hinder the king's pleasure in connection either with his divorce or with Papal supremacy. When the king first asked him for his opinion about the divorce, he had told him that he was not convinced that the marriage to Catherine was unlawful, so the king decided to employ other counsellors to work for the divorce. Since then, he had never said anything about the divorce to anyone; and he had refused to read a book that Catherine's confessor, Abel, had written against the divorce. Now that the king had married Anne Boleyn, whom More called 'this noble woman really anointed Queen', he would 'neither murmur at it, nor dispute upon it', but would pray for both Henry and Anne and the children of their marriage like all other faithful subjects. As for Papal supremacy, he said that he had never felt particularly strongly in favour of it until he read the arguments supporting it in Henry's book *The Assertion of the Seven Sacraments*.[27]

More's name was deleted from the bill of attainder, and he remained at liberty. Fisher was sentenced by the Act to life imprisonment for misprision of treason, but was pardoned by the king after paying a substantial fine. He was, in fact, guilty of a more serious offence than any with which he had been charged, for he had been secretly urging the emperor to invade England and save the realm from schism and heresy.[28]

Parliament also passed the Act of Succession, which enacted that the king's commissioners might require anyone to swear an oath to uphold the statute and the right of the children of Henry and Anne to succeed to the throne. Anyone who refused to take the oath when he was required to do so would be guilty of misprision of treason with the usual consequences. The oath was taken first by the members of the king's council, by the bishops, and by the highest dignitaries in the country; afterwards it was put to JPs, and by them to heads of households; and many heads of households administered it to their family and servants. By these means, Henry forced all the leading persons in England either to swear to support the divorce and the right of Anne's children to succeed to the crown, or to disclose their opposition and suffer imprisonment for life. More was one of the first to be asked to take the oath. He was served with a notice to appear before the commissioners at Lambeth Palace on Monday 13 April 1534.

On 5 March More had written to Henry and Cromwell promising that he would never do anything to hinder Henry's marriage to Anne or the repudiation of Papal supremacy. Thirty-nine days later, he refused to take the oath of succession, knowing that it meant imprisonment for life. He had made statements in the House of Lords in favour of the divorce which he knew were untrue; he had refused to give any encouragement to the opponents of the divorce, or even to read their books; and he had promised not to do anything against the divorce. But he would not swear to uphold it. On this issue More, who had so often compromised and lied, would not compromise and would not lie. He had quite made up his mind about this, and was determined not to give way. When he received the order to appear before the commissioners at Lambeth, he said to Roper: 'The field is won';[29] for he knew now where he stood and that nothing would induce him to compromise his conscience for any worldly consideration. He had argued that it was seditious for a Protestant to refuse to burn the Bible when ordered to do so by the king; but he would now refuse to take an oath when ordered to do so by the king. He had always refused to recognise the right of an individual to put his conscience before obedience to authority; but now he would claim that his conscience forbade him to obey authority. The persecutor was ready to endure persecution.

On the Monday morning, a very warm spring day, More presented himself at Lambeth Palace. A number of London clergymen had also been summoned to take the oath that day; but though they had arrived before More, he was interviewed first as a sign of respect due to him as a former Lord Chancellor. Cranmer, Cromwell, Audley and the other commissioners invited him to take the oath; but he refused. They tried to persuade him to change his mind, but as he was adamant, they suggested that he should walk in the garden and take time to reconsider his attitude. In view of the heat of the day, he preferred to wait indoors, while the priests who had been summoned were interviewed by the commissioners and required to swear.

When More was invited in again, the commissioners told him that all the others had sworn, and again urged him to do so. He said that he would not criticise anyone who had sworn, but would not swear himself unless the oath could be redrafted in a form which would make it compatible with his conscience for him to swear it. Cranmer argued that if More would not criticise those who swore, he must be in some doubt as to whether to swear or not; but it was certain that a subject should obey his prince, and the king had ordered him to swear. The certainty of the duty to obey the king should prevail over the doubt which More felt about swearing, and More should therefore take the oath. More was impressed by this argument, but said that the logical consequence of it was that if a man had any doubts as to what his conscience required him to do, an order from the king would settle it, and he could not accept this proposition. Eventually the commissioners ordered him to be placed in the custody of the Abbot of Westminster, and after being held prisoner for a few days in the abbot's house, he was sent to the Tower.[30] On the Tuesday, Fisher refused to take the oath, and he, too, was sent to the Tower.

More was a prisoner in the Tower for fifteen months. He was not ill-treated, though his health deteriorated in prison, where he suffered from pains in the chest and cramp in his legs. He was allowed books and writing materials until the last three weeks of his imprisonment, and had a servant to wait on him, like every gentleman in prison. He was regularly visited by his daughter Margaret, and at least once by his wife. He had to endure her attempts to persuade him to submit and take the oath, and thus regain his freedom and the family property. Margaret Roper, too, tried hard to persuade him to save himself by taking the oath. She herself had sworn it with the qualification that she took it as far as the law of God allows. It was an escape clause which the authorities were prepared to give to her but not to More, and he would not have accepted it if he had been offered it. He repeatedly stated that he would not condemn anyone who took the oath, but he would not take it himself. Nor would he tell anyone, not even Meg, why he refused to take it.[31]

He wrote several books in the Tower, some in Latin and some in English. His lengthy *Of the Sorrow, Weariness, Fear and Prayer of Christ before His capture (De Tristitia Christi)* was in Latin. The longest book in English was *A Dialogue of Comfort against Tribulation*. His *Treatise upon the Passion*, which he had probably begun to write before his imprisonment, was shorter; and the two other works, *A Treatise to receive the Blessed Body of our Lord* and *A Godly Instruction*, were very brief. He also wrote letters to his friends, especially to his daughter Margaret Roper. The books and letters contain no trace of More the humanist, More the lawyer, More the king's counsellor, or More the persecutor of heretics, but only of the More who had wished, long ago, to spend his life in a Carthusian monastery, and the More who spent Fridays in the New Building at Chelsea in prayer and mortification of the flesh.

In these books which he wrote in the Tower, More reveals his inner feelings and his vision of the world in their most tortured form. He sees life, as he did in *The Four Last Things*, as a place of suffering. 'Before we come to the fruitful Mount of Olives', he wrote in *De Tristitia Christi*:

> we must (I say) cross over the valley and stream of Cedron, a valley of tears and a stream of sadness whose waves can wash away the blackness and filth of our sins. But if we get so weary of pain and grief that we perversely attempt to change this world, this place of labour and penance, into a joyful haven of rest, if we seek Heaven on earth, we cut ourselves off for ever from true happiness, and will drown ourselves in penance when it is too late to do any good, and in unbearable, unending tribulations as well.[32]

He was obsessed by suffering, especially the sufferings of Christ, arguing that Christ endured far greater pain than any other martyr, even than those whose sufferings might appear to have been greater and more prolonged; for More was sure that Christ used his divine powers to ensure that he suffered far greater pain than any ordinary man would have experienced in similar circumstances.[33] He wrote about the sufferings of the Christians under the rule of the Turks in Hungary,[34] which had perhaps disturbed him in the days when, as a member of the Council, he saw Henry and Wolsey shrug off the Pope's appeals to them to end the wars against France or the Empire in order to launch a crusade to liberate Hungary from the Turk.

He also wrote about the fall of Adam and Eve, which was brought about because the woman talked too much, and because, like many gentlewomen, she was prepared to speak to strangers, instead of saying: 'My husband shall answer you'.

> And because that the woman's preaching and babbling to her husband did so much harm in the beginning, and would if it were suffered to proceed do always more and more, therefore St Paul commandeth that a woman shall not take upon her to teach her husband, but that her husband should teach her; and that she should learn of him *in*

Thomas Bilney plucked from the pulpit, from Foxe's *Book of Martyrs*

Thomas Cromwell, after the portrait by Holbein

silentio, that is in silence, that is to wit, she should sit and hear him, and hold herself her tongue. For St Paul well foresaw, that if the wife may be suffered to speak too, she will have so many words herself that her husband shall have never one.[35]

In November 1534 Parliament passed the Act of Supremacy which enacted that the king was Supreme Head of the Church of England. Another Act was passed which made it high treason to seek to deprive the king of any of his titles. As a result of these two Acts, a man could be executed as a traitor if he stated that the king was not Supreme Head of the Church. In addition to the oath of the succession, the king's subjects could now be required to take the oath of supremacy and to swear that they believed the king to be Supreme Head of the Church of England; those who refused to take the oath would be guilty of high treason through having denied the king's titles.

In April 1535 the priors of the Charterhouses of London, Beauvale in Nottinghamshire, and the Isle of Axholme in Lincolnshire, and a Carthusian monk of Sion, were asked to swear the oath of supremacy. They replied that they would not acknowledge the king to be the Head of the Church of England. This was enough to convict them of high treason, and they were tried and sentenced on 29 April. They were hanged, drawn and quartered at Tyburn on 4 May. Three other monks of the Charterhouse of London refused to take the oath, and were imprisoned in the Tower. They were kept for a time chained up by the leg and neck to the posts in their dungeon, where they were secretly visited by More's adopted daughter, Margaret Clement, who brought them food. On 30 April, the day after the trial of the first Carthusians, More was examined in the Tower by Cromwell and several lawyers in the service of the council. Cromwell asked him whether he would acknowledge the king to be Supreme Head of the Church; but he refused to answer. Fisher was also interrogated in the Tower and asked whether he accepted that the king's divorce and his marriage to Anne were valid and that he was Head of the Church. He asked to be excused from replying, as the answer might incriminate him.[36]

On 3 June More was again examined in the Tower by Cromwell, Cranmer, Audley, Suffolk and Wiltshire. He was informed that the king ordered him to say whether he agreed that the king was Head of the Church; but again he refused to answer. When pressed, he replied that the question was like a double-edged sword. If he did not believe the king to be Supreme Head of the Church – and he would not say whether he did or not – then, by swearing that he believed it, he would perjure his soul, and by refusing to swear he would endanger his life. He did not think it right that a man should be forced to answer a question, in such circumstances, as to what he believed. Cromwell said that More, when he was Lord Chancellor, had forced persons suspected of heresy to answer whether or not they believed that the Pope was Head of the Church, knowing that they would violate their conscience by saying Yes and would be burned if they said No; so why should More not be forced to answer the question as to whether he believed the king to be Head of the Church? More said that there was a distinction between the two cases, because at the time when he was examining heretics the law of every country in Christendom laid down that the Pope was the Head of the Church, whereas now the doctrine that the king was Head of the Church was accepted in only one country and rejected in every other country in Christendom.[37]

A few days later, the authorities discovered that More had been writing letters to Fisher, which were carried by More's servant. In several of these letters, which More wrote at the end of May, he had told Fisher that he was refusing to reply when asked for his opinions about the king's supremacy over the Church, but suggested that Fisher should not adopt the same line in case it was taken as proof that they had conspired together. As a result of the discovery of his letters to Fisher, he was deprived of writing materials on 12 June, and apparently also of his books. He could hardly complain of this, for when he was Lord Chancellor he had ordered that heretics should not be allowed books or writing materials in prison. When he was questioned on 14 June about his letters to Fisher, he said that he had written only to comfort Fisher, knowing that he was a fellow-prisoner in the Tower. He also told his interrogators that he had written to his daughter Margaret to tell her that there was no need to worry about him, because he was afraid that Meg, who was pregnant, might panic and attempt to flee to avoid arrest if she thought that he had been proceeded against for treason. He told them that Margaret had repeatedly urged him to submit and acknowledge the king's supremacy over the Church.[38]

On 22 May Pope Paul III, hearing that Fisher was in danger of being sentenced to death, created him a cardinal. The Pope afterwards stated that his chief motive in doing this was to save Fisher's life by a public demonstration of support which would deter Henry from offending all the powers of Europe by executing a cardinal. It had the opposite effect. Henry was infuriated when he heard the news, and is said to have declared that he would cut off Fisher's head and send it to Rome to have the cardinal's hat put on it. Fisher was brought to trial on 17 June on a charge of high treason for depriving the king of one of his titles by denying that he was Supreme Head of the Church of England. He admitted that he did not accept Henry as Head of the Church but argued that he was not guilty, for the statute enacted that it was high treason to deny the king's title 'maliciously', and he had not acted out of malice.[39] This argument was rejected, as it had been in the case of the Carthusian monks, and Fisher was sentenced to death. Three more Carthusians were hanged, drawn and quartered at Tyburn on 19 June; and on the 22nd Fisher, whose sentence had been commuted by Henry to death by the axe, was beheaded on Tower Hill.

More was brought to trial on the same charge in Westminster Hall on 1 July before special Commissioners sitting with a London jury. The judges were hardly impartial, for Cromwell, Norfolk, Suffolk, and Anne Boleyn's father and brother, Wiltshire and Rochford, were among the commissioners, with the Lord Chancellor, Audley, presiding. Unlike Fisher and the Carthusians, More denied that he had ever said that the king was not Head of the Church, but claimed that he had always refused to answer the question, and that silence could never constitute an act of high treason. When the prosecution argued that silence implied consent, he replied that if this was so, his silence must be interpreted as consenting to the Act which made Henry Head of the Church. Thus while Fisher and the Carthusians, when facing their judges, took their stand for the Papal Supremacy, More rested his defence on a legal quibble. The prosecution cited the statement that he had made to Cromwell and the other commissioners on 3 June, and in his letter to Fisher, that the Act was like a two-edged sword in requiring a man either to swear against his conscience or to suffer death for high treason; but More had been careful, in making this statement, to put it as a hypothetical case, without admitting that he himself was in this predicament.

It was difficult for the prosecution to maintain that anything that More had said or done constituted a malicious denial of the king's title as Supreme Head. But the Solicitor-General, Sir Richard Rich, then gave evidence of a conversation that he had had with More on 12 June, when he visited More in the Tower in another attempt to persuade him to take the oath of supremacy, and also, apparently, to remove More's writing materials and books.*

Rich said to More that the king in Parliament could enact any law and that all subjects were bound to obey. He asked More whether, if Parliament passed an Act requiring everyone to swear allegiance to Rich as king, More would be compelled by law to comply. More admitted that he would be forced to obey such a law, but said that this

---

* The official report of Rich's evidence at the trial differs in some respects from Roper's account of the incident. In his evidence, Rich said that he visited More on 12 June to persuade him to take the oath; Roper does not give the date, but states that it took place when Rich came, with Southwell and Palmer, to remove More's books.

was a light case, and he would put a higher case to Rich: if Parliament passed an Act that God should no longer be God, would this Act take effect? Rich agreed that no Act of Parliament could prevent God from being God, but put a half-way case to More: if Parliament enacted that the king was Supreme Head on earth of the Church of England, why should not More accept this, just as he would accept an Act which made Rich king? According to Rich, More replied that the cases were not similar, because a king can be made by Parliament and deprived by Parliament, 'to which every subject present in Parliament could give his consent'; but as to the supremacy over the Church, a subject cannot be bound, 'because he cannot give his consent to that in Parliament; and although the king is so accepted in England, yet many foreign countries do not affirm the same'.

More denied that Rich was speaking the truth, but, adhering to his policy of silence, did not give his own account of the conversation. It has generally been assumed that Rich committed perjury, in connivance with Cromwell and the prosecution, in order to provide the evidence necessary to convict More. This is, on the whole, the most likely explanation. Rich was at the beginning of a long career in which he would do all that was required of him by the authorities at every turn in royal policy.* After providing the evidence which Cromwell needed to convict More in 1535, he and his associate, Wriothesley, gave evidence against Cromwell when Cromwell was executed in 1540; in 1547 he stepped in to become Lord Chancellor when Wriothesley fell; and he played his part in enforcing the royal supremacy against Catholics under Edward VI, in burning Protestants under Mary, and once more in enforcing the royal supremacy under Elizabeth, before he died, a respected JP and landowner in Essex, in 1567.

It is unlikely that Rich succeeded in trapping More into making an unguarded statement on 12 June; but his evidence that, on this occasion, More said that the king was accepted as Supreme Head of the Church only in England and not in many foreign countries, is very similar to the statement which More himself, in his letter to Margaret Roper, states that he made to Cromwell and the commissioners on 3 June. He then argued that it was legitimate to force a man to violate his conscience as the alternative to being burned, in order to uphold a law which was universally recognised throughout Christendom, but not in the case of a

---

* The unforgettable scene in Robert Bolt's play *A Man for all Seasons*, in which More is informed that Rich has been rewarded for his perjury at the trial by being appointed Attorney-General for Wales, is a justifiable piece of dramatic licence. Rich had previously been Attorney-General for Wales, but in October 1533 had been promoted to be Solicitor-General (for England) – the second law officer of the Crown.

law that was recognised only in England. His argument meant that a law of the English Parliament did not in all circumstances have the binding effect of the accepted doctrines of the international Church; and it did not perhaps need a very great exaggeration by Rich to distort what More really said on 12 June into what Rich said that he said. But even if Rich's evidence had been true, it was obviously straining the law to hold that a man was maliciously seeking to deprive the king of his title, and was consequently to be hanged, drawn and quartered as a traitor, because he had said to the Solicitor-General, in a private conversation, that a subject is not bound on the question of the supremacy over the Church 'because he cannot give his consent to that in Parliament'.

The jury were out for only a quarter of an hour before giving their verdict of 'Guilty'. There is no evidence that the jury was packed; but although most Londoners had a high opinion of More and a low opinion of Queen Anne Boleyn, they had no sympathy with anyone who resisted the king's proceedings against that foreign priest, the Bishop of Rome. More and the handful of Papalist supporters who opposed the breach with Rome had even less support in London than the obstinate heretics who preached doctrinal innovation in religion and preferred to be burned rather than to recant. The jury were obviously not impressed by More's legalistic hair-splitting; it was clear enough, from his whole conduct during the preliminary examinations and at the trial, that he was refusing to accept the king as Supreme Head of the Church of England.

Audley was about to sentence him to death, when More reminded him that in the days when he was a judge it was usual to ask a convicted prisoner if he had anything to say before sentence was passed. After Audley had given him leave to speak, he said everything that he believed about the supremacy but had been careful not to say until the jury had given their verdict. There are two versions of his speech. One was published in Paris a few weeks after the trial; the other is Roper's version in his book about More, written about twenty years later, and repeated shortly afterwards by Harpsfield. The two accounts agree in substance. More declared that Parliament had no power to abolish the Papal supremacy over the Church. When Audley interrupted to say that most learned doctors took the opposite view, More said that for every bishop supporting the royal supremacy, there were a hundred learned men throughout Christendom who supported his position; and that against the Act of Parliament were the opinions of all the General Councils of the Church for the last thousand years. 'Not only have you no authority, without the common consent of Christians all over the world, to make laws and frame statutes, Acts of Parliament or Councils against the said union of Christendom, but you and the others sin capitally in doing so.'

In Roper's and Harpsfield's account, More said that just as the city of London could not make laws which contravened the laws of the realm, so the English Parliament could not make valid laws which contravened the general law of Christendom. Norfolk intervened to comment that More's statement had made his wickedness plain.

According to the version published in Paris, More added that he had only been proceeded against because of his constant opposition to Henry's marriage to Anne Boleyn. Roper and Harpsfield say nothing about this, even though they were writing in Mary's reign, when any condemnation of the divorce of Mary's mother and the marriage to Anne would have been very popular with the queen and the authorities. If More did in fact say this, it was of course untrue. Whatever More may have thought, he had not publicly opposed Henry's marriage to Anne, and had often pointed this out to Henry and Cromwell; and though More had been sentenced to life imprisonment for refusing to swear an oath supporting the marriage, he was sentenced to death for refusing to recognise that the king was Supreme Head of the Church of England. The supremacy had become the essential issue by 1535, and even if More had been an enthusiastic supporter of the divorce, he would have been executed for refusing to accept the royal supremacy. The Paris report is therefore probably wrong, and Roper and Harpsfield right, on this point.

When More had finished, Audley passed sentence of death – the full sentence required by law, that More was to be hanged, cut down while still living, castrated, his entrails cut out and burned before his eyes, and then beheaded.[40] As he was being taken back to the Tower, Margaret Roper and his son John broke through the cordon of guards to embrace him. After he had bidden them farewell, as he moved away, Margaret ran back, again broke through the cordon, and embraced him again. At the Tower, he was informed that he was to die before 9 a.m. on 6 July, the Eve of St Thomas of Canterbury's Day, and that the king, in his mercy, had commuted the sentence to death by the headsman's axe. On the night before his execution, he sent Margaret his hairshirt, so that no one should see it on the scaffold and so that she could treasure that link that was a secret between the two of them. He wrote her a last letter with the piece of coal that he had used for writing during the three weeks since they had removed his books and writing materials.[41]

In his letter, he asked Meg to give his farewell messages to his son, his daughter-in-law and their children, to his daughter Cecily Heron, to Margaret Clement, and to several of her maidservants; but he sent no message to his wife. He told Meg that he was happy to die on the eve of Becket's feast day and in the week after St Peter's Day; and he praised her courage in breaking through the cordon of guards to bid him farewell.

I cumber you, good Margaret, much, but I would be sorry if it should be any longer than tomorrow. For it is St Thomas Even and the utas of St Peter; and therefore tomorrow long I to go to God; it were a day very mete and convenient for me. I never liked your manner toward me better than when you kissed me last; for I love when daughterly love, and dear charity, hath no leisure to look to worldly courtesy. Farewell, my dear child, and pray for me, and I shall for you and all your friends, that we may merrily meet in Heaven.[42]

Only in his relationship with his daughter Margaret did this strange, tortured, cruel man reveal a tenderness and a capacity to love.

Next day, on the morning of 6 July 1535, he was beheaded on Tower Hill. Margaret Roper could not bring herself to attend the execution, and Margaret Clement, alone of all More's family and household, was present. As he walked to the scaffold, carrying a red cross in his hand, people noticed that he had allowed his beard to grow in prison. On the way he was accosted by an embittered woman who felt aggrieved by a judgment which he had given against her when he was Lord Chancellor. He told her that he remembered her case well, and believed that he had given the right decision. He was also approached by more friendly strangers. One of them offered him a glass of wine, which he refused, because Jesus had been offered only gall on the cross.

He had been told that the king expected him to make only a very short speech on the scaffold, and he complied with Henry's last order to him. After telling the people to pray for the king, he told them that he died the king's servant, but God's first.[43]

Margaret Clement took the headless corpse to Margaret Roper, who was waiting at the church of St Peter ad Vincula in the Tower. They had been given permission to bury the body there. The head was boiled, as usual, to preserve it and to add terror to its appearance before exhibiting it on London Bridge. More's head was boiled too much, and turned black. It was put on the pole on London Bridge which Fisher's head had occupied for the past fortnight. After a few days, Margaret Roper bribed a constable of the watch to take it down and give it to her. The boiling had made it almost unrecognisable, but she identified it without hesitation as More's head because of the missing tooth which had been extracted during his lifetime.[44] She hid the head in some place where no one found it.

Things were not easy for More's family after his death. His property had been forfeited to the king on his conviction for misprision of treason when he refused to take the oath of the succession; if it had not already been forfeited then, it would have been forfeited on his conviction for high treason. Like the families of all convicted traitors, they had to rely on the king's generosity, and hope that in due course he would give some of the property back to them. Dame Alice successfully petitioned Cromwell to grant her a small pension,[45] and John More and the married daughters had property of their own; but in 1540 Cecily's husband, Giles Heron, was executed as a Papist traitor, and his property, too, was forfeited. Both Roper and John More were arrested within a few years of More's death, and questioned as to the whereabouts of More's papers, as well as about their loyalty to the king. Roper gave nothing away, and saved More's manuscripts and letters for the Catholics in Mary's reign and for future historians and biographers. For the time being, nothing written by More could be published; and the traitor's family had no redress when his *History of King Richard III* was published in 1544 by Grafton as part of Harding's *Chronicle*, without mentioning that More was the author.

Margaret Roper did not live to see the day when her father would once more be respected in England. She died in 1544, when she was probably aged thirty-nine, and was buried with her mother in the parish church at Chelsea where More had hoped to lie. Roper continued to preserve More's head. The family kept the secret even in Mary's reign, when More was acclaimed by the authorities as a martyr for the Catholic Church. They knew that the Catholic queen was childless; that her sister Elizabeth, the daughter of Anne Boleyn, was suspected of being a secret heretic; and that evil days might come again in England. Their fears were well grounded. Margaret Clement escaped abroad after Elizabeth's accession, and lived to a great age under the protection of Philip II of Spain among the English Catholic refugees in the Netherlands. Roper lived on in Elizabeth's kingdom, being summoned before the council and forced to give recognisances for his good behaviour, but otherwise unmolested by rulers who were more tolerant of religious dissent than his father-in-law had been. When he died in 1578 he was buried in the Roper family vault in St Dunstan's church in Canterbury. They somehow managed secretly to bury More's head in the vault with him without anyone knowing about it; and no official of Elizabeth's government found it and destroyed it.

More's head remained safely hidden in the Roper vault in St Dunstan's Canterbury. In 1835 the vault was opened, and someone saw a box which might have contained the head; but it was left in place. The vault was again opened and the head inspected on the five-hundredth anniversary of More's birth in 1978. It had nearly crumbled to dust, and could not definitely be identified as More's; but it was possible to see that a tooth was missing.[46]

CHAPTER 17

THE VERDICT OF HISTORY

In the course of less than five years between 1530 and 1535, Henry VIII had two of his former Lord Chancellors arrested and charged with high treason. Wolsey died, as he would have wished, before he could be executed; More, as *he* would have wished, died a martyr's death for the Catholic Church and Papal supremacy.

Both men have been remembered for four hundred and fifty years after their deaths, but the public image which they have posthumously presented has varied over the centuries. Wolsey, who had been envied and hated during the last years of his life, was out of favour with both Catholics and Protestants after his death. For John Foxe in 1563, his pomp and worldly pride epitomised all the vices of Papist prelates. But Nicholas Harpsfield, whom Foxe denounced as one of the most cruel persecutors of Mary's reign, could at least agree with Foxe in condemning Wolsey. Harpsfield thought that Wolsey was responsible for the divorce of Catherine of Aragon and all the evils which flowed from it, having persuaded Henry to divorce Catherine out of spite, because Charles V had refused to back his candidature for the Papacy.[1]

A lone voice was raised on Wolsey's behalf in 1557, when his gentleman-usher George Cavendish wrote a short book about his recollections of Wolsey. Cavendish, who joined Wolsey's household about 1522, described the embassy to Amiens and Compiègne in 1527, but his book was largely devoted to Wolsey's fall and his conduct during the last year of his life. The book showed Wolsey in a very sympathetic light, and revealed the love and devotion which his gentlemen and servants felt for him. As time passed, the story of the rise of the butcher's son of Ipswich to unparalleled power and wealth and his fall to utter disaster became increasingly fascinating to the people. Seventy years after his death, Shakespeare, who had obviously read Cavendish's book and followed it closely in his play *Henry VIII*, could express the point of view and even arouse sympathy for the arrogant cardinal, as he could in the case of the grasping Jew, Shylock, and the regicide usurper, Macbeth.

By the eighteenth and nineteenth centuries, it was possible to take a more detached view of the religious and political conflicts of the Tudor period, and Wolsey was regarded in a different light. Fiddes's very long biography in 1724 presented a sympathetic picture of an able statesman. A hundred and fifty years later, Victorian historians saw Wolsey as a great Foreign Secretary who, in the days before Britannia ruled the waves, had raised English prestige and power abroad, and had shown himself, in more difficult circumstances than those that faced his successors, to be a worthy predecessor of Chatham, Pitt, Canning, Palmerston and Disraeli. The historians of the late nineteenth and early twentieth centuries saw him as a great patriot who gave many years of invaluable service to his king, only to be shamefully betrayed and sacrificed by him to gratify a scheming mistress and jealous courtiers.[2]

The posthumous fate of Thomas More has been stranger and more controversial. In the weeks and months that followed his execution, he was hailed as a martyr by Catholics abroad, while the English government set out to blacken his memory and to blackguard his reputation in nearly as unpleasant a way as More himself had vilified the memory of the Protestant martyrs who had been burned when he was Lord Chancellor.[3] But for the Catholic propagandists, More took second place to Fisher. The executions in England during the summer of 1535 aroused great indignation in Catholic Europe; but it was the martyrdom of Fisher, a venerable bishop who had just been created a cardinal, which angered the Catholics most, for it was interpreted, as Henry had intended it to be, as a challenge and affront to the Pope, to the emperor, and to all their European allies and secret supporters in England. The preachers and writers in Rome, Brussels, Paris and Madrid, who denounced the execution of Fisher, did not forget to add that Henry had also put to death Sir Thomas More, a former Lord Chancellor and an author and scholar of international standing, as well as a number of holy abbots and monks; but Fisher, both as a cardinal and bishop, and as the most fearless and consistent opponent of the divorce and supporter of Queen Catherine, held a position in the estimation of Catholics with which More could not compete.[4]

Within twenty years of the executions of Fisher and More, a Catholic queen had reunited England to the Church of Rome, had acknowledged Papal supremacy over the Church of England, and had begun to burn Protestant heretics on a bigger scale than had ever been seen in the days of Henry VIII. Among the victims of her persecution was Cranmer, who had examined both Fisher and More in 1534 and 1535, and had reluctantly played his part in the proceedings which led to their execution. When he was burned at Oxford in 1556, a new precedent in savagery was established, for he was burned despite the fact that he had recanted, although he was not a relapsed heretic. Dr Cole, who preached the sermon before Cranmer was burned, felt it necessary to justify this step. The text of his sermon, which was recorded not only by the Protestant John Foxe, but by Cole's Catholic colleague, Alan Cope, contains a remarkable and shocking passage. According to Foxe, Cole said that it was necessary for the heretics to atone for the deaths of those two holy martyrs, More and Fisher; that while the execution by Mary of the Duke of Northumberland had atoned for the death of More, the executions of Hooper, Ferrar and Ridley were insufficient to atone for the death of so holy a man as Fisher, and Cranmer must therefore make a fourth in order to make the balance. If Foxe's account is correct, an official Catholic spokesman in 1556 thought that Fisher was worth four times as much as More. No such imbalance appears in Cope's version of Cole's speech; he states merely that Cole said that as the death of the layman Northumberland had atoned for the layman More's, so the cleric Cranmer's must atone for the cleric Fisher's. Though Cope, who was present in Oxford at the time of Cranmer's burning, is more likely to be correct than Foxe, the fact that Foxe thought that Cole had put a four-to-one value on Fisher as against More almost certainly shows that Catholics had been talking in this way.[5]

It was perhaps in order to redress this balance that Roper, in Mary's reign, wrote his short book about More. Roper was now the MP for Canterbury, and he showed his manuscript to the Archdeacon of Canterbury, Nicholas Harpsfield. Although Harpsfield was very busy burning heretics in the diocese of Canterbury, he took time off to write his *Life and Death of Sir Thomas More, Knight*, which closely followed Roper's manuscript. More's family also arranged for the publication in 1557 by his nephew William Rastell and the official government printer, Cawood, of *The Works of Sir Thomas More, Knight, sometime Lord Chancellor of England, written by him in the English tongue*, in a volume of over a thousand pages. It included More's early works and poems, his translation of the life of Pico della Mirandola, *Richard III*, all the polemical books against Tyndale and the English heretics, and the spiritual works which he wrote as a prisoner in the Tower, including a translation of *De Tristitia Christi* by More's granddaughter Mary Basset, who was Margaret Roper's daughter. Apart from the Tower tracts, it did not include the books which More had written in Latin, like *Utopia* and the *Answer to Luther*. More's letters to Margaret Roper from the Tower were published at the end of the book. His Latin works were published at Louvain in 1565, including *Utopia*, which had been frequently reprinted on the Continent since the first edition of 1516.

Two more short biographies of More were published before the end of the century. Stapleton, who was born in the month in which More died, included More in his book *Tres Thomae* as one of the three Thomases, with St Thomas the Apostle and Thomas Becket. During his years of exile in the Netherlands, Stapleton got to know his fellow-refugee, Margaret Clement, who died aged over eighty only a few years before Stapleton published *Tres Thomae* at Douai in 1588. Stapleton included several anecdotes and other additional information about More which are not to be found in either Roper or Harpsfield. He undoubtedly obtained much of his information from Margaret Clement; but not all his additions to Roper and Harpsfield are reliable. In 1599 another biography of More was written by a young Catholic refugee in the Netherlands who signed himself 'Ro.Ba.', but cannot be identified.[6] Ro.Ba. adds only a few details to Roper, Harpsfield and Stapleton. In 1631 More's great-grandson, Cresacre More, wrote another biography of More, in which he added traditional family gossip – not always true – to the narratives of the earlier biographers.

Meanwhile thousands of Englishmen could read, in successive editions of Foxe's book in their cathedrals, churches and homes, about More, 'accounted a man both witty and learned, but whatsoever he was besides, a bitter persecutor he was of good men and a wretched enemy against the truth of the Gospel';[7] how he flogged Protestant martyrs tied to trees in his garden; and how at last he met with his well-deserved punishment.

John Fisher Bishop of Rochester and Sir Thomas More, in King Henry's time, after they had brought John Frith, Bayfield and Bainham, and divers other to their death, what great reward won they thereby with Almightly God? Did not the sword of God's vengeance light upon their own necks shortly after, and they themselves made a public spectacle at the Tower Hill of bloody death, which before had no compassion of the lives of others? Thus ye see the saying of the Lord to be true, 'He that smiteth with the sword shall perish with the sword.'[8]

Foxe also wrote that he was sure that Fisher and More, who were acclaimed by the Pope as Catholic martyrs, would after a hundred years 'be also shrined and porthosed, dying as they did in the quarrel of the Church of Rome, that is, in taking the Bishop of Rome's part against their own ordinary and natural prince'.[9] But More and Fisher had to wait more than a hundred years for canonisation. In 1572 Pope Gregory XIII declared that relics of More and Fisher could be used to dedicate altars when no relics of early Christian martyrs were available; but no further official step was taken towards their canonisation till 29 December 1886, when, on the anniversary of Becket's murder, they were beatified by Leo XIII along with fifty-two other English Catholics who had been executed for their devotion to the Church of Rome in the reigns of Henry VIII and Elizabeth I.[10] This was followed by the first comprehensive modern biography of More, *Life and Writings of Blessed Thomas More*, by the Catholic author, the Reverend T. E. Bridgett, which was published in 1891. Although religious controversy between Protestants and Catholics was much more acute in Victorian England than it is today, particularly where the history of the Reformation was concerned, the beatification of More was generally welcomed by English Protestants as well as Catholics. Surprisingly, and certainly illogically, More has always been held in higher regard by English Protestants than Fisher and the other Catholic martyrs of the sixteenth century, perhaps because of his *Utopia* and the beauty and pathos of his letters from prison to his daughter. Froude was almost alone among English nineteenth-century historians in justifying his execution, and even Froude was much more hostile to 'the miserable old man'[11] Fisher than to More. Some of More's most fervent admirers have been, not Roman Catholics, but conservative-minded Anglicans, like Gairdner at the end of the nineteenth century and Chambers in the 1930s, who have admired him for his constancy and integrity, and not least for his resistance to the forces of religious radicalism and revolution.[12]

But More was also championed in a new and surprising quarter. In 1887 the German Social-Democrat and Marxist, Karl Kautsky, published his *Thomas More and his Utopia*. Kautsky was beginning to establish his reputation as the leading international Marxist theoretician on whom the mantle of Marx and Engels had fallen – a position which he retained until he opposed the Bolshevik revolution of 1917 and was violently denounced by Lenin and Trotsky as 'the renegade Kautsky' in a series of vitriolic books and pamphlets which were worthy of the polemicists of the Reformation period. Kautsky saw More as the founder of modern socialism, as well as a great humanist, a champion of the merchant class and of the historically progressive bourgeoisie, an upholder of the pre-Jesuitical Catholicism of the people of feudal times, and a martyr for freedom of conscience and resistance to royal despotism. Like other admirers of More, he reached the surprising conclusion that More was incapable of telling a lie. Kautsky believed that 'only in modern times, with the rise of scientific Socialism, has it become possible to do full justice to More the Socialist. . . . Although *Utopia* is more than four hundred years old,* the ideals of More are not vanquished, but still lie before striving mankind.'[13]

The revival of Roman Catholicism in England after 1850, and the efforts of its leaders, Cardinal Wiseman and Cardinal Manning, had

---

* This statement appears in the 1927 English edition of Kautsky's book.

been largely responsible for More's beatification in 1886. His canonisation in 1935 was chiefly due to the further extension of Catholic influence under Ronald Knox, Hilaire Belloc and G.K. Chesterton. In his speech at the More Memorial Exhibition in Chelsea in 1929, Chesterton declared that More was more important today than at any time since his death, but not as important as he would be in a hundred years' time; he hailed More as 'the greatest Englishman, or, at least, the greatest historical character in English history'.[14] On 19 May 1935, in the quadricentenary year of their martyrdom, both More and Fisher were canonised by Pope Pius XI.

In the same year, Professor R.W. Chambers's great biography of More appeared. Although Chambers was a professor of English literature, not of history, he made himself a specialist in studies of More, and his biography has had a great impact; its partiality and its distorting selectivity cannot detract from its sincerity and charm, and from the vivid and moving, if inaccurate, picture which it presents of Thomas More. In 1965 Father Bernard Basset, S.J., wrote a warm biography of More; and in 1968 another Catholic writer, E.E. Reynolds, followed up his biography of Margaret Roper and several studies of More with another strongly sympathetic biography. But the influence of the biographers was eclipsed by that of Robert Bolt, who in his very successful play, *A Man for all Seasons*, in 1960, and in the film that was made from it in 1966, presented, with the help of a great performance by Paul Scofield, an image of More which is even more misleading than Chambers's – a brilliant and moving portrayal of More as he ought to have been but unfortunately was not. There is only one criticism that can be made of *A Man for all Seasons* – that the splendidly upright hero of the play should not have been named Thomas More.

The socialists, Chambers, and Bolt have reversed the position of 1535, when More took second place to Fisher in Catholic martyrology. Yet surely Fisher is a more praiseworthy hero for the Catholics than More. Fisher, like More, was a persecutor of heretics; he, too, believed, like all Catholics and Protestants of his time, that the fact that the blessed martyr Polycarp was burned to death as a Christian in the second century did not mean that the Protestant heretics who were burned by the Catholic Church in the sixteenth century were martyrs; for it was the cause for which a man died, not the manner of his death, which made him a martyr. But Fisher denounced his heretical victims and opponents with a restraint and dignity which were far removed from the scurrilous lies and obscene abuse which More levelled at them; and he faced the prospect of martyrdom with far more resolution than More. Fisher never compromised about the divorce, as More did; and when he was required to take the oath of supremacy, he bravely declared that he did not believe that the king was Supreme Head of the Church, instead of hoping, like More, to save his life by an evasion and legal casuistry.

More was much more reluctant to be a martyr than a persecutor. The books that he wrote in the Tower contain several passages which justify reluctance to undergo martyrdom – that Christ urged those persecuted in one city to flee into another, that a man must not try to run before he has learned to walk, that no man should rush in to win the glory of martyrdom until he is sure that God has called him to do so – all the arguments put forward by those Protestants whom More mocked as cowards because they, too, sought reasons for avoiding or postponing martyrdom.[15] But More must not be denied the credit of dying for his principles; for despite all the reluctance and evasions, he ultimately chose martyrdom, when he could have saved his life, his family's property and even his position at court and in public life by taking the oaths of the succession and supremacy, like his friend Tunstal and nearly everyone else.

More died for his principles – but for what principles? If in fact he said, as the Paris news-letter reported, that he died because of his opposition to Henry's marriage to Anne Boleyn, this was untrue. Some have claimed that he died to uphold the Papal supremacy over the Church of England; others have pointed out that he never expressly said that he believed in Papal supremacy, and died for denial of the royal supremacy, not for asserting the supremacy of anyone else. But More repeatedly declared that he never had, and never would, oppose either the marriage to Anne or the establishment of the royal supremacy over the Church. He baulked only at taking the oath. He died because he believed that, though a man was entitled to lie and forge in the interests of the Church and the struggle against heresy, he would imperil his immortal soul if he swore an oath which he did not believe to be true.

It is an irony that More stood for almost the opposite of everything for which he is admired today. He is remembered as the champion of the cause of human freedom against tyranny, and of the conscience of the individual against government orders to comply; and Protestants honour him as a gesture of goodwill to Catholics in the cause of interdenominational understanding and ecumenicalism. There was nothing of which More more strongly disapproved than freedom, individual conscience, and religious toleration. He may not have flogged heretics in his garden, and may have been no worse a persecutor than many bishops; but as J.A. Guy has pointed out, his particular contribution to the anti-heresy drive was the importance which he attached to censorship.[16] Perhaps because he was first and foremost a writer, he thought that books were the chief carriers of the plague of heresy, and passionately believed in the banning, seizure and burning of unorthodox books. As for the ecumenical movement, he believed that it was as necessary to burn heretics as to kill Turks, and hoped that the day would never come when Catholics would be reduced to asking Protestants to grant them toleration instead of being in a position where they could persecute Protestants. He claimed that the international Church was entitled to force an individual to violate his conscience, and denied the right only to a national government and Parliament when it was seeking to intimidate individuals whose views were upheld by the majority opinion in Christendom.[17] It would be truer to see him as a champion of the Common Market than of freedom of conscience.

Wolsey, like all his contemporaries, suppressed heresy and prosecuted heretics, and would not have shrunk from burning them in certain circumstances; but compared to More he was tolerant and merciful. He was a man of the old régime, of the international Church as it existed on the eve of the Reformation – easy-going, self-indulgent, corrupt, wholly lacking in both idealism and fanaticism, and relatively tolerant. His fall was the signal for the beginning of a religious, political and social revolution. It left the field free for the revolutionaries and counter-revolutionaries, both of whom rejected Wolsey and the old régime. More considered Luther and even Tyndale to be revolutionaries, and he would not have been surprised had he known that they would be succeeded in the next generation and the next century by far more determined and ruthless revolutionaries like John Knox and Oliver Cromwell.

More himself was their leading opponent, the most perfect expression of counter-revolution. Three hundred and thirty years after his death Louis Veuillot, the leading representative of French Catholic Ultramontanism, defined the enemy which was assailing the Church as 'the Revolution'. Three times the Church had been assaulted by the Revolution: the first time by the Reformation under Luther; the second, by the Enlightenment under Voltaire; the third time by socialist atheism under Garibaldi. If Veuillot had lived fifty years later, he would have referred to the Revolution's fourth attack under Lenin, even if he would not have mentioned Kautsky, who lamented the fact that Voltaire did not share his admiration for More.[18]

Even in the earliest stages of the revolutionary movement, More thought that Lutheranism meant anarchy, mob violence, and the overthrow of law and order, discipline, the social fabric, and all the religious and moral values which he worshipped. He believed that this threat must be fought and defeated by every available means, and that all means would be justified by the end for which he would employ them. If young heretics could be deterred by savage whippings from continuing to believe in the doctrines which would lead them to the stake, well and good; if not, then, reluctantly, he would mete out to them the 'terrible death' that the law rightly prescribed for heretics as a necessary deterrent to others.[19]

By contrast to More the fanatical counter-revolutionary, Wolsey is the balanced, cynical, efficient administrator and power-politician. One can imagine him in any country in any century, entering the Church, making a fortune in business by the time he was thirty, winning a seat in the House of Commons, or joining the Communist Party, whichever was the necessary step to success in the society in which he found himself. He could easily have adapted himself to life in the twentieth century. After spending a few days taking stock of the new situation – that heralds are no longer sent to declare war, that it takes a few minutes, and not six weeks, for news to be sent from Madrid to London, and that it is more important to win the goodwill of trade union leaders than of bishops – he would have set to work, and would in no time have become the chairman of a nationalised industry in Britain, a leading corporation executive in America, or a member of the Politburo in the Soviet Union. He would have attended as many directors' lunches and party meetings as were necessary to maintain and increase his influence, but no more than were necessary. He would have paid himself an enormous salary and allotted himself the greatest privileges and perks, but would have managed things extremely well and have been worth every penny that was paid to him.

One can also imagine Thomas More in the twentieth century, and it is sad that this is a far more frightening picture. It is a picture of a sincere and well-meaning idealist and a brilliant intellectual, whose principles and flawless logic, combined with a repressed but deeply-engrained emotionalism, have turned him into a fanatic determined to crush what he considers to be the forces of evil. One can imagine him, after writing books about socialism and planning, becoming more and more obsessed with the menace of the enemy who was assaulting civilisation, and reaching the point where he justified, by specious arguments, the liquidation of millions of human beings as a regrettable but necessary measure in the fight against Jewish Bolshevism or Trotskyist deviationism, or the extermination of three-quarters of the world's population by nuclear weapons in order to protect his way of life. In the midst of the unparalleled dangers which confront mankind in the last quarter of the twentieth century, our greatest hope is that our fate will lie in the hands of a modern Wolsey and not of a modern Thomas More.

BIBLIOGRAPHY

MANUSCRIPT SOURCES

British Library:
  Cotton MSS., Caligula D vii, viii
             Galba, B ix
             Vitellius B ix, xi, xx
  Additional MSS. 28578
Public Record Office:
  State Papers I/2, 17, 23, 27, 42

PRINTED WORKS

ALLEN, P.S. and H.M. (eds.). *Opus Epistolarum Des. Erasmi Roterodami* (Oxford, 1906–58).

Archaeologia, vol. XXV (London, 1834).

BASSET, B. *Born for Friendship* (London, 1965).

Bishop Cranmer's Recantacyons (*Miscellanies of the Philobiblon Society*, vol. XV) (London, 1877–84).

BRADFORD, W. (ed.). *Correspondence of the Emperor Charles V* (London, 1850).

BRIDGETT, T.E. *Life and Writings of Blessed Thomas More* (3rd ed.) (London, 1924).

BRIXIUS, G. *Antimorus* (Basle, no date (1520?)).

BUCHOLTZ, F.B VON. *Geschichte der Regierung Ferdinand des Ersten* (Vienna, 1831–8).

BURNET, G. *The History of the Reformation of the Church of England* (ed. N. Pocock) (Oxford, 1865).

Calendar of Letters, Documents and State Papers relating to the Negotiations between England and Spain in Simancas and elsewhere (ed. G.A. Bergenroth, P. de Goyangos, G. Mattingly) (London, 1866–1947) (cited as '*Span. Cal.*').

Calendar of State Papers and Manuscripts relating to English Affairs in the Archives of Venice and other Libraries in Northern Italy (ed. Rawdon Brown, Cavendish Bentinck, etc.) (London, 1864–1947) (cited as '*Ven. Cal.*').

CAMERON, T.W. 'The Early Life of Thomas Wolsey' (*English Historical Review*, vol. III, London, 1888).

CAMUSAT, N. *Meslanges historiques* (Troyes, 1619).

Captivité de François Ier (ed. A. Champollion-Figeac) (Paris, 1847).

CAVENDISH, G. *Thomas Wolsey, late Cardinall, his lyffe and deathe* (ed. Richard S. Sylvester) (Early English Text Society) (London, 1959).

CHAMBERS, R.W. *Thomas More* (London, 1945 ed.). See also *The Fame of Blessed Thomas More*; More, *English Works*; *Shakespeare's Hand in the Play of Sir Thomas More*.

CHARLES V. Correspondence. See Bradford; Lanz.

CHESTERTON, G.K. 'A Turning Point in History'. See *The Fame of Blessed Thomas More*.

CREIGHTON, M. *A History of the Papacy from the Great Schism to the Sack of Rome* (London, 1897 ed.).

DERRETT, J. DUNCAN M. 'The "New" Document on Thomas More's Trial', including E.E. Reynolds's reply (*Moreana*, vol. III, Angers, 1964).

— 'Sir Thomas More and the Nun of Kent' (*Moreana*, vol. XV, Angers, 1967).

Dictionary of National Biography (Oxford, 1885–1900).

EHSES, S. *Römische Dokumente zur Geschichte der Ehescheidung Heinrichs VIII von England* (Paderborn, 1893).

ELLIS, H. *Original Letters illustrative of English History* (London, 1824–46).

ELTON, G.R. 'Sir Thomas More and the Opposition to Henry VIII' (*Moreana*, vol. XV, Angers, 1967). See also *Essential Articles*.

Encyclopaedia Britannica (London and New York, 1910 ed.).

English Historical Review, vols. III, VII (London, 1888 and 1892).

ERASMUS, D. *Collected Works of Erasmus* (Toronto, 1974–9).

— *Praise of Folly and Letter to Martin Dorp 1515* (ed. A.H.T. Levi) (London, 1971).

— *The Whole Familiar Colloquies* (London and Glasgow, 1877).

See also Allen.

Essential Articles for the study of Thomas More (ed. R.S. Sylvester and G.P. Marc'hadour) (Hamden, Conn., 1977).

The Fame of Blessed Thomas More (ed. R.W. Chambers) (London, 1929).

FIDDES, R. *The Life of Cardinal Wolsey* (London, 1724) (Part II, *Collections*, cited as 'Fiddes, *Collections*').

FISH, S. *A Supplicacyon for the Beggers*. See *Four Supplications*.

FISHER, J. *R.D.D. Ioannis Fischerii . . . Opera* (Würzburg, 1597) (reprint, Farnborough, Hants, 1967).

Four Supplications 1529–1553 A.D. (Early English Text Society) (London, 1871).

FOXE, J. *Actes and Monuments of these latter and perillous dayes* (London, 1563) (1st English edition of *The Book of Martyrs*).

— *The Ecclesiasticall History, containing the Actes and Monuments of thynges passed* (London, 1570) (2nd English edition of *The Book of Martyrs*).

— *The Acts and Monuments of John Foxe* (ed. J. Pratt) (London, 1877) (containing all the first and second English editions of *The Book of Martyrs*). (All references are to the 1877 edition.)

FROUDE, J.A. *History of England from the fall of Wolsey to the death of Elizabeth* (London, 1870 ed.)

GARDINER, S. 'Defence of Fisher's Execution'. See Janelle.

— *De Vera Obedientia*. See Janelle.

GARRARD, P.H. See Tatton-Brown.

GRANVELLA, A.P. DE. *Papiers d'État du Cardinal de Granvelle* (ed. C. Weiss) (Paris, 1841–52).

GREEN, MRS A.E. *Letters of Royal and Illustrious Ladies of Great Britain* (London, 1846).

Greyfriars Chronicle. – *Chronicle of the Greyfriars of London* (ed. J. Gough Nichols) (Camden Society) (London, 1852).

GRYNAEUS, S. *Platonis Omnia Opera* (Basle, 1534).

GUY, J.A. *The Cardinal's Court: The Impact of Thomas Wolsey in Star Chamber* (Hassocks, 1977).

— *The Public Career of Sir Thomas More* (Brighton, 1980).

— 'Sir Thomas More and the Heretics' (*History Today*, vol. XXX, London, 1980).

HALL, E. *Chronicle* (London, 1809 ed.)

HARPSFIELD, N. *The Life and death of Sr Thomas More, knight* (ed. Elsie Vaughan Hitchcock) (Early English Text Society) (London, 1932).

HENRY VIII. *Assertio Septem Sacramentorum* (ed. Rev. L. O'Donovan) (New York, 1908 ed.)

— *The Love Letters of Henry the Eighth* (ed. L. Black) (London, 1933).

HERBERT OF CHERBURY, LORD. *The Life and Raigne of King Henry the Eighth.* See Kennet.

HERBRÜGGEN, H. SCHULTE. *Sir Thomas More: Neue Briefe* (Münster, 1966).

HESS, S. *Erasmus von Rotterdam, nach seinem Leben und Schriften* (Zürich, 1790).

HUGHES, P. *The Reformation in England* (London, 1950–4).

JANELLE, P. (ed.). *Obedience in Church and State* (Cambridge, 1930).

KAUTSKY, K. *Thomas More and his Utopia* (London, 1927 ed.)

KENNET, W. *A Complete History of England with the lives of the Kings and Queens thereof* (London, 1706).

KRONENBERG, M.E. 'A Printed letter of the London Hanse Merchants (3 March 1526)' (in *Oxford Bibliographical Society Publications, New Series*, vol. I, Oxford, 1947).

LANZ, K. *Correspondenz des Kaisers Karl V* (Leipzig, 1844–6).

LEADAM, I.S. *Select Cases before the King's Council in the Star Chamber* (Selden Society) (London, 1903).

— *Select Cases in the Court of Requests* (Selden Society) (London, 1898).

LE GLAY, M. *Négociations diplomatiques entre la France et l'Autriche durant les trente premières années du XVIe siècle* (Paris, 1845).

LE GRAND, J. *Histoire du Divorce de Henry VIII Roy d'Angleterre et de Catherine d'Arragon* (Paris, 1688).

Letters and Papers (Foreign and Domestic) of the Reign of King Henry VIII (ed. J. Brewer, J. Gairdner and A.E. Stamp) (London, 1862–1929) (cited as '*L.P.*')

Letters and Papers illustrative of the Reigns of Richard III and Henry VII (ed. J. Gairdner) (London, 1861).

Lettres du Roy Louis XII et du Cardinal G. d'Amboise, avec plusieurs autres lettres (Brussels, 1712).

Love Letters of Henry VIII. See Henry.

LUTHER, M. *Antwortt deutsch Mart. Luthers auff König Henrichs von Engelland buch* (Wittenberg, 1522).

MACKINNON, J. *Luther and the Reformation* (London, 1925–30).

MARC'HADOUR, G. 'Thomas More's Birth: 1477 or 1478?' (*Moreana*, vol LIII, Angers, 1977). See *Essential Articles*.

MORE, ALICE. 'Supplique de Dame Alice More au Chancelier Audley' (*Moreana*, vol. IV, Angers, 1964).

MORE, CRESACRE. *The Life of Sir Thomas More K^l* (London, 1726).

MORE, THOMAS. *The Complete Works of St Thomas More* (ed. Richard S. Sylvester, Craig R. Thompson, John M. Headley, Louis A. Schuster, Richard C. Marius, James P. Lusandi, Richard J. Schoeck, J.B. Trapp, Louis C. Martz, Frank Maclay, Gerry E. Haupt, and Clarence H. Miller) (vols. II, III(i), V, VIII, IX, XII, XIII, XIV) (New Haven and London, 1963–79) (cited as *More's Works*).

— *The Correspondence of Sir Thomas More* (ed. Elizabeth Frances Rogers) (Princeton, N.J., 1947) (cited as 'Rogers').

— *The English Works of Sir Thomas More* (ed. W.E. Campbell, A.W. Reed, R.W. Chambers, W.A.G. Doyle-Davidson) (London, 1931) (facsimile reprint of 1557 edition) (cited as '*More's English Works*').

— *St Thomas More: Selected Letters* (ed. Elizabeth Frances Rogers) (New Haven and London, 1961) (cited as '*More's Selected Letters*').

— *St Thomas More: Utopia* (ed. E. Surtz) (New Haven and London, 1964).

— *Sir Thomas More: Neue Briefe*. See Herbrüggen.

— *Thomae Mori, Angliae, ornamenti eximii Lucubrationes* (Basle, 1563).

— *The Workes of Sir Thomas More Knyght, sometyme Lorde Chancellour of England, wrytten by him in the English tongue* (London, 1557) (cited as '*More's English Works*', the pagination of both this edition and the 1931 edition being given).

Moreana (Angers, 1963–78). See Derrett; Elton; Marc'hadour; More, Alice; Reynolds; Zeeveld.

MORICE, R. See Nichols.

MURNER, T. *Ob der künig vsz engelland ein lügner sey oder der Luther* (no place (Strasbourg ?), 1522).

NICHOLS, J.G. *Narratives of the Days of the Reformation* (Camden Society) (London, 1859).

Notes and Queries, 5th Series, vols. II, V (London, 1874 and 1876).

Paris News Letter (Paris, 1535). See Harpsfield.

PARMITER, G. DE C. *The King's Great Matter* (London, 1967).

PETER MARTYR D'ANGHIERA. *Opus Epistolarum Petri Martyris Anglerii Medidanensis* (Paris, 1670).

PINKERTON, J. *The History of Scotland from the Accession of the House of Stuart to that of Mary* (London, 1797).

POCOCK, N. *Records of the Reformation: The Divorce 1527–1533* (Oxford, 1870).

POLLARD, A.F. *Wolsey* (London, 1929).

RASTELL, W. 'Certen Breef Notes apperteyning to Bushope Fisher, collected out of Sir Thomas Moores Lyfe, writt by Master Justice Restell'. See Harpsfield.

REDSTONE, V.R. 'The Parents of Cardinal Wolsey' (*The Athenaeum*, vol. I, London, 1900).

REYNOLDS, E.E. *The Field is Won* (London, 1968).

— *Margaret Roper* (London, 1953).

— *Saint John Fisher* (London, 1955).

— *The Trial of St Thomas More* (London, 1964).

— 'An Unnoticed Document' (*Moreana*, vol. I, Angers, 1963). See also Derrett.

RO. BA. *The Lyfe of Syr Thomas More* (ed. Elsie Vaughan Hitchcock, Mgr. P.E. Hallett, and A.W. Reed) (Early English Text Society) (London, 1950).

ROGERS, E.F. 'Sir Thomas More's Letter to Bugenhagen' (in *The Modern Churchman*, vol. XXXV, London, 1946). See *Essential Articles*; More, *Correspondence*; More, *Selected Letters*.

ROPER, W. *The Lyfe of Sir Thomas Moore, knighte* (Early English Text Society) (London, 1935).

ROSCOE, W. *The Life and Pontificate of Leo the Tenth* (London, 1846).

ROY, W. *Rede me, and be nott wrothe; For I saye no thynge but trothe* (in *Harleian Miscellany*, vol. IX, London, 1812).

RYMER, T.W. *Foedera, Conventiones, Literae, Et Cujuscunque Generis Acta Publica inter Reges Angliae* (London, 1704–17).

SAVADA, P.A. 'Laus Potentiae or the Praise of Realpolitik? Hermann Oncken and More's Utopia' (in *Moreana*, vol. XV, Angers, 1967).

SCARISBRICK, J.J. *Henry VIII* (London, 1968).

Shakespeare's Hand in the Play of Sir Thomas More (A.F. Pollard, etc.) (London, 1923).

SKELTON, J. *The Poetical Works of John Skelton* (ed. A. Vyce) (London, 1843).

SMITH, PRESERVED. *Erasmus* (New York, 1923).

Spanish Calendar. See *Calendar of Letters, Documents and State Papers . . . in Simancas.*

STAPLETON, T. *The Life and Illustrious Martyrdom of Sir Thomas More* (translated by Mgr. P. Hallett from 'Vita et illustre Martyrium Thomae Mori', in *Tres Thomae*) (London, 1928).

State Papers during the Reign of Henry VIII (London, 1831–52).

Statutes of the Realm (London, 1810–24).

STOW, J. *Annales* (London, 1631).

STRYPE, J. *Ecclesiastical Memorials* (Oxford, 1822 ed.)

TATTON-BROWN, T. 'The Roper Chantry in St. Dunstan's Church, Canterbury' (*The Antiquaries Journal*, vol. LX, Oxford, 1980).

TEULET, A. *Papiers d'État, Pièces et Documents relatifs à l'histoire de l'Ecosse au XVIᵉ siècle* (Paris, 1851–60).

THEINER, A. *Vetera monumenta Hibernorum et Scotorum historiam illustrantia 1216–1547* (Rome, 1864).

Twentieth Century Interpretations of Utopia (ed. W. Nelson) (Englewood Cliffs, N.J., 1968).

Valor Ecclesiasticus temporis Regi Henrici Octavi (London, 1810–34).

VAN ORTROY, Fr. *Vie du Bienheureux Martyr Jean Fisher* (Brussels, 1893).

Venetian Calendar. See *Calendar of State Papers . . . in the Archives of Venice.*

WHITTINTON, R. *Vulgarie Roberti Whitintoni* (in *The Vulgaria of John Stanbridge and the Vulgaria of Robert Whittinton*) (Early English Text Society) (London, 1932).

WILKINS, D. *Concilia Magnae Britannicae et Hiberniae* (London, 1737).

WILLIAMS, N. *The Cardinal and the Secretary* (London, 1975).

WILLOW, MARY EDITH. *An Analysis of the English Poems of St Thomas More* (Nieuwkoop, 1974).

WODMORE, J.E. 'Tonbridge Priory' (*Archaeologia Cantiana*, vol. XIV (Kent Archaeological Society), London, 1882).

ZEEVELD, W.G. 'Apology for an Execution' (*Moreana*, vol. XV, Angers, 1967). See also *Essential Articles*.

REFERENCES

Chapter 1 – Thomas Wolsey of Ipswich

1. Pollard, *Wolsey*, pp. 12, 276n.; Cameron, 'The Early Life of Thomas Wolsey' (*English Historical Review*, III. 460–1); Williams, *The Cardinal and the Secretary*, pp. 5–6.
2. Chambers, *Thomas More*, pp. 48–49.
3. Cameron, op. cit., III. 459–60.
4. Redstone, 'The Parents of Cardinal Wolsey' (*The Athenaeum*, I. 400–1).
5. Cameron, op. cit., III. 461–2.
6. Hughes, *The Reformation in England*, I. 371–5.

Chapter 2 – Thomas More of London

1. For More's father and grandfather, see Chambers, pp. 52–53.
2. Notes to *More's Works*, XIV. 742–3.
3. Roper, *The Lyfe of Sir Thomas Moore, knighte*, p. 5; Harpsfield, *The Life and Death of Sir Thomas More*, pp. 10–11; Chambers, pp. 56–60.
4. *More's Works*, II. 92–93.
5. Stapleton, *The Life and Illustrious Martyrdom of Sir Thomas More*, p. 9; Ro. Ba., *The Lyfe of Syr Thomas More*, p. 22; Chambers, pp. 65–66.
6. Roper, p. 5; Harpsfield, p. 12; Chambers, pp. 66–68.
7. Erasmus to Prince Henry (autumn 1499); Erasmus to Botzheim, 30 Jan. 1523 (Allen, *Opus Epistolarum Des. Erasmi Roterodami*, I. 6, 239–41; Erasmus, *Collected Works*, I. 195–7).
8. Preserved Smith, *Erasmus*, p. 64.
9. See Erasmus to More, 28 Oct. 1499 (Erasmus, *Collected Works*, I. 227).

Chapter 3 – The Ambitious Priest

1. Cavendish, *Thomas Wolsey, late Cardinall, his lyffe and deathe*, pp. 4–5.
2. Ibid, p. 5; Cameron, op. cit., III. 462–4; Williams, p. 6.
3. Cameron, op. cit., III. 463; Williams, p.6.
4. Williams, p. 7; Pollard, p. 12.
5. Cameron, op. cit., III. 464; Pollard, p. 12.
6. Cavendish, p. 5; Cameron, op. cit., III. 494–5.
7. Cavendish, pp. 5–6; Cameron, op. cit., III. 465–7.

8. Cameron, op. cit., III. 467; Rymer, *Foedera*, XII. 783–4.
9. Tout, 'Deane, Henry', in *Dictionary of National Biography*.
10. Cavendish, pp. 6–7; Pollard, p. 13; Cameron, op. cit., III. 468.
11. Cameron, op. cit., III. 470.
12. Cavendish, pp. 7, 9.
13. Darcy to Wolsey, 15 Jan. (1514) (*L.P.*, I. 4652).
14. For Wolsey's mission to Scotland, see (Wolsey) to Henry VII (Apr. 1508) (Pinkerton, *History of Scotland*, II. 445–50); Gairdner, Pref. to *Letters and Papers illustrative of the Reigns of Richard III and Henry VII*, I. pp. lxi–lxii; Cameron, op. cit., III. 471–2.
15. Cavendish, pp. 7–9; Cameron, op. cit., III. 470–1.
16. Henry VII to Wolsey (Oct.) and Nov. 1508; Maximilian I to Henry VII (Oct. 1508); Wolsey to Henry VII, 4, 23 Oct., 1 Nov. 1508 (Gairdner, op. cit., I. 425–52).
17. Rymer, XIII. 217–18; Cameron, op. cit., III. 470, 473; *Notes and Queries* (5th Ser.), II. 148; V. 413–14.
18. Cameron, op. cit., III. 474.
19. Ibid, III. 475–6; Gairdner, 'Wolsey', in *D.N.B*.

Chapter 4 – Lawyer, Humanist or Monk?

1. Roper, p. 6; Harpsfield, pp. 13, 17; Erasmus to Hutten, 23 July 1519 (Allen, IV. 17).
2. Ibid (Allen, IV. 18).
3. Roper, p. 6; Harpsfield, pp. 18–19.
4. Erasmus to Hutten, 23 July 1519 (Allen, IV. 18); Erasmus, *Colloquies*, p. 131 ('The Uneasy Wife'); Chambers, pp. 95–96.
5. Erasmus, *Praise of Folly*, pp. 136–7; Chambers, p. 184.
6. Chambers, p. 98.
7. Erasmus to Hutten, 23 July 1519 (Allen, IV. 18); More's Epitaph (1532) (More, *Selected Letters*, pp. 182–3).
8. Erasmus to Hutten, 23 July 1519 (Allen, IV. 19).
9. Ibid.
10. Roper, pp. 8–9; Harpsfield, p. 20.
11. Roper, pp. 7–8; Harpsfield, pp. 14–17.
12. More to Ruthall (undated) (*More's Works*, III (i). 2–9).
13. *More's English Works*, I. 327–44.
14. More, 'A merry jest how a sergeant would learne to playe the frere' (*More's English Works*, I. 329–30, 332; c. ii).
15. Lucian's Greek text and More's translation of 'The Cynic', 'Menippus', and 'The Lover of Lies' (*More's Works*, III (i). 10–77).
16. Lucian's Greek text and More's translation of 'Tyrannicide' (*More's Works*, III (i). 78–93).
17. Notes to *More's Works*, III (i)., pp. xxviii, xxxvii, xl, lv–lxvii.
18. More, 'Declamatio Thomae Mori Lucianicae Respondens' (*More's Works*, III (i). 94–127).

19. More to Ruthall (undated) (*More's Works*, III (i). 4–7).
20. More, 'The Life of John Picus, Earl of Mirandola' (*More's English Works*, I. 347–96).
21. Ibid, I. 9–10, 361–2.
22. A.W. Reed's Introduction to *More's English Works*, I. 18.
23. Cresacre More, *The Life of Sir Thomas More*, pp. 18–19.
24. More, 'Life of John Picus' (*More's English Works*, I. 10, 362).

Chapter 5 – The Cardinal of York

1. Caroz to King Ferdinand of Aragon, 29 May 1510 (*Span.Cal.*, II. 44).
2. Cavendish, pp. 12–13.
3. Ibid.
4. Ibid, p. 38; Rymer, XIII. 293; *L.P.*, I. 1359, 1506, 4747, 5607; Cameron, op. cit., III. 475–6; Gairdner, 'Wolsey', in *D.N.B.*
5. Warham's note, 26 May 1511 (*L.P.*, I. 1685).
6. Henry VIII to Darcy (Mar. 1511) (P.R.O., S.P. 1/2 f. 44); Stile to Henry VIII, 5 Aug. 1512 (*L.P.*, I. 3355); Knight to Wolsey, 5 Aug. 1512 (*Ellis' Letters*, II(i). 188); Ferdinand of Aragon's correspondence, Oct.–Nov. 1512 (*Span.Cal.*, II. 68, 70, 72).
7. Knight to Wolsey, 5 Aug. 1512 (Ellis, II (i). 188).
8. Wolsey to Foxe, 30 Sept. 1512 (Fiddes, *Collections*, pp. 8–9).
9. 'The King's Book of Payments', 1st, 2nd and 3rd year of Henry VIII (*L.P.*, II., pp. 1441–1518).
10. Erasmus to Jonas, 13 June 1521 (Allen, IV. 525–6).
11. Brixius, *Antimorus*, passim; More to Brixius (1520) (Rogers, pp. 212–39); More to Erasmus, 3 Sept. 1516; (Mar.) and (May 1520); Erasmus to Brixius (Aug. 1517); Erasmus to More, 26 Apr. 1520; Erasmus to Hermann (Aug. 1520); Erasmus to Budaeus, 9 Aug. 1520; 16 Feb., (Sept.) 1521 (Allen, II. 339–40; III. 41; IV. 217–32, 239–41, 250–5, 323–6, 442–3, 575–80).
12. Bregilles to Margaret of Austria, 2 Aug. 1513 (*Lettres de Louis XII*, IV. 190–1).
13. Catherine of Aragon to Wolsey, 26 July; 13, 25 Aug.; 16 Sept. 1513 (Ellis, I (i). 79–85, 89–91).
14. Tuke to Pace, 22 Sept. 1513 (*Ven.Cal.*, II. 316).
15. Papal Bull, 6 Feb. 1514 (*L.P.*, I. 4722).
16. Treaty of St Germain-en-Laye, 9 July 1514 (*Span.Cal.*, II. 178); Peter Martyr to Furtado, 4 Oct. 1514 (*Pet.Martyr Epist.*, p. 297).
17. Louis XII's orders for payments to Suffolk, Wolsey, etc., Nov.–Dec. 1514 (*Span.Cal.*, II. 191, 193–6, 198–200, 203–4).
18. Gigli to Wolsey, 26 Aug. 1514; Leo X's Bulls for Wolsey, 15 Sept. 1514; Gigli to Ammonio (Sept. 1514) (*L.P.*, I. 5354, 5411–16, 5464).
19. Henry VIII to Leo X, 12 Aug. 1514; Leo X to Henry VIII, 24 Sept. 1514 (*L.P.*, I. 5318, 5445).
20. Wolsey to Mary, Queen of France (Jan. 1515); Spinelly to Wolsey, 22 Feb.

1514/5; Sampson to Wolsey, 27 Feb. 1514/5; Suffolk to Wolsey, 3, 8 Feb.; 5 Mar. 1515; Wolsey to Suffolk (Feb. 1515) (*L.P.*, II. 15, 106, 113, 134, 180, 197, 223).

21. Wolsey to Suffolk (Mar. 1515); Suffolk to Henry VIII, (Mar.), 22 Apr. 1515; Mary, Queen of France to Henry VIII, four letters of Mar. 1515; Suffolk to Wolsey, 12 Mar., 17 Apr. 1515; receipts, etc., by Mary, Queen of France and Suffolk, Apr. 1515 (Green, *Letters of Royal Ladies*, I. 187; Ellis, I (i). 121–2; *L.P.*, II., Pref., pp. xii–xiii, xviii–xix, xxiii–xxix, xxxi–xxxiii; Nos. 224–30, 237, 281, 283, 318–20, 329, 331).

22. Wolsey to Gigli (June, July, 1 Aug. 1515); Gigli to Wolsey, 7 Sept. 1515; Hadrian to Wolsey, 10 Sept. 1515; Henry VIII to Leo X, 30 Sept. 1515 (*L.P.*, 648, 763, 780, 887, 893, 960).

23. Anon. account of Wolsey's consecration as Cardinal (Fiddes, *Collections*, pp. 251–3).

24. Foxe to Wolsey, 23 Apr. 1516 (*L.P.*, II. 1814).

25. Giustiniani to the Doge, 2 Jan. 1516 (*Ven.Cal.*, II. 671).

26. Leo X to Wolsey, 17 May, 27 July 1518 (Rymer, XIII. 606, 609); Gigli to Wolsey, 1 Sept. 1519 (*L.P.*, III. 444).

27. Leo X to Albany, 18 Jan. 1518 (*L.P.*, II. 3889).

28. Plan for banquet, 7 July 1517; Giustiniani to Doge, 10 July 1517; Chieregato to Isabella d'Este, 10 July 1517 (*L.P.*, II. 3446, 3455; *Ven.Cal.*, 918, 920).

29. Treaty of Westminster, 9 July 1518 (Rymer, XIII. 632, 642); Bonnivet etc. to François I, 4 Oct. 1518 (*L.P.*, II. 4479).

30. Gigli to Wolsey, 12 June, 8 Nov., 10 Dec. 1517; 27 Feb. 1518 (*L.P.*, II. 3352, 3781, 3828, 3973); Minio to Doge, 18 Aug. 1517; 13, 29 Apr.; 13 July 1518 (*Ven.Cal.*, II. 954, 1023, 1026, 1045); Cardinal Medici to Wolsey, 5 July 1518; Leo X to Wolsey, 30 July 1518 (Rymer, XIII. 607–10); Creighton, *History of the Papacy*, V. 279–86.

31. Treaty of London, 2 Oct. 1518 (Rymer, XIII. 624); Giustiniani to Doge, 5 Oct. 1518; anon. report to Mantua, 9 Oct. 1518 (*L.P.*, II. 4481; *Ven.Cal.*, II. 1085, 1088); Hall, *Chronicle*, pp. 594–6.

Chapter 6 – Utopia *and* Richard III

1. More to Henry VIII (June 1509) (Rogers, pp. 14–15); Chambers, pp. 99–100.

2. More to Dorp, 21 Oct. 1515 (Rogers, p. 36); Roper, p. 8; Harpsfield, p. 17; Chambers, p. 98.

3. For Erasmus, see especially Preserved Smith, *Erasmus*, passim.

4. Erasmus, *Praise of Folly*, pp. 55–61; Erasmus to Hutten, 23 July 1519 (Allen, IV. 16).

5. More to Dorp, 21 Oct. 1515 (Rogers, pp. 28–74).

6. Erasmus to Hutten, 23 July 1519 (Allen, IV. 13–22).

7. Ibid, IV. 20

8. Commission to Tunstal, More, etc., 2 Oct. 1515 (*L.P.*, II. 986).

9. Sampson to Wolsey, 27 Feb. 1514/5, 14 June, (July) 1515 (*L.P.*, II. 199, 581, 769).
10. More, *Utopia*, pp. 9–11.
11. *More's Works*, II., pp. lxiii–lxv.
12. *Utopia*, pp. 9–10.
13. More, *A Treatise upon the Passion*; More, *A godly instruction*; More, *A Dialogue of Comfort against Tribulation* (*More's Works*, XII. 304; XIII., 42, 212).
14. Erasmus to Hutten, 23 July 1519 (Allen, IV. 21).
15. *Utopia*, pp. 24–34.
16. Ibid, pp. 61, 65–81, 84–85, 97–98, 108–12, 114.
17. Ibid, p. 112.
18. Ibid, pp. 118–24, 129.
19. Ibid, pp. 82–83.
20. Ibid, pp. 130–5.
21. More, *A godly instruction* (*More's Works*, XIII. 212).
22. *Utopia*, p. 135.
23. Ibid, p. 92.
24. Ibid, p. 140.
25. Ibid, pp. 137–41.
26. Ibid, pp. 147–8.
27. Chambers, p. 125.
28. *Utopia*, pp. 150–1.
29. Ibid, pp. 151–2.
30. More to Peter Gilles (Oct. 1516) (Rogers, pp. 79–80).
31. *More's Works*, II., pp. lxiii–lxv.
32. Chambers, p. 117.
33. More, *Richard III* (*More's Works*, II. 83, 86).
34. Ibid, II. 3–4.
35. Ibid, II. 54–57.
36. Ibid, II. 91.
37. Ibid, II. 92–93.
38. *Utopia*, pp. 16–18.
39. For Evil May Day, see Giustiniani to Doge, 5, 12 May 1517; Chieregato to San Pietro, 19 May 1517; Sagudino to Foscari, 19 May 1517 (*Ven.Cal.*, II. 879, 883, 887, 910; *L.P.*, II. 3204, 3230, 3259); More, *Apology* (*More's Works*, IX. 156); *Greyfriars Chronicle*, p. 30; Hall, pp. 588–91.
40. Chambers, pp. 45–46.
41. Roper, pp. 9–11; Harpsfield, p. 23.
42. Commission to Wingfield, Knight and More, 26 Aug. 1517 (*L.P.*, II. 3634).
43. Chambers, pp. 170–1; and see Guy, *The Public Career of Sir Thomas More*, pp. 6–8.
44. More, *Dialogue of Comfort against Tribulation* (*More's Works*, XII. 219–20); Harpsfield, pp. 94–95.

Chapter 7 – The Field of Cloth-of-gold

1. For Erasmus's New Testament, see Preserved Smith, pp. 159–77.
2. More to Dorp, 21 Oct. 1515; More to Lee, 1 May 1519 (Rogers, pp. 28–74, 138–54); Preserved Smith, pp. 175–6.
3. Preserved Smith, pp. 74–77.
4. Ibid, p. 127; Chambers, pp. 114–15, 217.
5. Preserved Smith, pp. 127–8.
6. Mackinnon, *Luther and the Reformation*, I. 281–305; II. 1–270.
7. Erasmus to Wolsey, 18 May 1519, 7 Mar. 1522; Erasmus to Mountjoy (1521) (Allen, III. 587–93; IV. 542–5; V. 27–28); Preserved Smith, pp. 215–23.
8. For the election at Frankfurt, see Pace to Wolsey, 3 July 1519 (B.L., Vit. B. xx, p. 149); correspondence of Pace, Giustiniani, Albert of Brandenburg, Charles V, etc., May–July 1519 (*L.P.*, III. 100, 235–6, 240–1, 274, 283, 296–7, 299–300, 302, 304, 307–8, 318, 320, 323, 326, 339, 348, 352–4, 371, 412, 416; *Ven.Cal.*, II. 1220, 1249; Ellis, I (i). 154, 179, 194; *State Papers of Henry VIII*, I. 2, 8; Brewer, in *L.P.*, III. Pref., pp. i–xviii).
9. For the negotiations and arrangements for the Field of Cloth-of-gold, see correspondence of Wolsey, Sir Richard Wingfield, Worcester, Bonnivet, François I, etc., Aug. 1519–May 1520 (*L.P.*, III. 415–16, 514, 592, 609, 622–5, 632–3, 642–3, 645, 666, 673, 677, 681, 692, 698–700, 702–4, 738, 746, 764, 778, 797, 806–9, 821, 830–3, 835, 841–2; Rymer, XIII. 691, 695; *St.Pap.*, VI. 54; Ellis, I (i). 168–74).
10. Correspondence of Sir Richard Wingfield, François I, Bonnivet and Wolsey, Apr. 1520 (*L.P.*, III. 697, 722–7, 733–6).
11. Correspondence of Charles V, Mesa, and Margaret of Austria, Apr.–May 1520 (*L.P.*, III. 637, 689–90, 696, 728, 731–2, 739–42, 770–1, 773–4, 776, 788–9, 798, 803–4, 814–15; *Span.Cal.*, II. 274).
12. Charles V's grants, Mar. 1520–July 1522; Leo X to Wolsey, 4 July 1520; Campeggio to Wolsey, 4 July, 10 Dec. 1520; La Roche to Wolsey, 17 July 1520; Charles V to Wolsey, 6 Oct. 1520 (Rymer, XIII. 714, 725–6, 769–71; *L.P.*, III. 709, 803, 899–900, 921, 1094, 2307, 2361).
13. More to Erasmus, 26 May 1520 (Allen, IV. 266–9); Memorandum on those attending interview with French King (Mar. 1520); Account of meetings of Henry VIII with Charles V and François I (May–July 1520); correspondence of Giustiniani, Cornaro, etc. (*L.P.*, III. 702(2), 803, 824; *Ven.Cal.*, III. 50, 53–56, 58–59); Hall, pp. 603–5.
14. Memoranda on those attending interview with French King (Mar. 1520) (Rymer, XIII. 710–14; *L.P.*, III. 702(2) and (3)).
15. Letter to Montemerlo, 18 June 1520 (*Ven.Cal.*, III. 88); *L.P.*, III., Pref., pp. lviii, lxxii.
16. Two accounts of the Field of Cloth-of-gold (June 1520) (*L.P.*, III. 869–70); Hall, pp. 605–20.
17. For Field of Cloth-of-gold, see four accounts (June 1520); correspondence of Budaeus, Soardino, Giustiniani, etc. (*L.P.*, III. 869–70, 878; *Ven.Cal.*, III. 50, 67–69, 80–85, 88–94); Hall, pp. 605–20.

18. Soardino to Marquis of Mantua, 26 June 1520 (*Ven.Cal.*, III. 94).
19. Memorandum of François I's ministers (May 1520) (Teulet, *Papiers d'État*, I. 17); Treaty of Ardres, 6 June 1520 (Rymer, XIII. 721–2); François I to d'Aubigny (Jan. 1521) (*L.P.*, III. 1127).
20. List of noblemen and others to attend the king at Gravelines (July 1520) (*L.P.*, III. 906).
21. For the meeting at Gravelines, see memoranda of May 1520 (*L.P.*, III. 803–4); Ludovico Spinelli to Gasparo Spinelli, 12 July 1520 (*Ven.Cal.*, III. 106); Hall, pp. 620–2.
22. More to Erasmus, 26 May 1520; Erasmus to More (June 1520); Erasmus to Wolsey, 7 Aug. 1520 (Allen, IV. 266–70, 324–5); Myconius to Clivanus, 20 Nov. 1520 (Hess, *Erasmus von Rotterdam*, II. 607–8); Preserved Smith, p. 230 and n.
23. Preserved Smith, pp. 227–31.
24. Cardinal Medici to Gambara (Nov. 1520); Campeggio to Wolsey (Jan.), 30 Mar. 1521; Leo X to Wolsey, 6 Jan., 16 Mar., 1, 17 Apr. 1521; Warham to Wolsey, 8 Mar., 3 Apr. 1521; Cardinal Medici to —— (Mar. 1521) (Rymer, XIII. 734–5, 739–44; *St.Pap.*, VI. 67; Ellis, III (i). 239–47; *L.P.*, III. 1080, 1123–4, 1193, 1197, 1208, 1210, 1216, 1218, 1234).
25. Fisher's sermon, 12 May 1521 (Fisher, *Opera*, pp. 1375–92); anon. account (May 1521) (Roscoe, *Leo X*, II. 420–1); Wolsey to Booth, 14 May 1521 (Wilkins, *Concilia*, III. 690–3); Suriano to Doge, 13 May 1521; Ludovico Spinelli to Gasparo Spinelli, 14–17 May 1521 (*Ven.Cal.*, III. 210, 213).
26. Clerk's speech in Consistory (2 Oct. 1521); Leo X's Bull, 11 Oct. 1521; Leo X to Henry VIII, 4 Nov. 1521 (in Henry VIII, *Assertio Septem Sacramentorum*, pp. 156–79; Rymer, XIII. 760); Clerk to Wolsey, 10 Oct. 1521 (Ellis, I (i). 292).
27. Roper, p. 67; Henry VIII to Leo X, 21 May 1521 (in Henry VIII, op.cit., pp. 152–5); Brewer's Pref. to *L.P.*, I., pp. ccccxix–ccccxxv; Notes to *More's Works*, V. 720–1.
28. For Buckingham's arrest, trial and execution, see documents connected with Buckingham's trial; value of Lord Abergavenny's lands (May 1521); Wolsey to Henry VIII, 20 May 1521; Wolsey to Jerningham, 20 May 1521 (*L.P.*, III. 1284–8, 1290–3); Ludovico Spinelli to Gasparo Spinelli, 14–17 May 1521; Suriano to Doge, 21 May 1521 (*Ven.Cal.*, III. 213, 219); Juan Manuel to Charles V, 22 May 1521 (*Span*.Cal., II. 336); Hall, pp. 622–4; Brewer's Pref. in *L.P.*, III., pp. cviii–cxxxvii).
29. Wolsey to Jerningham, 20 May 1521 (*L.P.*, III. 1293).
30. More, 'The Four Last Things' (*More's English Works*, p. 86).
31. Grant of lands to More, 23 Mar. (1522) (*L.P.*, III. 2239).
32. Paris News-letter, 23 July 1535 (in Harpsfield, p. 266); Harpsfield, p. 23.
33. Ammonio to Erasmus, 18 Feb. 1516 (Allen, II. 200–1).

Chapter 8 – The Calais Conference

1. Sormano to Doge, 23 May 1516; Giustiniani to Doge, 2 Jan., 1 Nov. 1516 (*L.P.*, II. 1380; *Ven.Cal.*, II. 671, 732, 801).

2. Giustiniani's report to the Senate, 10 Oct. 1519 (*Ven.Cal.*, II. 1287).

3. More, *A Dialogue of Comfort against Tribulation* (*More's Works*, XII 213–14).

4. Henry VIII's and Wolsey's instructions to Tunstal and Sir Richard Wingfield; Charles V's instructions to Mesa and Hanneton (Jar.–July 1521); Wolsey to Henry VIII (Mar.), 20 July 1521; Charles V to Henry VIII, 20 July 1521 (*L.P.*, III. 1150, 1162, 1213–14, 1340, 1362, 1371, 1395, 1418, 1422, 1424, 1432; *St.Pap.*, I. 11, 19).

5. Account of Wolsey's landing at Calais (Aug. 1521); Wolsey to Henry VIII, 1 Aug. 1521 (*St.Pap.*, I. 25; *L.P.*, III. 1453, 1458).

6. Duprat etc. to François I, 5, 8 Aug. 1521; Charles V to Wolsey, 7 Aug. 1521 (Le Glay, *Négociations diplomatiques entre la France et l'Autriche*, II. 535–42; *L.P.*, III. 1467, 1475, 1478).

7. Wolsey to Henry VIII (Aug. 1521); Minutes of Calais Conference by Charles V's envoys, (Nov. 1521) (*Papiers d'État de Granvelle*, I. 128–241; *L.P.*, III. 1479, 1816).

8. Duprat etc. to François I, 8 Aug. 1521; Duprat to Louise of Savoy, 19 Aug. 1521; Bonnivet to Duprat, 15 Aug. 1521 (Le Glay, II. 483–6, 540–2; *L.P.*, III. 1478, 1489). See also Suriano to Doge, 10 Aug. 1521 (*Ven.Cal.*, III. 293).

9. Spinelly to Wolsey, 9 Aug. 1521 (*L.P.*, III. 1482).

10. Contarini to Doge, 13, 16 Aug. 1521 (*Ven.Cal.*, III. 294, 298); Wolsey to Henry VIII, 14 Aug. 1521; French report of Calais Conference (Le Glay, II. 529–86; *L.P.*, III. 1488, 1817).

11. For Wolsey's visit to Bruges and the negotiations there, see Contarini to Doge, 16, 19, 22, 24 Aug. 1521 (*Ven.Cal.*, III. 298, 302, 310, 312); Wolsey to Henry VIII (two letters of Aug. 1521) (*St.Pap.*, I. 38–40; *L.P.*, III. 1491, 1493–4); Charles V to Juan Manuel, 20 Aug. 1521 (*Span.Cal.*, II. 353).

12. Wolsey to Henry VIII (Aug. 1521), 24 Aug. 1521 (*St.Pap.*, I. 39, 43).

13. Sir Richard Wingfield to Wolsey, 22 July 1521; Gattinara to Charles V, 30 July 1521; Treaty of Bruges, 25 Aug. 1521 (Le Glay, II. 473–82; *L.P.*, III. 1446, 1508).

14. Wolsey to Henry VIII (Aug. 1521) (*St.Pap.*, I. 36–38); Contarini to Doge, 16 Aug. 1521 (*Ven.Cal.*, III. 298).

15. Charles V to Mesa, 16 Dec. 1521; Charles V to Wolsey, 17 Dec. 1521; Margaret of Austria to Wolsey, 17 Dec. 1521 (Bradford, *Correspondence of the Emperor Charles V*, pp. 21–25; *L.P.*, III. 1876–7, 1880).

16. Erasmus to Warham, 23 Aug. 1521 (Allen, IV. 567).

17. Treaty of Bruges, 25 Aug. 1521 (*L.P.*, III. 1508).

18. Contarini to Doge, 16, 19, 22, 24, 26 Aug. 1521 (*Ven.Cal.*, III. 298, 302, 310, 312–13, 315).

19. Contarini to Doge, 26 Aug. 1521 (op.cit., III. 316).

20. Duprat etc. to Wolsey, 26 Aug. 1521; Duprat etc. to François I, 28 Aug.

1521; French report of Calais Conference (Le Glay, II. 487–92, 529–86; *L.P.*, III. 1511, 1513, 1817).

21. Duprat etc. to François I, 28 Aug., 7, 8 Sept. 1521; Gattinara to Charles V, 1 Sept. 1521; Wolsey to Henry VIII, 4 Sept. 1521; Minutes of Calais Conference by Charles V's envoys (Aug.–Nov. 1521), and French report (Le Glay, II. 487–92, 494–520, 529–86; *Granvelle*, I. 125–241; *L.P.*, III. 1513, 1534, 1544, 1552, 1555, 1816–17).

22. Duprat etc. to François I, 8 Sept. 1521 (Le Glay, II. 512–13).

23. Duprat to François I (Sept. 1521) (Le Glay, II. 514–20).

24. Ibid, p. 519.

25. For the negotiations at Calais, see the correspondence of Charles V, Gattinara, Wolsey, Worcester etc. (Sept.–Nov. 1521); Minutes of Calais Conference by Charles V's envoys, and French report (Le Glay, II. 529–86; Granvelle, I. 125–241; *L.P.*, III. 1549, 1553, 1557, 1560, 1605–6, 1615–16, 1620, 1622, 1625, 1634–5, 1638, 1667, 1670, 1683, 1689, 1693–6, 1705, 1724, 1729, 1732, 1736, 1738, 1742, 1746, 1748, 1753, 1816–17).

26. Gattinara etc. to Charles V, 10 Sept. 1521 (*L.P.*, III. 1560).

27. For Wolsey's illness, see Gattinara etc. to Charles V, 15, 18, 20, 24 Sept. 1521; Minutes of Calais Conference by Charles V's envoys, and French report (*Granvelle*, I. 125–241; Le Glay, II. 529–86; *L.P.*, III. 1580, 1590, 1595, 1816–17).

28. Charles V to Wolsey, 16 Nov. 1521; Charles V to Hanneton, 16 Nov. 1521; Treaty of Calais, 24 Nov. 1521; François I to Duprat, etc., 24 Nov. 1521 (*L.P.*, III. 1769–70, 1802–3).

29. French report of Calais Conference; Henry VIII to Wolsey (Nov. 1521) (*L.P.*, III. 1814, 1817).

30. Campeggio to Wolsey, 15, 17 Dec. 1521; Clerk to Wolsey (Dec. 1521), 4 Jan. (1522) (*L.P.*, III. 1869, 1879, 1895, 1932); Juan Manuel to Charles V, 2 Dec. 1521; Report of Conclave (Jan. 1522) (*Span.Cal.*, II. 366, 375).

31. Mesa to Charles V, 19 Dec. 1521; Charles V to Mesa, 16 Dec. 1521; Charles V to Wolsey, 17, 27 Dec. 1521; Charles V to Henry VIII, 27 Dec. 1521 (Bradford, pp. 14–15, 17–32; *L.P.*, III. 1876–7, 1884, 1906–7).

32. Charles V to Henry VIII, 27 Dec. 1521 (Bradford, pp. 27–29).

33. Margaret of Austria to Wolsey, 17, 27 Dec. 1521 (*L.P.*, III. 1880, 1904).

34. Charles V to Juan Manuel (Dec. 1521); Juan Manuel to Charles V, 27, 31 Aug.; 6, 26 Sept. 1521; Margaret of Austria to Berghes (Nov. 1521) (*L.P.*, III. 1766, 1908; *Span.Cal.*, II. 356–9); Suriano to the Doge, 27 Jan. 1522 (*Ven.Cal.*, III. 396); Brewer's Pref. to *L.P.*, III., pp. clxxxvii–ccvi.

35. For the conflicting reports of the Conclave, see Clerk to Wolsey (Dec. 1521), 4, 13 Jan. (1522); Campeggio to Wolsey, 9, 10 Jan. 1522 (Ellis, III (i). 304–16; *L.P.*, III. 1895, 1932, 1945, 1952, 1960); Report of Conclave (Jan. 1522) (*Span.Cal.*, II. 375).

36. Adrian VI to Wolsey, 16 May, 1522 (*L.P.*, III. 2260).

37. Pace to Wolsey, 1, 9, (20) Sept.; 4 Oct. 1521; Wolsey to Henry VIII, 4, 28 Sept. (undated); François I to Duprat, 19 Nov. 1521; Clarencieux's declaration of war, 29 May 1522 (*St.Pap.*, I. 47–48, 51–52, 54–69; Le Glay, II. 584; *L.P.*, III. 1533, 1544, 1558, 1577, 1594, 1611, 1629–30, 1780, 2292).

38. For Charles V's visit to England, see correspondence and memoranda of Ruthall, Sir Richard Wingfield, Charles V, Salinas, Contarini and Suriano, May–July 1522 (Rymer, XIII. 767–8; *L.P.*, III. 2283, 2289, 2306, 2309; *Span.Cal.*, II. 420, 437, 441; *Ven.Cal.*, III. 462–3, 465–7, 470, 484, 486, 493, 495); Hall, pp. 634–42.
39. Clarencieux's declaration of war, 29 May 1522 (*L.P.*, III. 2292).
40. Treaties of Windsor, 16, 19 June 1522; Treaty of Bishop's Waltham, 2 July 1522 (*L.P.*, III. 2322, 2333, 2360; *Span.Cal.*, II. 442).
41. Charles V's grants and correspondence, Apr. 1522–Mar. 1523 (*Span.Cal.*, II. 409, 538); Suriano etc. to Doge, 10 June 1524 (*Ven.Cal.*, III. 835).
42. Memorandum on grants by the spiritualty (Aug. 1522) (*L.P.*, III. 2483).
43. Surrey to Henry VIII, 3 Sept. 1522; Wolsey to Surrey (9 Sept. 1522); Sandys to Henry VIII, 10 Sept. 1522; (*L.P.*, III. 2499, 2526, 2530).
44. Sandys to Henry VIII, 10 Sept. 1522 (*L.P.*, III. 2530).
45. Sandys to Wolsey, 12 Sept. 1522 (*L.P.*, III. 2541).
46. For the campaign in France, see reports of Surrey and Sandys to Henry VIII and Wolsey, Sept.–Oct. 1522; Wolsey to Surrey (Sept. 1522) (*L.P.*, III. 2530, 2540–1, 2549, 2551, 2560, 2568, 2579, 2581, 2592, 2614); Wolsey to Henry VIII, 21 Oct. 1522 (*St.Pap.*, I. 112); Badoer to Doge, 8–13 Oct. 1522 (*Ven.Cal.*, III. 565); Hall, pp. 646–8.
47. Commissions to Shrewsbury and Wolsey, correspondence of Shrewsbury and Dacre, July–Sept. 1522 (Rymer, XIII. 772–3; *L.P.*, III. 2439 (1) and (6), 2503, 2531, 2536).
48. Correspondence of Wolsey, Margaret Queen of Scots, Albany and Dacre, Sept.–Oct. 1522 (*St.Pap.*, I. 107–9; VI. 106–7; *L.P.*, III. 2537–8, 2564, 2565 (5) and (6), 2567 (5), 2571–2, 2574).
49. Wolsey to Albany (Oct. 1522) (*L.P.*, III. 2573).

Chapter 9 – More versus Luther

1. Preserved Smith, p. 47.
2. Ibid, pp. 327–34.
3. More to a monk (1520?) (Rogers, pp. 165–206; see More, *Selected Letters*, pp. 121–2, for the passages quoted).
4. More to Erasmus, 15 Dec. (1516) (Allen, II. 420–1).
5. Chambers, p. 178.
6. Ibid, pp. 182–4.
7. Ro. Ba., p. 129.
8. For the sweating sickness and its symptoms, see Chieregato to Bartolomeo, 6 Aug. 1517 (*Ven.Cal.*, II. 945); Tuke to Vannes, 14 July 1528 (*L.P.*, IV. 4510).
9. Roper, pp. 28–29.
10. More to Gonell, 22 May 1518 (Rogers, pp. 120–3); Chambers, pp. 182–3; Basset, *Born for Friendship*, pp. 119–21, 127–31.
11. Erasmus to Hutten, 23 July 1519 (Allen, IV. 19).
12. Chambers, pp. 284–5; Cresacre More, p.187.
13. Stapleton, pp. 95–96.

14. Stapleton, pp. 74–75; Bouge to —— (1535) (*E.H.R.*, VII. 713–15); Roper, pp. 48–49; Harpsfield, pp. 65–66.
15. More, 'The Four Last Things' (*More's English Works.*, I. 60, 72, 79–80, 82, 460, 471–2, 475–6).
16. Ibid, I. 77, 468.
17. Ibid, I. 78, 468.
18. Ibid, I. 78, 469.
19. Ibid, I. 97, 494.
20. Ibid, I. 95–96, 493.
21. Ibid, I. 102, 499.
22. Roper, p. 67; Notes to *More's Works*, V. 720–3.
23. Luther, *Antwortt deutsch Mart. Luthers auff König Henrichs von Engelland buch*, Ai, B, Biii, Diii, Fiii.
24. Henry VIII to Duke John of Saxony, 20 Jan. 1523 (*L.P.*, IV. 40, where it is wrongly dated 1523/4); Murner, *Ob der köning vsz engelland ein lügner sey oder der Luther*; Fisher, *Assertionis Lutheranice Confutatio*; Eck, *Assertio Hic Invictissime Angliae regis über de secciatis & calumnis & impietatibus Lutheri*; Fisher, *Defensio regis assertionis contra Babyloniam capitatem*; Notes to *More's Works*, V. 726–31, 791–3.
25. More to Cromwell, 5 Mar. (1534) (Rogers, p. 496).
26. Preserved Smith, p. 278; Notes to *More's Works*, V. 825.
27. Stapleton, p. 34.
28. More, *Responsio ad Lutherum* (*More's Works*, V. 41, 57, 79, 181, 223, 225, 227, 311, 341, 355, 403, 429, 437, 439, 611, 677, 683).
29. Ibid, V. 61, 685, 689, 691.
30. Ibid, V. 687, 689.
31. Ibid, V. 313.
32. Ibid, V. 317, 499.
33. Notes to *More's Works*, V. 823–5.
34. Carcellius to the Reader (ibid, V. 3–5).
35. Ibid, V. 13.
36. Chambers, p. 277.
37. *More's Works*, V. 141.
38. Ibid, V. 691.
39. Harpsfield, pp. 84–86.

Chapter 10 – With the Emperor against France

1. Hannibal to Wolsey, 14 Mar. (1523); Cardinal Medici to Wolsey, 23 Mar., 3 Apr. 1523; Adrian VI's Bull, 26 Mar. 1523; Campeggio to Wolsey, 30 Mar. 1523; Cardinal Medici to Henry VIII, 3 Apr. 1523 (Rymer, XIII. 783–4; *L.P.*, III. 2891, 2910, 2913, 2918, 2928–9).
2. Praet and Marnix to Charles V, 1 June 1523 (Bradford, p. 53).
3. For the negotiations with Venice, see correspondence of the Doge, Suriano and Contarini, Mar. 1522–July 1523; Wolsey to the Doge, 6 Sept. 1523 (*Ven.Cal.*, III. 426, 429, 463, 467, 470, 474–6, 480, 482, 484, 486, 494–5,

502, 506–7, 512–17, 522, 528, 531–2, 537–8, 541, 550, 552, 555, 562, 567, 570–1, 574, 582–4, 590, 593, 595–8, 601, 608, 618, 621, 623, 637, 650, 654–5, 671, 683, 687, 694, 700–1, 720); Wolsey to Henry VIII, 17 Aug. 1523 (*St.Pap.*, I. 119–20).

4. Wolsey to Dacre (18 June 1523) (*L.P.*, III. 3114–15).

5. Wolsey to Sampson and Jerningham, 30 Aug. 1523 (*St.Pap.*, VI. 170).

6. Ibid, VI. 173.

7. Surrey to Henry VIII (3 Nov. 1523) (Ellis, I (i). 232–5).

8. For the negotiations with Bourbon, see Agreement between Henry VIII and Bourbon, 4 Aug., 6 Sept. 1523 (Le Glay, II. 589–92; *St.Pap.*, VI. 174–5); More to Wolsey, 13 Sept. 1523 (Rogers, pp. 286–8); and correspondence between Charles V, Bourbon, Wolsey, and the Imperial and English Ambassadors, May–Oct. 1523 (Bradford, pp. 53–71, 80–82; *St.Pap.*, I. 133–4; VI. 131–41, 151n., 174–5; *L.P.*, III. 3030, 3055, 3064, 3123, 3225, 3257, 3307–8, 3326, 3335, 3386, 3388; *Span.Cal.*, II. 583, 602; *Further Supp.*, pp. 236–41, 274–6).

9. Draft of Wolsey's speech (Apr. 1523) (*L.P.*, III. 2957).

10. For More's action as Speaker and the incident with Wolsey, see Roper, pp. 12–20; Harpsfield, pp. 26–33; Proceedings in Parliament, 15 Apr.–31 July 1523 (*L.P.*, III. 2956); Wolsey to Henry VIII (July 1523) (*St.Pap.*, I. 116–17).

11. Wolsey to Henry VIII, 24 Aug. 1523 (*St.Pap.*, I. 124).

12. Adrian VI's Bull, 30 Apr. 1523 (Rymer, XIII. 790–2); correspondence of Adrian VI, Campeggio and Ghinucci, Feb.–June 1523 (*L.P.*, III., 2848–9, 2865, 2871–3, 2984, 2996, 3107).

13. Charles V to Adrian VI, 22 Aug. 1523 (*Span.Cal.*, II. 588).

14. *More's Works*, XII. 6–7, 191–3, 303–4.

15. More, 'The Four Last Things' (*More's English Works*, I. 459).

16. Articles between Henry VIII and Bourbon, 4 Aug. 1523 (Le Glay, II. 589–92).

17. Treaty of Valladolid, 2 July 1523; Sampson and Jerningham to Wolsey, 3 July 1523 (*L.P.*, III. 3149–50; *Span.Cal.*, II. 561).

18. More to Wolsey, 20 Sept. 1523 (Rogers, pp. 289–95).

19. More to Wolsey, 12 Sept. 1523 (ibid, pp. 284–6).

20. Ibid; correspondence between Wolsey, Margaret of Austria, Charles V, and the Ambassadors, Sept. 1523 (*L.P.*, III. 3315–18, 3320, 3371; *Span.Cal.*, *Further Supp.*, pp. 274–6).

21. More to Wolsey, 20 Sept. 1523 (Rogers, pp. 293–4).

22. For the campaign in France, see Roeulx to Margaret of Austria (Sept. 1523); More to Wolsey, 30 Oct. 1523; 'Action of the army in France'. 19 Sept.–7 Nov. 1523 (Rogers, pp. 299–301; *L.P.*, III. 3348, 3485, 3516); Hall, pp. 667–72.

23. Wolsey to Henry VIII, 30 Sept., 1 Oct. 1523 (Burnet, *History of the Reformation of the Church of England*, VI. 11–14).

24. Wolsey to Clerk, Pace etc., 4 Oct. 1523 (L.P., III. 3389).

25. Account of Conclave (Nov. 1523); Clerk, Pace and Hannibal to Wolsey, 2 Dec. 1523; Charles V to Henry VIII, 12 Dec. 1523; Charles V to Wolsey,

16 Dec. 1523 (*St.Pap.*, VI. 195–201; *L.P.*, III. 3547, 3592, 3629, 3647; *Span.Cal.*, II. 611); Brewer's Pref., in *L.P.*, III, pp. ccclxxxiv.

26. Clerk etc. to Wolsey, 2 Dec. 1523 (*St. Pap.*, VI. 200–1).

27. Wolsey to Henry VIII, 6 Dec. 1523 (Burnet, VI. 15–16).

28. Wolsey to Sampson and Jerningham, 24 Jan. (1524) (*St.Pap.*, VI. 242–54).

29. Bourbon to Henry VIII, 18 Jan. (1524) (ibid, VI. 241).

30. Louise d'Angoulême to Brinon and Vaulx, (Apr. 1524), 16 Feb. 1524/5; Wolsey to Sampson, 4 June, (Nov.) 1524; Wolsey to Henry VIII, 5 Feb. (1525) (*Captivité de François Ier*, pp. 53–57; *St.Pap.*, I. 153–6; VI. 305–11, 364–72; *L.P.*, IV. 271, 841, 1093, 1263); Praet to Charles V, 31 July; 8, 16 Aug. 1524 (*Span.Cal.*, Further Supp., pp. 367–75).

31. Treaty of 25 May 1524 (*L.P.*, IV. 365); Wolsey to Pace, 28 May 1524 (*St.Pap.*, VI. 289).

32. Pace to Wolsey, 25 June, 5, 16 July 1524 (*L.P.*, IV. 441, 471, 503); Wolsey to Pace, 28 June 1524 (*St.Pap.*, VI. 314–20).

33. Wolsey to Pace, 17 July 1524 (*L.P.*, IV. 510).

34. See Praet's correspondence with Margaret of Austria and Charles V, Jan. 1524–Jan. 1525 (*Span.Cal.*, Further Supp., pp. 298–306, 316–28, 354–7, 388–94, 399–408, 418–21, 426–33).

35. Praet to Charles V, 3 Jan. 1525 (*Span.Cal.*, III. 1).

36. Praet to Charles V, 19 Jan. 1525 (ibid, III. 5).

37. For the Praet incident, see Wolsey to Sampson (13 Feb. 1525); Sampson to Wolsey, 15 Mar. (1525); Margaret of Austria to Wolsey, 6 Apr. 1524/5; Margaret of Austria to Henry VIII, 7 Apr. 1524/5 (*L.P.*, IV. 1083, 1190, 1247–8); Praet to Charles V, 25 Feb. 1525; 'Justification des Anglais' (7 Mar. 1525); Wolsey to Charles V, 8 Mar. 1524/5; Henry VIII to Charles V, 8 Mar. 1524/5; Bourgogne etc. to Margaret of Austria, 9 Mar. 1525 (*Span.Cal.*, III. 20, 28, 32–33); Charles V to Praet, 26 Mar. 1525 (Lanz, *Correspondenz des Kaisers Karl V.*, I. 157–9).

38. Brinon and Vaulx to Louise d'Angoulême, 6 Mar. (1525) (*L.P.*, IV. 1160).

39. *Greyfriars Chron.*, p. 32; Norfolk to Wolsey, 1 Apr. 1525 (Ellis, III (i). 376–81); Hall, pp. 692–3.

40. Tunstal etc. to Wolsey, 2 June 1525; Wingfield to Wolsey, 2 June 1525 (Ellis, III (ii). 13–18; *L.P.*, IV. 1379–81).

41. Memoranda of Charles V, Henry VIII and their ministers (June–Aug. 1525) (*Span.Cal.*, Further Supp., pp. 443–7).

42. Correspondence of Brinon and Vaulx, and of Louise d'Angoulême, July–Oct. 1525 (*L.P.*, IV. 1525, 1531, 1537, 1606, 1609, 1669, 1692, 1903; *Captivité de François Ier*, pp. 359–63; Rymer, XIV. 189–92).

43. Treaty of The Moor, 30 Aug. 1525; ratification of the treaty by French cities, and Louise d'Angoulême's correspondence, Oct. 1525–Mar. 1526 (*L.P.*, IV. 1617, 1711, 1770, 1783, 1788; *Captivité de François Ier*, pp. 349–52, 378–9).

Chapter 11 – With France against the Emperor

1. Clerk to Wolsey, 31 May 1526; Wolsey to Henry VIII, 21 July 1528 (*St.Pap.*, I. 163, 320); Suriano to the Doge, 11 Sept. and undated (Sept) 1521 (*Ven.Cal.*, III. 335–6).
2. Giustiniani to the Doge, 15, 17 Aug. 1517 (*Ven.Cal.*, II. 951, 953); Du Bellay to Montmorency, 24 May, 21 Aug. 1528 (Le Grand, *L'histoire du Divorce*, III. 102; *L.P.*, IV. App. 196).
3. For Wolsey's policy towards enclosures, see Pollard, pp. 77–87.
4. For Wolsey's actions in the Court of Star Chamber, see Guy, *The Cardinal's Court*, passim.
5. Corresondence of Wolsey, Northumberland and Dacre, June 1524–Apr. 1528 (*St.Pap.*, IV. 493; *L.P.*, IV. 405, 1223, 4133–4, 4203).
6. Correspondence of Wolsey, Oxford and Lady Oxford, Feb. 1524–July 1528 (*L.P.*, IV. 106, 4586–7).
7. Foxe, IV. 173–246, 557.
8. Ibid, IV. 657; Roy, *Read me and do not grudge* (*Harleian Misc.*, IX. 78–81).
9. Foxe, V. 415–17.
10. Hansa Merchants in London to Mayor of Cologne, 3 Mar. 1526 (New Style) (in Kronenberg, 'A printed letter of the London Hanse Merchants' (*Oxford Bibliographical Society Publications*, New Series, I. 25–26)).
11. Examinations of Hansa merchants and of Prickness, 8 Feb. (1526) (*L.P.*, IV. 1962).
12. Foxe, V. 417–19; *Greyfriars Chron.*, p. 33; Dalewyn's recantation, 6 Apr. 1526 (*L.P.*, IV. 2073).
13. Hansa Merchants in London to Mayor of Cologne, 3 Mar. 1526 (op.cit., I. 26–27).
14. Foxe, IV. 622.
15. Ibid, V. 117.
16. Hacket to Wolsey, 24 Nov., 1 Dec. 1526; 12 Jan. 1526/7 (*L.P.*, IV. 2652, 2677, 2697); Nix to Warham, 14 June 1527 (Ellis, III (ii). 91–92); Foxe, IV 670–1; Hall, pp. 762–3.
17. Hacket's correspondence, June–Sept. 1528 (*L.P.*, IV. 4431, 4580, 4650, 4714, 4746); Hacket to Friar West, 31 Dec. 1528 (B.L., Galba B. ix. 155).
18. Wolsey's commissions to suppress Bayham Abbey and St Frideswide's, and his grants to Cardinal's College, Oxford, Apr. 1525–Sept. 1526 (*L.P.*, IV. 1252, 1468, 1688, 1695, 1913, 1964, 2538).
19. Longland to Wolsey, 11 Aug. 1526; Benet to Wolsey, 9 Mar. (1528); Kirtin to Wolsey, 13 Mar. (1528) (*L.P.*, IV. 2391, 4047, 4056).
20. Sir E. Guildford to Sir H. Guildford, 8 June 1525; Warham to Wolsey, 2 July 1525 (*L.P.*, IV. 1397, 1470).
21. *Greyfriars Chron.*, p. 32; correspondence of Norfolk and Wolsey, Mar.–Apr. 1525 (*L.P.*, IV. 1199, 1249, 1261).
22. Correspondence of Warham, Norfolk, Suffolk, Henry VIII and Wolsey, Apr.–May 1525 (Ellis, III (i). 359–75; III (ii). 3–12; Fiddes, *Collections*, p. 29; *L.P.*, IV. 1260, 1295, 1305–6, 1318–19, 1329, 1343).

23. Proclamations of 14 July, 28 Nov. 1526; Longland to Wolsey, 30 Sept. 1528 (*L.P.*, IV. 2318, 2660, 4796); Pollard, pp. 85–86.

24. Skelton, *Why come ye not to Court ?*, (in Skelton, *Poetical Works*, II. 26–67); Williams, *The Cardinal and the Secretary*, pp. 68–71.

25. Articles of the House of Lords against Wolsey (1 Dec. 1529) (in Lord Herbert, *Henry VIII*, in Kennet, *A Complete History of England*, II. 128).

26. Fiddes, *Collections*, pp. 227–8; Pollard, p. 309 and n.; Clerk to Wolsey, 13 Sept. 1526 (*L.P.*, IV. 2482).

27. Orio to the Doge, 1 Dec. 1525 (*Ven.Cal.*, III. 1175); French memorandum (Jan. 1526); Wolsey to Fitzwilliam and Tayler, 18 Jan. (1526) (*L.P.*, IV. 1879, 1902).

28. Treaty of Madrid, 14 Jan. 1525/6 (Rymer, XIV. 308–26); Taylor to Wolsey, 18, 19 Mar. (1526) (Ellis, II (i). 331–7).

29. Correspondence of Wolsey, Lee and Henry VIII, July 1525–May 1526 (*Span.Cal.*, III. 127; *L.P.*, IV. 1926, 2036, 2039, 2148, 2688).

30. Treaty of 8 Aug. 1526 (Rymer, XIV. 185–7).

31. Correspondence of Henry VIII, Clement VII, Ladislaus II, Ghinucci, Spinelli, Hacket, Wallop and Ferdinand I, Mar.–Sept. 1526 (*St.Pap.* VI. 532–3, 572–6, 581–3; Ellis, II (i). 341–3; *L.P.*, IV. 2105, 2118, 2130, 2268, 2272, 2463, 2485, 2960–1, 3067–8, 3095, 3126; *Ven.Cal.*, III. 1371).

32. Correspondence of Wolsey, Clement VII, Campeggio, Gilberti, the Doge, Spinelli and Knight, May–Sept. 1526 (*L.P.*, IV. 2148, 2228, 2231–3, 2261, 2266–7, 2320, 2408, 2422; *Ven.Cal.*, III. 1324, 1362, 1366, 1371, 1393, 1406; *St.Pap.*, I. 169–75; Rymer, XIV. 187; Theiner, *Vetera Monumenta*, p. 553).

33. Correspondence of Harvel, Ghinucci, Gambara and Knight, June–Oct. 1526 (*L.P.*, IV. 2244, 2296, 2466, 2477; *St.Pap.*, I. 181–3).

34. Correspondence of Campeggio, Gilberti, Casale and Russell, Feb. 1527 (*L.P.*, IV. 2857, 2866, 2868, 2875–6).

35. John of Almain to Wolsey, 17 Sept. 1526; Wolsey to Lee, 19 Sept. 1526; Lee to Wolsey, 2 Dec. 1526 (*L.P.*, IV. 2489, 2493, 2682).

36. Lee to Wolsey, 31 Jan., 9 Feb., 25 Mar., 13 Apr. (1527) (*L.P.*, IV. 2830, 2865, 2987, 3040).

37. For the negotiations for the Anglo-French treaty, see Vaulx, etc. to François I, 21 Mar. (1527); Memorandum by Turenne, etc. (May 1527) (*L.P.*, IV. 2974, 3105); Turenne to Albany, 1 May 1527 (Teulet, I. 62).

38. Treaties of 30 Apr., 29 May 1527 (*L.P.*, IV. 3080, 3138).

39. Memorandum by Turenne, etc. (May 1527) (*L.P.*, IV. 3105).

40. Henry VIII's Instructions to Poyntz (May 1527) (*L.P.*, IV. 3143).

41. Russell and Casale to Wolsey, 26 Apr. 1527 (*L.P.*, IV. 3065, 3068).

42. Memorandum on sack of Rome (May 1527) (*L.P.*, IV. 3114); Sanga to Nuncio in England, 27 June 1527 (P.R.O., S.P., I/42, 121–2).

Chapter 12 – The King's Secret Matter

1. Cavendish, pp. 29–34.
2. Charles V's answer to Clarencieux (27 Jan. 1528) (Le Grand, III. 45–46); Mendoza to Charles V, 18 May 1527 (*Span.Cal.*, III. 69); Hall, pp. 755–6; Harpsfield, pp. 40–42; Stapleton, pp. 197–8; MS 'Life of Fisher' (in Van Ortroy, *Vie du Bienheureux Martyr Jean Fisher*, pp. 159–61); Stow, *Annals*, pp. 543–4.
3. Wolsey to Henry VIII, 5 July 1527 (*St.Pap.*, I. 197).
4. Examination of Bishop Foxe, 5, 6 Apr. 1527 (Depositions in Legatine Court) (*L.P.*, IV. 5791).
5. Judicial proceedings before Wolsey and Warham, 17–31 May 1527 (*L.P.*, IV. 3140).
6. Wolsey to Henry VIII, 1 July 1527 (*St.Pap.*, I. 194–5).
7. Fisher to Wolsey (June 1527) (Fiddes, *Collections*, p. 185).
8. Wolsey to Henry VIII, 2 June (1527) (*St.Pap.*, I. 189–90).
9. Wolsey to Ghinucci, Lee and Poyntz (June 1527) (*St.Pap.*, I. 585–7); English clergy to Spanish clergy (Sept. 1527) (*L.P.*, IV. 3436).
10. Wolsey to Henry VIII, 29 July 1527 (*St.Pap.*, I. 230–3); Knight to Wolsey (Aug. 1527) (*L.P.*, IV. 3363); Wolsey's articles for government of the Church during the Pope's captivity (Sept. 1527) (Pocock, *Records*, I. 19–21).
11. Mendoza to Charles V, 18 May 1527 (*Span.Cal.*, III (ii). 69).
12. List of Wolsey's suite (July 1527) (*L.P.*, IV. 3216).
13. Wolsey to Henry VIII, 5 July 1527 (*St.Pap.*, I. 196–204).
14. Ibid; Wolsey to Henry VIII, 8, 11 July 1527 (ibid, I. 205, 212).
15. Wolsey to Henry VIII, 11, 16, 18 July 1527 (ibid, I. 212–13, 216, 219).
16. Cavendish, pp. 47–48.
17. Wolman to Wolsey, 26 July 1527 (*L.P.*, IV. 3304); Knight to Wolsey, 9 July 1527 (*St.Pap.*, I. 209).
18. Wolsey to Henry VIII, 22, 24 July 1527 (*L.P.*, IV. 3289; *St.Pap.*, I. 221–3); François I's commission to Wolsey (July 1527) (Rymer, XIV. 202–3); Cavendish, pp. 48–50.
19. Wolsey to Henry VIII, 24, 31 July 1527; Wolsey to Ghinucci and Lee, 1 Aug. 1527 (*St.Pap.*, I. 223–5; VI. 594–6).
20. Browne to Wolsey, 1 Aug. 1527 (*L.P.*, IV. 3328); Wolsey to Henry VIII, 9 Aug. 1527 (*St.Pap.*, I. 235).
21. For Wolsey's reception at Amiens, see Wolsey to Henry VIII, 9, 16, 19 Aug. 1527 (*St.Pap.*, I. 235–53, 256–60, 262–4); Correspondence of Canal and Camillo, Aug. 1527 (*Ven.Cal.*, IV. 148, 151, 156); Cavendish, pp. 51–54.
22. Wolsey to Henry VIII, 29 July, 9 Aug. 1527 (*St.Pap.*, I. 230–3, 242–3); François I to Wolsey, 24 July 1527 (*L.P.*, IV. 3298).
23. Wolsey to Henry VIII, 11, 19 Aug., 5 Sept. 1527 (*St.Pap.*, I. 254–6, 262–4, 267–77).
24. Treaty of 18 Aug. 1527 (Rymer, XIV. 203–18); Wolsey to Henry VIII, 19 Aug. 1527 (*St.Pap.*, I. 262–4); Cavendish, pp. 57–62.

25. Wolsey to Henry VIII, 5 Sept. 1527 (*St.Pap.*, I. 267–77); Wolsey to Ghinucci etc. (Sept. 1527); François I to his Ambassadors in Spain (Sept. 1527); memorandum of François I's final offer to Charles V (Sept. 1527); Charles V's reply to English Ambassadors, 15 Sept. 1527 (*L.P.*, IV. 3412, 3415, 3430–1).

26. Cavendish, pp. 62–63.

27. Wolsey to Henry VIII, 5 Sept. 1527 (*St.Pap.*, I. 267–77).

28. Knight to Henry VIII, 12, 13 Sept. 1527; Wolsey to Henry VIII, 13 Sept. 1527 (*St.Pap.*, I. 277–9; VII. 1–3); Henry VIII to Wolsey (Sept. 1527) (Burnet, VI. 22).

29. Wolsey to Henry VIII, 21 Sept. 1527; Browne to Henry VIII, 18 Sept. 1527 (*St.Pap.*, I. 279; VII. 6); Giustiniani to the Doge, 18 Sept. 1527 (*Ven.Cal.*, IV. 168).

30. Charles V to Mendoza, 29 July 1527 (*L.P.*, IV. 3312); Navagero to the Doge, 27 July 1527 (*Ven.Cal.*, IV. 142).

31. Mendoza to Charles V, 18 May 1527; Mendoza's memorandum (Dec. 1527) (*Span.Cal.*, III (ii). 252).

32. Charles V to Mendoza, 30 Sept. 1527 (*L.P.*, IV. 3464).

33. Mendoza to Charles V, 26 Oct. 1527 (*Span.Cal.*, III (ii). 224).

34. Foxe, IV. 621–42.

35. Foster's recantation, 5 Dec. 1527 (*L.P.*, IV. 3639); memorandum of 5 Jan. 1527/8 (Pocock, I. 54); Vernier to the Doge, 27 Nov. 1527; Spinelli to ——, 8 Jan. (1528) (*Ven.Cal.*, IV. 210, 225).

36. Clarencieux's declaration to Charles V (22 Jan. 1528) (*Granvelle*, I. 310–46).

37. Charles V's reply to Clarencieux (27 Jan. 1528) (Le Grand, III. 27–48); Charles V to Margaret of Austria, 28 Mar. 1528 (*L.P.*, IV. 4112).

38. Wolsey to Henry VIII, 2 Mar. 1528 (*St.Pap.*, I. 186–8); Ghinucci and Lee to Wolsey, 28 July 1528 (*L.P.*, IV. 4564).

39. Correspondence of Margaret of Austria, Windsor Herald, Hacket, Wolsey, Ghinucci and Venier, Feb.–May 1528 (*L.P.*, IV. 3966, 4008, 4147, 4153, 4256; *St.Pap.*, I. 288; *Ven.Cal.*, IV. 97–98).

40. Treaty of Hampton Court, 15 June 1528; Proclamation by Sheriff of London, 27 June 1528 (*L.P.*, IV. 4376, 4426).

41. Wolsey to Margaret Queen of Scots (Apr. 1528) (*L.P.*, IV. 4131).

42. Correspondence of Angus, Northumberland, Wolsey and Magnus, Mar.–Nov. 1528 (*St.Pap.*, IV. 517–41; *L.P.*, IV. 4116, 4830, 4859, 4892–3, 4924–5, 4986).

43. Wolsey to G. Casale, 5 Dec. 1527 (Burnet, IV. 19–33).

44. Wolsey to G. Casale, 6 Dec. 1527 (*St.Pap.*, VII. 18–21).

45. Wolsey to G. Casale, 27 Dec. 1527 (ibid, VII. 29–34).

46. Knight to Wolsey, 1 Jan. 1528; Knight to Henry VIII, 1 Jan. 1528 (Burnet, IV. 34–39); Clement VII to Henry VIII, 1 Jan. 1528 (*St.Pap.*, VII. 35–36); Clement VII's dispensation, 23 Dec. 1527 (Ehses, *Römische Dokumente*, pp. 14–16); Parmiter, *The King's Great Matter*, pp. 29–30n.

47. Wolsey to Gardiner and Fox (Feb. 1528) (*L.P.*, IV. 3913).

48. Ibid.

49. Correspondence of Gardiner, Fox and G. Casale, Feb.–Mar. 1528

(Pocock, I. 73–77, 83–93, 95–119; *St.Pap.*, VII. 52–56, 59–61, 63–64; Strype, *Mem.*, I (ii). 66–92; *L.P.*, IV. 3925, 3932–3, 3954, 4003, 4007, 4076–8, 4090, 4103, 4118, 4120).

50. Gardiner to Wolsey, 13 Apr. 1528 (Strype, *Mem.*, I (ii). 92–108).

51. Draft commissions to Wolsey, Warham and Campeggio (undated) (Pocock, I. 28–32; *L.P.*, IV. 3643, 3694).

52. Fox to Gardiner, 11 May 1528 (Strype, *Mem.*, I (ii). 112–27).

53. Wolsey to G. Casale, 10, 23 May 1528; Wolsey to Campeggio, 11, 23 May 1528 (Pocock, I. 163–5; *St.Pap.*, VII. 68–69; *L.P.*, IV. 4246, 4249, 4288–9).

54. G. Casale to Wolsey, 15 June 1528 (Pocock, I. 172–3); Gardiner to Henry VIII, 11 June 1528 (*St.Pap.*, VII. 77–79); Muxetula's protest, 20 July 1528; Clement VII's pollicitation, 23 July 1528 (*L.P.*, IV. 4535, 4550); Parmiter, pp. 57–58.

Chapter 13 – Cambrai and Blackfriars

1. Fox to Gardiner, 11 May 1528 (Strype, *Mem.*, I (ii). 117); Charter of Cardinal's College, Ipswich, 3, 28 July 1528; Giustiniani to the Doge, 12 Sept. 1517 (*L.P.*, II. 3675; IV. 4461, 4572).

2. Clement VII's Bulls, (Apr.), 14, 31 May 1528 (Rymer, XIV. 240–4; *L.P.*, IV. 4229).

3. Grants to Ipswich College, Apr. 1528–May 1529 (*L.P.*, IV. 4229, 4423–4, 4460, 4574–7, 5280, 5286, 5293–4).

4. Norfolk to Wolsey, 1, 15 Dec. 1527; Memorandum on food shortage (Jan. 1528); Sir E. Guildford to Wolsey, 24 June 1528 (*L.P.*, IV. 3625, 3664, 3761, 4414); Venier to the Doge, 27 Nov. 1527 (*Ven.Cal.*, IV. 210).

5. Memorandum, 13 Feb. (1528); Sandys to Wolsey, 9 Mar. (1528); Capell etc. to Long, 3 Apr. 1528; Boswell's examination, 5 Apr. 1528; Wolsey to Rochford (Apr. 1528) (*L.P.*, IV. 3926, 4043, 4141, 4145, 4189).

6. Norfolk to Wolsey, 9 Mar. (1528) (*L.P.*, IV. 4044)

7. Petition to Warham (Apr. 1528); Correspondence of Warham and Wolsey, Apr. 1528 (*L.P.*, IV. 4173, 4188–90).

8. Correspondence of Sir E. and Sir H. Guildford, and of Rochford; Depositions at Goudhurst and Cranbrook, May–June 1528 (*L.P.*, IV. 4287, 4296, 4299–4301, 4310, 4331).

9. Correspondence of Tuke, Hennege, Henry VIII, Anne Boleyn, and Du Bellay, June–July 1528 (*St.Pap.*, I. 296–301, 303–4, 310–12; *Love Letters of Henry VIII*, Nos. IX, XII; Burnet, IV. 103; *L.P.*, IV. 4480, 4510, App. 180, 185; Le Grand, III. 129–42, 150–7).

10. Correspondence of Benet, Hennege and Bell, Apr.–July 1528 (*L.P.*, IV. 4197, 4408; *St.Pap.*, I. 312–15); Henry VIII to Anne Boleyn (July 1528) (*Love Letters*, No. XIII).

11. Henry VIII to Wolsey, 14 July 1528 (Fiddes, *Collections*, pp. 174–6).

12. Ibid; Hennege to Wolsey, 14 July 1528 (*St.Pap.*, I. 316–17).

13. Henry VIII to Wolsey (July 1528) (Lord Herbert, p. 67).

14. Wolsey to Henry VIII (July 1528) (*St.Pap.*, I. 317–18).

15. Bell to Wolsey, 18 July 1528 (*St.Pap.*, I. 314n.); Isabel Jordan to Wolsey (July 1528) (*L.P.*, IV. 4529).

16. Lady Oxford to Wolsey, 8, 22 July 1528 (*L.P.*, IV. 4484, 4548).

17. Wolsey to G. Casale, 23 May 1528 (*St.Pap.*, VII. 68–69).

18. Correspondence of G. Casale, Wolsey and Henry VIII, Aug.–Oct. 1528 (*L.P.*, IV. 4655, 4681, 4683–4; *St.Pap.*, VII. 95–101).

19. Wolsey to Henry VIII, 6 Oct. 1528 (*St.Pap.*, I. 328–9).

20. Pollard, pp. 310–11.

21. Du Bellay to Montmorency, 25 Dec. 1528 (Le Grand, III. 260).

22. Correspondence of Campeggio and Wolsey, Oct.–Nov. 1528 (Theiner, pp. 570–4, *L.P.*, IV. 4857–8, 4875, 4881; *St.Pap.*, VII. 95–115; Pocock, I. 174–80).

23. Wolsey to G. Casale, 1 Nov. 1528 (*St.Pap.*, VII. 102–15).

24. Mendoza to Charles V, 4 Feb. (1529) (B.L., Add. MSS. 28578, c. 16); Catherine of Aragon to Charles V, 9 Jan. (1529); Abel to Charles V (Jan. 1529); Wolsey to Gardiner, 14 Mar. (1529); Memorandum (Mar. 1529) (*L.P.*, IV. 5154 (i) and (ii), 5375–6); Wolsey to a Cardinal (Jan. 1529) (Pocock, I. 187–8); Scarisbrick, *Henry VIII*, pp. 219–21.

25. Henry VIII to Gardiner etc. (Feb. 1529) (*L.P.*, IV. 5270).

26. Wolsey to Gardiner, 7 Feb. (1529) (Fiddes, *Collections*, pp. 211–12).

27. Du Bellay's correspondence (Feb.–Dec. 1528); Henry VIII to the Doge (Aug. 1528) (Le Grand, III. 210–11, 237; *L.P.*, IV. 4684, App. 149, 158, 203).

28. Du Bellay to François I, 22 June 1528 (*L.P.*, IV. 5702); Falier to ——, 22–29 June 1529 (*Ven.Cal.*, IV. 482); Stow, *Annals*, pp. 543–4.

29. Campeggio to Salviati, 29 June 1529 (Theiner, p. 585).

30. Depositions at Blackfriars trial (July 1529) (*L.P.*, IV. 5774).

31. Wolsey to Vannes and G. Casale, 22 June 1529 (B.L., Vit. B. xi, f. 175).

32. Du Bellay to ——, 22 May 1529 (Le Grand, III. 313–22).

33. Du Bellay to Montmorency, 28 May 1529 (*L.P.*, IV. 5601).

34. Suffolk to Henry VIII, 4 June 1529 (*St.Pap.*, VII. 182–4).

35. Du Bellay to Montmorency, 23 Aug. 1529 (Le Grand, III. 337–48).

36. Campeggio to Salviati, 16, 29 June 1529 (Theiner, pp. 583–4, 586–7); Du Bellay to Montmorency, 22, 30 June 1529 (Le Grand, III. 327–36); Wolsey to —— (June 1529); Wolsey to Louise d'Angoulême, 2 July 1529 (*L.P.*, IV. 5710, 5733).

37. Du Bellay to François I, 1 Sept. 1529 (*L.P.*, IV. 5911).

38. Treaty of Cambrai, 5 Aug. 1529 (Rymer, XIV. 326–44); Tunstal, More and Hacket to Henry VIII, 5 Aug. 1529 (Rogers, pp. 419–20).

39. Correspondence of Benet, Clement VII and G. Casale, July 1529 (Burnet, IV. 122–5; Le Grand, III. 336; *L.P.*, IV. 5779–80).

40. Wolsey to Benet, G. Casale and Vannes, 27 July 1529 (*St.Pap.*, VII. 193–7).

41. Cavendish, pp. 89–90.

Chapter 14 – The Fallen Cardinal

1. Suffolk to Wolsey, 7 Jan. (1528) (Ellis, III (i). 200–2).
2. Campeggion to Sanga, 3 Apr. 1529 (*L.P.*, IV. 5416); Foxe, IV. 257–8.
3. Memoranda about Wolsey (June 1529) (*L.P.*, IV. 5749–50).
4. Wolsey to Benet, G. Casale and Vannes, 27 July 1529 (*St.Pap.*, VII. 193–7).
5. Correspondence of Gardiner and Wolsey, Aug.–Sept. 1529 (*L.P.*, IV. 5816–17, 5819, 5821, 5825, 5831, 5844, 5865–9, 5875, 5882–4, 5890–1, 5893–4, 5897, 5918, 5923, 5925, 5928).
6. Chapuys to Charles V, 1 Sept. 1529; Chapuys to Margaret of Austria, 18 Sept. 1529 (*Span.Cal.*, IV. 132, 152).
7. Chapuys to Charles V, 4 Sept. 1529 (ibid, IV. 134).
8. Du Bellay to Montmorency, 16 Sept. 1529 (Le Grand, III. 354–9).
9. Phillips to Wolsey, 31 Aug. 1529; Coke to Butts, 10 Sept. 1529 (*L.P.*, IV. 5898, 5933).
10. Gardiner to Wolsey, 12 Sept. 1529 (*St.Pap.*, I. 344).
11. Chapuys to Charles V, 21 Sept. 1529 (*Span.Cal.*, IV. 160).
12. Cavendish, pp. 92–97.
13. Henry VIII to Campeggio, 22 Oct. 1529 (*L.P.*, IV. 6016); Du Bellay to Montmorency, 12 Oct. 1529 (Le Grand, III. 364–9).
14. Cavendish, p. 97; Hall, p. 760; Bill of indictment against Wolsey, 12 Oct. 1529 (*L.P.*, IV. 6035).
15. Cavendish, p. 98.
16. Memorandum, 25 Oct. 1529 (Rymer, XIV. 349); Chapuys to Charles V, 8 Nov. 1529 (*Span.Cal.*, IV. 211).
17. Indenture between Henry VIII and Wolsey, 22 Oct. 1529 (*L.P.*, IV. 6017).
18. Cavendish, pp. 98–104.
19. Ibid, pp. 114–16.
20. Ibid, pp. 116–19, 124–5.
21. Articles of House of Lords against Wolsey (1 Dec. 1529) (Lord Herbert, in Kennet, II. 125–9).
22. Grants by Wolsey and Winter (Dec. 1529); Paulet to Wolsey, 6 June 1530 (*L.P.*, IV. 6082, 6094, 6115).
23. Extracts from undated letters of Cromwell and Wolsey (*L.P.*, IV. 6076).
24. Wolsey to Cromwell (June 1530) (Ellis, II (ii). 29).
25. Cavendish, pp. 110–12, 119–20.
26. Ibid, pp. 120–2; Falier to the Doge, 29 Jan. 1530 (*Ven.Cal.*, IV. 563).
27. Wolsey's undated letters to Cromwell and Gardiner (Jan.–Feb. 1530) (*St.Pap.*, I. 354–8; Ellis, I (ii). 1–13).
28. Pardon and Grant to Wolsey, 10, 14 Feb. 1529/30 (Rymer, XIV. 366–76); Cavendish, p.123.
29. Cavendish, p. 130.
30. Ibid, pp. 127–8.
31. Capon to Wolsey, 9, 20 July 1530; Tresham to Wolsey, 7, 11 Oct. 1530 (*L.P.*, IV. 6510, 6523, 6666, 6679); Chapuys to Charles V, 20–22 Feb. 1530 (*Span.Cal.*, IV. 265).

32. Vaulx to François I, 15 Mar. 1530 (Le Grand, III. 411).
33. Chapuys to Charles V, 16 Mar. 1530; Vaulx to François I, 27–29 Mar., 1530 (*Span.Cal.*, IV. 270, 279).
34. Cavendish, pp. 131–2; Wolsey to Henry VIII (Apr. 1530); Stubbs to Wolsey, 17 May 1530 (*L.P.*, IV. 6344, 6390).
35. Cavendish, pp. 132–5, 138; Henry VIII to Dacre, 28 Mar. 1530; Magnus to Wolsey, 18 Apr. 1530 (Ellis, III (ii). 172–6); Orders to Abbot of Peterborough, etc. (Mar. 1530); Clayburgh to Wolsey, 29 Mar. 1530 (*L.P.*, IV. 6294, 6299).
36. Dolphine to Wolsey, 19 Apr. 1530; Wolsey to Percy (Apr. 1530); Smith to Wolsey, 10 June 1530 (*L.P.*, IV. 6343, 6345, 6447).
37. Cromwell to Wolsey, 18 Aug. 1530 (*St.Pap.*, I. 366); Smith to Wolsey, 10 June 1530 (*L.P.*, IV. 6447).
38. Confessions of Lawrence and Turner, 20 June 1530; Henry VIII to Wolsey, 21 June 1530; Wolsey to —— (July 1530) (*L.P.*, IV. 6466, 6473, 6749).
39. Wolsey to Henry VIII (July 1530) (*L.P.*, IV. 6467).
40. House of Lords to Clement VII, 13 July 1530 (Rymer, XIV. 405–7).
41. Capon to Wolsey, 11 Apr. 1530 (*L.P.*, IV. 6230).
42. Inquisition of Wolsey's property since 2 Dec. 1523, 14 July 1530 (Rymer, XIV. 402–4).
43. Wolsey to Henry VIII (July 1530) (Ellis, II (ii). 33).
44. Letters of Tresham, Capon and Higham to Wolsey, July–Oct. 1530 (*L.P.*, IV. 6377, 6510, 6579, 6666, 6679); Wolsey to Gardiner, 23 July 1530 (Strype, *Mem.*, I (ii). 137–8); Wolsey to Cromwell (July 1530) (*St.Pap.*, I. 370–1).
45. Capon to Wolsey, 20 July 1530 (*L.P.*, IV. 6523).
46. Wolsey to Cromwell (July 1530) (*St.Pap.*, I. 362).
47. Arundell to Wolsey, 17 Oct. 1530 (*L.P.*, IV. 6688).
48. Chapuys to Charles V, 15, 29 June; 20 Aug. 1530 (*Span.Cal.*, IV. 354, 366, 411).
49. Chapuys to Charles V, 11 July 1530 (ibid, IV. 373).
50. Chapuys to Charles V, 27 Nov. 1530 (*L.P.*, IV. 6738; *Span.Cal.*, IV. 509).
51. Ibid; Scarpinello to the Duke of Milan, 17 Nov., 2 Dec. 1530; Giustiniani to the Doge, 18 Nov. 1530 (*Ven.Cal.*, IV. 632–3, 637).
52. Chapuys to Charles V, 5 Sept. 1530 (*Span.Cal.*, IV. 422).
53. Cavendish, pp. 138–44; Cromwell to Wolsey, 18 Aug. 1530 (*St.Pap.*, I. 365–8).
54. Cavendish, pp. 144–52.
55. Northumberland to Wolsey, 26 Apr. 1529 (*L.P.*, IV. 5497).
56. Cavendish, pp. 152–5.
57. Ibid, pp. 155–74.
58. Chapuys to Charles V, 27 Nov. 1530 (Bradford, pp. 319–20).
59. Bryan to Henry VIII, 21 Nov. 1530 (*St.Pap.*, VII. 211–15).
60. Cavendish, pp. 177–9.
61. Ibid, p. 179.
62. Ibid, pp. 179–81.

63. Ibid, pp. 181–3, 185–6; Falier to the Doge, 8 Dec. 1530 (*Ven.Cal.*, IV. 639).
64. Giustiniani to the Doge, 14 Dec. 1530 (*Ven.Cal.*, IV. 641); Chapuys to Charles V, 4 Dec. 1530 (Bradford, pp. 331–7).

Chapter 15 – Lord Chancellor More and the Heretics

1. More to Cochlaeus (1528) (Rogers, p. 395).
2. More to Cromwell (May 1534) (Rogers, p. 488); Stapleton, p. 213.
3. For the history of the portrait, and its date, see Chambers, pp. 219–22.
4. Foxe, IV. 622.
5. More to Bugenhagen (1526) (Rogers, pp. 325–65); see also Rogers, 'Sir Thomas More's letter to Bugenhagen', in *Modern Churchman*, XXXV. 350–60.
6. Preserved Smith, pp. 279–80, 331–3, 342–6.
7. More to Erasmus, 18 Dec. 1526 (Allen, VI. 441–3).
8. More to Cromwell, 5 Mar. 1534 (Rogers, p. 493); Roper, pp. 31–32.
9. More to Cromwell, 5 Mar. 1534 (Rogers, p. 496).
10. Tunstal's licence to More, 7 Mar. 1527/8 (ibid, pp. 387–8).
11. More, *Dialogue concerning Heresies* (*More's English Works*, pp. 173, 179, 203, 209).
12. Ibid, pp. 257–9.
13. Ibid, p. 274.
14. Ibid, p. 275.
15. Ibid, pp. 214, 217, 285.
16. Ibid, p. 258.
17. Campeggio to Wolsey, 28 Apr. 1527 (*L.P.*, IV. 3072).
18. More, *Dialogue concerning Heresies* (*More's English Works*, pp. 262–72).
19. Fish, *A Supplication for the Beggars* (in *Four Supplications*, p. 7; Foxe, IV. 661); More, *Supplication of Souls* (*More's English Works*, pp. 288–359).
20. Memorandum, 26 Oct. 1529 (Rymer, XIV. 349–50); Du Bellay to Montmorency, 22, 27 Oct. 1529 (Le Grand, III. 376, 379–80; *L.P.*, IV. 6018); Chapuys to Charles V, 25 Oct., 8 Nov. 1529 (Bradford, pp. 256–98; *Span.Cal.*, IV. 211); Falier to the Doge, 28 Oct. 1529; Scarpinello to Duke of Milan, 15 Aug. 1530 (*Ven.Cal.*, IV. 521, 601).
21. Roper, pp. 20–21.
22. Ibid, pp. 56–57.
23. Hall, p. 764.
24. Chapuys to Charles V, 8 Nov. 1529 (*Span.Cal.*, IV. 211).
25. Articles of House of Lords against Wolsey (1 Dec. 1529) (*L.P.*, IV. 6075).
26. Whittinton, *Vulgaria*, p. 64.
27. Falier's report to the Senate, 10 Nov. 1531; Capello to the Doge, 8 Jan. 1532 (*Ven.Cal.*, IV. 694, 718).
28. Roper, pp. 40–43, 61–64; Guy, *The Public Career of Sir Thomas More*, pp. 81–82, 91.
29. Pollard, p. 86; but see Guy, *The Public Career of Sir Thomas More*, pp. 80–93.
30. 'An Act concerning punishment of beggars and vagabonds' (*Statutes of the*

Realm, 22 Hen. VIII, c. 12).

31. Morice's statement (*Narratives of the Reformation*, pp. 240–2); Foxe, VIII. 6–7).
32. House of Lords to Clement VII, 13 July 1530 (Rymer, XIV. 405–7).
33. List of heretical opinions, 24 May 1530; Proclamation of 22 June 1530 (Wilkins, III. 727–37, 740–2); Hall, p. 771.
34. Correspondence of Vaughan and Cromwell, Jan.–May 1531 (*St.Pap.*, VII. 302–4; *L.P.*, V. 65 (i) and (ii), 153, 201, 248).
35. More, *The Confutation of Tyndale's Answer* (*More's Works*, VIII. 14–17).
36. Roper, pp. 43–44.
37. More to Lady More, 3 Sept. 1529 (Rogers, pp. 422–3).
38. Roper, p. 51.
39. More, *The Apology of Sir Thomas More* (*More's Works*, IX. 118).
40. Ibid.
41. Ibid, IX. 119; Foxe, IV. 689.
42. More, *Apology* (*More's Works*, IX. 117).
43. Guy, 'Sir Thomas More and the Heretics' (*History Today*, XXX. 14–15).
44. Foxe, IV. 670–1; More, *Confutation of Tyndale's Answer*; More, *Apology* (*More's Works*, VIII. 18–20; IX. 118–19).
45. Foxe, IV. 698.
46. Ibid, IV. 705.
47. Ibid, IV. 689.
48. Ibid, IV. 698.
49. Ibid, V. 5–7, 9; *Letter of Sir Thomas More impugning the erroneous writings of John Frith* (Rogers, pp. 440–64).
50. Tunstal's protest (Jan. 1532) (Wilkins, III. 745); Henry VIII to Tunstal (Feb. 1532) (*L.P.*, V. 820).
51. Chapuys to Charles V, 21 Feb., 1, 22 Mar., 2 Apr. 1531 (*L.P.*, V. 112, 120, 148, 171; *Span.Cal.*, IV. 641, 664); Charles V to More, 11 Mar. 1531 (Schulte Herbrüggen, *Sir Thomas More: Neue Briefe*, p. 97).
52. Chapuys to Charles V, 2 Apr. 1531 (*L.P.*, V. 171).
53. Roper, p. 35.
54. Chapuys to Charles V, 13, 22 May 1532 (*L.P.*, V. 1013, 1046); Submission of the Clergy, 15 May 1532 (Wilkins, III. 754–5); Memorandum, 16, 20 May 1532 (Rymer, XIV. 433–4).
55. Roper, pp. 103–4; but see Chambers, pp. 287–90.

Chapter 16 – Thomas More the Martyr

1. More to Erasmus, 14 June 1532 (Allen, X. 31–34).
2. More's Epitaph (1533) (Ibid, X. 260–1).
3. More to Erasmus (June 1533) (ibid, X. 258–60).
4. More to Erasmus, 14 June 1532 (ibid, X. 33); Grynaeus, *Platonis Omnia Opera*, Pref., B4.
5. More, *The Confutation of Tyndale's Answer* (*More's Works*, VIII. 3, 11).
6. Ibid, VIII. 17–21.

7. Ibid, VIII. 23–26; Foxe, IV. 643–56.

8. *More's Works*, VIII. 91–92.

9. Ibid, VIII. 64–65.

10. Ibid, VIII. 143–5, 164–77.

11. Ibid, VIII. 177.

12. Ibid, VIII. 177–9.

13. Strype, *Mem.*, I (ii). 172.

14. *More's Works*, VIII. 16, 62, 123–4.

15. Ibid, VIII. 29.

16. Ibid, VIII. 29–30, 56.

17. Ibid, VIII. 31–32.

18. Ibid, VIII. 27.

19. Roper, pp. 57–58.

20. *The Apology of Sir Thomas More (More's Works*, IX. 45, 60).

21. More to Cromwell (Mar. 1534) (Rogers, pp. 480–8).

22. More to Elizabeth Barton (1533) (ibid, pp. 465–6).

23. Cromwell to Fisher (Feb. 1534) (Burnet, IV. 195–201).

24. More to Cromwell, 1 Feb. 1533/4 (Rogers, pp. 467–9).

25. More to Cromwell (Feb. and Mar. 1534) (ibid, pp. 470, 480–8).

26. More to Henry VIII, 5 Mar. (1534) (ibid, pp. 488–91).

27. More to Cromwell, 5 Mar. (1534) (ibid, pp. 492–501).

28. Chapuys to Charles V, 10 Oct. 1533 (*L.P.*, VI. 1249; *Span.Cal.*, IV. 1133).

29. Roper, p. 73.

30. More to Margaret Roper (17 Apr. 1534) (Rogers, pp. 501–7).

31. Margaret Roper to Lady Alington (Aug. 1534); More to Wilson (two letters, Jan.–Mar. 1535) (ibid, pp. 514–38); Roper, pp. 82–84; Ro. Ba., pp. 211–12; Harpsfield, p. 175.

32. More, *De Tristitia Christi* (*More's Works*, XIV. 17–21).

33. Ibid, XIV. 229–37.

34. More, *A Dialogue of Comfort against Tribulation* (*More's Works*, XII. 189–209).

35. More, *A Treatise upon the Passion* (*More's Works*, XIII. 20).

36. More to Margaret Roper (May 1535) (Rogers, pp. 550–4); Fisher's replies to interrogatories, 12, 14 June 1535 (*Archaeologia*, XXV. 94–99; *St.Pap.*, I. 431–2).

37. More to Margaret Roper (3 June 1535) (Rogers, pp. 555–9); More's replies to interrogatories, 3 June 1535 (*L.P.*, VIII. 814).

38. More's replies to interrogatories, 14 June 1535 (*St.Pap.*, I. 432–6).

39. Chapuys to Charles V, 16 June 1535; Trial of Fisher, 17 June 1535 (*L.P.*, VIII. 876, 886 (i), (ii), (viii); *Span.Cal.*, V. 14).

40. For More's trial, and Rich's evidence, see report of trial, 1 July 1535; *L.P.*, VIII. 974); Spanish report (Aug. 1535) (*Span.Cal.*, V. 180); the Paris News-letter, 23 July 1535 (in Harpsfield, pp. 258–64); Roper, pp. 86–97; Harpsfield, pp. 183–97.

41. Roper, pp. 97–99.

42. More to Margaret Roper, 5 July 1535 (Rogers, pp. 563–5).

43. Spanish report (Aug. 1535) (*Span.Cal.*, V. 180); the Paris News-letter, 23

July 1535 (in Harpsfield, p. 266); Roper, pp. 100–3; Harpsfield, pp. 201–4; Stapleton, pp. 208–11.

44. Stapleton, pp. 213, 215.
45. Lady More to Henry VIII (Christmas 1534); Lady More to Cromwell (May 1535) (Rogers, pp. 547–8, 554–5); Cromwell's memorandum (Aug. 1535) (*L.P.*, IX. 218).
46. Bridgett, *Life and Writings of Blessed Thomas More*, pp. 435–7; Tatton-Brown, 'The Roper Chantry', and Garrard, App. 4 (*The Antiquaries Journal*, LX. 227–46).

Chapter 17 – The Verdict of History

1. Foxe, IV. 587–617; Harpsfield, pp. 39–43.
2. For historians' assessments of Wolsey, see Pollard, pp. 1–8.
3. Memorandum drafted by Wriothesley (July 1535); Morison to Cromwell (27 Aug. 1535) (*L.P.*, VIII. 1118; IX. 198); Cromwell to G. Casale, 30 Sept. 1535 (*St.Pap.*, VII. 633–6); Zeeveld, 'Apology for an Execution' (in *Moreana*, XV. 353–71).
4. Chapuys to Granvelle, 11 July 1535; Pio to Ambrogio, 18, 24, 29 July 1535; Ortiz to Empress Isabel, 20 July 1535; Paul III to Ferdinand I (July), 26 July 1535; Nicerinus to Montanus, 23 July 1535; Chapuys to Charles V, 25 July 1535; Paul III to François I, 26 July 1535; G. Casale to Cromwell, 27 July 1535 (*St.Pap.*, VII. 618–22; Bucholtz, *Ferdinand I*, IX. 15–16; Camusat, *Meslanges historiques*, Part 2, pp. 27–29; *Span.Cal.*, V. 181, 183; *L.P.*, VIII. 1019, 1060, 1075, 1095–6, 1104–5, 1116–17).
5. *Bishop Cranmer's Recantacyons*, pp. 96–97; Foxe, VIII. 85.
6. See E.V. Hitchcock's Introduction to Ro. Ba., op.cit., pp. xxiv–xxv.
7. Foxe, V. 99.
8. Ibid, VIII. 635–6.
9. Ibid, V. 100.
10. Decree of the Congregation of Sacred Rites, 29 Dec. 1886 (in Bridgett, pp. xxix–xxxii).
11. Froude, *History of England*, II. 96.
12. For historians' assessments of More, see Chambers, pp. 351–6.
13. Kautsky, *Thomas More and his Utopia*, pp. 79, 125–6, 129, 171, 250.
14. G.K. Chesterton, 'A Turning Point in History' (in *The Fame of Blessed Thomas More*, p. 63).
15. More, *The Confutation of Tyndale's Answer*; *A Dialogue of Comfort against Tribulation*; *De Tristita Christi* (*More's Works*, VIII. 17–21; XII. 247; XIV. 63, 83, 237–51).
16. Guy, 'Sir Thomas More and the Heretics' (*History Today*, XXX. 14).
17. Roper, pp. 225–6; More, *Confutation of Tyndale's Answer* (*More's Works*, VIII. 128); More to Margaret Roper (3 June 1535) (Rogers, pp. 557–8).
18. Kautsky, p. 78.
19. More, *Dialogue concerning Heresies* (*More's English Works*, p. 274).

INDEX